Discover Florida

Experience the best of Florida

This edition written and researched by

Adam Karlin,
Jennifer Rasin Denniston, Paula Hardy, Benedict Walker

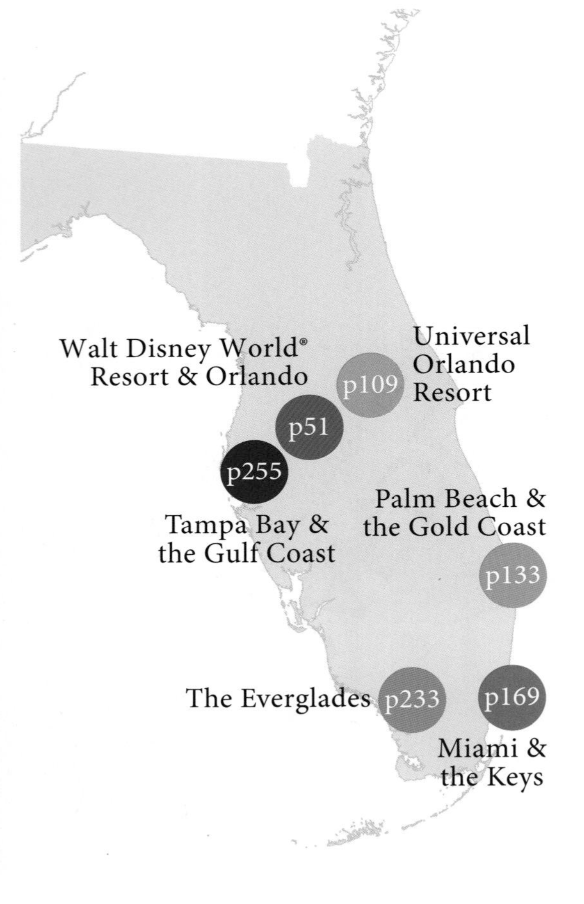

Palm Beach & the Gold Coast

- Fort Lauderdale
- Hollywood Beach & Broadwalk
- Flagler Museum
- Morikami Museum & Japanese Gardens
- Gumbo Limbo Nature Center

Miami & the Keys

- Miami Art Deco Historic District
- Key West
- Hemingway House
- Little Havana
- Overseas Highway Cycling

Walt Disney World® Resort & Orlando

- Disney's Parades & Light Shows
- Epcot
- Fantasyland
- Sunset Boulevard
- Animal Kingdom

Universal Orlando Resort

- Wizarding World of Harry Potter
- Islands of Adventure
- Universal Studios
- Production Central
- Springfield

The Everglades

- Everglades National Park
- Big Cypress National Preserve
- Hell's Bay
- Chickee Camping
- Everglades International Hostel

ampa Bay &
he Gulf Coast

Contents

Plan Your Trip

Discover

Walt Disney World® Resort & Orlando 51

Universal Orlando Resort 109

Contents

Discover Florida

In Focus

Survival Guide

This Is Florida

Florida is the USA's playground. Florida is bracken wetlands that melt under soul-searing sunsets. Florida is blue lakes, teal oceans and green rivers cutting a tropical plain into parcels of romantic beauty. Florida is sand like snow. Florida is cities that have dedicated themselves to giving you food, shopping, nightlife and enjoyment. Florida is waiting.

This state exudes a powerful attraction. Generation after generation of travelers keeps coming back. Our grandparents had retirement cottages here. Our parents can recall childhood visions of mermaids and manatees and Mickey that their children remember with a similar warm-hearted nostalgia, and want to pass on to the next generation and the next.

These recollections encapsulate what many deem 'Old Florida.' But Old Florida sits alongside the new here as the state is constantly pushing itself to reinvent the best in tourism. If you want it, Florida has it, in every color, size and shape.

There are malls near Fort Myers where you can live out your most lurid consumer fantasies. Thanks to demand for the local, organic and indigenous, those malls are a few miles from neighborly farmer's markets. There are theme parks galore in Orlando, while in the Everglades to the south and Apalachicola to the north, there are state and national parks where a unique subtropical environment is protected by dedicated citizens settling new frontiers in conservation and environmentalism.

There are miles of beach in Miami. And beyond sun and sun, a world class, daring arts district. There are the latest toys and trends of the wealthy in Palm Beach, and a few hours south, simple pleasures and parades dedicated to flights of fantasy in Key West.

And everywhere you go there is the backbone of Florida: visitors. They can find anything here, and often, more than what they expected. Get ready to join their satisfied ranks.

> "Florida is the USA's playground"

Lifeguard stand, Miami (p178)

10 ST
NO
LIFEGUARD
ON
DUTY

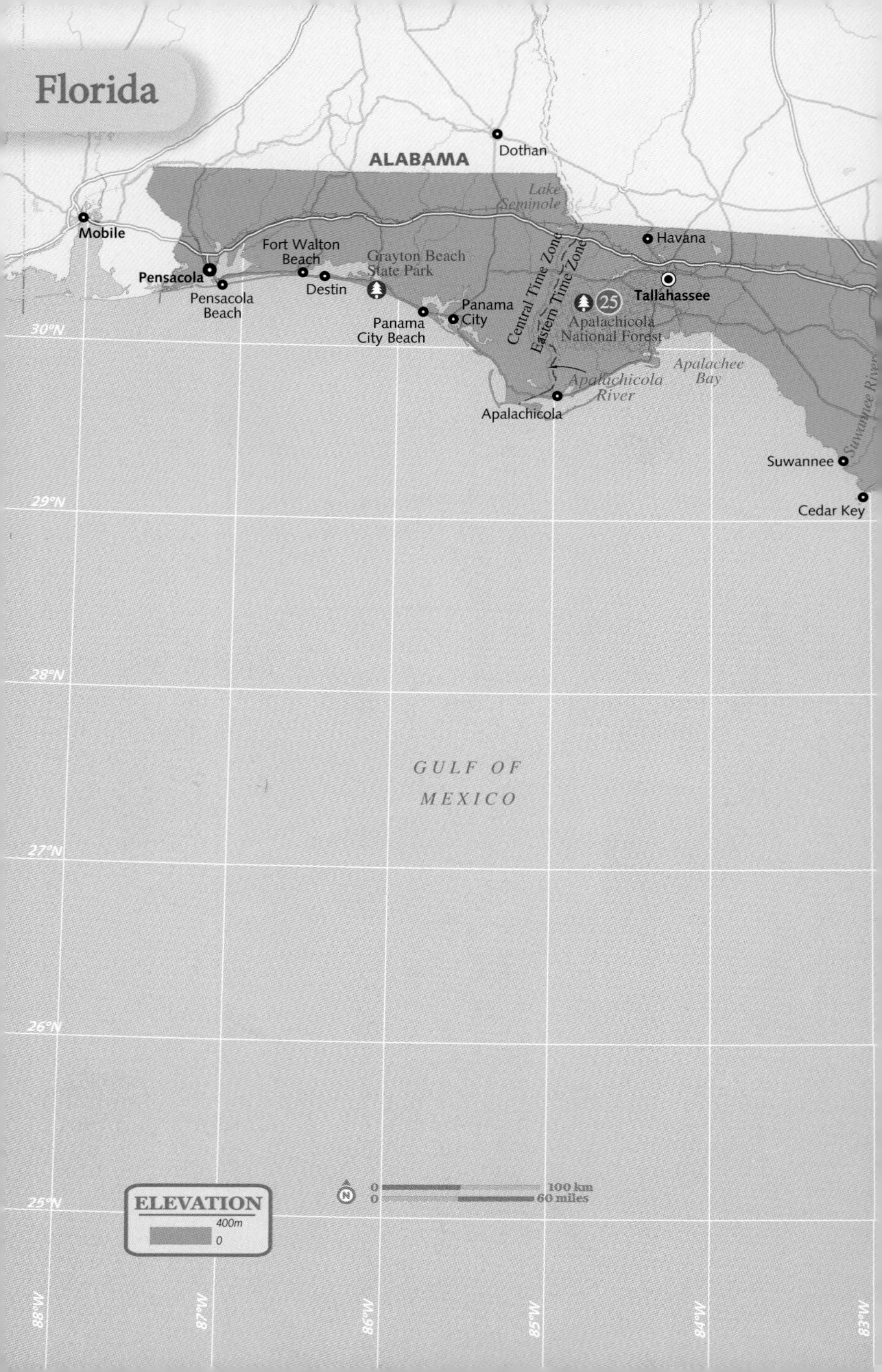

Florida
ALABAMA
Dothan
Lake Seminole
Mobile
Havana
Fort Walton Beach
Grayton Beach State Park
Pensacola
Pensacola Beach
Destin
Tallahassee
Central Time Zone
Eastern Time Zone
25
Apalachicola National Forest
Panama City
Panama City Beach
Apalachee Bay
Apalachicola River
Apalachicola
Suwannee River
Suwannee
Cedar Key
30°N
29°N
28°N
27°N
26°N
25°N
GULF OF MEXICO
ELEVATION
400m
0
0
100 km
0
60 miles
88°W
87°W
86°W
85°W
84°W
83°W

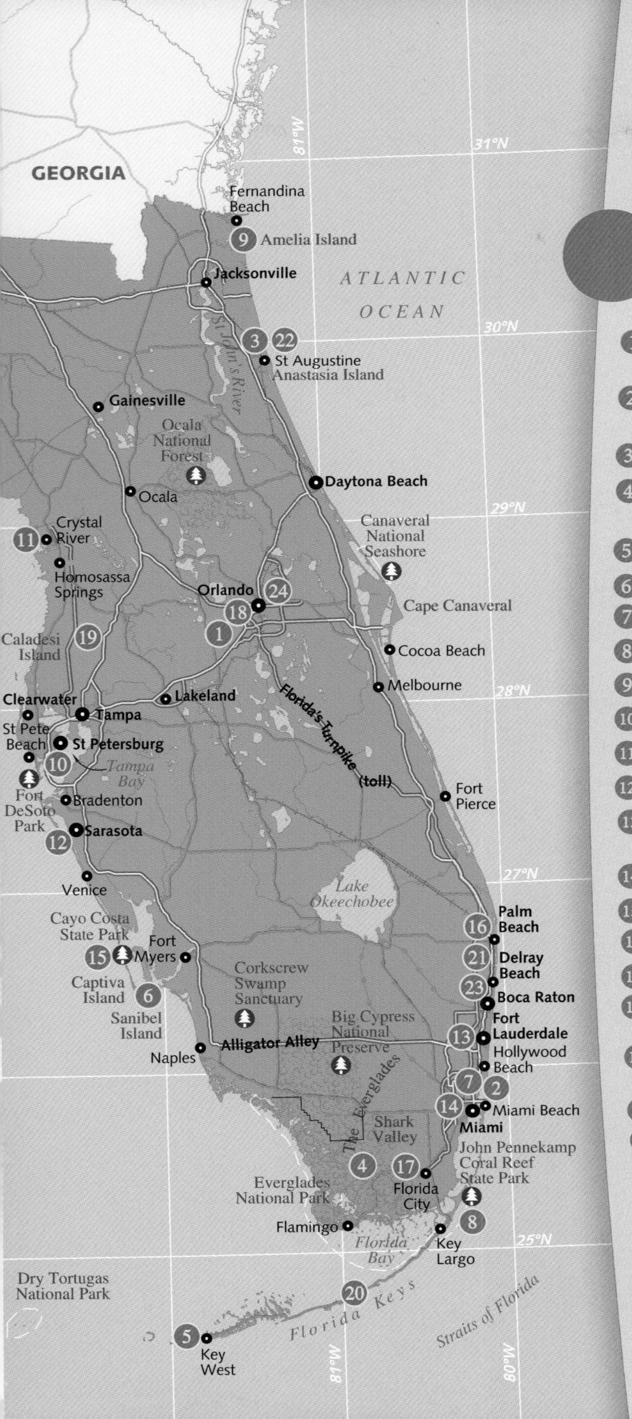

25 Top Highlights

1. Walt Disney World® Resort
2. Miami Art Deco Historic District
3. Spanish Quarter Museum
4. Wildlife in the Everglades National Park
5. Key West
6. Shelling on Sanibel Island
7. Hollywood Beach
8. Snorkeling in the Keys
9. Amelia Island
10. Salvador Dalí Museum
11. Swimming with Manatees
12. Mote Marine Laboratory
13. Gondola Ride through Fort Lauderdale
14. Miami Art Scene
15. Exploring the Gulf Islands
16. Shopping in Palm Beach
17. Robert Is Here
18. Wizarding World of Harry Potter
19. Weeki Wachee Springs State Park
20. Overseas Hwy Road Trip
21. Blowing Rocks Preserve
22. St Augustine Ghost Tours
23. Morikami Museum & Japanese Gardens
24. Winter Park
25. Apalachicola National Forest

25 Florida's Top Highlights

Walt Disney World® Resort

Florida's basic reason for being is to function as the world's best playground, and nowhere is this truer than Walt Disney World® Resort (p60). Mickey's home is one of the world's original theme parks, the embodiment of imagination and flights of fancy. Children can explore a bright realm that caters to their every need, and adults quickly revert back to childhood. Yes, it gets crowded, but it's the gold standard in all-American fun for a reason. Besides, if you don't go your kids will never, ever forgive you. Below: Expedition Everest (p69)

1

RICHARD GREEN/ALAMY ©

2

Miami Art Deco Historic District

Art deco isn't just distinctive in Miami. In the Art Deco Historic District (p179), it's definitive. An early 20th-century expression of aesthetic that embodies seemingly contradictory impulses – modernity with nostalgia, streamlining with embellishment, subdued colors and riots of pastel – whatever your take on deco may be, you'll be hard-pressed to find a better concentration of a style that simply screams 'South Florida' outside of Miami and Miami Beach.

Colonial Quarter

New England and Virginia like to claim they're the oldest parts of America, but the record for a contiguously inhabited city in the continental USA is held by St Augustine. The local Colonial Quarter (p249) covers two acres of grounds and one specific era of history: 1740. Costumed re-enactors go the extra mile by sleeping in scratchy period clothing in camps outside of the complex, so you know you're getting an authentic peek into Florida's – and America's – earliest European roots.

3

The Best... Theme Parks

WALT DISNEY WORLD® RESORT
The king of all theme parks wears a mouse-eared crown. (p60)

UNIVERSAL STUDIOS
A cutting-edge theme park with the most innovative rides. (p121)

ADVENTURE ISLAND
Hours of fun at this 30-acre water park. (p294)

BUSCH GARDENS
Themed around Africa, this park melds wildlife with family fun. (p294)

WEEKI WACHEE SPRINGS STATE PARK
The local mermaids are a font of nostalgic Florida romance. (p290)

The Best...
Historical Sites

ART DECO HISTORIC DISTRICT
Miami Beach's art deco district encompasses the best of South Beach. (p179)

EDISON & FORD WINTER ESTATES
The original snowbird mansions for two Amer ican barons of industry. (p286)

HEMINGWAY HOUSE
Where the great author lived, loved, drank, fought and wrote. (p223)

INDIAN KEY HISTORIC STATE PARK
Vine-encrusted ruins of a once-inhabited island only accessible by boat. (p220)

VIZCAYA MANSION
The greatest, grandest and most imaginative of Miami's wedding-cake mansions. (p196)

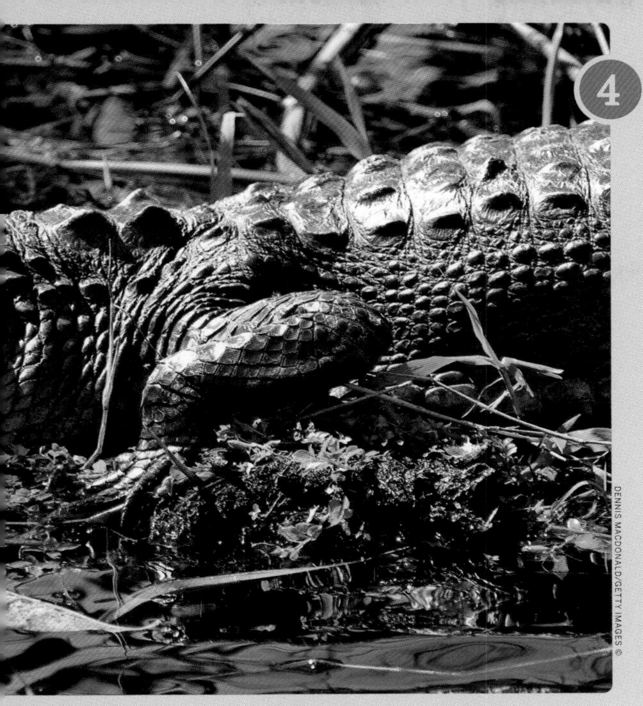

DENNIS MACDONALD/GETTY IMAGES ©

4 Wildlife in the Everglades National Park

No one can contend with the Sunshine State when it comes to Jurassic-era tropical primeval goodness. At the Royal Palm Visitor Center (p245), peek past trees standing sentinel in wine-dark water, and you'll see great flapping pterodactyl-esque herons, snapping turtles basking under an almost Pleistocene sun, and dozens of alligators. Nature's perfect grinning predator, leathery carnivores found a working design and haven't changed it for millions of years. Left: Alligator

DENNIS K JOHNSON/GETTY IMAGES ©

5 Key West

Here's an island that balances two poles of travel. It's a mangrove-cloaked kingdom where almost anything goes, leading to tolerance of creative types. Yet, Key West is also family friendly, a sunny shelter for folks who want a civilized escape amid stately tropical architecture, excellent dining and innocent (if eccentric) Americana. See both sides of the Key West experience at Mallory Square's (p223) daily sunset street festivals. Left: Entertainer, Mallory Square

Shelling on Sanibel Island

6

Sanibel Island (p289) has one of the heaviest concentrations of shells in the world. This highlight already sounds like a tongue twister, and just to add some more 'S' sounds, if you visit Sanibel you'll develop the distinctive 'Sanibel stoop' from bending over to inspect little creamy rainbow gems on the sand.

7

Hollywood Beach

In Hollywood Beach (p166), there are loads of beautiful people who resemble LA celebrities, and some nights, a few real celebrities strolling about, too. But Hollywood Beach consciously makes an effort to be all accommodating and family friendly. You can shop for a corny souvenir and then run across a gaggle of models heading to the local ice-cream parlor on the boardwalk.

Snorkeling in the Keys

The continental USA has one coral reef to boast of, and Florida is where it's at. Drive to Key Largo, northernmost of the Florida Keys, and head to John Pennekamp Coral Reef State Park (p218). The trick is getting under the surface of the park – literally. Take a trip from the marina onto and into the water, where you'll find bursts of rainbow-colored fish and water so clear it could be a window. If you don't dive, getting SCUBA-certified here is the capstone of any Florida vacation.

The Best... Beaches

HOLLYWOOD BEACH
A bare minimum of atti tude, a whole lot of swagger. (p166)

BAHIA HONDA STATE PARK
Wild, windswept and wonderful; a perfect slice of the Keys. (p222)

BOWMAN'S BEACH
Sparkling sand and family-friendly shelling on quiet Sanibel Island. (p289)

FORT LAUDERDALE BEACH
Open views and the Atlantic Ocean combine into a beach exemplar. (p159)

SOUTH BEACH
South Beach is sand, celebrities and sexiness sizzling under the sun. (p179)

Amelia Island

North Florida is part of the Deep South, and one of the more charming reminders of this geographic trivia is Amelia Island (p298). A moss and magnolia draped sea island located just 13 miles south of the Georgia border, Amelia's hub, Fernandina Beach, is as gorgeous a cluster of preserved historical goodness as you'll find between here and the Mason Dixon line. Did we mention cute restaurants and cafes, plenty of Civil War–era history, stately groves of oak trees and gorgeous beaches? Because that's all here, too.

The Best... Outdoors

SHELLING ON SANIBEL
Get a suntan, your knees bent and some rare shells. (p289)

CYCLING MIAMI
The flat terrain of Miami is perfect for bicycle-bound adventures. (p200)

PADDLING THE PANHANDLE
Take a kayak along the waters of Apalachicola National Forest. (p300)

HIKING IN THE EVERGLADES
Long hauls and short-jaunt trails prevail in this park. (p247)

CAYO COSTA STATE PARK
This semi-isolated island is begging to be explored. (p282)

10 Salvador Dalí Museum

It's hard to create a museum dedicated to a specific artist. But it's even more difficult to make that museum as clever and creative as the body of said artist's work. And that's where the Salvador Dalí Museum (p275), designed by architect Yann Weymouth, in St Petersburg, one of the finest modern art museums in Florida, deserves a lot of credit. This innovative experience lures you into Dali's creative process via architectural tricks (like a contemplation room and sitting garden) on the one hand, and excellent, knowledgeable staff on the other.

11 Swimming with Manatees

The manatee, ponderous icon of the Florida conservation movement, is one of the more interesting species in the world. They're not what you'd call magnificent, or even cute in a conventional sense. But their bulk is immensely endearing – manatees appear kind – and at Crystal River (p294) you can swim a slow, sweet ballet with these gentle giants. The time to come is winter, when hundreds of manatees float their unhurried way into the blue waters of Kings Bay.

STEPHEN FRINK/GETTY IMAGES ©

12

Mote Marine Laboratory

Maybe you don't like aquariums. Maybe you think there's too much flash and not enough science, or the opposite: the science isn't presented in an easily understood way. If either of these criticisms apply to you, or if, on the other hand, you love aquariums, come to the Mote Marine Laboratory (p283) in Sarasota. Part research facility, part aquarium, all educational, and accessible to everyone from scholar to layman, this is one of the finest aquariums in a state that does the genre well.

FREE PRESS PHOTO

13

Gondola Ride through Fort Lauderdale

If Las Olas Blvd is the heart of Fort Lauderdale, then the hundreds of canals that spread throughout the city are the city's veins and capillaries. The best way to explore South Florida's second city is via gondola (p161). These narrated tours offer nice insight and are a good peek under Lauderdale's skin, although you're welcome to opt for a silent gondola tour for a more romantic experience.

Miami Art Scene

Miami's masterstroke of urban planning has been to use the arts as an engine for city renewal. The move has taken the form of projects like the Adrienne Arsht Center for the Performing Arts and the magnificent New World Center, and marketing the heck out of Midtown Miami, the location of dozens of art galleries and studios. Every weekend of the month you can find arts walks (p178) throughout Miami's many neighborhoods, giving you the chance to stroll and peruse paintings, all usually accompanied by a drink. Below: Art Basel (p45), Miami, mural by Mr. Brainwash, all rights reserved

14

The Best... Nightlife Hotspots

DOWNTOWN/MIDTOWN MIAMI
The best local hotspots in Miami can be found here. (p187)

ORLANDO
Downtown and Greater Orlando have a pumping party scene. (p89)

YBOR CITY
Tampa flexes her dancing and entertainment muscles in this district. (p265)

KEY WEST
Key West, to put it lightly, really likes to party. (p223)

MIAMI BEACH
Beautiful, brash, sexy and celebrity-studded – and yet sometimes, surprisingly down to earth! (p185)

The Best... Culture & Arts

SALVADOR DALÍ MUSEUM
Fascinating modern art museum and exploration of one surrealist's life. (p275)

ADRIENNE ARSHT CENTER FOR THE PERFORMING ARTS
This wonderful venue bestrides Miami like a set of seashells. (p187)

MORIKAMI MUSEUM & JAPANESE GARDENS
Delray Beach's excellent oasis of Japanese arts and aesthetic sensibility. (p154)

STRAZ CENTER FOR THE PERFORMING ARTS
Tampa's gem, this is the Gulf Coast's finest theater venue. (p272)

ORLANDO MUSEUM OF ART
Once you're done at Disney, absorb fantastic high culture here. (p90)

Exploring the Gulf Islands

Florida's Atlantic Coast gets lots of attention from visitors, and rightly so, but the state's Gulf Coast is quintessentially Floridian. Calm, cozy and still like a warm bath, one of the joys of the Gulf Coast – besides considerable wildlife, good beaches and pretty shoreside towns – are its offshore islands. From calm colonies of low-impact seaside developments like Sanibel and Captiva to bubbly hamlets like Siesta Key, to the Zen-induced physical serenity of Cayo Costa (p282), there's a Gulf Coast island made just for you. Left: Beach, Santa Rosa Island

16 Shopping in Palm Beach

If you ever waltz into a Grimm's fairy tale and meet the famed emperor who had no clothes, let his highness know he should pop on over to Worth Ave (p146) in Palm Beach to restock his closet. Shopping doesn't get much more aristocratic than this, but you don't need a fat wallet to appreciate Palm Beach (although it helps). Just walking Worth Ave gives a sense of joining, if ever so briefly, the jet set and all the glamour and attitude that world contains.

Right: Worth Ave, Palm Beach

HOBERMAN COLLECTION/UIG VIA GETTY IMAGES ©

17 Robert Is Here

We know: why get excited about a farmers' stand? Well, Robert Is Here (for more on the origin of the funny name, see p251) is more than a produce shack. It's a quirky, long-standing emblem of South Florida agriculture and Old Florida eccentricity. It's a petting zoo, a roadside attraction and a place to get some of the best orange juice in the world. Basically, Robert Is Here is an experience, and if you're driving around Homestead, you should be Here, too.

Wizarding World of Harry Potter

Florida is where the frontiers of the theme park experience are getting pushed waaay past roller coasters. Enter: the Wizarding World of Harry Potter in Universal Studios (p122). Folks, short of buying a magic broomstick and taking to the Quidditch field, this is as close as you'll come to immersing yourself in Hogwarts. The most jaded theme-park cynics are wowed by the wonder of the Wizarding World, and if you've got any sense of imagination, prepare to have it stimulated to new heights. Below: Hogwarts

18

The Best... Shopping

WORTH AVENUE
The glitziest shopping strip in Florida is a luxury-goods paradise. (p146)

DESIGN DISTRICT
Miami's mecca for unique furniture, *objects d'art* and designer homewares. (p191)

ST ARMAND'S CIRCLE
More than a mall, St Armand's is Sarasota's social center. (p285)

KEY WEST
Look no further for quirky, art-inspired gifts, crafts and souvenirs. (p231)

CITYPLACE
West Palm Beach adores its own lovely outdoor shopping mall megaplex. (p146)

The Best... Food Scenes

TAMPA
The capital of the Gulf Coast boasts international-quality restaurants (p267)

FORT LAUDERDALE
Lauderdale's food scene trots the globe and showcases local goodness. (p162)

MIDTOWN MIAMI
Forget South Beach; locals go here for Miami's best food. (p208)

KEY WEST
This little island has some incredibly diverse eating options. (p228)

ST PETERSBURG
The Gulf Coast's second city has a sophisticated dining scene. (p276)

Weeki Wachee Springs State Park

19

We give Florida credit for keeping nostalgic travel romance alive and well. Nostalgia is basically the name of the game at Weeki Wachee Springs (p290), where 'mermaids' have entertained travelers such as Elvis Presley and Esther Williams since 1947. This isn't just impressive underwater ballet (although it is very much that), it's a window into the past and the kitschy sort of attractions that established Florida as America's playground back in the day. Right: Mermaid show

AURORA PHOTOS/ALAMY ©

DANITA DELIMONT/GETTY IMAGES ©

20 Overseas Hwy Road Trip

Traveling around the USA is all about road trips, which we usually associate with mountains, waving grain and other America the Beautiful imagery. But how about a road trip (p226) that traverses over 100 miles of bridges and causeways and pretty mangrove islets, all scattered throughout the twin teal and blue brackets of Florida Bay and the Gulf of Mexico? This is the Overseas Hwy, which connects the Florida Keys to the mainland, and you to all the quirks, characters and sunny sensibilities of Keys life. Left: Seven Mile Bridge, Pigeon Key

Blowing Rocks Preserve

21

Blowing Rocks (p158) is a natural wonder: a limestone outcrop perfectly positioned on the state's southeastern Atlantic Coast where water occasionally spews through like a raging geyser. What we really love about this spot is its isolation. Blowing Rocks is far from South Florida's rampant development. Within the protected area of the preserve, you'll find pristine biomes that give you a good feel for the wild heart of the state.

22

St Augustine Ghost Tours

St Augustine has been around for almost 500 years and been a haven for conquistadors, smugglers, pirates and (gasp) politicians. For a taste of noir in paradise, get with the folks at St Augustine City Walks (p298). They run fine walking tours of their home that show off plenty of pride, quirks and more than a few spots supposedly haunted by ghosts of St Augustine past. Above: Castillo de San Marcos National Monument (p298), St Augustine

Morikami Museum & Japanese Gardens

Delray Beach is not the sort of spot where we expect to find a gateway unto Zen wisdom and Japanese aesthetics, but hey, Florida is full of surprises like that. If you're in the area, do yourself a favor and visit the heart-wrenchingly beautiful Morikami Museum and Japanese Gardens (p154), the best collection of Japanese art in the state and a fine example of landscaping. The history behind the gorgeous gardens is as poignant as the rows of pruned shrubbery and bonsai plants.

23

The Best... Wildlife

HOMOSASSA SPRINGS WILDLIFE STATE PARK
A semi-safari of the best of native Florida wildlife. (p293)

EVERGLADES NATIONAL PARK
See gators, waterfowl, snakes and Florida at her most beautiful. (p242)

JN 'DING' DARLING NATIONAL WILDLIFE REFUGE
A quiet slice of pristine Gulf Coast nature and fauna. (p289)

JOHN PENNEKAMP CORAL REEF STATE PARK
Get a glimpse of the wildlife that lies beneath Florida's surface. (p218)

SWIMMING WITH MANATEES
Take a cool, refreshing dip with Florida's own gentle giants. (p294)

Winter Park

Orlando's theme parks are the main tourism draw in Central Florida, and with good reason. But if you can find the time to take a break from Disney and Universal, we highly recommenc a day spent browsing the quiet bookshops and pretty art galleries of Winter Park (p96). This well-kept suburb is a gem, a good spot to while away the day engaging in understated pleasantries, sipping coffee at nice cafes, snacking at excellent restaurants and perusing the latest arts walks and gallery showcases.

The Best... Parks

EVERGLADES NATIONAL PARK
This wild, wet wilderness is Florida's most unique natural treasure. (p242)

BISCAYNE NATIONAL PARK
An almost entirely underwater park with superb diving and boating. (p251)

JOHN PENNEKAMP CORAL REEF STATE PARK
Dive, snorkel or boat around Key Largo's own coral reef. (p218)

CAYO COSTA STATE PARK
A jewel of an off-shore island ripe for low-key adventures. (p282)

WEKIWA SPRINGS STATE PARK
Near Orlando you'll find this slice of interior Florida nature. (p91)

24

25

Apalachicola National Forest

Most visitors to Florida don't know of her natural wilderness treasures outside of the Everglades. In that case, said visitors should discover this forest (p300), the largest national forest in the state, which boasts over half a million acres of sylvan prettiness. Within the pine country and wetlands of this North Florida treasure, one can find miles of hiking trails, fishing opportunities, bears, coyotes, foxes, alligators, flocks of bird life and gorgeous strands of old growth Cypress and Tupelo swamp.

Florida's Top Itineraries

Islands of Adventure to Downtown Disney

5 DAYS

Theme Park Party

This Orlando itinerary is tailored to give you time to trip around some of the best theme parks in the world while still giving you a window to enjoy the fine dining, shopping and lifestyle goodness found within said park properties.

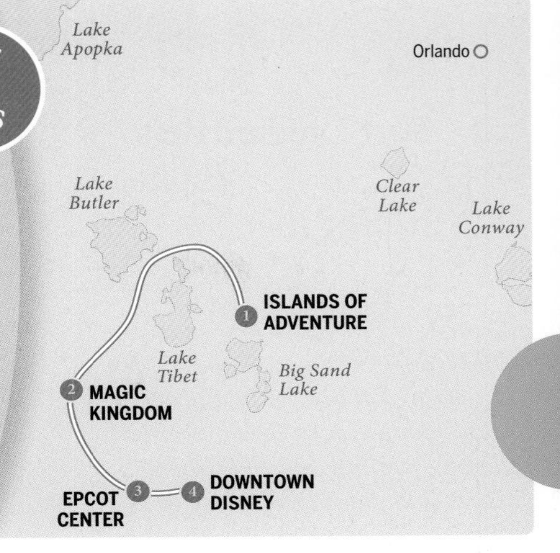

1 Islands of Adventure (p118)

We'll start this theme-park parade with Florida's most daring park design at Islands of Adventure. Part of Universal Studio Resort, Islands appeals to older children and adults who are kids at heart. The centerpiece of the park is the **Wizarding World of Harry Potter**, at the time of writing the most impressive theme-park experience we've encountered. Have dinner (try the barbeque) at the brilliant **Yellow Dog Eats** in nearby Windermere.

ISLANDS OF ADVENTURE ➔ MAGIC KINGDOM

30 minutes The easiest route between parks is I-4E.

2 Magic Kingdom (p60)

Move on to the Magic Kingdom, Walt Disney World® Resort's foundation stone. **Cinderella's Castle** still graces princess dreams, while the **Pirates of the Caribbean** awaits, along with thrilling **Space Mountain**. Hop on the **monorail**, and have a vintage Americana meal at the **50's Prime Time Cafe** for good-deal Disney dining.

Big Thunder Mountain Railroad (p61), Walt Disney World®
PETER PTSCHELINZEW/GETTY IMAGES ©

MAGIC KINGDOM ➔ EPCOT CENTER

One hour Connect via monorail, bus or boat through the Transportation & Ticket Center.

3 Epcot Center (p65)

Have breakfast at the artsy **White Wolf Café** in Orlando, then head back to the park. Dominated by its geodesic dome, Epcot is an old-school version of what Disney once considered the future to be. The **World Showcase** is also one of the better places to eat in the park. Stick around for the brilliant **Illuminations** light show. If you head back into Orlando, check out the **Ravenous Pig**, a fun, delicious gastropub.

EPCOT CENTER ➔ DOWNTOWN DISNEY

One hour Connect via monorail, bus or boat through the Transportation & Ticket Center.

4 Downtown Disney (p72)

An enormous shopping, eating and hotel complex, **Downtown Disney** is where adults can engage in indulgences galore. Dining here is some of the best within the park. If you have time later in the day, leave the park and go swimming at **Typhoon Lagoon**.

Fort Lauderdale to Jupiter
Digging Up the Gold Coast

Southeast Florida is known as the Gold Coast, a tribute to the golden coins left behind by European shipwrecks. Today the title references yellow sands, burnished sunsets and gilt-edged lifestyles of towns like Palm Beach.

1 Fort Lauderdale (p159)

South Florida's second city has a wonderful stretch of sand in the form of the **Fort Lauderdale Beach and Promenade**. Have a walk by the water, then get around *on* the water via **gondola** so you can explore Fort Lauderdale's many canals. Make sure you take time to stroll the breezy **Riverwalk** and **Las Olas Riverfront**, and take a tour of the city's lovely harbor on the good ship **Carrie B**.

FORT LAUDERDALE ➔ DELRAY BEACH

30 minutes Delray Beach is north of Fort Lauderdale on I-95.

2 Delray Beach (p154)

Drive north of Fort Lauderdale and pop into Boca Raton to take in the **Gumbo Limbo Nature Center**, a wonderful preserve that includes a sea turtle rehabilitation center. Have lunch and laze the day away in pretty **Mizner Park**. Further north is Delray Beach, home of the **Morikami Museum and Japanese Gardens**, a vale of meditative serenity and *objets d'art* from across Japan. Head to nearby **Joseph's Wine Bar** for some fine Mediterranean fare.

DELRAY BEACH ➔ PALM BEACH

30 minutes Palm Beach is north of Delray Beach on I-95.

3 Palm Beach (p142)

Make sure you stop at **Lake Worth Beach**, the midway point between Delray and Palm Beach, widely considered one of the best beaches in south Florida. You can enjoy half the day here wandering slowly along the seashore. Have some excellent seasonal Italian cuisine at **Paradiso Ristorante**. In Palm Beach, marvel at the opulence of the rich and famous in the **Flagler Museum**, on ritzy Ocean Blvd, and along posh **Worth Ave**. The next morning make sure to have some of the best brunch around at the famous **Circle** restaurant at the Breakers Resort.

PALM BEACH ➔ JUPITER

1 ½ hours Head north via US 1 or I-95.

4 Jupiter (p158)

Just a quick, scenic drive north of Palm Beach, you'll find the attractive beach town of Jupiter, one of Florida's better surfing sites. Nearby you can find the state's version of Old Faithful: the gushing geyser of water at **Blowing Rocks Preserve**. Just north of here is **Hobe Sound National Wildlife Refuge**, where you can find 3½ miles of pristine beach that sea turtles use for nesting in June and July.

Blowing Rocks Preserve (p158)
JUDD PATTERSON/GETTTY IMAGES ©

Tampa to Universal Studios
From Gulf to Gryffindor

On this trip we're taking in the arts, culture, kitsch and natural beauty of the Gulf Coast, the becalmed, bathwater-warm alternative to the showy Atlantic Coast, and then turning inland to enjoy the rides and resorts of Universal Studios.

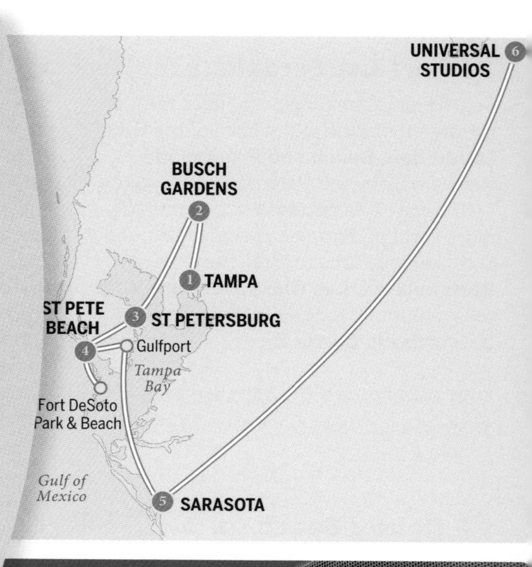

1 Tampa (p264)

Experience Tampa's family-friendly and cultural sides of the city by taking in the **Lowry Park Zoo** and checking out the **Tampa Museum of Art** – you can do both in a day, with a break for lunch at **Columbia Restaurant**. In the evening, if you're feeling up for cigars and beer (or bright lights), go to Cuban-influenced **Ybor City**.

TAMPA ➜ BUSCH GARDENS

20 minutes Take I-275 north; Busch Gardens is off exit 50.

2 Busch Gardens (p294)

A quick drive north of downtown Tampa is **Busch Gardens**, with nine 'African' regions, roller coasters, an open savannah populated by African animals and nearby **Adventure Island** water park. Eating options are OK, but you'll find a better dinner at the **Refinery** in Tampa.

BUSCH GARDENS ➜ ST PETERSBURG

40 minutes Take I-275 to St Petersburg, 32 miles to the south.

3 St Petersburg (p274)

'St Pete' is filled with good culture, good food and good times. Walk around charming historic **Coffee Pot Bayou**, then go forward in time to the ultramodern **Dalí Museum**. During the day have an elegant French-Vietnamese lunch at **Alesia**.

ST PETERSBURG ➜ ST PETE BEACH

25 minutes St Pete Beach is nine miles west of downtown St Petersburg. **45 minutes** Pinellas Suncoast Transit Authority (PSTA) offers a day pass for $4.50.

4 St Pete Beach (p280)

Fort DeSoto Park and Beach is one of the best beaches on the Gulf Coast. Make a side trip to **St Pete Beach**, a lovely seaside escape packed with restaurants and bars. Spend the night in the amiable artists' colony of **Gulfport**.

ST PETERSBURG ➜ SARASOTA

45 minutes Go south of St Petersburg via I-275 and US-301.

5 Sarasota (p283)

Have Sarasota's best breakfast at the **Jim's Small-Batch Bakery**, then spend the day at the **Mote Marine Laboratory**, a research center that doubles as a superlative aquarium. In the evening, wander **St Armand's Circle**, an attractive outdoor shopping area.

SARASOTA ➜ UNIVERSAL STUDIOS

2 ½ hours I-75N from Sarasota, exit 261 to take I-4E toward Orlando.

6 Universal Studio Resort (p121)

Depart the laidback Gulf Coast for flashy **Universal Studio Resort**. We recommend **Islands of Adventure**, which boasts some of the best rides and themed 'zones' of any Orlando-area park. Make sure to explore the wonderful **Wizarding World of Harry Potter**, where an actual sorting hat assigns you to Hufflepuff, Ravenclaw, Slytherin (boo) or Gryffindor (yay!).

The Tampa Museum of Art (p265), designed by architect Stanley Saitowitz

IMAGE: RICHARD CUMMINS/GETTTY IMAGES ©

Miami to Key West
South Florida's Finest

You're taking in lots of beauty on this trip: Miami's beautiful people and skyline, Miami Beach's sand and architecture, the ethereal splendor of the Everglades and the funky, quirky good looks of Key West and her sister islands.

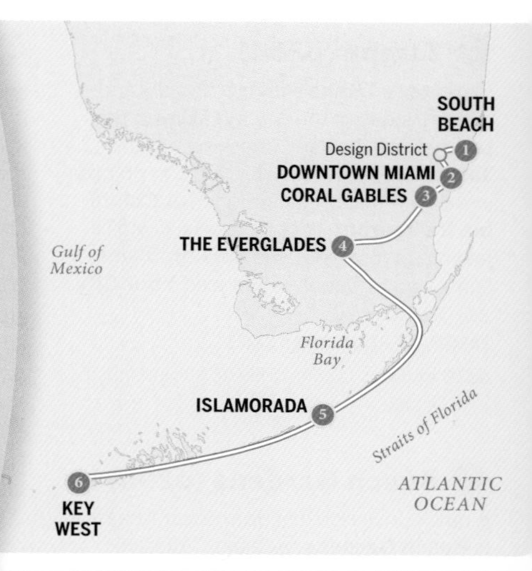

1 South Beach (p179)

Tour the **Art Deco Historic District** and afterwards, pop into the **Wolfsonian-FIU** to learn more about Miami design and architecture. At night, wander up the neon avenue of **Ocean Dr**. When you're worn out from sightseeing, have a delicious Caribbean dinner at Haitian **Tap Tap**.

SOUTH BEACH ➔ DOWNTOWN MIAMI

30 minutes The MacArthur and Venetian causeways connect South Beach to Downtown. **30 minutes to one hour** Bus routes A, C, S, M and 120; see www.miamidade.gov/transit for more.

2 Downtown Miami (p187)

In Downtown Miami, ride the free monorail, the **Metromover**, for a tour of the city skyline. In the evening, head to the **Design District** to sample Miami's best restaurants and nightlife; we recommend the small plates menu at innovative **Michy's**.

DOWNTOWN MIAMI ➔ CORAL GABLES

15 to 30 minutes Located just south of Downtown Miami.

3 Coral Gables (p197)

The official heart of Miami's Cuban community is Little Havana; stop by **Maximo Gomez Park** to see old-timers play chess and dominoes. Next door, Coral Gables is full of Mediterranean-style homes, designer shops on **Miracle Mile**, and grand structures like the nearby **Vizcaya Mansion**. Make sure to browse the shelves at **Books and Books**, the best independent book store in Miami.

CORAL GABLES [➔] EVERGLADES

One hour Go south on US 1 or SW 177th Ave/Krome Ave.

4 The Everglades (p242)

In this unique wetland you can spot dozens of alligators at the **Royal Palm Visitor Center,** go for a hike along the **Pinelands** trail or watch the sunset from the **Pa-hay-okee Overlook**.

EVERGLADES ➔ ISLAMORADA

1 ½ hours Go south on US 1, which becomes Overseas Hwy in Key Largo. **Two to three hours** Commuter buses go from Homestead to the Keys; expect long rides.

5 Islamorada (p219)

The drive across the Keys is one of the USA's great road trips. In Key Largo, take a glass-bottom boat ride at **John Pennekamp Coral Reef State Park.** Further south in Islamorada, feed the giant fish at **Robbie's Marina**.

ISLAMORADA ➔ KEY WEST

Two hours The drive on the Overseas Hwy is simply gorgeous. **Two to three hours** Commuter buses exist, but the schedule is spotty.

6 Key West (p223)

Check out the **Turtle Hospital** on Marathon. Tiny deer on **Big Pine Key** are on the road to Key West. On Key West, enjoy the evening visiting the fantasy-inspired nightly carnival in **Mallory Sq**.

Pa-hay-okee Overlook (p246)

Fort Lauderdale to Orlando
Florida: Coast to Coast

On this two-week journey we take a loop through Florida, from the Atlantic Coast of south Florida to the tepid serenity of the Gulf Coast to the theme-park paradise of Orlando. Oh, and we're throwing in a gator-inhabited park to add some Jurassic diversity.

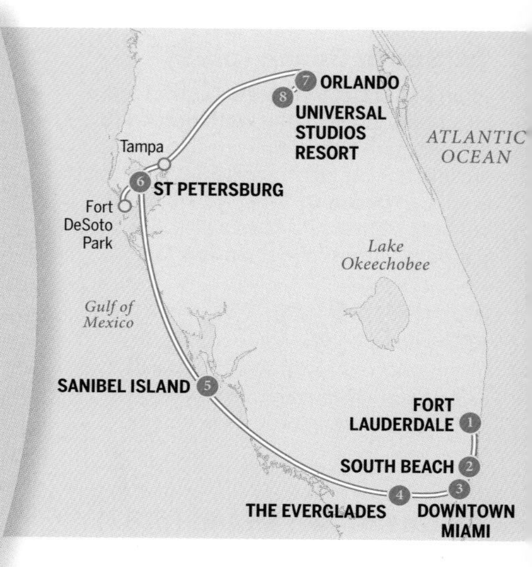

1 Fort Lauderdale (p159)

South Florida's canal-crisscrossed second city has been called the 'Venice of America.' Have a shopping and dining stroll on **Las Olas** and be sure to spend a good chunk of your day wandering the lovely beach **Promenade**.

FORT LAUDERDALE ➔ SOUTH BEACH

45 minutes I-95S is the quickest way down, but a longer, more scenic route takes in all of Collins Ave.

2 South Beach (p179)

South Beach is simply one of the most beautiful seaside neighborhoods in the country. Take as much in as possible, from the white sands and ocean to the **Art Deco Historic District** to the beautiful people preening on **Lincoln Rd**.

SOUTH BEACH ➔ DOWNTOWN MIAMI

30 minutes Five causeways link Miami Beach to Miami proper. **30 minutes to one hour** Bus routes include A, C, S, M and 120; check www.miamidade.gov/transit.

3 Downtown Miami (p187)

Downtown Miami is bracketed by fascinating **Little Havana**, the heart of the Miami Cuban community, **Wynwood**, and the **Design District**, Miami's official neighborhoods for the arts. Speaking of which, make sure to admire the architecture of the stunning **Adrienne Arsht Center for the Performing Arts**.

DOWNTOWN MIAMI ➔ EVERGLADES

One hour Take Tamiami Trail/US 41/8th St from Miami to Shark Valley.

4 The Everglades (p242)

The Everglades constitute the wild, natural heart of Florida. At **Shark Valley**, you can ride a family-friendly tram, cycle, or walk a flat trail that runs by dozens of alligators and flocks of waterfowl. Check out the photography at the **Clyde Butcher Gallery** on your way out of the park. You can camp in the park, or find good-value lodging in **Everglades City**.

EVERGLADES ➔ SANIBEL ISLAND

Three hours Take US-41 to Naples, then I-75N to Sanibel.

White-sand beach, Sanibel Island (p289)
DANITA DELIMONT/GETTY IMAGES ©

5 Sanibel Island (p289)

Sanibel Island is a pretty Gulf Island connected to the Florida mainland by causeway. The development here is low-impact, so you can appreciate the island scenery as you potter around. We recommend driving through the **JN 'Ding' Darling Wildlife Refuge** to connect with Florida's natural beauty, and collecting shells on the white sand beaches – the **shelling** here is considered world class.

SANIBEL ISLAND ➔ ST PETERSBURG

Three hours I-75N is the easiest way to get to St Petersburg.

6 St Petersburg (p274)

Take a detour to check out St Pete's beaches, especially **Fort DeSoto Park**, family friendly and pretty as a postcard. In St Petersburg, avail yourself of fine dining and be sure to visit the Salvador Dalí Museum, an excellent modern arts institution, or catch a show at nearby Tampa's wonderful **Straz Center**.

ST PETERSBURG ➔ ORLANDO

Two hours Take I-4E to get to Orlando.

7 Orlando (p89)

Orlando is much more than theme parks. Wander around the art galleries and cafes of **Winter Park**, and if you want to experience more creativity, go to the extensive, educational **Orlando Museum of Art**. Organic, French fare can be had at cozy **Bikes, Beans & Bordeaux**.

ORLANDO ➔ UNIVERSAL STUDIOS

20 minutes Take I-4W to get to Universal Studios.

8 Universal Orlando Resort (p109)

You can pick whatever theme park you want to visit in Orlando, but we love Universal Orlando Resort for the **Wizarding World of Harry Potter.** Of course, if **Disney World** is more your speed, you should spend time wandering around the nostalgic lanes of the **Magic Kingdom** or the semifuturistic realms of **Epcot Center**.

Florida Month by Month

Top Events

- **Carnaval Miami**, March
- **Fantasy Fest**, October
- **SunFest**, May
- **Goombay Festival**, June
- **Gay Days**, June

January

College Football Bowl Games

On January 1, New Year's Day, Floridians go insane for college football. Major bowls are played in Orlando (Capital One Bowl), Tampa (Outback Bowl) and Jacksonville (Gator Bowl), while Miami's Orange Bowl (January 3) often crowns the collegiate champion.

February

Edison Festival of Light

For two weeks, Fort Myers celebrates the great inventor Thomas Edison with a block party, concerts and a huge science fair. February 11, Edison's birthday, culminates with an incredible Parade of Light (www.edisonfestival.org).

Speed Weeks

During the first two weeks of February, up to 200,000 folks rev their engines for two major car races – the Rolex 24 Hour Race and Daytona 500 – and party full throttle.

Florida State Fair

Over a century old, Tampa's Florida State Fair is classic Americana: two mid-February weeks of livestock shows, greasy food, loud music and old-fashioned carnival rides.

South Beach Wine & Food Festival

No paper-plate grub-fest, this late-February event is a Food Network–sponsored culinary celebration of food, drink and celebrity chefs (www.sobefest.com).

Mardi Gras

Whether it falls in late February or early March, Fat Tuesday inspires parties statewide. Pensacola Beach is Florida's best.

Left: October Fantasy Fest
WENDELL METZEN/GETTY IMAGES ©

March

Spring Break

Throughout March to mid-April, Colleges release students for one-week 'spring breaks.' Coeds pack Florida beaches for debaucherous binges – but hey, it's all good fun. The biggies? Panama City Beach, Pensacola, Daytona and Fort Lauderdale.

Baseball Spring Training

Through March, Florida hosts Major League Baseball's spring training 'Grapefruit League.' Thirteen pro baseball teams train and play exhibition games, drawing fans to the Orlando area, the Tampa Bay area, and the southeast.

Carnaval Miami

Miami's premiere Latin festival takes over for nine days in early March: there's a Latin drag-queen show, in-line-skate competition, domino tournament, the immense Calle Ocho street festival, Miss Carnaval Miami and more (www.carnavalmiami.com).

Florida Film Festival

In Winter Park, near Orlando, this March celebration of independent films is fast becoming one of the largest in the southeast.

Captain Robert Searle's Raid

St Augustine meticulously re-creates Robert Searle's infamous 1668 pillaging of the town in March. Local pirates dress up again in June for Sir Francis Drake's Raid. Volunteers are welcome!

St Patrick's Day

Ireland's patron saint gets his due across Florida on March 17 (any excuse to drink, right?). Miami turns the greenest.

Winter Music Conference

For five days in late March, DJs, musicians, promoters and music-industry execs converge on Miami to party, strike deals, listen to new dance music and coo over the latest technology (www.wmcon.com).

April

Interstate Mullet Toss

In late April on Perdido Key, near Pensacola, locals are famous for their annual ritual of tossing dead fish over the Florida–Alabama state line. Distance trumps style, but some have lots of style.

May

Sea Turtle Nesting

Beginning in May and extending through October, sea turtles nest on Florida beaches; after two months (from midsummer through fall), hatchling runs see the kids totter back to sea.

Isle of Eight Flags Shrimp Festival

On May's first weekend, Amelia Island celebrates shrimp, art and pirates, with an invasion and lots of scurvy pirate talk – aaarrrrgh!

SunFest

Over five days in early May, a quarter million folks gather in West Palm Beach for South Florida's largest waterfront music and arts festival (www.sunfest.com).

Memorial Day Circuit Party

For late May's Memorial Day weekend, Pensacola becomes one massive three-day gay party, with lots of DJs, dancing and drinking.

June

Gay Days

Starting on the first Saturday of June, and going for a week, upwards of 40,000 gays and lesbians descend on the Magic Kingdom and other Orlando theme parks, hotels and clubs. Wear red (www.gaydays.com).

Goombay Festival

In Miami's Coconut Grove, this massive four-day, early-June street party draws over 300,000 to celebrate the city's Bahamian culture with music, dancing and parades; it's one of America's largest black-culture festivals (www.goombayfestivalcoconutgrove.com).

July

Fourth of July

America's Independence Day is the cause for parades and fireworks, large and small, across the state. Miami draws the biggest crowd for the best fireworks and laser show.

Steinhatchee Scallop Season

The opening day of scallop season in Steinhatchee can draw a thousand folks, who take to the waters to harvest this delectable bivalve by hand. Anyone can join the following two-month treasure hunt.

August

Miami Spice

Miami's restaurants join together in August to offer prix-fixe lunches and dinners in an attempt to draw city residents from their apartments.

September

Mickey's Not-So-Scary Halloween Party

At Disney World on select evenings over two months (starting in September), kids can trick or treat in the shadow of Cinderella's Castle, with costumed Disney favorites and a Halloween-themed parade.

October

Fantasy Fest

Key West pulls out all the stops for this weeklong costumed extravaganza culminating in Halloween. Everyone's even crazier than usual, and Key West's own Goombay Festival competes for attention the same week.

MoonFest

West Palm Beach throws a rockin' block party for Halloween, October 31. Guests are encouraged to come in costume, and dozens of the best local bands play for free.

November

White Party

A raucous gay and lesbian celebration (and HIV/AIDS fundraiser), the White Party is actually a series of parties and nightclub events in Miami Beach and Fort Lauderdale over a week in late November (www.whiteparty.net). And yes, wear white.

Tampa Cigar Heritage Festival

Tampa's Ybor City has a long history as the cigar-making capital of the US. That heritage, and the cigars themselves, are celebrated in this one-day festival (www.cigarheritagefestival.com).

St Arrrgustine Pirate Gathering

Put on an eye patch and dust off your pirate lingo for this hokey celebration of scurvy dogs and seafaring rascals in St Augustine for three days in mid-November.

December

High season begins for South Florida beaches. Manatees arrive in warm-water springs.

Art Basel Miami Beach

Very simply, early December sees one of the biggest international art shows in the world, with over 150 art galleries represented and four days of parties (www.artbaselmiamibeach.com).

Victorian Christmas Stroll

The landmark 1891 Tampa Bay Hotel (now a museum) celebrates Christmas, Victorian-style, for three weeks in December, with folks in period costume.

King Mango Strut

Miami's Coconut Grove rings in the New Year with this wacky, freak-alicious, after-Christmas parade, which spoofs current events and local politics (www.kingmangostrut.org).

Far left: June Goombay Festival;
Left: July 4th of July, Miami

What's New

For this new edition of Discover Florida, our authors have hunted down the fresh, the transformed, the hot and the happening. These are some of our favorites. For up-to-the-minute recommendations, see www.lonelyplanet.com/florida.

1 **NEW FANTASYLAND**
The Magic Kingdom is the oldest part of Walt Disney World® Resort, and Fantasyland has long been the most nostalgic corner of the Magic Kingdom. But by the time you read this, the New Fantasyland will be open and offering a Snow White–themed roller coaster and Be Our Guest – the only restaurant in the Magic Kingdom that serves booze (wine and beer only). Parents celebrate! (p63)

2 **PÉREZ ART MUSEUM MIAMI**
After many years, Miami's home-grown art museum and its accompanying Museum Park are open to the public. The tropical-moderne facade is already an iconic part of Miami's waterfront. (p190)

3 **DECOBIKE**
Peddle around South Beach in style (and help combat the emissions belched out by all of those classic cars and Hummers) on your own lovely DecoBike. (p201)

4 **COLISEUM BALLROOM**
After an extensive renovation, St Petersburg's historic Coliseum Ballroom is reopening to the public. Don't miss the lavish interior of this events space, originally built in 1924. (p279)

5 **LEGACY TRAIL**
See blue waterways and green subtropical woodland on two unhurried wheels on the Legacy Trail, a bike path that runs from Sarasota to Venice. (p285)

6 **GREAT CALUSA BLUEWAY**
Experience the serenity of Southwest Florida's gentle waters on the Buck Key Paddling Trail, a reopened ecological playground of mangroves, beaches and wetlands within the Great Calusa Blueway. (p286)

7 **WIZARDING WORLD OF HARRY POTTER AT UNIVERSAL ORLANDO RESORT**
Muggles rejoice! The Gringotts vaults and Harry Potter's London have arrived at Universal Orlando Resort's Diagon Alley. There's even a Hogwarts Express to transport you to the *other* Wizarding World (Hogsmeade) at Islands of Adventure. (p122)

8 **SPRINGFIELD**
If you've wanted to walk the streets of Springfield, drink a Duff, quaff a Flaming Moe and down a Krusty Burger, don't miss this *Simpsons*–themed addition to Universal Orlando Resort. (p121)

9 **WOOD TAVERN**
This welcome addition to the Miami nightlife scene manages to combine casual service, a huge outdoor area, artsy clientele and an enormous beer menu. (p214)

10 **WET WALKS**
Want to see the Everglades up close and personal? Embark on a wet walk into the heart of the wetlands. Nothing says adventure like an alligator-adjacent stroll. (p243)

Get Inspired

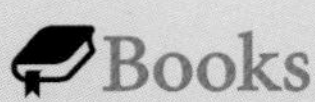

Books

- **Swamplandia!** (2011) Karen Russell's surreal, tragicomic saga of a family of alligator wrestlers.
- **Sick Puppy** (2000) This Carl Hiaasen comedy-tropical-noir novel stars the stupidest Labrador retriever in literature.
- **Continental Drift** (1985) Moving tale by Russell Banks about a blue-collar worker who flees to Florida.
- **The Everglades: River of Grass** (1947) Beautifully written tribute to the Everglades by activist/environmentalist/feminist Marjory Stoneman Douglas.

Films

- **There's Something About Mary** (1998) Hilarious Farrelly Brothers take on love, Miami and hair gel.
- **Key Largo** (1948) Humphrey Bogart and Lauren Bacall classic.
- **Monster** (2003) Charlize Theron portrays the dark side of the Florida dream.
- **Scarface** (1983) A Cuban gangster goes from rags to riches to... well, trouble.

Music

- **Primitive Love** (1985) Gloria Estefan puts Cuban-American music on the map.
- **Losing Streak** (1996) Less Than Jake rocks out with ska-punk goodness.
- **Changes in Latitudes, Changes in Attitudes** (1977) Jimmy Buffet's quintessential album.
- **R.O.O.T.S** (2009) Flo Rida's second album is full of massive production and party tracks.
- **Ocean Avenue** (2003) Yellowcard's pop-punk doesn't get any sweeter and/or sadder.

Websites

- **Tampa Bay News/St Pete Times** (www.tampabay.com) Website for the *St Petersburg Times,* one of the best newspapers in the state.
- **Florida State Parks** (www.floridastateparks.org) Gateway site for Florida state parks.
- **Just Florida** (www.justflorida.org) Exhaustive website on Florida travel.
- **Florida Division of Cultural Affairs** (www.florida-arts.org) Portal into the local arts scene.

Short on time?

This list will give you instant insight into the region.

Read *Hoot,* by Carl Hiaasen, is a funny, moving tale of growing up and fighting off rapacious land developers – themes the author likes.

Watch *The Birdcage,* a Robin Williams classic that captures everything silly and lovable about Florida, especially Miami Beach.

Listen Lynyrd Skynyrd's (pronounced *'lĕh-'nérd 'skin-'nérd*) debut is the opus of American Southern (and Florida Swamp) rock and roll.

Log on www.visitflorida.com is the state's incredibly comprehensive official tourism portal.

Gazebo, Key Largo (p218)
CRISTIAN LAZZARI/GETTY IMAGES ©

Need to Know

Currency

US dollars ($)

Language

English, also Spanish.

Money

ATMs widely available. Credit cards widely accepted.

Visas

Nationals qualifying for the Visa Waiver Program allowed a 90-day stay sans visa; all others need a visa.

Cell Phones

Europe and Asia's GSM 900/1800 standard is incompatible with the USA's cell-phone systems.

Wi-Fi

Common in midrange and top-end hotels, cafes, libraries and malls.

Internet Access

Common in midrange and top-end hotels. Internet cafes prevalent in towns.

Tipping

Tipping (15% to 20%) is mandatory. Bartenders, taxi drivers and hotel staff expect small tips (a few dollars).

For more information, see Survival Guide (p337).

When to Go

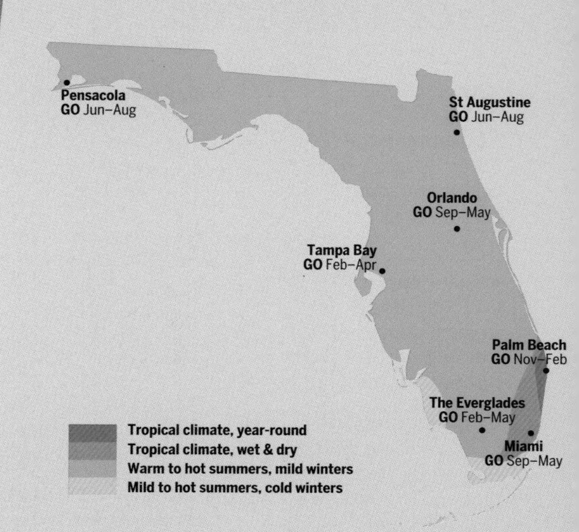

High Season (Mar–Aug)

- South Florida beaches peak with Spring Break.
- Panhandle and northern beaches peak in summer.
- Orlando theme parks peak in summer.

Shoulder (Feb & Sep)

- In South Florida, February has ideal dry weather, but no Spring Break craziness.
- Northern beaches/theme parks less crowded, still hot.
- Prices drop from peak by 20–30%.

Low Season (Oct–Jan)

- Some beach towns virtually close until winter snowbirds arrive.
- Hotel prices can drop from peak by 50%.
- Winter dry season runs November to April.

Advance Planning

- **Three months before** Start plotting out your overarching itineraries, including routes between major destinations. For good rates, now is the time to book plane tickets and reserve hotel rooms.
- **One month before** Make reservations at high-end restaurants and get car rental (or bus tickets) sorted out.
- **One week before** Check the internet to see if any concerts, plays or other live events are on when you visit.

Your Daily Budget

Budget up to $150

- Dorm beds/camping: $25-50
- Supermarket self-catering and cheap eats

Midrange $150–300

- Budget to midrange hotels: $80-150
- Target theme park and beach shoulder seasons
- Rental car: $40-80 a day, more with insurance

Top End over $300

- Boutique hotel and theme parks: $200-500
- High-season beach hotel/resort: $250-400
- All-inclusive, four- to seven-day theme-park blowout: $1500-4000

Exchange Rates

Australia	A$1	$0.87
Canada	C$1	$0.88
Europe	€1	$1.24
Japan	Y100	$0.86
New Zealand	NZ$1	$0.79
UK	UK£1	$1.57

For current exchange rates see www.xe.com.

What to Bring

- **Sunscreen** Florida sun is strong and unrelenting, so bring the right sunscreen.
- **Sweater/Sweatshirt** Come winter, it can get nippy at night, even in Miami (plus it gets downright cold in northern Florida).
- **ID** Always bring ID if heading out at night. Florida bouncers rigorously check ID at the door.
- **GPS** A good GPS is invaluable, especially for getting around back roads.

Arriving in Florida

- **Miami International Airport**

Metrobus Every 30 minutes 6am-11pm daily; 35 minutes to Miami Beach

Shuttle Vans $20–26

Taxis $38 to South Beach

- **Orlando International Airport**

Lynx Bus Lynx bus $2. Every 30 minutes 6am-10:30pm daily; 40 minutes downtown, 70 minutes Walt Disney World® Resort

Shuttle Vans $20–30

Taxis $50–60. Higher rates to Walt Disney World® Resort

- **Tampa International Airport**

HART Buses Hart bus $2. Every 15 minutes 5:30am-11:30pm weekdays, every half-hour 7am-8:30pm weekends; 40 minutes to downtown

Shuttle Vans $12–32

Taxis $30

Getting Around

- **Car** An extensive road network criss-crosses Florida; some major highways have tolls.
- **Bus** Greyhound serves major cities and some midsized towns across the state.
- **Train** Amtrak serves Florida's largest cities.
- **Air** Short hop flights are possible, but expensive.
- **Boat** Ferries connect Key West to Ft Myers and Marco Island.

Accommodations

- **Boutique Hotels** Smaller, independently owned hotels, many with creative flair.
- **Resorts** Large, sometimes all-inclusive properties with multiple activities on offer.
- **Hotels** Includes larger, business-style and corporate-geared accommodation.
- **B&B** Small properties, often converted homes where (of course) breakfast is included.
- **Hostels** Dorm-style budget rooms.
- **Motels** Budget, usually located near highways.

Be Forewarned

- **Hurricanes** Official hurricane season lasts from June 1 to November 30.
- **Traffic** Tends to be awful in large Florida cities.
- **Wildlife** Jellyfish are a beach annoyance; gators less so, but never feed them.

Walt Disney World® Resort & Orlando

Walt Disney World® is what happens when innocence meets imagination. If Florida promises to fulfill your desires, Walt Disney World® is your dreams made manifest. Surrounding this movable fantasy feast is Orlando, Theme Park Capital of the World. Then again, if Orlando holds said title, it's because the Theme Park crown is a pair of mouse ears. From nostalgic Magic Kingdom to faux-modern Epcot to glamorous Hollywood Studios, everything in Walt Disney World® makes good on the guarantees of childhood: 'X' marks the spot, the princess will be rescued, true love will triumph and good will beat evil. What accompanies this promise? Illusion and magic and rides; shows and parades; escape from the everyday, the ordinary, the real. Still, when you're ready for the real world again, explore Orlando's world-class museums and excellent parks – still wonderful, if in the shadow of Cinderella's Castle.

Epcot Center (p65)

Splash Mountain (p61) ride
HELEN SESSIONS/ALAMY ©

Walt Disney World® Resort & Orlando

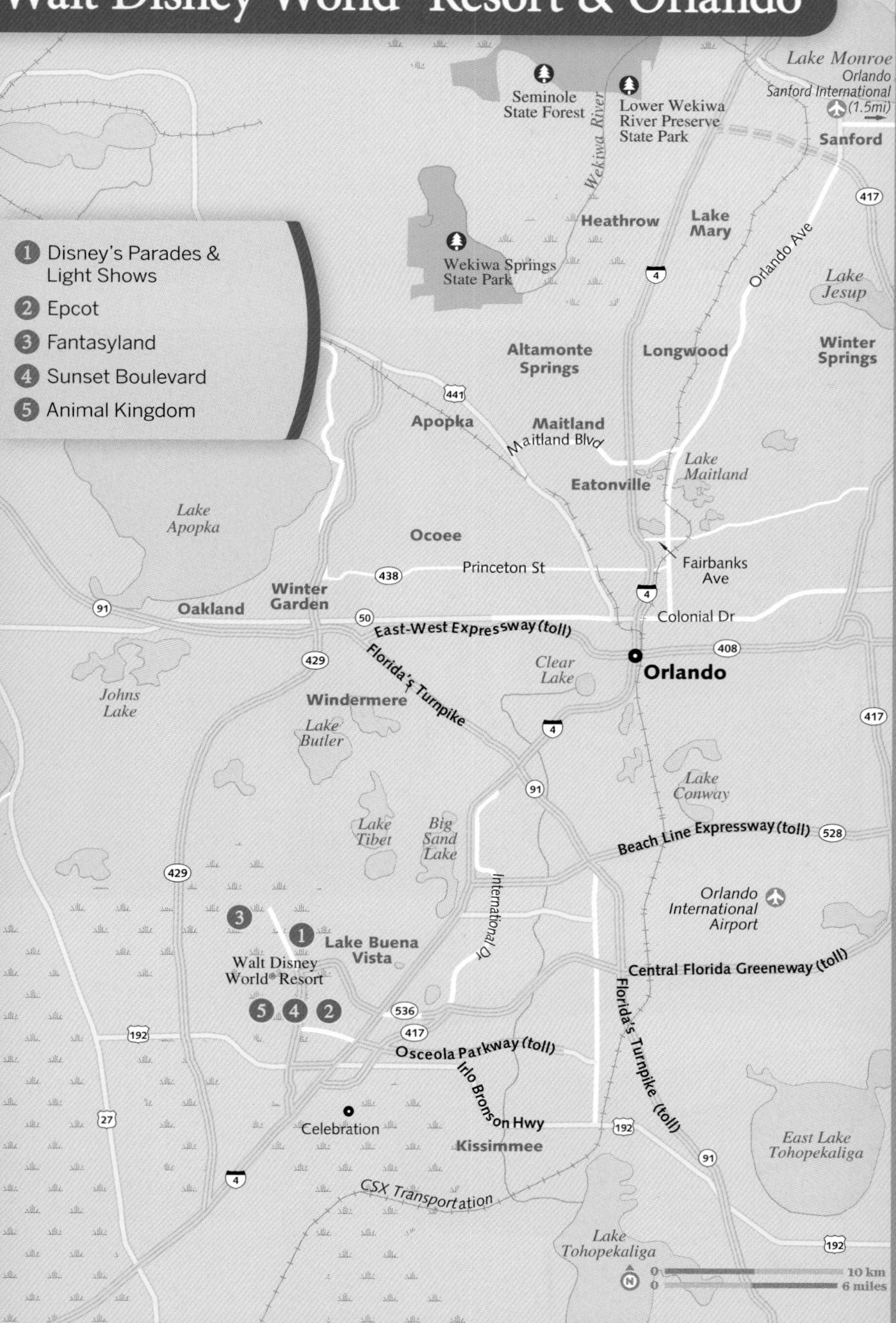

Walt Disney World® Resort & Orlando's Highlights

Disney's Parades & Light Shows

In the theme park dedicated to Disney films and the dreams they've inspired, you can see those flights of fancy come alive during daily shows. By day, watch your favorite characters bounce along in the Main Street Electrical Parade and Celebrate a Dream Come True; at night, watch the skies come alive with lasers, fireworks and loud noises during Fantasmic! and IllumiNations. Cinderella Castle during the Main Street Electrical Parade (p68)

1

2 Epcot

If the Magic Kingdom brings fantasy to life, Epcot opts for science fiction and geographic flights of fancy. In Future World the tech-tastic attractions are a Disney-fied glimpse into brave new worlds unlocked by science and exploration. The World Showcase brings us back to Earth in the form of (admittedly) clichéd depictions of the global stage, from Moroccan belly dancing to Norwegian Viking longboats. Mission Space (p65)

BLAINE HARRINGTON III/CORBIS ©

3 Fantasyland

Fantasyland is as good as Disney gets when it comes to little kids and their parents. Rides and attractions are gentle and there's a quiet, old-school charm that gives this section of the Magic Kingdom a little more warmth and heart than other parts of the park. That said, you'd be remiss to not check out Mickey's PhilharMagic, a 3-D journey into the heart of the Disney experience.

Dumbo ride

MARK GREEN/ALAMY ©

4 Sunset Boulevard

What to do with older kids who are embarrassed to pose with Dumbo, but aren't independent adolescents yet? Take them to Sunset Boulevard in Hollywood Studios. The Rock 'n' Roller Coaster and Twilight Zone Tower of Terror provide a bit of a thrill, which should make most kids feel mature enough to leave the Magic Kingdom (but scared enough to still need mom and dad).

5 Disney's Animal Kingdom

The Animal Kingdom is great fun. There are roller coasters and Lion King–inspired parades, but you can also spot gorillas and lions on jeep safari, or do jungle treks past tigers and real dragons. So while plenty of Disney magic goes on behind the curtains (or bamboo partition) it feels authentically wild at the end of the day, too. Gorilla

Walt Disney World® Resort & Orlando's Best...

Rides & Attractions

- **It's a Small World** This old-school ride brings out the kid in everyone.
- **Twilight Zone Tower of Terror** A legitimately scary thrill!
- **Turtle Talk with Crush** *Finding Nemo's* Crush leads this awesome interactive experience.
- **Expedition Everest** A Nepalese roller coaster of a ride.
- **Toy Story Midway Mania!** Another incredible Pixar-based interactive extravaganza.

Dining

- **Yellow Dog Eats** Fine barbecue in a laid-back former general store. (p102)
- **Dandelion Communitea Cafe** Vegetarians will rejoice in this organic eatery. (p103)
- **Sci-Fi Dine-in Theater** Out-of-this-world (*groan*; sorry) themed Disney dining. (p81)
- **La Hacienda de San Angel** Latin flavors infuse this World Showcase favorite. (p79)

Hotels

- **EO Inn & Spa Serene B&B** for those seeking crowd escapes. (p97)
- **Bay Hill Club & Lounge** Old-time charm and warm service. (p98)
- **Disney's Grand Floridian Resort & Spa** Disney's poshest resort, all Old Florida charm. (p76)
- **Disney's Animal Kingdom Lodge** Our favorite themed hotel recalls the aesthetic of *The Lion King*. (p77)

Shows

- **Finding Nemo: The Musical** Innovative set and costume design make this the best show at Disney. (p88)
- **IllumiNations** The Earth's history presented as a flashy light show. (p68)
- **Jammin' Jungle** Animal puppets and African dancing. (p68)
- **Fantasmic!** Disney villains take on Mickey Mouse. (p68)
- **Main Street Electrical Parade** A nostalgic favorite: light show meets parades meets Disney characters. (p68)

Left: Parade, Main Street, USA (p61); **Above:** Seas With Nemo & Friends Pavilion (p66)

Need to Know

BE FOREWARNED

I-4 is the main highway in the Orlando metro area. From the hours of 8am to 10am and 4pm to 6pm it can be an absolute nightmare for traffic, boasting some of the worst gridlock in the nation.

ADVANCE PLANNING

- **Hotels** If you're planning on staying in Walt Disney World® Resort, or visiting the area during any kind of festival, you'll want to book lodging early.
- **Car rentals** Try to organize at least one month in advance; car rentals book out fast in Orlando.
- **Restaurants** The top-end dining places we list, plus themed dining like eating with Disney characters, requires advance reservations.
- **Babysitters** If you need time to yourself, try to organize a sitter service soon; see www.kidsniteout.com.
- **Tickets** Get a Fastpass as early as possible in order to bypass Disney's famously long lines.

RESOURCES

- **The Orlando Sentinel** The best newspaper covering the region: includes good listings for live shows, arts events, nightlife etc; www.orlandosentinel.com
- **The Daily Disney** The *Orlando Sentinel*'s eye on Walt Disney World®, with peeks into the behind-the-scenes workings of the park; www.orlandosentinel.com/the-daily-disney
- **All Ears** An unofficial guide to getting around Walt Disney World®; allears.net

GETTING AROUND

- **Car** I-4 is the main highway that runs through Orlando.
- **Monorail** Three monorail routes intersect the heart of the Disney resort.
- **Boat** Multiple ferry services link Disney's major subparks and resort areas.
- **Bus** All areas of Walt Disney World® save the Magic Kingdom are connected by bus.

Walt Disney World® Resort & Orlando Itineraries

You've got a couple kingdoms, 11 nations in Epcot and several dimensions of fantasy. And then there's Orlando: a city that warrants some exploration.

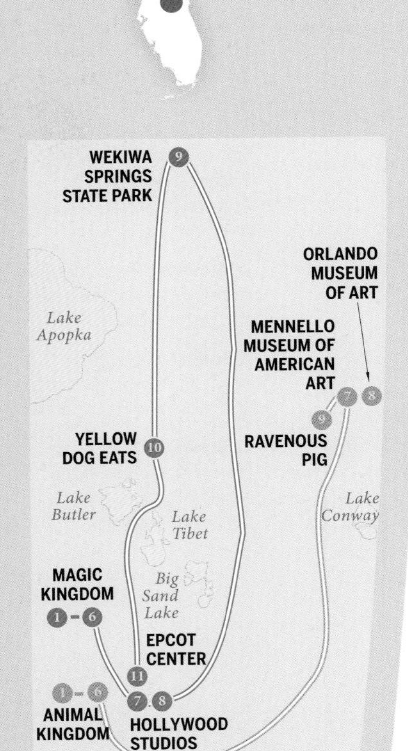

4 DAYS

KIDS' QUEST

MAGIC KINGDOM TO ORLANDO

This is an itinerary tailored for families with young children (10 or under). We'll start in the ❶ **Magic Kingdom**, where you should spend your first day wandering from ❷ **Fantasyland** to ❸ **Adventureland** and everywhere around and in between. If you plan a bit in advance, you should organize ❹ **character dining** for your kids. Make sure to catch the ❺ **Spectromagic** parade and the ❻ **Wishes Nighttime Spectacular** fireworks show in the evening.

The next day, you'll go to Hollywood Studios; ❼ **Pixar Pals Countdown for Fun** showcases familiar characters, while ❽ **Toy Story Midway Mania** puts you in the middle of a video game. On your third day, tube around ❾ **Wekiwa Springs State Park** in Orlando during the day and have dinner at the scrumptious ❿ **Yellow Dog Eats**, which boasts a menu even young ones with picky appetites can handle. If you don't think kids will enjoy a day in Orlando, head to ⓫ **Epcot Center**: there's plenty more Disney to be had.

Top Left: Mad Tea Party ride, Magic Kingdom (p60);
Top Right: Splash Mountain (p61)

OLDER KIDS & ADULTS

ANIMAL KINGDOM TO WINTER PARK

We start in ❶ **Animal Kingdom**; ❷ **Expedition Everest** is a great roller coaster that ought to keep your toes curled in excitement, but the focus here is (duh) animal encounters. So walk past tigers and (Komodo) dragons on the ❸ **Maharajah Jungle Trek** and drive on a fun ride-meets-zoo-meets-safari trip via ❹ **Kilimanjaro Safari**. If you book in advance, get the ultimate animal encounter by embarking on the ❺ **Wild Africa Trek**. Also, don't miss ❻ **Finding Nemo: the Musical**; it's a fun theatrical experience with giant puppets, goofy voice acting and lots of color.

The next day, go to Orlando and Winter Park. If you don't have kids, visit the ❼ **Mennello Museum of American Art**; if you do, the ❽ **Orlando Museum of Art** has more exhibits for young ones. Make sure to finish the day with dinner at the excellent ❾ **Ravenous Pig**.

Discover Walt Disney World® Resort & Orlando

At a Glance

- **Magic Kingdom** (p60) Low on thrills and high on nostalgia, with Cinderella's Castle and nightly fireworks.
- **Epcot** (p65) A handful of rides to one side, country-based food, shopping and attractions to the other.
- **Animal Kingdom** (p67) Part zoo and part county fair, with a heavy dusting of Disney-styled Africa.
- **Orlando** (p89) Cultured, cosmopolitan, but likes to let its hair down at night.

Cinderella's Castle, Magic Kingdom

MEL LONGHURST/ROBERT HARDING ©

WALT DISNEY WORLD® RESORT

Minutes before the Magic Kingdom opens, Alice in Wonderland, Cinderella, Donald Duck and others stand where all can see them, sing 'Zippidee Doo Dah' and throw sparkly Mickey Mouse confetti into the crowds. They dash off on an open-windowed train, the gates open, and children, adults, honeymooners, grandparents and everyone in between enter the park, some strolling, others dashing down the impeccably clean Main Street toward Cinderella's Castle. That iconic image is as American as the Grand Canyon, a place as loaded with myth and promises of hope as the Statue of Liberty. If only for these few minutes, this is indeed the Happiest Place on Earth.

Yes, there will be seemingly endless lines. You'll get back to the hotel exhausted and aching, and swear next time you'll take a real vacation... Until those last minutes before you fall asleep. You see your child's face staring adoringly at Winnie the Pooh, or reaching out to grab the Donald Duck that pops out from the 3-D movie. And it's OK. That vacation can wait.

Sights

Walt Disney World® Resort covers over 40 sq miles, and includes four separate theme parks and two water parks, all connected by a complicated system of monorail, boat and bus, and intersected by highways and roads.

MAGIC KINGDOM

When most people think of Walt Disney World® Resort, they're thinking of the **Magic Kingdom** (**Map p62; ☎407-939-5277; www.disneyworld.disney.go.com; 1180 Seven Seas Dr;**

adult/child 3-10yr $95/89; 9am-9pm, hours vary; Disney, Disney, monorail Disney). This is Disney of commercials, Disney of princesses and pirates, Disney of dreams come true and Tinker Bell, quintessential old-school Disney with classic rides like It's a Small World and Space Mountain.

Main Street, USA Landmark

(Map p62; www.disneyworld.disney.go.com; theme park admission required; 9am-9pm, hours vary; ; Disney, Disney, Lynx 50, 56) Fashioned after Walt Disney's hometown of Marceline, MO, Main Street, USA, is best experienced with an aimless meander. Peruse the miniature dioramas of Peter Pan and Snow White in the street windows; pop in to catch the black-and-white movie reels of old Disney cartoons and browse the hundreds of thousands of must-have Disney souvenirs.

Adventureland Ride, Show

(Map p62; www.disneyworld.disney.go.com; theme park admission required; 9am-9pm, hours vary; ; Disney, Disney, Lynx 50, 56) Adventure Disney-style means pirates and jungles, magic carpets and tree houses, whimsical and silly representations of the exotic locales from storybooks and imagination. Don't miss **Pirates of the Caribbean** – the slow-moving boat through the dark and shadowy world of pirates remains one of the most popular attractions at Disney.

Frontierland Ride, Show

(Map p62; www.disneyworld.disney.go.com; theme park admission required; 9am-9pm, hours vary; ; Disney, Disney, Lynx 50, 56) Wild West Disney-style. **Splash Mountain** depicts the misadventures of Brer Rabbit, Brer Bear and Brer Fox, complete with chatty frogs, singing ducks and other critters. The 40mph drop into the river makes for one of the biggest thrills in the park, and you will get very wet! With no steep drops or loop-dee-loops, mild **Big Thunder Mountain Railroad** coaster is a great choice for little ones.

Liberty Square Ride, Show

(Map p62; www.disneyworld.disney.go.com; theme park admission required; 9am-9pm,

Local Knowledge

Walt Disney World® Resort Don't Miss List

DEWAYNE BEVIL, REPORTER, ORLANDO SENTINEL

1 MAGIC KINGDOM

Don't miss Magic Kingdom (p60), the theme park that changed Florida tourism. Nostalgia and classic attractions dominate, and Disney has upgraded favorites such as Haunted Mansion and the Enchanted Tiki Room. Magic Kingdom is a winner with little princesses.

2 TOY STORY MIDWAY MANIA

There are always lines outside this ride. Once inside and aboard, guests are effectively shrunk into a video game with characters from the Pixar movies, amid rapid-fire virtual carnival games. Most people get off wanting to get on again, so go directly to Toy Story (p70) to secure a free FastPass, which allows you to come back at a specific time.

3 WILD AFRICA TREK

A behind-the-scenes tour (p69) at Disney's Animal Kingdom gives guests unique behind the scenes experience on Kilimanjaro Safaris. Only a few dozen folks are allowed each day, so it's priced from $189 per person, on top of regular admission to Animal Kingdom.

4 EPCOT INTERNATIONAL FOOD & WINE FESTIVAL

This event in September spotlights global cuisine in kiosks scattered throughout World Showcase. Food is served up tapas-style across six weeks.

5 FIREWORKS

Major pyrotechnics are a nightly event at Walt Disney World® Resort. The 'Wishes' (p68) show, complete with real-life Tinker Bell flying out of Cinderella Castle, caps off the day at Magic Kingdom, while 'IllumiNations' is the impressive finale at Epcot.

Walt Disney World® Resort

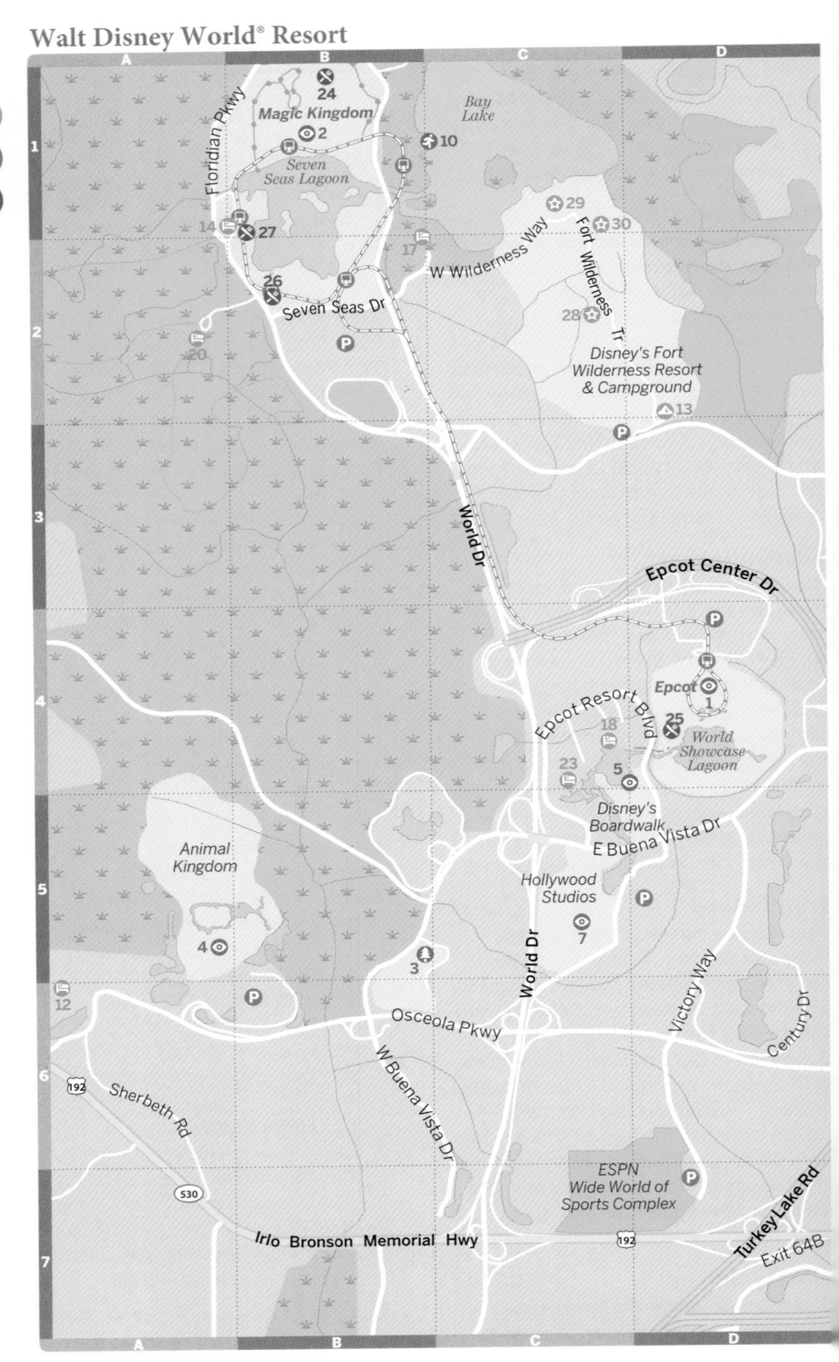

hours vary; Disney, Disney, Lynx 50, 56) The ramblin' 19th-century **Haunted Mansion**, another classic piece of low-on-thrill and high-on-silly fun, and the only real ride in Liberty Sq. Cruise slowly past the haunted dining room, where apparitions dance across the stony floor, but beware of those hitchhiking ghosts – don't be surprised if they jump into your car uninvited.

Fantasyland

Ride, Show

(Map p62; www.disneyworld.disney.go.com/new-fantasyland; Magic Kingdom; theme park admission required; 9am-9pm, hours vary; ; Disney, Disney, Lynx 50, 56) Quintessential Disney, Fantasyland is the highlight of any Disney trip for both the eight-and-under crowd and grown-ups looking for a nostalgic taste of classic Disney. Tweens too cool for fairy tales and teens looking for thrills may turn up their noses. Disney began introducing all kinds of changes here in 2013, such as *Beauty and the Beast*–themed attractions and the new *Snow White*–themed coaster, the **Seven Dwarfs Mine Train**.

Tomorrowland

Ride, Show

(Map p62; www.disneyworld.disney.go.com; Magic Kingdom; theme park admission required; 9am-9pm, hours vary; ; Disney, Disney, Lynx 50, 56) Though the theming as a Jetsons-inspired peek into the future falls flat, Tomorrowland holds a few wildly popular Disney highlights. Come first thing or use a FastPass+ for **Space Mountain**, an indoor coaster into the star-studded galaxies of outer space, and **Buzz Lightyear's Space Ranger Spin**, a cross between a ride and a video game.

Rose Garden

Gardens

(Map p62; www.disneyworld.disney.go.com; Magic Kingdom; theme park admission required; 9am-9pm, hours vary; Disney, Disney, Lynx 50, 56) For a bit of downtime, the covered waterside pavilion just off the bridge to the right of Cinderella's Castle makes a perfect place to pull out those goldfish snacks and take a quiet rest. It's pictured but not labeled on the Magic Kingdom map. Look for this quiet treasure on your way into Tomorrowland.

Walt Disney World® Resort

Don't Miss Sights

1 Epcot D4
2 Magic Kingdom B1

Sights

Adventureland .... (see 2)
Africa .... (see 4)
Asia .... (see 4)
3 Blizzard Beach B5
Characters in Flight .... (see 6)
Club Cool .... (see 1)
Dinoland .... (see 4)
Discovery Island .... (see 4)
DisneyQuest Indoor Interactive Theme Park .... (see 6)
4 Disney's Animal Kingdom A5
5 Disney's BoardWalk D4
6 Downtown Disney F4
Ellen's Energy Adventure .... (see 1)
Fantasyland .... (see 2)
Frontierland .... (see 2)
7 Hollywood Boulevard & Echo Lake C5
Liberty Square .... (see 2)
Main Street, USA .... (see 2)
Mission Space .... (see 1)
Oasis .... (see 4)
8 Old Town F7
Pixar Place & Mickey Avenue .... (see 7)
Rafiki's Planet Watch .... (see 4)
Rose Garden .... (see 2)
Seas with Nemo & Friends Pavilion .... (see 1)
Soarin' .... (see 1)
Spaceship Earth .... (see 1)
Star Tours: The Adventure Continues .... (see 7)
Sunset Boulevard .... (see 7)
Test Track .... (see 1)
Tomorrowland .... (see 2)
9 Typhoon Lagoon E5

Activities, Courses & Tours

Animation Academy .... (see 7)
Fort Wilderness Tri-Circle-D Ranch .... (see 13)
10 Sammy Duvall's Watersports Centre C1
Surrey Bikes at the Boardwalk .... (see 5)

Sleeping

11 Barefoot Suites F7
12 Disney's Animal Kingdom Lodge A6
Disney's BoardWalk Inn .... (see 5)
13 Disney's Fort Wilderness Resort D2
14 Disney's Grand Floridian Resort & Spa B1
15 Disney's Old Key West Resort E4
16 Disney's Port Orleans French Quarter and Riverside Resorts E4
17 Disney's Wilderness Lodge B2
18 Disney's Yacht Club Resort and Disney's Beach Club Resort C4
19 Hilton Orlando Bonnet Creek E5
20 Shades of Green Resort A2
21 Villas of Grand Cypress E2
22 Waldorf Astoria E5
23 Walt Disney World Swan & Dolphin Hotels C4

Eating

50's Prime Time Café .... (see 7)
Be Our Guest .... (see 2)
Biergarten .... (see 1)
Chefs de France .... (see 1)
Cheshire Cafe .... (see 2)
Cinderella's Royal Table .... (see 2)
Earl of Sandwich .... (see 6)
Flying Fish .... (see 5)
Fresh-A-Peel .... (see 6)
24 Gaston's Tavern B1
Jiko .... (see 12)
Kouzzina by Cat Cora .... (see 5)
La Cava del Tequila .... (see 1)
La Hacienda de San Angel .... (see 1)
25 Le Cellier Steakhouse D4
Les Halles Boulangerie Patisserie .... (see 1)
26 'Ohana B2
Paradiso 37 .... (see 6)
Restaurant Marrakesh .... (see 1)
Rose & Crown .... (see 1)
San Angel Inn .... (see 1)
Sci-Fi Dine-In Theater .... (see 7)
Teppan Edo .... (see 1)
Via Napoli .... (see 1)
27 Victoria & Albert's B1
Writer's Stop .... (see 7)
Yak and Yeti .... (see 4)

Drinking & Nightlife

Belle Vue Room .... (see 5)
Big River Grille & Brewing Works .... (see 5)
Jellyrolls .... (see 5)
Raglan Road .... (see 6)

Entertainment

28 Chip 'n' Dale Campfire Singalong C2
Cirque du Soleil La Nouba .... (see 6)
29 Hoop-Dee-Doo Musical Revue C1
House of Blues .... (see 6)
30 Mickey's Backyard Barbecue C1
Spirit of Aloha .... (see 26)

Shopping

Bibbidee Bobbidee Boutique .... (see 2)
Lego Imagination Center .... (see 6)
Once Upon a Toy .... (see 6)
World of Disney .... (see 6)

Getting There & Around

The only direct way to get to Magic Kingdom is by boat or monorail from Disney's Magic Kingdom resorts of Grand Floridian, Grand Polynesian Resort, Contemporary Resort, Fort Wilderness Resort or Wilderness Lodge, or by 600-passenger ferry or monorail from the Transportation & Ticket Center. There is no parking, so if you drive, you have to park at the Transportation & Ticket Center and then take the monorail or the ferry to the park.

With its massive parking lot and endless lines for bus shuttles, the Transportation & Ticket Center, however, can be unbearable. Instead, consider hopping the monorail or water launch to Disney's Contemporary Resort, Grand Floridian or Polynesian Resort, and then taking a cab to your hotel.

EPCOT

With no roller coasters, no parades, no water rides, and plenty of greenery, things here run a bit slower, with a bit less va-voom, than the rest of Walt Disney World® Resort. Slow down and enjoy. Smell the incense in Morocco, listen to the Beatles in the UK, sip miso in Japan – then rocket into the future.

World Showcase — Attraction

(www.disneyworld.disney.go.com; Epcot; theme park admission required; 9am-6pm, hours vary; Disney, Disney, monorail Disney) Who needs the hassle of a passport and jet lag when you can travel the world right here at Walt Disney World®? World Showcase, one of two themed sections of Epcot, comprises 11 countries arranged around a lagoon. Watch belly dancing in Morocco, eat pizza in Italy and buy personally engraved bottles of perfume in France, before settling down to watch fireworks about world peace and harmony. Disney was right. It truly is a small world after all.

Soarin' — Ride

(Map p62; www.disneyworld.disney.go.com; Future World, Epcot; theme park admission required; 9am-6pm, hours vary; Disney, Disney, monorail Disney) Soar up and down, hover and accelerate as the giant screen in front of you takes you over California's citrus groves, golf courses, mountains, coasts, rivers and cities and, finally, into the fireworks over Cinderella's Castle at Disney Lane. You can smell the oranges and your feet almost touch those surfers below.

Mission Space — Ride

(Map p62; www.disneyworld.disney.go.com; Future World, Epcot; theme park admission required; 9am-6pm, hours vary; Disney, Disney) One of two thrill rides at Future World, Epcot, Mission Space straps you into a tiny

FastPass

A FastPass is a free paper ticket that allows you to return to an attraction during a designated time window, thereby jumping the mind-numbingly long lines and hopping right on. This is the lowdown: if a ride has a FastPass option, there will be automated ticket machines at the ride entrance. Swipe your park ticket and out pops your FastPass with your return time. Return to the ride within the designated time frame, show your paper FastPass ticket at the FastPass line, and zip right onto the ride with no more than a 15-minute wait. The catch? Check the bottom of your FastPass to find out when you are eligible to swipe your card for another FastPass – the crowd level determines whether or not you can get a second one before your allocated time to use the first one, and you are never allowed more than two at a time. FastPasses for the most popular attractions can run out by midday, and don't be surprised if your return time isn't for upwards of five hours from the time you get your pass. If you really want to see something, get your FastPass as soon as possible.

four-person spaceship cockpit and launches you into, you guessed it, space. While this is a simulated experience and not a high-speed ride, the special effects can be nauseating and the dire warnings are enough to scare away even the most steel-bellied folk. There are two ride options, one with less intensity than the other.

Ellen's Energy Adventure — Ride

(Map p62; 407-939-5277; www.disneyworld.disney.go.com; Future World, Epcot; theme park admission required; 9am-6pm, hours vary; Disney, Disney, monorail Disney) This 45-minute ride is the oddest attraction in Orlando, perhaps in the entire state of Florida. It begins with a movie during which Ellen DeGeneres dreams that she is playing *Jeopardy!* with Jamie Lee Curtis. Determined to outsmart her know-it-all opponent, Ellen joins Bill Nye the Science Guy on a trip through history to learn about energy sources. At this point, you board a 96-passenger vehicle and lurch slowly through the darkness into the Cretaceous period.

Spaceship Earth — Ride

(Map p62; www.disneyworld.disney.go.com; Future World, Epcot; theme park admission required; 9am-6pm, hours vary; Disney, Disney) Inside the giant golf-ball landmark at the entrance to Disney's Epcot, Spaceship Earth is a strange, kitschy slow-moving ride through time that is surprisingly cool and enjoys a cult following.

Seas with Nemo & Friends Pavilion — Ride, Show

(Map p62; www.disneyworld.disney.go.com; Future World, Epcot; theme park admission required; 9am-6pm, hours vary; Disney, Disney, monorialDisney) Kids under 10 won't want to miss the two *Nemo*-themed attractions at Epcot's Future World. Ride a clamshell through the ocean with Nemo on **Seas with Nemo & Friends** and talk face-to-face with Crush in the interactive **Turtle Talk with Crush**, a Disney highlight.

Test Track — Ride

(Map p62; www.disneyworld.disney.go.com; Future World, Epcot; theme park admission re-

Left: Kilimanjaro Safaris (p69); **Below:** Monorail
(LEFT) D. TROZZO/ALAMY ©; (BELOW) IAN DAGNALL/ALAMY ©

quired; 9am-6pm, hours vary; Disney, Disney) Board a car and ride through heat, cold, speed, braking and crash tests. At one point a huge semi with blinding lights heads right for you, its horn blaring. When testing the acceleration, the car speeds up to 60mph within a very short distance, but there are few turns and no ups and downs like a roller coaster. At the ride's entrance you can virtually design your own car, and at the exit you'll find all kinds of car-themed games and simulators.

Getting There & Around

A pleasant, well-lit paved waterfront path or boat shuttle connects Epcot to Hollywood Studios, Disney's BoardWalk and the following Epcot resorts: Walt Disney World® Swan & Dolphin, Disney's Yacht Club and Disney's Beach Club, and Disney's BoardWalk Inn. The monorail runs a direct line between Epcot and the Transportation & Ticket Center; from there, catch a monorail or ferry to Magic Kingdom. Disney buses depart from outside Epcot to Disney resorts, Hollywood Studios and Animal Kingdom.

Within the park, a boat shuttles folks to and from Morocco and Germany from two boat docks at Showcase Plaza, just outside Future World.

Club Cool (Map p62; www.disneyworld.disney.go.com; Future World, Epcot; theme park admission required; 9am-6pm, hours vary; Disney, Disney) Free samples of soft drinks from other countries that aren't sold in the USA. Try Smart Watermelon from China, Vegitabeta from Japan and Beverley from Italy, among others.

ANIMAL KINGDOM

Set apart from the rest of Disney both in miles and in tone, **Animal Kingdom (Map p62; 407-939-5277; www.disneyworld.disney.go.com; 2101 Osceola Pkwy, Walt Disney World® Resort; adult/child $90/84; 9am-6pm, hours vary; Disney)** attempts to blend theme park and zoo, carnival and African safari, all stirred together with a healthy dose of Disney characters, storytelling and transformative magic.

HELEN SESSIONS/ALAMY ©

Don't Miss

Walt Disney World® Resort Parades & Shows

It takes a little bit of planning to coordinate your schedule to hit Disney's parades and nighttime spectaculars. Note that times vary according to day and season. In addition to the following cornerstones, check www.disneyworld.disney.go.com for holiday celebrations and specialty parties.

The **Wishes Nighttime Spectacular** (8pm) may be the most iconic Disney event bar none. Jiminy Cricket narrates this display of pomp, fireworks and general wonderment over Cinderella's Castle at Magic Kingdom.

Introduced in 2014, **Festival of Fantasy** (morning & afternoon, hours vary) features elaborate floats and dancing characters, including Peter Pan and Sleeping Beauty.

The fiery **IllumiNations** (nightly, hours vary), famed for its light show and fireworks, centers around a massive globe in the center of Epcot's World Showcase Lagoon.

Thousands of twinkling lights, covering various floats and favorite Disney characters, glimmer and sparkle through the park during the **Main Street Electrical Parade** (nightly, hours vary). Highlights include a massive Pete and his dragon, and Alice in Wonderland on top of a giant mushroom.

At **Celebrate the Magic** (nightly, hours vary), a seasonally changing light-and-music performance at Cinderella's Castle highlights Disney movies and characters in the Magic Kingdom.

Huge folk-art animal puppets and Disney characters in safari motif star in **Jammin' Jungle** (daily, hours vary), held at Animal Kingdom.

Fantasmic (nightly) is dramatic, overhyped and very popular. This water, music and light show centers on a vague and confusing plot in which Mickey Mouse proves victorious over a cast of Disney villains. Seating begins 90 minutes in advance, and even though the outdoor ampitheater seats more than 6000 people, it's always crowded.

Oasis
Zoo

(Map p62; www.disneyworld.disney.go.com; Animal Kingdom; theme park admission required; 9am-6pm, hours vary; ; Disney) Oasis is the first themed section of Animal Kingdom. It has cool critters, including a giant anteater, but it's best to move along to other attractions and pause to enjoy the animals on your way out and home.

Discovery Island
Show

(Map p62; www.disneyworld.disney.go.com; Animal Kingdom; theme park admission required; 9am-6pm, hours vary; Disney) The only attraction here is the *Bugs' Life*–themed **It's Tough to Be a Bug!**, a 4-D movie that includes periods of darkness, dry-ice and flashing lights. Though it's a lot of fun and very cute, it can terrify little ones – you will definitely hear children crying by the end.

Africa
Ride, Show

(Map p62; www.disneyworld.disney.go.com; Animal Kingdom; theme park admission required; 9am-6pm, hours vary; Disney) Board a jeep and ride through the African Savannah on **Kilimanjaro Safaris**, pausing to look at zebras, lions, giraffes and more, all seemingly roaming free. This is one of the Animal Kingdom's most popular attractions, so come early or use your FastPass+. The **Festival of the Lion King**, a *Lion King*–themed song and dance performance, earns rave reviews, but we were underwhelmed.

Asia
Ride, Show

(Map p62; www.disneyworld.disney.go.com; Animal Kingdom; theme park admission required; 9am-6pm, hours vary; Disney) Home to two of Animal Kingdom's three most popular rides: **Expedition Everest**, a great roller coaster with a yeti twist; and **Kali River Rapids**, a water ride. Owls and peregrine falcons dazzle audiences at **Flights of Wonder**. It's got some cheesy dialogue, but the animals are spectacular as they zoom around over your head.

Dinoland
Ride, Attraction

(Map p62; www.disneyworld.disney.go.com; Animal Kingdom; theme park admission required; 9am-6pm, hours vary; Disney) This bizarre dinosaur-themed section seems more like a tired carnival than Disney Magic, with garish plastic dinosaurs, midway games and 'Trilo-Bite' snacks. But little ones will like the kids' coaster **Primeval Whirl**, and **Dinosaur** is a really fun water ride with a *Jurassic Park* twist. Be warned – a giant T-Rex pops out just before you plummet, and you will get wet.

Rafiki's Planet Watch
Zoo

(Map p62; www.disneyworld.disney.go.com; Animal Kingdom; theme park admission required; 9am-6pm, hours vary; ; Disney) Veterinarians care for sick and injured animals at the **Conservation Station**, and sometimes there are animal interactions. You can check out the adorable, fist-sized tamarin monkeys and pet sheep and goats at **Affection Section**. But ultimately, the **Wildlife Express Train** you take to get here might just be the best part of this Disney enigma.

Around the World in 80 Minutes (or so)

The best way to experience the World Showcase is to simply wander as the mood moves you, poking through stores and restaurants, and catching what amounts to Bureau of Tourism promotional films and gentle rides through some of the countries. Donald Duck and his comrades take you through Mexico in Gran Fiesta Tour Starring the Three Caballeros; Norway's rather odd boat-ride Maelstrom meanders past Vikings, trolls and waterfalls; and the American Adventure show features audio-animatronic figures presenting a simplified interpretation of US history. The featured countries from left to right around the water are Mexico, Norway, China, Germany, Italy, the USA (The American Adventure), Japan, Morocco, France, the UK and Canada.

Getting There & Away

Disney buses stop at Animal Kingdom, but note the ride here can be up to 45 minutes, maybe longer. There is parking just outside the park gates.

HOLLYWOOD STUDIOS

Hollywood Studios offers none of the nostalgic charm of Magic Kingdom, the sophisticated delights of Epcot or the kitschy fun of Animal Kingdom. It's meant to conjure the heydays of Hollywood, with a replica of Graumann's Chinese Theatre and Hollywood Brown Derby, but most of the attractions find their inspiration from unabashed 21st-century energy.

The 122ft Sorcerer's Hat serves as the park's primary focal point. Make a right onto Sunset Blvd to hit the roller coasters, the Beauty and the Beast show and Fantasmic (a nighttime spectacular), and left towards New York for the movie-based attractions.

Sunset Boulevard — Rides, Shows

(Map p62; www.disneyworld.disney.go.com; Hollywood Studios; theme park admission required; Hollywood Studios hours; ; Disney, Disney) The simple and sweet outdoor theater performance of **Beauty and the Beast – Live on Stage** follows the storyline, incorporates the classic songs, and doesn't fall back on any special effects or crazy shenanigans. It's a rock-solid classic hit with the Disney-princess-loving crowd. For thrills and chills rather than frills, two of Disney's most talked about rides are in Sunset Blvd.

Pixar Place & Mickey Avenue — Rides, Shows

(Map p62; www.disneyworld.disney.go.com; Hollywood Studios; theme park admission required; Hollywood Studios hours; ; Disney, Disney) Lines are always long at **Toy Story Mania!** (FastPass+), where folks don 3-D glasses and shoot their way through midway games trying to score points, and the walk-through **The Legend of Captain Jack Sparrow** is a must for *Pirates of the Caribbean* fans.

Hollywood Boulevard & Echo Lake — Rides, Shows

(Map p62; www.disneyworld.disney.go.com; Hollywood Studios; theme park admission required; Hollywood Studios hours; ; Disney, Disney) This is where you'll find the *Star Wars*-themed **Star Tours** (FastPass+), one of Disney's newest and best 3-D

Aerosmith guitar, Rock 'n' Roller Coaster

HELEN SESSIONS/ALAMY ©

Best of Hollywood Studios

Within hours of the park opening, FastPass return times for Tower of Terror and Rock 'n' Roller Coaster can be after dark, so get to the park when the gates open and turn right at the Sorcerer's Hat. Immediately pick up a FastPass to one, and get in line for the other.

Twilight Zone Tower of Terror Elevator free fall through a haunted hotel, this is classic Disney thrills.

Rock 'n' Roller Coaster Indoor roller coaster and one of the most popular at any park.

Beauty and the Beast – Live on Stage Outdoor stage show of the princess tale; one of the best at Disney.

Voyage of the Little Mermaid Charming black light live performance, but frustratingly short.

Toy Story Mania! Ride-through video game.

Pixar Pals Countdown to Fun parade Pixar characters dance through the streets.

Sci-Fi Dine-In Theater (p81) Burgers and glow-in-the-dark drinks served drive-in movie style.

50's Prime Time Café (p81) Disney theme dining at its absolute best.

simulated experiences. the over-the-top stunt-show **Indiana Jones Epic Stunt Spectacular** (Fastpass+), held in a huge outdoor theater, and **American Idol**. There are several American Idol competitions daily – see the website for details on how to become a contestant.

Star Tours: The Adventure Continues — Ride

(Map p62; www.disneyworld.disney.go.com; Hollywood Studios; theme park admission required; Hollywood Studios hours; ; Disney, Disney) Board a Star Speeder 1000 and blast into the galaxy at this 3-D *Star Wars*–themed simulation ride.

Getting There & Away

A paved waterfront walkway or a boat shuttle connects Hollywood Studios to Disney's BoardWalk and the following Epcot resorts: Walt Disney World® Swan & Dolphin, Disney's Yacht Club and Disney's Beach Club, and Disney's BoardWalk Inn. Disney buses provide transportation to other parks and hotels, sometimes requiring a transfer.

TYPHOON LAGOON & BLIZZARD BEACH

In addition to the four theme parks, Disney boasts two distinctly themed water parks. Of the two, Blizzard Beach boasts the better thrills and speed, but Typhoon Lagoon has the far superior wave pool, a fantastic lazy river and tots' play area, and plenty of room to splash on the beach.

Typhoon Lagoon — Water Park

(Map p62; 407-939-5277, 407-560-4120; www.disneyworld.disney.go.com; 1145 Buena Vista Dr, Walt Disney World® Resort; adult/child $53/45, admission incl in Water Park Fun & More with Magic Your Way theme park ticket; hours vary; Disney) An abundance of palm trees, a zero-entry pool with a white sandy beach, high-speed slides and the best wave pool in Orlando make this one of the most beautiful water parks in Florida. Little ones will love floating along **Castaway Creek** and splashing at **Ketchakiddee Creek**.

Animation Academy

In this day of Photoshop and computer-driven animation, it's hard to imagine the painstaking process behind classic Disney animation. Try your hand at drawing a Disney character at Hollywood Studio's **Animation Academy** (Map p62; from 10:30am, on the half-hour;), a short course hosted by a Disney animator. There are about 40 drafting tables, equipped with paper and pencil, and your drawing may be one of the best souvenirs of the trip! Classes start at 10:30am and are held every half-hour at the Magic of Disney Animation.

Blizzard Beach Water Park

(Map p62; 407-560-3400, 407-939-5277; www.disneyworld.disney.go.com; 1534 Blizzard Beach Dr, Walt Disney World® Resort; adult/child $53/45, admission incl in Water Park Fun & More with Magic Your Way theme park ticket; hours vary; Disney) The newer of Disney's two water parks, themed as a melted Swiss ski resort complete with a ski lift, **Blizzard Beach** is the 1980s Vegas Strip hotel to Typhoon Lagoon's Bellagio. At its center sits **Mt Gushmore**, from which waterslides burst forth.

Information

Swimsuits with buckles or metal parts aren't allowed on most of the rides. Hours vary by day and by season; call the individual parks for current hours. From October through March, only one Disney water park is open at a time. Disney's two water parks are included in the price of a Water Park Fun & More ticket.

Getting There & Away

Disney buses stop at both Typhoon Lagoon and Blizzard Beach, and there is complimentary self-parking at both parks.

DISNEY'S BOARDWALK

Far less harried and crowded than Downtown Disney, the very small **Disney's BoardWalk** (Map p62; 407-939-5277; www.disneyworld.disney.go.com; 2101 Epcot Resorts Blvd, Walt Disney World® Resort; Disney, Disney) area across from Epcot and along Crescent Lake echoes waterfront boardwalks of turn-of-the-century New England seaside resorts. On Thursday to Saturday evening street performers like magicians, jugglers and musicians give a festive vibe. Pick up a doughnut or cute little Mickey Mouse cakes at the bakery, and toot around on a two-passenger surrey-with-the-fringe-on-top bike.

Information

Public areas at Disney's BoardWalk are open from 8am to 2am.

Getting There & Away

A well-lit paved walking path and small boats connect Disney's BoardWalk to Epcot and Hollywood Studios, as well as to the following Epcot resorts: Walt Disney World® Swan & Dolphin and Disney's Yacht Club and Disney's Beach Club. Disney buses stop at the Boardwalk Resort, a low-lying clapboard hotel at the center of the boardwalk.

DOWNTOWN DISNEY

Stretching along the water, **Downtown Disney** (Map p62; 407-939-6244; www.disneyworld.disney.go.com; 1490 E Buena Vista Dr, Walt Disney World® Resort; 8:30am-2am; Disney, Disney, Lynx 50) is an outdoor mall that lures tourists with three districts of shops, restaurants, music venues and more shops: **West Side** is home to a multiplex dine-in theater and the stage show Cirque du Soleil La Nouba, **Marketplace** features the largest Disney store in the world, and **Pleasure Island** has several restaurants, bars and clubs. There's a Disney-styled party atmosphere here, particularly on the weekends, with folks walking around sipping margaritas from paper cups, street performers dancing on stilts and parents pushing strollers loaded down with Disney shopping bags.

Disney is in the midst of completely overhauling Downtown Disney,renaming it Disney Springs and revamping the restaurants, stores and offerings. The new **Disney Springs** is expected to be completed in 2016.

DisneyQuest Indoor Interactive Theme Park Arcade

(Map p62; ☎407-828-3800; www.disneyworld.disney.go.com; Downtown Disney; adult/child $48/42, admission incl in Water Park Fun & More with Magic Your Way theme park ticket; ⏰11:30am-10pm Mon-Fri, to 11pm Sat & Sun; 👪; 🚌Disney, ⛴Disney, 🚌Lynx 50) With five dizzying floors of exhibits designed to indulge video-game addicts, this 'interactive theme park' makes the perfect place to wile away a rainy or hot afternoon. Virtual-reality attractions include a trip on Aladdin's magic carpet over Agrabah and a float down a river into the Mesozoic Age. You can design and 'ride' your own roller coaster, or simply lose yourself for hours in old-school video games and pinball machines.

Characters in Flight Ride

(Map p62; ☎407-939-7529; www.disneyworld.disney.go.com; Downtown Disney; adult/child $18/12; ⏰8:30am-midnight; 🚌Disney, ⛴Disney, 🚌Lynx 50) Guests climb on board the basket of this massive tethered gas balloon and ascend 400ft into the air for 360-degree views.

Information

Public areas at Downtown Disney are open from 8am to 2am.

Getting There & Around

Downtown Disney is accessible by boat from Downtown Disney resorts and by bus from everywhere else. There is complimentary self-parking, but no direct Disney transportation to any of the theme parks. You can walk from one end of Downtown Disney to the other, or catch a boat shuttle that stops at each district.

Activities

Disney offers a dizzying array of recreational activities, many based at Disney hotels and none requiring park admission. Call Walt Disney World® Recreation (☎407-939-7529) for reservations and details; for general information on activities at Walt Disney World® Resort, check www.disneyworld.disney.go.com.

Disney's BoardWalk at twilight

BLAINE HARRINGTON III/ALAMY ©

Meeting Disney Characters

Folks of all ages pay a lot of money and spend a lot of time in line to get their photo taken with Winnie the Pooh, Snow White and other Disney favorites. Note that any character experiences in the resort hotels do *not* require theme-park tickets.

FREE MEETINGS

In addition to permanent character-greeting locations in Epcot and Animal Kingdom, look on individual maps for the pointing white finger and check the *Times Guide* for details. Each theme park has specific places where characters hang out, and you can simply hop in line to meet them and have your photo taken. Not all parks, however, have the same characters. Mickey, Minnie, Pluto, Donald and Goofy are everywhere, but Pixar characters are at Hollywood Studios, which is also where you're most likely to find any new folk, and your best bet to catch a princess is at Magic Kingdom.

CHARACTER DINING

Make reservations up to six months (yes, six!) in advance either online or by calling Walt Disney World® Dining (407-939-3462) for any of the many character-dining meals in the theme parks and resort hotels. Disney's Grand Floridian Resort features a buffet breakfast with Winnie the Pooh, Mary Poppins and Alice in Wonderland, as well as lunch, tea or dinner with the princesses; there's a jam-packed breakfast and dinner with Goofy and pals at Chef Mickey's in Disney's Contemporary Resort; and the 100-Acre-Wood folk come to Magic Kingdom's Crystal Palace for three meals a day. Probably the most coveted seat is Cinderella's Royal Table (p78) inside Cinderella's Castle at Magic Kingdom. Cinderella greets guests and sits for a formal portrait (included in the price), and a sit-down meal with the princesses is served upstairs. Note that character meals are not fine-dining experiences, nor are they intimate affairs – they can be rather loud and chaotic. Characters rotate around the room, stopping for a minute or so at each table to pose for a photograph and sign autograph books.

BIKING

Trails along the shores of Disney's lagoons and past woods, resorts and golf courses make for some lovely family-friendly biking, and several Disney hotels rent two-wheel bikes (hour $9, day $18) and old-fashioned surreys ($22 per half-hour).

Surrey Bikes at the Boardwalk Bicycle Rental

(Map p62; 407-560-8754; www.disneyworld.disney.go.com; Disney's BoardWalk; per 30min $22; Disney, Disney) Toot around the waterfront on cute four-wheel bikes with candy-striped surrey on top.

HORSEBACK RIDING

Carriage rides are also available at Disney's Port Orleans Resort.

Fort Wilderness Tri-Circle-D Ranch Horseback Riding

(Map p62; 407-824-2832; www.disneyworld.disney.go.com; 4510 N Wilderness Trail, Disney's Fort Wilderness Resort & Campground; per 30min $10-45; Disney, Disney) Guided trail, pony, wagon, hay and carriage rides.

WATER SPORTS

More than 10 Disney hotels rent kayaks, canoes, jet skis and pontoons, among other things.

Sammy Duvall's Watersports Centre Water Sports
(Map p62; ☎407-939-0754; www.sammyduvall.com; 4600 World Dr, Disney's Contemporary Resort; personal watercraft per hour $135, waterskiing, wakeboarding & tubing up to 5 people per hour $165 ; 10am-5pm; Disney, Disney, monorail Disney) Lessons, rentals and parasailing.

Sleeping

Disney resort hotels are divided according to location, and Disney-provided transportation to *that* location is often included. Prices vary drastically according to season, and there are 20 (!) different seasons; plus, deluxe resorts can have upwards of 10 different 'room types.' Prices given here are for value/peak weekends; note that weekdays will be a bit less.

In a category all its own, **Shades of Green Resort** (Map p62; ☎407-824-3400; www.shadesofgreen.org; 1950 W Magnolia Palm Dr; r $90-150, ste $235-250; ; Disney) sits within Walt Disney World® Resort but is owned by the Armed Forces Recreation Center. Only active and retired members of the US Armed Services (including National Guard) and their widows and widowers can stay here, and rates are divided into three categories according to rank.

MAGIC KINGDOM

The number-one advantage to staying at one of these hotels on Bay Lake is that they are one easy monorail or boat ride from Magic Kingdom – you can get to classic Disney with no need for transfers.

Down Time: Nature Trails

Short trails around Discovery Island lead to quiet spots along the water, where a handful of benches make a great place to relax with a snack. Keep your eye out for animals like tortoises and lemurs in and around the water.

Walt Disney World® Resort Swan & Dolphin Hotels (p76)

TIM E WHITE/ALAMY ©

Disney's Fort Wilderness Resort
Campground, Cabin $$

(Map p62; ☎407-824-2900, 407-939-5277; www.disneyworld.disney.go.com; 4510 N Fort Wilderness Trail; value/regular/peak tent sites $55/79/91, RV sites $74/102/130, 6-person cabins $330/403/456; ; Disney, Disney) Located in a huge shaded natural preserve, Fort Wilderness caters to kids and families with its hay rides, fishing and nightly campfire sing-alongs. Cabins sleep up to six and are hardly rustic, with cable TV and full kitchens, and while cars aren't allowed within the gates, you can rent a golf cart to toot around in.

Disney's Grand Floridian Resort & Spa
Resort $$$

(Map p62; ☎407-824-3000, 407-939-5277; www.disneyworld.disney.go.com; 4401 Floridian Way; r value/regular/peak $550/606/714, 6-person ste from $1412; P; Disney, Disney, monorail Disney) One easy monorail stop from Magic Kingdom, the Grand Floridian rides on its reputation as the grandest, most elegant property in Disney World, and it does indeed exude a welcome calm and charm. The four-story lobby, with a live orchestra playing jazz (and yes, Disney classics), oozes all the accoutrements of Old Florida class and style.

Disney's Wilderness Lodge
Resort $$$

(Map p62; ☎407-824-3200, 407-939-5277; www.disneyworld.disney.go.com; 901 Timberline Dr, Walt Disney World® Resort; r value/regular/peak $325/394/471, 6-person ste from $688; P; Disney, Disney) The handsome lobby's low-lit tepee chandeliers, hand-carved totem pole and dramatic 80ft fireplace echo national-park lodges of America's old West. Though it's meant to feel as if you're in John Muir country, with its wooded surrounds and hidden lagoonside location, the fake geyser and singing waiters in the lobby restaurant dispel the illusion mighty quick.

EPCOT

One of the best parts about this cluster of hotels is their easy access to restaurants and entertainment in Epcot, Hollywood Studios and Disney's BoardWalk.

Disney's BoardWalk Inn
Resort $$$

(Map p62; ☎407-939-5277, 407-939-6200; www.disneyworld.disney.go.com; 2101 Epcot Resorts Blvd; r value/regular/peak $411/477/569, 6-person ste & cottages from $756; P; Disney, Disney) This resort embodies the seaside charm of Atlantic City in its heyday, with a waterfront the color of saltwater taffy, tandem bicycles with candy-striped awnings, and a splintery boardwalk. The lovely lobby features sea-green walls, hardwood floors and soft floral vintage seating areas. Elegant rooms have a terrace or balcony.

Walt Disney World Swan & Dolphin Hotels
Resort $$

(Map p62; ☎Dolphin 407-934-4000, Swan 407-934-3000; www.swandolphin.com; 1200 & 1500 Epcot Resorts Blvd; r $160-380; Disney, Disney) These two Michael Graves–designed high-rise luxury hotels, which face each other on Disney property and share facilities, offer a distinctly toned-down Disney feel but all the Disney perks, including Disney transportation and Magic Hours (where a theme park opens early and closes late for guests at Disney hotels only).

Disney's Yacht Club Resort & Disney's Beach Club Resort
Resort $$$

(Map p62; ☎Beach Club 407-934-8000, Walt Disney World 407-939-5277, Yacht Club 407-934-7000; www.waltdisneyworld.disney.go.com; 1700 & 1800 Epcot Resorts Blvd, Walt Disney World® Resort; r value/regular/peak $400/465/554, 8-person ste from $1633; ; Disney, Disney) These handsome sister resorts, pleasantly located along the water and a five-minute walk from Epcot, strive for old New England beachside charm. The pools, boasting sandy shores and a slide off the mast of a ship, earn rave reviews, but we found them cramped and in need of a face-lift.

ANIMAL KINGDOM

To get from these hotels to Epcot, Hollywood Studios, Animal Kingdom, Downtown Disney and Disney's BoardWalk, you must take a bus (or drive), and to get to Magic Kingdom you'll need to take a bus and then a monorail or boat.

Disney's Animal Kingdom Lodge Resort $$$

(Map p62; 407-939-5277, 407-938-3000; www.disneyworld.disney.go.com; 2901 Osceola Blvd; r value/regular/peak $319/389/465, 6-/8-person ste from $930/1697; P ❄ @ ☰ ≋; Disney) With an abutting 33-acre savannah parading a who's who of Noah's Ark past hotel windows and balconies, park rangers standing ready to answer questions about the wildlife, and African-inspired food served at the recommended restaurants, this resort offers particularly fun and quirky theming.

DOWNTOWN DISNEY

While these hotels offer easy and pleasant boat access to Downtown Disney, the only Disney transportation to the theme parks and Disney's BoardWalk is by bus.

Disney's Port Orleans French Quarter and Riverside Resorts Resort $$

(Map p62; French Quarter 407-934-5000, Riverside 407-934-6000; www.disneyworld.disney.go.com; 1251 Riverside; r value/regular/peak $182/211/237; P ❄ @ ☰ ≋; Disney, Disney) Lush gardens and a jubilant Mardi Gras–motif blend in an effort to create a Louisiana feel to these sister resorts. Though the result sometimes falls flat and the simple rooms feel dated, the resort is a mecca for activities and includes a sea-serpent waterslide, boat rental, horse-drawn-carriage rides and evening s'mores. This is one of the biggest resorts at Disney; a boat connects the two properties, or it's a 15-minute walk.

Disney's Old Key West Resort Resort $$$

(Map p62; 407-827-7700, 407-939-5277; www.disneyworld.disney.go.com; 1510 N Cove Rd; studios value/regular/peak $327/368/431, 1-bedroom villas $452/508/556, 2-bedroom villas $618/742/903; P ❄ @ ☰ ≋; Disney, Disney) Victoriana oozes from every gingerbread-accented pastel corner, every palm-tree enclave and from the azure-blue waters. This is an 'all villa' resort. Studios sleep four; one- and two-bedroom villas sleep eight; and three-bedroom villas sleep 12.

Eating

Table-service restaurants accept 'priority seating' reservations up to 180 days in advance unless otherwise noted. Call Disney Dining at 407-939-3463 or go to www.disneyworld.disney.go.com to peruse menus and make reservations.

Disney's Animal Kingdom Lodge
NIK WHEELER/ALAMY ©

MAGIC KINGDOM

Eating at Magic Kingdom is less about great food than theming, festive environs and character-dining opportunities. You certainly won't starve, as there are snacks, fast-food eateries and table-service restaurants at every turn, but there's little here worth seeking out.

Be Our Guest American $$

(Map p62; 407-939-3463; www.disneyworld.disney.go.com; Magic Kingdom; mains lunch $9-14, dinner $18-32; 10:30am-2:30pm & 4-9:30pm, hours vary; ; Disney, Disney, Lynx 50, 56) Disney's newest and hottest restaurant, set inside the Beast's marvelously detailed castle, is a must for *Beauty and the Beast* fans. Options include braised pork, carved turkey and the most talked about dessert at Disney, the Master's Cupcake. But it's the attention to theming that is the real draw.

Gaston's Tavern American $

(Map p62; www.disneyworld.disney.go.com; Magic Kingdom; mains $6-10, theme park admission required; 9am-park closing; ; Disney, Disney, Lynx 50, 56) Homage to that superego Gaston, with pork shanks, giant cinnamon rolls and hummus. It's an odd mix of quick-service options, but the re-created tavern with the giant portrait of Gaston is well done, and the food is pretty good. Try Le Fou's Brew, Disney's counter to Universal's run-away hit Butterbeer.

Cinderella's Royal Table American

(Map p62; 407-934-2927; www.disneyworld.disney.go.com; Cinderella's Castle, Magic Kingdom; adult $60-75, child $36-45; 8-10:40am, 11:45am-2:40pm & 4-10pm; ; Disney, Disney, Lynx 50, 56) Cinderella greets guests and sits for a formal portrait (included in the price), and a sit-down meal with princesses is served upstairs. This is the only opportunity to eat inside the iconic castle – make reservations six months in advance. Hours vary.

Cheshire Cafe Bakery $

(Map p62; www.disneyworld.disney.go.com; Magic Kingdom; cake-cups $4-10, theme park admission required; 9am-park closing; Disney, Disney, Lynx 50, 56) Delectably sweet and charmingly cute cake-cups, which are basically cupcake parfaits with several layers of rich butter-cream frosting topped with *Alice in Wonderland*–themed decorations, are big enough to share.

Rose & Crown

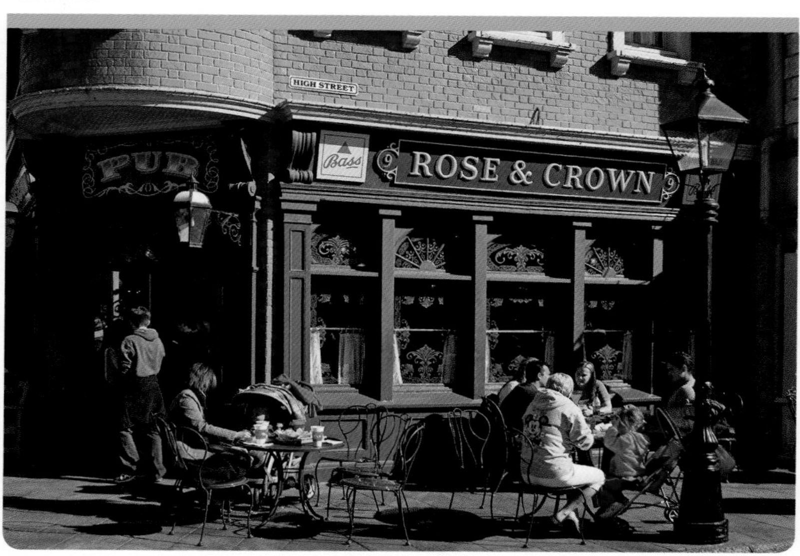

MEL LONGHURST/ALAMY ©

Victoria & Albert's: No-Kids-Allowed Dining

When Disney announced that children under 10 would no longer be allowed at Victoria & Albert's, the crème de la crème of Orlando's dining scene, headlines roared with news of Disney's ban on children and the internet gaggle was nothing short of horrified indignation. But with almost 100 other restaurants to choose from, families shouldn't have a problem finding alternatives to this three-hour, seven-course dinner ($150 per person, wine pairing costs an additional $65). Indulge yourself with exquisite food and top-notch service in the Victorian-inspired decor of earthy creams. Along with Cinderella's Table, this place, located inside Disney's Grand Floridian Resort, books up months in advance; make reservations at 407-939-3463 the morning of the 180th day before you want to dine.

EPCOT

Eating at Epcot is as much about the experience as the food, and many of the restaurants go overboard to create an atmosphere characteristic of their country.

La Cava del Tequila — Mexican $

(Map p62; 407-939-3463; www.disneyworld.disney.go.com; Epcot; tapas $6-12, theme park admission required; noon-park closing; Disney, Disney, monorail Disney) Pop in for a cucumber, passion fruit or blood-orange margarita. Can't decide? Try a flight of margaritas or shots. The menu features more than 70 types of tequila and a limited tapas menu, and it's a cozy, dark spot, with tiled floors, Mexican-styled murals and a beamed ceiling. La Cava is connected to San Angel Inn, a full-service sit-down restaurant, but does not take reservations.

La Hacienda de San Angel — Mexican $$

(Map p62; 407-939-3463; www.disneyworld.disney.go.com; Epcot; mains $23-30, theme park admission required; 4pm-park closing; ; Disney, Disney, monorail Disney) Authentic Mexican rather than Tex Mex, this lagoonside eatery features corn tortillas made daily; mango and chipotle salsas; and on-the-rocks margaritas ranging from rose-infused Rosita to a classic with cactus lemongrass salt on the rim.

Via Napoli — Pizza $$

(Map p62; 407-939-3463; www.disneyworld.disney.go.com; Epcot; pizzas $13-22, theme park admission required; 11:30am-park closing; ; Disney, Disney, monorail Disney) The thin-crust pizza cooked in a wood-burning stove is tasty, and the toppings take things beyond run-of-the-mill pepperoni.

San Angel Inn — Mexican $$

(Map p62; 407-939-3463; www.disneyworld.disney.go.com; Epcot; mains $17-28, theme park admission required; 11:30am-park closing; ; Disney, Disney, monorail Disney) Set inside an Aztec pyramid and surrounded by a recreated Mexican market, with perpetual night skies twinkling with Disney stars. Excellent chips with freshly made salsa and *pico de gallo* (fresh salsa of tomatoes, onion and jalapeños), solid Mexican fare, and rice pudding with raisins and cinnamon for dessert. Ask about vegetarian options.

Rose & Crown — English $$

(Map p62; 407-939-3463; www.disneyworld.disney.go.com; Epcot; mains $13-21, theme park admission required; 11am-park closing; ; Disney, Disney, monorail Disney) Housed in a British pub, this little spot serves up ploughman's lunch, steak, fish and chips, and a tasty vegetable curry. Wash it down with Bass on tap and head across the path for a garden concert of the Fab Four, or settle on the patio for the nightly light show IllumiNations.

Chefs de France French $$

(Map p62; ☎407-939-3463; www.disneyworld.disney.go.com; Epcot; mains $19-35, theme park admission required; ⊙noon-3pm, 4:30-park closing; ; Disney, Disney, monorail Disney) Bright yellow and with lovely big windows, this bustling French brasserie features steak *frites* and other bistro classics. Four times a day, from Monday to Saturday, *Ratatouille*'s Remy makes an appearance. He won't stop at every table, like a traditional character meal, but he dances about, stopping randomly to visit with folk.

Biergarten German $$

(Map p62; ☎407-939-3463; www.disneyworld.disney.go.com; Epcot; buffet lunch adult/child $20/11, buffet dinner $27/13, theme park admission required; ⊙11am-park closing; ; Disney, Disney, monorail Disney) Satisfy a hearty appetite with traditional German foods (don't miss the pretzel bread) and a massive stein of brew. The restaurant interior is made to look like an old German village, with cobblestones, trees and a Bavarian oompah band in the evening.

Restaurant Marrakesh Middle Eastern $$$

(Map p62; ☎407-939-3463; www.disneyworld.disney.go.com; Epcot; mains $21-36, theme park admission required; ⊙11:30am-park closing; ; Disney, Disney, monorail Disney) Sparkling belly dancers shimmy and shake past the massive pillars and around the tables of the Sultan's Palace, magnificently decorated with mosaic tiles, rich velvets and sparkling gold. While the lamb kabobs, vegetable couscous and other basics are disappointing, the windowless elegance is a fun escape from the searing sun and kids love to join in the dancing.

Le Cellier Steakhouse Steak $$$

(Map p62; ☎407-939-3463; www.disneyworld.disney.go.com; Epcot; mains $21-35, theme park admission required; ⊙11am-park closing; ; Disney, Disney, monorail Disney) If you love meat, this place is for you. Try the buffalo. Dark and cavernous, with stone walls and lanterns, it makes a good spot to escape the heat, but the dense sauces and decadent desserts might not be the best fuel to get you through the day.

Teppan Edo Japanese $$

(Map p62; ☎407-939-3463; www.disneyworld.disney.go.com; Epcot; mains $16-29, theme park admission required; ⊙11am-park closing; ; Disney, Disney, monorail Disney) Chefs toss the chicken, fling the chopsticks and frenetically slice and dice the veggies in this standard cook-in-front-of-you eatery next to Japan's gardens.

Les Halles Boulangerie Patisserie French $

(Map p62; www.disneyworld.disney.go.com; Epcot; pastries & sandwiches $2-10, theme park admission required; ⊙9am-park closing; Disney, Disney) Most folks come for cakes, éclairs and cookies, but

Earl of Sandwich (p82)

JEFF GREENBERG/ALAMY ©

it also sells French-bread pizza, quiche and those baguette sandwiches that are ubiquitous in the real France, as well as wine and champagne.

ANIMAL KINGDOM

Yak and Yeti — Asian $$

(Map p62; 407-939-3463, 407-824-9384; www.disneyworld.disney.go; Animal Kingdom; mains $14-29, theme park admission required; 11am-park closing; ; Disney) Sharing the name of Kathmandu's exclusive digs in the real Nepal, decorated with a vaguely Nepalese-infused decor, and serving pan-fried noodles, pot stickers, tempura, and icy Tsingtao, this recommended getaway at the base of Mt Everest transports you from Disney to the Himalayas. The food is surprisingly good, and is one of the best bets for for eating inside the park.

HOLLYWOOD STUDIOS

50's Prime Time Café — American $$

(Map p62; 407-939-3463; www.disneyworld.disney.go.com; Hollywood Studios; mains $13-21, theme park admission required; 11am-park closing; ; Disney, Disney) Step into a quintessential 1950s home for a home-cooked meal, including Grandma's Chicken-Pot-Pie, Aunt Liz's Golden Fried Chicken and Mom's Old-Fashioned Pot Roast, served up on a Formica tabletop. Waitresses in pink plaid and white aprons banter playfully and admonish those diners who don't finish their meals, putting their elbows on the table with a sassy 'shame, shame, shame.'

Sci-Fi Dine-In Theater — American $$

(Map p62; 407-939-3463; www.disneyworld.disney.go.com; Hollywood Studios; mains $13-30, theme park admission required; 11am-park closing; ; Disney, Disney) Burgers, ribs and glow-in-the-dark drinks served drive-in movie style. Climb into your convertible cadillac, order from the car hop, sip on a Lunar Landing and sit back for a silly horror movie or sci-fi flick. This is Disney theming at its best.

Down Time: Magic Kingdom

The covered waterside pavilion in the rose garden just off the bridge to the right of Cinderella's Castle makes a perfect place to take a quiet rest amid the hectic theme-park crowds. Pictured but not labeled on Walt Disney World® Resort's Magic Kingdom map, look for it on your way into Tomorrowland.

Writer's Stop — Bakery $

(Map p62; www.disneyworld.disney.go.com; Hollywood Studios; mains $6-12, theme park admission required; 9am-park closing; ; Disney, Disney) Decent coffee and sweets in a small shop designed to look like an independent bookstore. If it's not too crowded, the few comfy chairs around a TV screening Disney cartoons make a good place to rest.

DISNEY'S BOARDWALK

Kouzzina by Cat Cora — Greek $$$

(Map p62; 407-939-3463, 407-939-2380; www.disneyworld.disney.go.com; Disney's BoardWalk; mains $15-35; 7-11am & 5-10:30pm; ; Disney) Though it can be rather loud and hectic, Kouzzina boasts a particularly interesting menu. Pop in for breakfast of blueberry-orange pancakes and chicken sausage on your way to Hollywood Studios, or cinnamon-stewed chicken and chilled ouzo on your way home!

Flying Fish — Seafood $$$

(Map p62; 407-939-2359, 407-939-3463; www.disneyworld.disney.go.com; Disney's BoardWalk; mains $26-39; 5-10pm; ; Disney) Flying Fish, specializing in complicated and innovative seafood dishes, consistently ranks as one of the best upscale dining spots at Disney. Make reservations well in advance for the limited-seating five-course prix-fix wine-pairing menu. Kids' meals are significantly less expensive (from $6 to $15),

Below: Downtown Disney; **Right:** Via Napoli (p79)

DOWNTOWN DISNEY

Paradiso 37 South American $$

(Map p62; 407-934-3700; www.paradiso37.com; Downtown Disney; mains $15-25; 11:30am-11pm Sun-Thu, to midnight Fri & Sat; P; Disney, Disney, Lynx 50) With more than 15 tequila flights on the menu, an impressive cocktail list and a menu representing 37 countries of North, South and Central America (or so they claim), this contemporary waterfront spot is one of Downtown Disney's best bets.

Earl of Sandwich Sandwiches $

(Map p62; www.disneyworld.disney.go.com; Downtown Disney; sandwiches $5-8; 8:30am-11pm; P; Disney, Disney, Lynx 50) Surprisingly good toasted sandwiches ranging from basic to exotic. One of the most satisfying lunches at Disney, with plenty of bang for your buck; but in the end, it's a fast-food sandwich chain.

Fresh-A-Peel American $

(Map p62; www.disneyworld.disney.go.com; Downtown Disney; mains $5-12; 9:30am-11:30pm, to midnight Fri & Sat; P; Disney, Disney, Lynx 50) With nitrate-free hot dogs served on whole-grain buns, veggie burgers, turkey burgers and 'popped chips,' this is the closest to health food you'll find at Disney.

RESORT HOTELS

Jiko African $$$

(Map p62; 407-939-3463, 407-938-4733; www.disneyworld.disney.go.com; 2901 Osceola Pkwy, Disney's Animal Kingdom Lodge; mains $24-35; 5:30-10pm; ; Disney) Excellent food, with plenty of grains, vegetables and creative twists, a tiny bar and rich African surrounds make this a Disney favorite for both quality and theming. You can relax with a glass of wine on the hotel's back deck, alongside the giraffes and other African beasts.

'Ohana American $$

(Map p62; ☎407-939-3463; www.disneyworld.disney.go.com; 1600 Seven Seas Dr, Disney's Polynesian Resort; mains $15-30; 7:30-11am & 5-10pm; ; Disney, Disney) The Polynesian's signature restaurant evokes a South Pacific feel with rock-art animals, a huge oak-burning grill cooking up massive kabobs of meat, and demonstrations of hula and limbo dancing, coconut racing and other Polynesian-themed shenanigans. The only thing on the menu is the all-you-can-eat family-style kabobs and veggies, slid off skewers directly onto the giant wok-like platters on the table. Breakfast is a Lilo and Stitch character meal.

Victoria & Albert's American $$$

(Map p62; ☎407-939-3463; www.disneyworld.disney.go.com; 4401 Floridian Way, Disney's Grand Floridian Resort; prix fixe $150, wine-pairing extra $65; 5-10:30pm; Disney, Disney, monorail Disney) Indulge yourself in the earthy, cream-colored Victorian-inspired decor at this elegant restaurant, the crème de la crème of Orlando's dining scene and one of its most-coveted reservations. The seven-course meal, complete with crystal and live cello music, oozes romance.

Dinner at the intimate Chef's Table or Queen Victoria's room includes ten courses. This is the only place in Disney that does not allow kids. If you have children, consider reserving a spot at **Disney's Children Activity Center** (**☎407-939-3463; www.disneyworld.disney.com.go; select Disney resort hotels; per child per hr $12, 2hr minimum, incl dinner; hours vary**) at Disney's Polynesian Resort, an easy two stops away on the monorail.

Drinking & Nightlife

Downtown Disney and the much smaller Disney's BoardWalk are Walt Disney World® Resort's designated shopping, drinking and entertainment districts, but you'll find bars and sometimes live music at most Disney resorts and within the theme parks. Magic Kingdom is the only place that does not sell alcohol.

If You Like... Dinner Theater

Disney's three dinner shows sell out early, so make your reservation up to 180 days in advance; you can cancel up to 48 hours in advance with no penalty. They are each held at a Disney resort, include beer and wine, and do not require theme park admission.

1 HOOP-DEE-DOO MUSICAL REVUE

(p85) This is one of Disney's longest-running shows and great fun once you grab your washboard and get into the spirit of it all.

2 SPIRIT OF ALOHA SHOW

(p85) Lots of yelling and pounding on drums while hula-clad men and women leap around stage, dance and play with fire in this South Pacific–style luau at Disney's Polynesian Resort.

3 MICKEY'S BACKYARD BARBECUE

(Map p62; 407-824-1593, 407-939-3463; www.disneyworld.disney.go.com; 4510 N Fort Wilderness Trail, Disney's Fort Wilderness Resort; adult $50-60, child $36-40; 6:30pm; Disney, Disney) The only dinner theater with Disney characters; expect country-and-western singin', ho-down style stompin,' fried chicken and goofy Mickey antics at this Disney favorite at Disney's Fort Wilderness Resort.

Belle Vue Room — Bar

(Map p62; 407-939-6200; www.disneyworld.disney.go.com; 2101 Epcot Resorts Blvd, Disney's BoardWalk Inn; 7-11am & 5pm-midnight; Disney, Disney) On the 2nd floor of Disney's BoardWalk Inn, this is an excellent place for a quiet drink. It's more like a sitting room than a bar: you can relax and play a board game, listen to classic radio shows like *Lone Ranger,* or simply take your drink to a rocking chair on the balcony and watch the comings and goings along Disney's BoardWalk.

Raglan Road — Pub

(Map p62; 407-938-0300; www.raglanroad.com; Downtown Disney; 11am-midnight, live music from 4pm; Disney, Disney) Traditional Irish ditties, Irish dancing, solid tasty Irish fare, cozy pub decor and beer flights with Guinness, Harp, Smithwicks and Kilkenny complete the leprechaun mood.

Big River Grille & Brewing Works — Brewery

(Map p62; 407-560-0253; www.disneyworld.disney.go.com; Disney's BoardWalk; 11:30am-11pm) Open-air microbrewery with outdoor seating along the water.

Entertainment

Disney has enough drinking and entertainment options to keep you busy with something different every night of the week for a month straight.

Cirque du Soleil La Nouba — Performing Arts

(Map p62; 407-939-7328, 407-939-7600; www.cirquedusoleil.com; Downtown Disney; adult $65-150, child $55-125; 6pm & 9pm Tue-Sat; Disney, Disney, Lynx 50) Disney's best live show features mind-boggling acrobatic feats expertly fused to light, stage and costume design to create a cohesive artistic vision. And of course, there's a silly Disney twist involving a princess and a frog. This is a small horseshoe theater, with roughly 20 rows from the stage to the top, and no balcony.

Chip 'n' Dale Campfire Singalong — Cinema

(Map p62; 407-939-7529; www.disneyworld.disney.go.com; 4510 N Wilderness Trail, Disney's Fort Wilderness Resort; 7pm winter, 8pm summer; Disney, Disney) One of Disney's best offerings, this intimate and low-key character experience offers singing and dancing with Chip and Dale, campfires for roasting marshmallows, and a free outdoor screening of a Disney film. Every night is a different movie, and Disney doesn't post a schedule on its website – call or search online.

House of Blues
Live Music

(Map p62; ☎407-934-2583; www.houseofblues.com; Downtown Disney; ⏰10am-11pm Mon-Thu, to midnight Fri & Sat, 10:30am-11pm Sun; ; Disney, Disney, Lynx 50) Top acts visit this national chain serving southern cooking and blues. It's particularly popular for the Sunday's Gospel Brunch buffet.

Spirit of Aloha
Dance

(Map p62; ☎407-939-3463; www.disneyworld.disney.go.com; 1600 Seven Seas Dr, Disney's Polynesian Resort; adult $60-75, child $30-40; ⏰5:15pm & 8:15pm; Disney, Disney, monorail Disney) Hula-clad men and women leap around the stage, dance and play with fire in this South Pacific–style luau at Disney's Polynesian Resort. Pulled pork, barbecue ribs and island-themed specialties like pineapple-coconut bread are served family-style.

Hoop-Dee-Doo Musical Revue
Comedy

(Map p62; ☎407-939-3463, 407-824-2803; www.disneyworld.disney.go.com; 4510 N Wilderness Trail, Disney's Fort Wilderness Resort; adult $55-70, child $28-36; ⏰4pm, 6:15pm & 8:30pm daily, hours vary; ; Disney, Disney) Nineteenth-century vaudeville show at Disney's Fort Wilderness Resort, with ribs delivered to your table in metal buckets, corny jokes, and the audience singing along to 'Hokey Pokey' and 'My Darling Clementine.'

Jellyrolls
Bar

(Map p62; ☎407-560-8770; www.disneyworld.disney.go.com; Disney's BoardWalk; admission $12; ⏰7pm-2am) Comedians on dueling pianos encourage the audience to partake in all kinds of musical silliness and sing-alongs.

ESPN Wide World of Sports
Spectator Sport

(☎407-939-4263, Visitors Center 407-541-5600; http://espnwwos.disney.go.com; 700 S Victory Way, Walt Disney World® Resort) This 230-acre sports facility at Walt Disney World® hosts Atlanta Braves spring training and hundreds of amateur and professional sporting events.

Shopping

Most stores are thematically oriented, so after the Winnie the Pooh ride you'll find lots of Winnie the Pooh stuff, and after the Indiana Jones ride you'll find, well, an Indiana Jones fedora, of course.

Bibbidee Bobbidee Boutique
Children

(Map p62; ☎407-939-7895; www.disneyworld.disney.go.com; Magic Kingdom; hair & makeup from $49; ⏰10am-8pm, hours vary) Inside Cinderella's Castle, fairy godmothers finalize your kid's transformation from shorts and T-shirt to bedazzling

Sculpture, House of Blues

Tickets

Walt Disney World® tickets are called **Magic Your Way**. The minimal base ticket, which allows access to one theme park for one day, costs adult $99, child aged three to nine $93. From that, you can add days and options either when you first purchase your ticket or any time within the 14 days after the ticket is first used.

Multiple Days up to 10 The per-day cost drops 50% if you buy a seven-day or longer base ticket. Multiple-day tickets allow unlimited admission to all four of Disney's theme parks (but not the water parks), so you can go in and out of a theme park as many times as you'd like, *but you can only go to one theme park a day*. They can be used anytime within 14 consecutive days. Adult tickets for 2/3/4/5/6/7/8/9/10 days cost $188/274/294/304/314/324/334/344/354. Tickets for children aged three to 10 cost $10-20 cheaper.

Water Park Fun & More ($60) Includes one admission per day to your choice of Blizzard Beach water park, Typhoon Lagoon water park, DisneyQuest Indoor Interactive Theme Park (at Downtown Disney), ESPN Wide World of Sports and Disney's Oak Trail Golf Course (with reserved tee time). You will be given one pass for each day of your Magic Your Way ticket, and you can use these passes to access whatever you'd like, whenever you'd like.

No Expiration Unused days of multiple-day tickets do not expire after 14 days. The price varies from $22 if added on to a two-day ticket, to $67 days if added on to a four-day ticket.

Park Hopper ($40-60) Allows unlimited access to any of the four theme parks during the course of one day, so you can spend the morning at Magic Kingdom, the afternoon at Animal Kingdom and head to Epcot for the evening. The cost is the same regardless of when you add this option and whether you are adding it to a one-day ticket or to a 10-day ticket.

princess with fanciful hairstyling and makeup.

Once Upon a Toy Children
(Map p62; ☎407-824-4321; www.disneyworld.disney.go.com; Downtown Disney; ⏰10am-11pm; 🚌Disney, ⛴Disney, 🚌Lynx 50) Design a personalized My Little Pony, build your own light saber and create your own tiara at one of the best toy stores anywhere. You'll find old-school classics such as Mr Potato Head and Lincoln Logs, board games, action figures, stuffed animals and more.

Lego Imagination Center Children
(Map p62; ☎407-828-0065; www.disneyworld.disney.go.com; Downtown Disney; ⏰9am-11pm; 🚌Disney, ⛴Disney, 🚌Lynx 50) Life-size Lego creations, tables to create your own masterpieces and a wall of individually priced Lego pieces.

World of Disney Souvenirs
(Map p62; ☎407-939-6224; www.disneyworld.disney.go.com; Downtown Disney; ⏰9am-11pm; 🚌Disney, ⛴Disney, 🚌Lynx 50) Room after room of Disney everything at this Disney megasuperduper store.

Information

Child Care

Baby-care centers are located in every park. They're air-conditioned, packed with toys, and some run Disney cartoons. You can purchase diapers, formula, baby powder and over-the-counter medicine. Walt Disney World® Resort uses **Kid's Nite Out** (☎407-828-0920, 800-696-8105; www.kidsniteout.com; 1/2/3/4 kids per

hr $16/18.50/21/23.50, 4hr minimum, plus $10 travel fee; ⏲sitters available 24/7) for private babysitting either in the hotel or in the parks.

Several Disney resorts offer drop-off children's activity centers ($11.50 per hour per child including dinner; two-hour minimum) for children aged three to 12, with organized activities, toys, art supplies, meals and a Disney movie to end the evening. You do not have to be a guest at the hotel to use the centers.

Kennels

With the exception of select campsites at Disney's Fort Wilderness Resort & Campground, pets are not allowed anywhere at WDW. **Best Friends Pet Care at Walt Disney World® (☎877-493-9738; www.bestfriendspetcare.com/waltdisneyworldresort; 2510 Bonnet Creek Pkwy; per day $18-72, overnight $38-78; ⏲1hr before Walt Disney World® parks open to 1hr after closing)**offers overnight boarding and day care for dogs, cats and 'pocket pets.' Rates vary based on your pet; call for details.

Medical Services

Medical facilities are located within each theme park and at both Disney water parks; see park maps for locations.

Park Hours

Theme park hours change not only by season, but day to day within any given month. Generally, parks open at 8 or 9am and close sometime between 6 and 10pm. At Walt Disney World® Resort, one of the four theme parks stays open or closes late for guests of Walt Disney World® Resort hotels only – these 'Magic Hours' are a perk of staying at a Disney hotel.

Parking

If you're staying at a Disney resort, parking at all the parks is free; otherwise, it costs $17 per day. You will find parking lots outside the gates of all the parks except for Magic Kingdom; if you're driving to Magic Kingdom, you have to park at the Transportation & Ticket Center and take a monorail or ferry to the park.

Stroller Rental

Strollers (single/double per day $15/31; multiday $13/27) are available on a first-come first-served basis at Magic Kingdom, Epcot, Animal Kingdom, Hollywood Studios and Downtown Disney, and you can also purchase umbrella strollers (folding strollers). There is no stroller rental at Disney's two water parks, Disney's BoardWalk or at the resort hotels.

Tourist Information

Guest Services is located at the entrance to each theme and water park, with maps and general information.

Any time you call Disney, you'll be prompted to give all kinds of information they use for customer research. Keep pressing '0' – just cut them off mid-sentence – and you'll get a real human being.

Travelers with Disabilities

The *Guidebook for Guests with Disabilities,* available at Guest Services at each park and on Disney's website, has maps and ride-by-ride guides with information on closed captioning and accommodating wheelchairs and seeing-eye dogs. On many rides, folks in wheelchairs will be waved to the front of the line. You can borrow braille guides and audiotape guides from Guest Services and rent wheelchairs ($12) and electronic convenience vehicles (ECV; $50) at each of Disney's theme parks and at Downtown Disney. All chairs are first-come, first-served; reservations are not possible.

Public transportation is wheelchair accessible and select resort hotels offer features and services for guests with disabilities. Call ☎407-824-4321 or ☎407-827-5141 for further information. For thorough information on navigating Disney in a wheelchair, go to www.themouseonwheels.com.

Websites

Google anything to do with Disney, and you'll find pages of blogs and websites offering planning tips, advice and mind-boggling details on restaurants and attractions. It's easy to get buried in

Help, I Lost My Ticket

Each person must use their own ticket, identified at theme-park gates by finger-print scan, so if you lose it, you're screwed. If, however, you photocopy or photograph the back of your ticket (the side with the magnetic strip), Guest Relations may be able to use this to issue you a new one.

information-overload, but some sites can be helpful. Here are some comprehensive and reputable favorites:

Walt Disney World® (www.disneyworld.disney.go.com) Official Walt Disney World® website.

Walt Disney World® Information (www.wdwinfo.com) Exceptionally readable and thorough.

All Ears (www.allears.net) News, menus and more.

MouseSavers (www.mousesavers.com) Disney discounts.

Build a Better Mousetrip (www.buildabettermousetrip.com) Movie schedules and planning.

Kenny the Pirate (http://kennythepirate.com) Everything you need to know about meeting Disney characters.

Disney Food Blog (www.disneyfoodblog.com) All things Disney dining, including lists of where to satisfy specific dietary needs.

Mouse on Wheels (www.themouseonwheels.com) Guide to navigating Disney in a wheelchair.

Getting There & Away

To/From Airport

If you have no urge to visit Orlando, you can arrange luxury bus transportation to and from the airport through Disney's Magical Express (p106).

Car & Motorcycle

Disney lies 25 minutes' drive south of downtown Orlando. Take I-4 to well-signed exits 64, 65 or 67. At the **Disney Car Care Center** (**407-824-0976, car-rental shuttle 407-824-3470; 1000 W Car Care Dr, Walt Disney World®; 6am-8pm Mon-Fri, to 6pm Sat & Sun**), near the parking exit of Magic Kingdom, there is a full-service garage and an Alamo car-rental desk. A second Alamo desk is inside the Walt Disney World® Dolphin Resort.

Shuttle

Call one day in advance to arrange personalized transport to/from Universal Orlando Resort and SeaWorld with Mears Transportation (p107). It costs $19 round-trip per person.

Taxi

Taxicabs can be found at hotels, theme parks (except for Magic Kingdom, where there is no road access), the Transportation & Ticket Center, ESPN Wide World of Sports and Downtown Disney.

Getting Around

The Transportation & Ticket Center operates as the main hub of this system. Note that it can take up to an hour to get from point A to point B using the Disney transportation system, and there is not always a direct route.

Boat

Water launches connect Magic Kingdom directly to Disney's Grand Floridian Resort & Spa and Disney's Polynesian Resort; a second route connects Magic Kingdom to Disney's Fort

Finding Nemo – The Musical

Arguably the best show at Walt Disney World® Resort, this sophisticated theater performance wows children and adults alike. The show is directed by Peter Brosius, artistic director of the Children's Theater Company of Minneapolis, and the spectacular puppets were created by Michael Curry, who helped design the puppets for Broadway's *The Lion King*. The music is fun, the acting is phenomenal, and narrative structure follows the vision and spirit of the movie. Make a lunch reservation for the Tusker House buffet between 1pm and 1:45pm and you'll be given reserved seating to the 3:15 performance, thus avoiding the lines. There's no extra fee, but be sure to ask when you make your lunch reservation. Oddly, Disney doesn't clump the Nemo-themed attractions in one park: Turtle Talk with Crush and the Seas with Nemo & Friends, both a Disney highlight for little ones, are in Epcot.

Wilderness Resort & Campground and Disney's Wilderness Lodge; and a third route, utilizing 600-passenger ferries, connects Magic Kingdom to the Transportation & Ticket Center. Boats also connect Epcot and Hollywood Studios to Disney's BoardWalk Inn & Villas Resort, Disney's Yacht Club Resort and Disney's Beach Club Resort, and Walt Disney World® Swan & Dolphin Resorts. Finally, boats connect Downtown Disney to Downtown Disney resort hotels.

Bus

Everything but Magic Kingdom is accessible by bus (city-bus style) from other areas, but not all destinations are directly connected.

Monorail

Three separate monorail routes service select locations within Walt Disney World®. The Resort Monorail loops between the Transportation & Ticket Center, Disney's Polynesian Resort, Disney's Grand Floridian Resort & Spa, Magic Kingdom and Disney's Contemporary Resort. A second monorail route connects the Transportation & Ticket Center to Epcot, and a third route connects the Transportation & Ticket Center to Magic Kingdom.

ORLANDO & AROUND

Orlando is both benefactor and victim of its theme parks. Those parks are the main reason people visit the Orlando area, of course, but so many visitors miss out on Orlando itself: pockets of tree-lined neighborhoods, established communities with an entrenched sense of history, a rich performing-arts scene and several fantastic gardens, parks and museums.

Sights

DOWNTOWN ORLANDO

Lake Eola Park Park

(Map p92; ☎407-246-2378; 195 N Rosalind Ave; ⏰6am-midnight; 👪) Pretty and shaded, this little city park sits between downtown Orlando and Thornton Park. A paved sidewalk circles the water; there's a waterfront playground; and you can rent swan paddleboats (per 30 minutes $15). On Saturday mornings, the park is home to the Orlando Farmers Market (p106).

Thornton Park Neighborhood

(Map p92) Trendy Thornton Park borders Lake Eola to the east. Though it's only a few blocks, you'll find several good restaurants, a handful of neighborhood bars, and a weekend energy of 20-somethings and young families.

Wells' Built Museum of African American History & Culture Museum

(Map p90; ☎407-245-7535; 511 W South St; adult/child $5/2; ⏰9am-5pm Mon-Fri) Dr Wells, one of Orlando's first African American doctors, came to Orlando in 1917. In 1921 he built a hotel for African Americans barred from Florida's segregated hotels, and soon after he built South Street Casino, a venue for African American entertainers. This small museum sits in the original hotel.

Gallery at Avalon Island Gallery

(Map p92; www.avalongallery.org; 39 S Magnolia Ave; ⏰11am-6pm Thu-Sat) FREE Contemporary art gallery housed in the oldest commercial building in Orlando (c 1886).

Orange County Regional History Center Museum

(Map p92; ☎407-836-8500; www.thehistorycenter.org; 65 E Central Blvd; adult/child 3-12yr/senior $10/3.50/6.50; ⏰10am-5pm Mon-Sat, from noon Sun; 👪) Orlando before Disney? Permanent exhibits cover prehistoric Florida, European exploration, race relations and citrus production, with a re-created pioneer home and 1927 courtroom.

City Arts Factory Gallery

(Map p92; ☎407-648-7060; www.cityartsfactory.com; 29 S Orange Ave; ⏰11am-6pm Mon-Sat) FREE Central hub to downtown Orlando arts' scene.

LOCH HAVEN PARK

Loch Haven Park, with 45 acres of parks, huge shade trees and three lakes, is home to several museums and theaters all concentrated within walking distance.

Greater Orlando

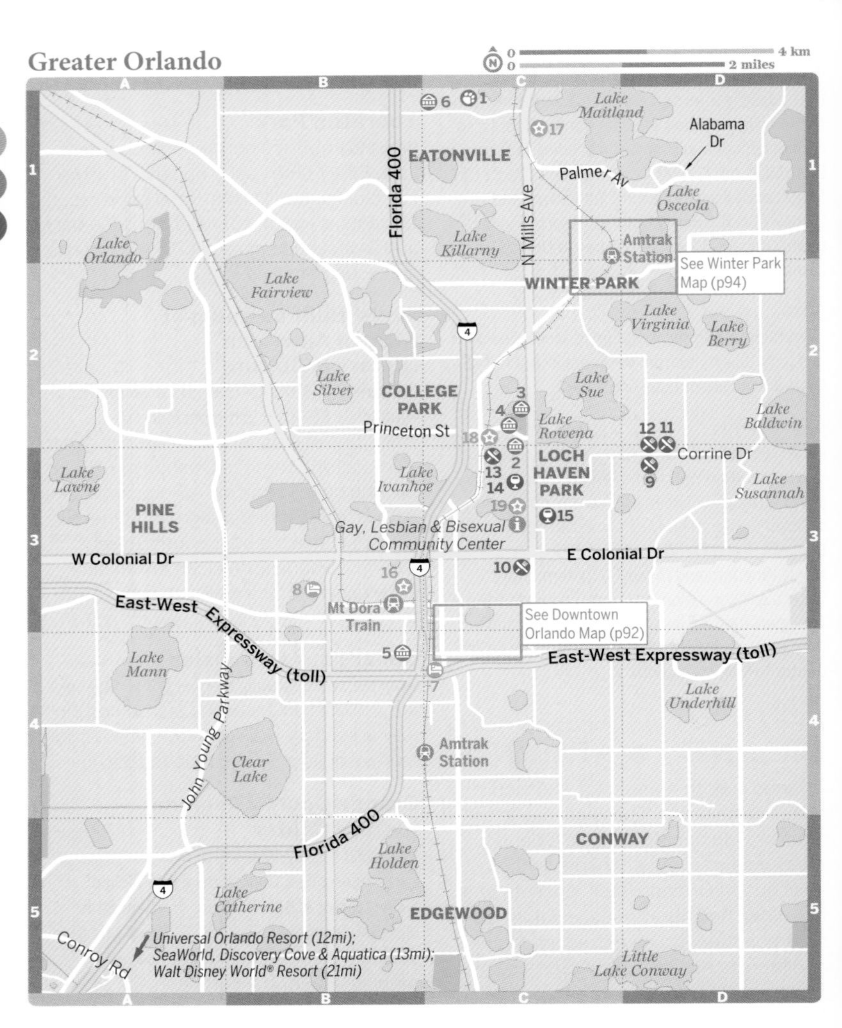

Orlando Museum of Art Museum

(Map p90; ☎407-896-4231; www.omart.org; 2416 N Mills Ave, Loch Haven Park; adult/child $8/5; ⏲10am-4pm Tue-Fri, from noon Sat & Sun; 👪; 🚌Lynx 125, 🚉Florida Hospital Health Village) Founded in 1924, Orlando's grand and blindingly white center for the arts boasts a fantastic collection, and hosts an array of adult and family-friendly art events and classes. The popular **First Thursday** ($10), from 6pm to 9pm on the first Thursday of the month, celebrates local artists with regional work, live music and food from Orlando restaurants.

Mennello Museum of American Art Museum

(Map p90; ☎407-246-4278; www.mennello museum.com; 900 E Princeton St, Loch Haven Park; adult/child 6-18yr $5/1; ⏲10:30am-4:30pm Tue-Sat, from noon Sun; 👪; 🚌Lynx 125, 🚉Florida Hospital Health Village) Tiny but excellent lakeside art museum featuring the work of Earl Cunningham, whose brightly colored images, a fusion of pop and folk

Greater Orlando

Sights

1 Audubon Center for Birds of Prey C1
2 Mennello Museum of American Art C3
3 Orlando Museum of Art C2
4 Orlando Science Center........................ C2
5 Wells' Built Museum of African American History & Culture B4
6 Zora Neale Hurston National Museum of Fine Arts C1

Sleeping

7 Aloft Orlando Downtown C4
8 Parliament House B3

Eating

9 Bikes, Beans & Bordeaux D3
10 Dandelion Communitea Café C3
11 East End Market D2
12 Stardust Video & Coffee........................ D2
13 White Wolf Café & Bar C3

Drinking & Nightlife

14 Matador C3
15 Wally's Mills Ave Liquors C3

Entertainment

16 Bob Carr Performing Arts Center B3
17 Enzian Theater....................................... C1
John & Rita Lowndes Shakespeare Center .... (see 3)
Orlando Repertory Theater........... (see 4)
18 Theatre Downtown................................ C2
19 Will's Pub C3

art, leap off the canvas. Visiting exhibits often feature American folk art.

Orlando Science Center Museum

(Map p90; 407-514-2000; www.osc.org; 777 E Princeton St, Loch Haven Park; adult/child $19/13; 10am-5pm Thu-Tue; ; Lynx 125, Florida Hospital Health Village) Changing exhibits on dinosaurs, the human body, the solar system and more offer candy-coated science education geared towards children ages 5 to 12. A giant tree grows through the four-story atrium, at the base of which you'll find alligators and a natural science discovery room.

GREATER ORLANDO

Wekiwa Springs State Park Outdoors

(407-884-2008407-884-2008; www.floridastateparks.org/wekiwasprings; 1800 Wekiwa Circle, Apopka; admission $6, campsites per person $5, hookups $24; 7am-dusk) Cool off in the icy spring-fed swimming hole, hike miles of trails and paddle the tranquil, still waters of the Wekiva River. **Nature Adventures (407-884-4311; www.canoewekiva.com; 1800 Wekiwa Circle, Wekiwa Springs State Park, Apopka; 2hr canoe/kayak $17, per additional hr $3; 8am-8pm;)**, inside the park, offers 2½-hour guided tours, rents kayaks and canoes (two hours $17, per additional hour $3) and supplies overnight camping supplies. Reserve primitive riverside campsites in advance.

Gatorland Zoo

(407-855-5496; www.gatorland.com; 14501 S Orange Blossom Trail/Hwy 17; adult/child $27/19; 10am-5pm; ; Lynx 108) With no fancy roller coasters or drenching water rides, this mom-and-pop park harkens back to Old Florida. It's small, it's silly and it's kitschy with, you guessed it, plenty of gators. A splintery wooden boardwalk winds past the hundreds of alligators in the breeding marsh and you can buy hot dogs to feed them.

Legoland Amusement Park

(863-318-5346; http://florida.legoland.com; 1 Legoland Way, Winter Haven; 1-/2-day tickets adult $84/99, child 9-12yr $75/92; 10am-5pm; ; Legoland Shuttle) With manageable crowds and lines, and no bells and whistles, lakeside Legoland maintains an old-school vibe – you don't have to plan like a general to enjoy a day here, and though it feels a bit dated, it is strikingly stress-free and relaxed. Rides and attractions, including the attached water park, are geared towards children aged two to 12. Booking online for a specific date can save you up to $15. Opening hours vary seasonally.

Bok Tower Gardens Gardens

(863-676-1408; www.boktowergardens.org; 1151 Tower Blvd, Lake Wales; adult/child $12/3, house tour $5; 8am-6pm, last admission 5pm;) Designed by Frederick Law Olmstead Jr and showcasing the meticulously carved 205ft stone bell tower, this 250-

Downtown Orlando

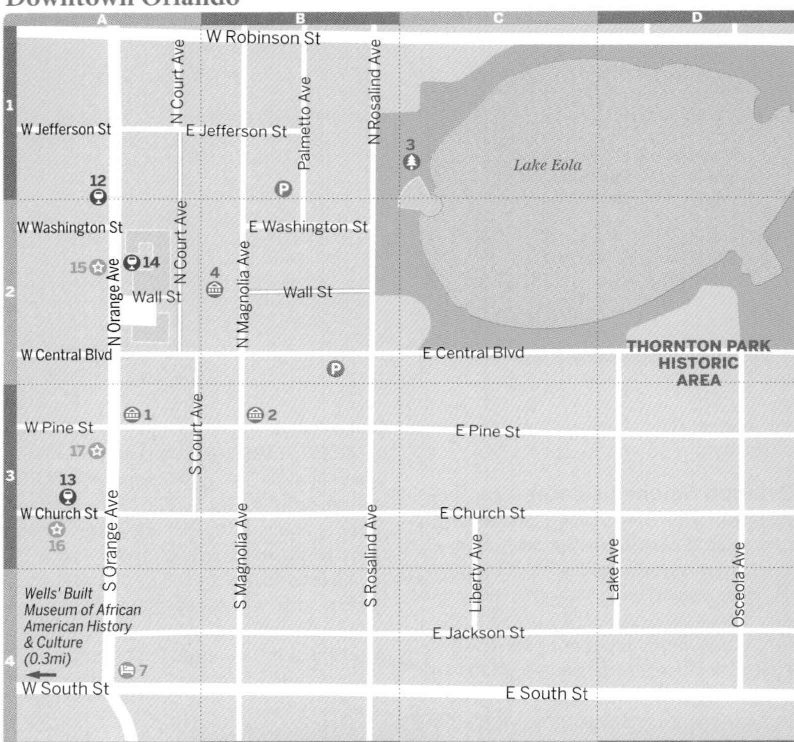

acre National Historic Landmark, about an hour south of Orlando, features beautiful gardens, twice-daily carillon concerts, the Mediterranean-style Pinewood Estates (circa 1930s) and a garden cafe. Kids can pick up special paper at the entry and make a treasure hunt out of looking for the iron rubbing posts, each with a different animal to rub. The gardens hosts outdoor classical-music concerts ($25).

SeaWorld — Theme Park

(☎888-800-5447; www.seaworldparks.com; 7007 Sea World Dr; adult/child $92/87, 14-day unlimited access incl with Discovery Cove ticket; 9am-7pm; ; Lynx 8, 38, 50, 111, I-Ride Trolley Red Line Stop 33) On top of the leaping dolphins, silly sea lions and splashing whales of SeaWorld's famous marine-animal shows, this park offers massive aquariums, opportunities to feed stingrays and dolphins, and two of the biggest thrill rides in town. While sea-animal encounters and shows remain as popular as ever, they have received criticism by animal welfare groups who claim the captivity of marine life is debilitating and stressful for the animals, and that this is exacerbated by human interaction.

Aquatica — Water Park

(☎407-351-3600; www.aquaticabyseaworld.com; 5800 Water Play Way; adult/child $56/41, advance online Splash & Save $19-28, 14-day unlimited access incl SeaWorld adult/child $119/114; 9am-6pm; ; Lynx 8, 38, 50, 111, SeaWorld shuttle, I-Ride Trolley Red Line Stop 34) A clean and pretty water park with tropical greenery offering a vague sense of Polynesia and some animal-viewing twists. Come here to splash, bob, float and zoom in lazy rivers, splash

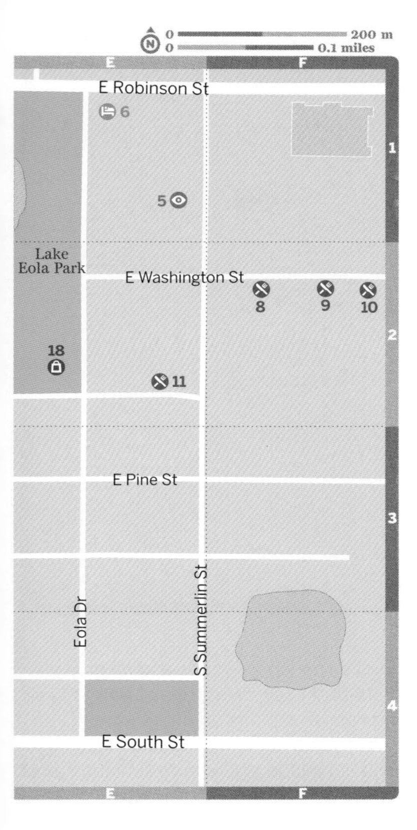

Downtown Orlando

zones, wave pools and slippery slides – that's what you do at water parks, and at Aquatica it's no different.

SeaWorld, which owns Aquatica, has come under scrutiny for its treatment of dolphins, and for their policies of keeping dolphins in captivity. Animal welfare organizations make compelling arguments against this practice.

Discovery Cove — Theme Park

(☎877-434-7268; www.discoverycove.com; 6000 Discovery Cove Way; incl 14-day unlimited access to SeaWorld & Aquatica tickets $169-280, incl dolphin swim $229-399, SeaVenture extra $59; ⏲8am-5:30pm, all-day experience, advance reservations required; 👪; 🚌Lynx 8, 38, 50, 111) At Discovery Cove, guests spend the day snorkeling in a fish- and ray-filled reef, floating on a lazy river through an aviary, and simply relaxing in an intimate tropical sanctuary of white-sand beaches. Sure, this island-getaway is all artificially made, but that's what Orlando does best. For an added price beyond the Resort Only package, you can swim with dolphins and walk along the sea floor.

Note that since the early 1990s, there has been a growing controversy regarding the ethics of dolphin captivity for the purposes of public display and human interaction. Both the Humane Society of the United States and the World Society for the Protection of Animals have come out strongly against the practice.

Audubon Center for Birds of Prey — Wildlife Reserve

(Map p90; ☎407-644-0190; http://fl.audubon.org/audubon-center-birds-prey; 1101 Audubon Way, Maitland; adult/child 3-12yr $5/4; ⏲10am-4pm Tue-Sun; 👪) Centered at a cool old house and very much off the beaten track, this little lakeside rehabilitation center for hawks, screech owls and

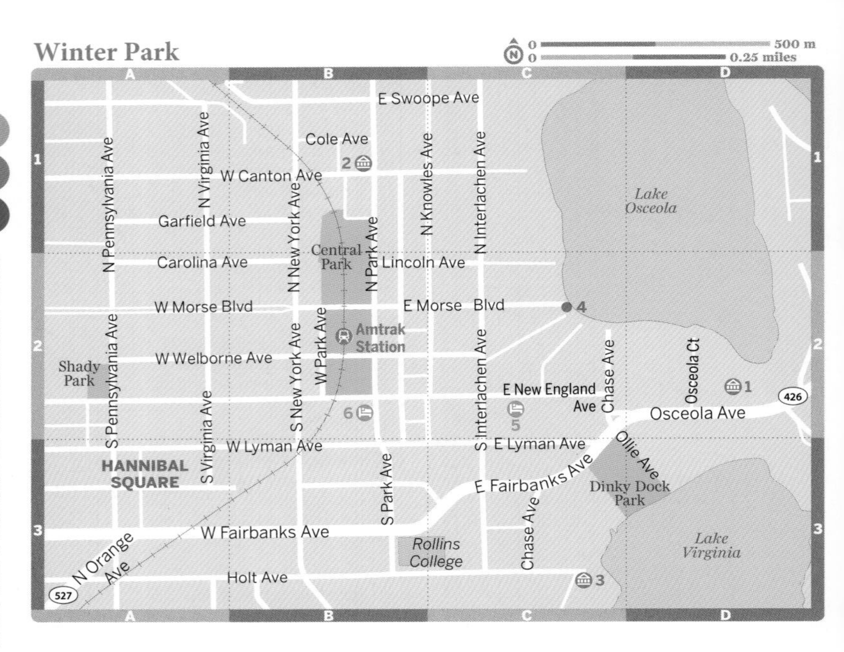

Winter Park

Sights

1 Albin Polasek Museum & Sculpture Gardens ... D2
2 Charles Hosmer Morse Museum of American Art ... B1
3 Cornell Fine Arts Museum ... C3

Activities, Courses & Tours

4 Scenic Boat Tour ... C2

Sleeping

5 Alfond Inn ... C2
6 Park Plaza Hotel ... B2

other talon-toed feathered friends offers plenty of opportunities to see the birds up close, just hanging out on the trainers' arms. Look out for Trouble the bald-eagle splashing and playing in his bathtub.

WonderWorks Museum

(**407-351-8800; www.wonderworksonline.com; 9067 International Dr; adult/child 4-12yr $25/20; 9am-midnight; ; Lynx 8, 38, 42, 50, 58, I-Ride Trolley Red Line Stop 23 or Green Line Stop 12**) Housed in a hard-to-miss, upside-down building, this bright, loud, frenetic landmark is a cross between a children's museum, a video arcade and an amusement park. Several stories of wall-to-wall interactive exhibits offer high-speed, multisensory education. Lie on a bed of nails, sit inside a hurricane simulator, and measure how high you can jump.

Zora Neale Hurston National Museum of Fine Arts Museum

(**Map p90; 407-647-3307; www.zoranealehurstonmuseum.com; 227 E Kennedy Blvd, Eatonville; 9am-4pm Mon-Fri, 11am-1pm Sat**) FREE Dedicated to Florida writer and anthropologist Zora Neale Hurston (1881–1960), born here in Eatonville and famous for her novel *Their Eyes Were Watching God*. This tiny one-room museum features changing exhibits by African American artists.

Nature Conservancy's Disney Wilderness Preserve Outdoors

(**407-935-0002; www.nature.org/florida; 2700 Scrub Jay Trail, Kissimmee; adult/child 6-17yr $3/2; 9am-5pm Mon-Fri; **) Hidden within Orlando's sprawl, this undeveloped and little-visited 11,500-acre preserve is the result of laws that required Walt Disney World® to compensate for the company's impact on (and devastation of) wetlands and sensitive natural habitats. The park's scrub, fields and woods are home to gopher tortoises, bald eagles, sandhill cranes and hundreds of other wildlife species.

Maitland Art Center Arts Center

(407-539-2181; www.maitlandartcenter.org; 231 W Packwood Ave, Maitland; adult/child $3/2; 11am-4pm Tue-Sun) Founded as an art colony in 1937 and listed on the National Register of Historic Places, this lovely little spot provides classes and studio space to area artists, galleries where they can display their work, and peaceful gardens.

Orlando Wetlands Park Outdoors

(407-568-1706407-568-1706; www.orlando wetlands.org; 25115 Wheeler Rd, Christmas; sunrise to sunset, closed Nov 15-Feb 1;) Woodlands, lakes and marshes flush with migrating birds, alligator, deer and all kinds of other critters. There are 20 miles of hiking trails and dirt roads, as well as restrooms, picnic tables and charcoal grills at the main entrance. Biking is limited to unpaved berm roads. The park, 30 miles east of downtown Orlando, sits about halfway between Orlando and Titusvile, home to Canaveral National Seashore and the Kennedy Space Center.

Old Town Amusement Park

(Map p62; 407-396-4888, 800-843-4202; www.myoldtownusa.com; 5770 W Irlo Bronson Memorial Hwy; admission free, per ride $2-6; noon-11pm; P ; Lynx 55, 56) Plopped among the exhaust, chain motels and the treeless landscape of Hwy 192, Old Town blends county fair and boardwalk with a touch of 1950s Americana. There are classic carnival rides, a spooky haunted funeral parlor, kitschy shops, live rock and roll, and old car cruises (Wednesday, Friday and Saturday at 8:30pm). Though it feels a bit run-down, lines for rides are short and there's no admission charge. Opening hours vary; see the website for a calendar of events. Free parking.

Local Knowledge

Winter Park Don't Miss List

ALICE MOULTON, WINTER PARK HISTORICAL ASSOCIATION & WINTER PARK SIDEWALK ART FESTIVAL BOARD MEMBER.

1 THE MORSE MUSEUM

The Charles Hosmer Morse Museum of American Art features the most comprehensive collection of works by Louis Comfort Tiffany in the world. A recent addition to the museum displays stained glass and architectural objects rescued from Tiffany's Long Island home, Laurelton Hall.

2 CORNELL FINE ARTS MUSEUM

The Cornell Fine Arts Museum on the Rollins College campus is home to one of the largest and most distinguished art collections in Florida. The permanent collection includes art by John Frederick Kensett, Henri Matisse, Pablo Picasso, Ed Ruscha, Tintoretto and Tiepolo, to name a few.

3 PARK PLAZA HOTEL

History buffs can't beat a stay at the Park Plaza Hotel, Winter Park's oldest and only downtown hotel. Originally known as the Hamilton Hotel when it was built in 1922, the hotel has been through major renovations, but retains the retro charm and historic significance of its past.

4 SCENIC BOAT TOUR

Nature-lovers won't want to miss the Scenic Boat Tour. The 18-passenger pontoon boat weaves through canals and across three lakes to give visitors a behind-the-scenes look at the lush tropical foliage, wildlife and magnificent lakefront estates of historic Winter Park.

5 WINTER PARK SIDEWALK ARTS FESTIVAL

The Winter Park Sidewalk Art Festival (www.wpsaf.org), set amid towering oaks and quaint shops, is a juried fine-arts show that attracts more than 300,000 visitors over three days during the third weekend in March.

MICHAEL DEFREITAS/ROBERT HARDING ©

Don't Miss Winter Park

Founded in 1858, this cozy college town concentrates some of Orlando's best-kept secrets.

The **Charles Hosmer Morse Museum of American Art** (407-645-5311; www.morsemuseum.org; 445 N Park Ave, Winter Park; adult/child $5/free; 9am-4pm Tue-Sat, from 1pm Sun, to 8pm Fri Nov-Apr;) houses the world's most comprehensive collection of Tiffany lead-glass lamps, windows, jewelry, blown glass, pottery and enamel.

Scattered through the grounds of the stately **Albin Polasek Museum & Sculpture Gardens** (www.polasek.org; 633 Osceola Ave, Winter Park; adult/child $5/free; 10am-4pm Tue-Sat, from 1pm Sun) are the works of Czech sculptor Albin Polasek. The small yellow villa perched on the shore of Lake Osceola was the artist's home.

The tiny **Cornell Fine Arts Museum** (www.rollins.edu/cfam; Rollins College, 1000 Holt Ave, Winter Park; adult/child $5/free; 10am-4pm Tue-Fri, noon-5pm Sat & Sun), on the campus of Rollins College, houses an eclectic collection of historic and contemporary art.

Brick walls, clean-lined wood furniture, antiques and luscious white cotton bedding give every room at the historic two-story Park Plaza Hotel (p98) a simple elegance.

One of the most talked-about foodie destinations in Orlando, the Ravenous Pig (p103) lives up to its reputation for creative, delicious food. Try the shrimp and grits or lobster taco.

A one-hour **Scenic Boat Tour** (407-644-4056; www.scenicboattours.com; 312 E Morse Blvd, Winter Park; adult/child $12/6; hourly 10am-4pm;) floats through 12 miles of tropical canals and lakes.

To get to Winter Park, take I-4 east to Fairbanks Ave, head east 2 miles to Park Ave and turn left.

Wet 'n Wild Water Park
(Map p120; 407-351-1800, 800-992-9453; www.wetnwildorlando.com; 6200 International Dr; adult/child 3-9yr $48/42, afternoons half-price; hours vary, call ahead; ; Lynx 8, 38, 42, 50, 58, I-Ride Trolley Red Line Stop 9 or Green Line Stop 5) Though not the most aesthetically pleasing water park in Orlando, this is the place to come for high-speed thrills. If you can tolerate the lines for rides, their twists, spins, dips and dives won't disappoint. For little ones, the fantastic one-acre **Blastaway Beach** offers all kinds of interactive water-spewing features and pint-sized slides. The park, owned by Universal Orlando Resort, is about a 10-minute walk from the theme parks. Parking costs $12. Wet 'n Wild participates in the Orlando Flex Ticket.

Kelly Park Swimming
(407-254-1902; 400 E Kelly Park Rd, Apopka; per vehicle $5; 8am-7pm Mar-Oct, to 5pm Nov-Feb;) Pick up an inner tube ($5) at the bar a half-mile before the entrance and float the shallow 1-mile stream formed by Rock Spring.

Activities

BIKING

Several resorts at Walt Disney World® Resort run their own cycling programs, including rentals and trails. One of the prettiest paths is between Disney's BoardWalk and Beach Club resorts – try it on a tandem candy-striped bike. Orlando's bike trails are in flux as the city develops a vast interconnected system of trails. **Outdoor Travels** (www.outdoortravels.com/biking_fl_overview_orlando.php) has descriptions of greater Orlando's bike trails. **Metro Plan Orlando** (www.metroplanorlando) has updated pdf maps.

West Orange Trail Bikes & Blades Cycling
(407-877-0600; www.orlandobikerental.com; 17914 State Rd 438, Winter Garden; bikes per hour $6-10, per day $30-50, per week $99-149, delivery/pick-up $40; 11am-5pm Mon-Fri, from 7:30am Sat & Sun) This bike shop lies 20 miles west of Orlando and sits at the beginning of the **West Orange Trail**. It offers bike rental and comprehensive information, both online and on-site, on biking in and around Orlando.

WATER SPORTS

Buena Vista Watersports Water Sports
(407-239-6939; www.bvwatersports.com; 13245 Lake Bryan Dr; per hour kayak, canoe or paddleboard $25, jetski $105, pontoon $125; 9am-6:30pm;) Just outside the Disney gates, with a low-key vibe. Waterski and tube riding include driver/instructor (per hour $95).

Sleeping

Rates outside theme park hubs are lowest from June through September and highest between Christmas and New Year, and in March and April. Prices quoted below are a range during high season. Most hotels offer complimentary shuttles to the theme parks,

DOWNTOWN

EO Inn & Spa Boutique Hotel $$
(Map p92; 407-481-8485; www.eoinn.com; 227 N Eola Dr, Thornton Park; r $129-229;) Small and understated hotel on the northeastern shore of Lake Eola, with an easy walk to Thornton Park and downtown Orlando bars and restaurants. The rooms vary dramatically in size.

Westin Grand Bohemian Luxury Hotel $$$
(Map p92; 407-313-9000; www.grandbohemianhotel.com; 325 S Orange Ave; r $179-299, ste $299-499, valet-only parking per day $24; P; Lymo) Downtown's most luxurious and elegant option has marble floors, a stunning art-deco bar with massive black pillars, weekend jazz and rich urban rooms. The small rooftop pool echoes 1950s Miami Beach.

Aloft Orlando Downtown Business Hotel $$
(Map p90; 497-380-3500; www.aloftorlandodowntown.com; 500 S Orange Ave; r $150-240, valet-only parking per day $20; P @) Open, stream-lined and decidedly modern, although the carefully constructed minimalist decor results in rooms that feel oddly empty, uninviting and unfinished, and the sleek little pool sits unpleasantly on the main road. But it is one of the few hotels within an easy walk to downtown Orlando's bars and restaurants.

GREATER ORLANDO

Bay Hill Club and Lodge Hotel $$
(888-422-9455, 407-876-2429; www.bayhill.com; 9000 Bay Hill Blvd; r $150-240; @) Quiet and genteel Bay Hill feels like a time-warp; as though you're walking into a TV set or your grandmother's photo album, into a time and place that is reassuringly calm and simple, and slightly bizarre. The staff is exceptionally gracious and accommodating, and handsome rooms are spread among a series of two-story buildings bordering the golf course.

Villas of Grand Cypress Resort $$$
(Map p62; 887-330-7370, 407-239-4700; www.grandcypress.com; 1 N Jacaranda Blvd; r from $165, 1-/2-/3-/4-bedroom villas from $280/395/555/725, resort fee per day $22;) Beautifully appointed rooms and villas, with natural cut stone, deep soaking tubs and outdoor patios, sit quietly along the Grand Cypress resort golf course. The least expensive option is the 'club suite,' a 650-sq-ft room with one king or two queen beds, a sleeper couch and a small patio. It feels cramped, but can work for a family of four.

Alfond Inn Boutique Hotel $$$
(407-998-8090; www.thealfondinn.com; 300 E New England Ave, Winter Park; r $170-$260; @) Contemporary white-walled elegance, a low-key welcoming vibe and a commitment to the arts combine to give this Winter Park gem a distinct style. Not only does it house the Alfond Collection of Contemporary Art, but all proceeds from hotel-room prices fund liberal-arts scholarships at nearby Rollins College. There's a lovely roof-top pool, an excellent locally sourced restaurant with courtyard tables, and well-appointed rooms.

Park Plaza Hotel Boutique Hotel $$$
(407-647-1072, 800-228-7220; www.parkplazahotel.com; 307 S Park Ave, Winter Park; r $180-220, ste $260-320;) Brick walls, spartan wood furniture, antiques and luscious white cotton bedding create a distinct arts-and-crafts sensibility at this historic two-story hotel. Rooms lining Park Ave share a narrow balcony, each with a private entrance and a few wicker chairs hidden from the street by hanging ferns, and are well worth the extra money.

Grande Lakes Orlando – JW Marriott & Ritz-Carlton Luxury Hotel $$$
(JW Marriott 407-206-2300, Ritz-Carlton 407-206-2400; www.grandelakes.com; 4012 Central Florida Pkwy (Ritz Carlton), 4040 Central Park Pkwy (JW Marriott); r $299-400, ste from $350, resort fee per-day $25, self/valet parking $19/26; P @) Two properties, one a Ritz and the other a Marriott, share facilities. The grounds, peaceful and elegant, with plenty of greenery and the best lazy river pool in Orlando, sit in a sheltered oasis of quiet and luxury. The spa is divine, the service impeccable, the food outstanding and most rooms have balconies overlooking the pool and golf course.

Hilton Garden Inn International Drive North Motel $$
(Map p120; 407-363-9332, 800-327-1366; www.hiltongardenorlando.com; 5877 American Way; r $100-225; @ ; I-Trolley Red Line Stop 7) With an airy garden-style lobby, a poolside tiki bar and an on-site restaurant, this makes an excellent midrange option for visiting Universal Orlando. It's less than a mile to the parks and, although it sits on I-4, it's quiet and set apart from the chaos of International Dr.

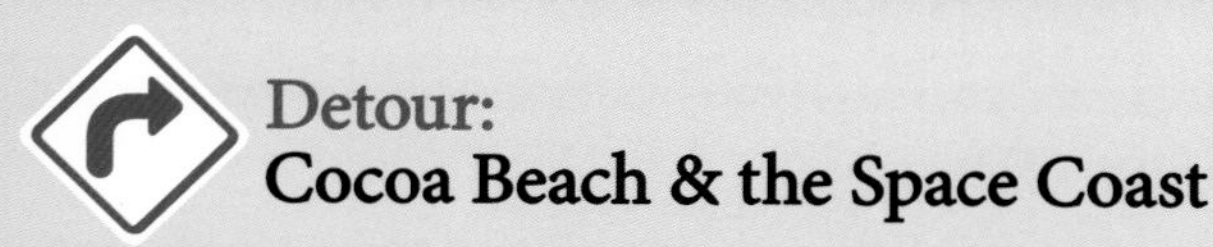

Detour: Cocoa Beach & the Space Coast

Cocoa Beach, an hour east of Orlando, is still a company town for NASA and the air-force base, but these days folks waiting to catch a cruise and surfers looking to party dominate the local scene. The town admirably balances Old Florida attitude with a brash, youthful sexiness that is quintessentially Central Florida. Cocoa Beach, birthplace and home of Kelly Slater, is one of the best spots for surfing in the state.

Three causeways – Hwy 528, Hwy 520 and Hwy 404 – cross the Indian River, Merritt Island and the Banana River to connect Cocoa Beach to the mainland.

Kennedy Space Center (☎866-737-5235; www.kennedyspacecenter.com; NASA Parkway, Merritt Island; adult/child 3-11yr $50/40; ⏰9am-7pm Apr-Aug, to 5pm Sep-Mar), the focal point of American space travel, has a small Visitor Complex that showcases the history and future of US space travel and research, and is the heart of the Kennedy Space Center. Here you'll find replicas of classic rockets and the space shuttle; an hour-long Astronaut Encounter, where a real astronaut fields questions from the audience; the beautiful Astronaut Memorial, which displays photos and names of those who died during shuttle disasters, plus IMAX films offering clear explanations of complicated science and cool footage of gravity-free life in space.

The two-hour Kennedy Space Center tour is the only way to see beyond the Visitor Complex without paying for an add-on tour. You'll see an LC 39 Observation Gantry, a 60ft observation tower with views of the twin launch pads and the astronauts' cramped living spaces at the International Space Station Center. Tours depart every 15 minutes from 10am to 2:45pm. Look for the coach buses and long lines to the right when you enter the Visitor Complex.

Merritt Island National Wildlife Refuge (☎321-861-0667; www.fws.gov/merrittisland; off FL-406; ⏰dawn-dusk) FREE This spectacular 140,000-acre refuge includes brackish marshes, mangrove swamps, pine flatlands and coastal dunes. More than 500 species of wildlife make this their home, including thousands of waterfowl stopping along their north–south migrations, alligators, otters and armadillos.

Brevard Zoo (☎321-254-9453; www.brevardzoo.org; 8225 N Wickham Rd, Melbourne; adult/child 2-12yr $16/12, Treetop Trek adult/small child $40/22; ⏰9:30am-5pm) Hand feed giraffes and lorikeets, who climb onto your head and arms in their enthusiasm, ride a train past camels and monkeys roaming free, and kayak through 22 acres of wetlands at this jewel of Old Florida zoos. Small, easily navigable, and boasting a great water-play area, this may just outshine the Kennedy Space Center for the under-10 crowd. Take I-95 exit 91 (Wickham Rd) 0.5 miles east.

Ron Jon Surf School (☎321-868-1980; www.cocoabeachsurfingschool.com; 150 E Columbia Lane, Cocoa Beach; per hr $50-65) Offers lessons for everyone from groms (that's surf talk for beginners) to experts, and there are plenty of other schools. For children five to 17.

Gay & Lesbian Orlando

In 1991 Orlando gay activist Doug Swallow and a handful of friends encouraged gays and lesbians to 'wear red and be seen' when visiting the Magic Kingdom. Some 2500 made it. Ever since, an estimated 40,000 to 50,000 red-shirted gay and lesbian visitors descend on Cinderella's Castle on the first Saturday in June. Though it explodes during Gay Days, there is a solid gay and lesbian community in Orlando year-round. Go to www.orlandogaycities.com for a thorough listing and reviews of bars and clubs, events, hotels, bathhouses and more.

Gay, Lesbian & Bisexual Community Center (Map p90; 407-228-8272; www.thecenterorlando.org; 946 N Mills Ave; 9am-4pm Mon & Thu, to 8pm Tue, Wed & Fri, noon-8pm Sat, noon-5pm Sun) General resource center, with tips on local hot spots and social events.

Parliament House (Map p90; 407-425-7571; www.parliamenthouse.com; 410 N Orange Blossom Trail; r & ste $66-106;) This legendary gay resort and an Orlando institution sits on Rock Lake and features several clubs and bars, a restaurant and some of the best drag shows south of the Mason-Dixon Line.

Pulse (407-649-3888; www.pulseorlandoclub.com; 1912 S Orange Ave; cover $5) Three nightclubs, each with its own distinct vibe but all ultramodern and sleek. Call for directions and hours.

Barefoot Suites Motel $$
(Map p62; 407-589-2127; www.thebarefootsuites.com; 2750 Florida Plaza Blvd, Kissimmee; ste $83-200, resort fee per day $7;) Bright and spacious one- and two-bedroom suites in a yellow six-story building. Low-key, friendly, under-the-radar and close to Disney, with kitchens and washer/dryers.

Embassy Suites Lake Buena Vista South Hotel $$
(407-597-4000; https://embassysuites3.hilton.com; 4955 Kyngs Heath Rd, Kissimmee; r $110-225;) Comfortable and modern two-room suites, complimentary cooked-to-order breakfasts and evening cocktails, as well as an on-site travel agent, Hertz car-rental desk, a market with food basics and coin laundry. Built in 2013, this is an excellent choice in a city overflowing with mediocre, aging and overrated chains.

Waldorf Astoria Luxury Hotel $$$
(Map p62; 407-597-5500; www.waldorfastoriaorlando.com; 14200 Bonnett Creek Resort Lane; r $200-400, ste $450-560, resort fee per day $25, valet-only parking $25; P@) Though this elegant classic doesn't offer the benefits of on-site Disney hotels, it's located within the gates of Walt Disney World® and, unlike Disney luxury, the quality of its rooms, amenities and service is impeccable. There's an excellent buffet breakfst, two grandly styled pools bordering the golf course, a Guerlain spa and divine beds. **Hilton Orlando Bonnet Creek** (Map p62; 407-597-3600; www.hiltonbonnetcreek.com; 14100 Bonnet Creek Resort Lane; r $130-300, resort fee per day $22, self/valet parking $16/24; P@), which has a lazy river and pool slide, shares amenities with the Waldorf, and rooms and packages there cost a bit less.

Palm Lakefront Hostel Hostel $
(407-396-1759; www.orlandohostels.com; 4840 W Irlo Bronson/Hwy 192, Kissimmee; dm/d/q $19/40/60; ; Lynx 56 & 55) This two-story roadside-motel-styled hostel sits among the traffic and chain restaurants of the Kissimmee strip. It doesn't look like much at first glance, but in the back, there's a grassy lakeside picnic and

BBQ area, a quiet fishing dock and a little pool. The public bus just outside connects directly to Disney's Transportation & Ticket Center.

Eating

Restaurant Row, a half-mile stretch of W Sand Lake Rd just west of Whole Foods and inside the strip mall Plaza Venezia, offers a concentration of diverse restaurants and high-end chains.

DOWNTOWN

Graffiti Junktion American Burger Bar Burgers $

(Map p92; 407-426-9503; www.graffitijunktion.com; 900 E Washington St, Thornton Park; mains $6-13; 11am-2am) This little neon graffiti-covered happenin' hangout, with courtyard dining and regular drink specials, is all about massive burgers with attitude. Top yours with a fried egg, artichoke hearts, chili, avocado and more.

Shari Sushi Japanese $$

(Map p92; 407-420-9420; www.sharisushilounge.com; 621 E Central Blvd, Thornton Park; mains $14-24; 5-10pm Sun-Wed, to 11pm Thu-Sat) Minimalist decor, huge sidewalk windows and a rather odd variety of tasty sushi, rolls and sashimi, but there's a limited selection of hot dishes. The elaborate drinks menu includes lemongrass *mojitos* and a cilantro-lime sake cocktail.

Dexters of Thornton Park American $$

(Map p92; Thornton Park 407-648-2777; www.dexwine.com; 808 E Washington St, Thornton Park; mains $10-17; 7am-10pm Mon-Thu, to 2am Fri, 11am-2am Sat, 10am-10pm Sun) Neighborhood restaurant with outdoor seating and wine by the flight, glass or bottle. The popular daily brunch includes interesting twists to breakfast mainstays, including pepper-jack grits, apple-pie french toast, duck bacon, and a selection of fruity mimosas including peach, mango and pineapple.

Benjamin French Bakery Bakery $

(Map p92; 407-797-2293; www.benjaminfrenchbakery.com; 716 E Washington St, Thornton Park; pastries $4, mains $6-12; 8am-7pm Tue-Sat, to 6pm Sun) Bright little French bakery featuring rustic sandwiches, salads and omelets. Your best bet, though, is a pastry and coffee to-go. Try the crusty home-made baguette or a coconut croissant.

INTERNATIONAL DRIVE (AROUND UNIVERSAL ORLANDO RESORT & SEAWORLD)

Thai Thani Thai $$

(407-239-9733; www.thaithani.net; 11025 International Dr; mains $9-22; 11:30am-11pm; ; I-Ride Trolley Red Line) Just past the gates to SeaWorld, Discovery Cove and Aquatica, this makes an ideal dinner

Orlando skyline from Lake Eola (p89)

choice after a day of dolphins and waterslides. It's friendly, cool and quiet, with gilded Thai decor and some tables with traditional floor seating. Good food, but watered-down spice – for a kick, ask for level 5.

Taverna Opa Greek $$

(**☎407-351-8660; www.opaorlando.com; 9101 International Dr; mains $12-25; ⏲noon-2am; ; I-Ride Trolley Red Line**) Great spot for Greek classics, including plenty of vegetarian options and fresh hummus made tableside. Can get loud and crazy late-night, when the belly dancer shimmies and shakes from table to table, and it isn't unusual for folks to climb onto the solid tables and kick up their heels. Nightly entertainment from 7pm.

TooJays Deli $

(**☎407-355-0340; www.toojays.com; 7600 Dr Phillips Blvd, Restaurant Row; sandwiches $4-7; ⏲8am-9pm Sun-Thu, to 10pm Fri & Sat;**) Excellent deli sandwiches to go, but nothing much in terms of ambience. If you feel a cold coming on, head here for quintessential homemade chicken noodle or matzah ball soup.

Cafe Tu Tu Tango Tapas $$

(**☎407-248-2222; www.cafetututango.com; 8625 International Dr; tapas $8-16; ⏲11:30am-11pm Mon, Wed, Thu & Sun, to midnight Tue, Fri & Sat; I-Ride Trolley Red Line Stop 20**) Local artwork, all for sale, crams the adobe-style walls of this bright Spanish eatery. Relax on the patio with cajun chicken egg rolls and a plate of alligator bites, washed down with a pitcher of sangria. On Tuesdays from 9pm to midnight, there's live music and $3 drinks.

GREATER ORLANDO

Yellow Dog Eats Barbecue $$

(**☎407-296-0609; www.yellowdogeats.com; 1236 Hempel Ave, Windermere; mains $7-14; ⏲11am-9pm;**) Housed in what was once a general store, with a tin roof, courtyard dining, an old boys' school locker filled with bottled beer, and an eclectic mix of quirky dog-inspired decor, this laid-back boho Orlando gem serves up excellent barbecue. Try the Florida Cracker (pulled pork with gouda, bacon and fried onions) with a side of Cuban black beans.

Aquatica (p92)

PER ANDERSEN/ALAMY ©

Ravenous Pig American $$$

(407-628-2333; www.theravenouspig.com; 1234 Orange Ave, Winter Park; mains $19-33; 11:30am-2pm & 5:30-9:30pm Tue-Sat) The cornerstone of Orlando's locally sourced restaurant trend, with giant black-and-white photos hanging from exposed ceiling pipes and a handful of sidewalk tables. Start with the bacon-infused bourbon old-fashioned and a plate of gruyère biscuits. Mains include a burger with truffle-oil fries, Florida seafood specialties, and quirky twists such as duck breast with 'dragon-tongue' beans.

Dandelion Communitea Café Vegetarian $

(Map p90; 407-362-1864; http://dandelioncommunitea.com; 618 N Thornton Ave; mains $6-10; 11am-10pm Mon-Sat, to 5pm Sun;) Unabashedly crunchy and definitively organic, this pillar of the sprouts and tofu, green-tea and soy-milk dining scene serves up creative and excellent vegetarian fare in a refurbished old house that invites folks to sit down and hang out.

Bikes, Beans & Bordeaux Cafe $

(Map p90; 407-427-1440; www.bikesbeansandbordeaux.com; 3022 Corrine Dr, Audubon Park; mains $6-12; 7am-10pm Mon-Fri, from 8am Sat, 8am-3pm Sun; P) The wine and beer list follows the international cycling season, with French Bordeaux during the Tour de France and so on. There's weekend live music, couches for lounging and local art. Try the hot feta dip or create your own flatbread concoction.

Stardust Video & Coffee Cafe $

(Map p90; 407-623-3393; www.stardustvideoandcoffee.wordpress.com; 1842 E Winter Park Rd, Audubon Park; mains $7-14; 7am-midnight Mon-Fri, from 8am Sat & Sun; P) Hipster-hippie hangout by day, with folks hunkered down behind laptops and books; craft cocktail and artisan beer hot spot by night. There's a Sunday brunch, fresh-squeezed juices, plenty of vegetarian options and, oddly, video rentals. Yes, videos. Paper lanterns and twinkly lights dangle from the ceiling and snapshot-style photographs hang haphazardly from the concrete walls.

White Wolf Café & Bar Diner $$

(Map p90; 407-895-9911; www.whitewolfcafe.com; 1829 N Orange Ave; mains $14-29; 8am-9pm Mon-Fri, to 3pm Sun; Lynx 102) Neighborhood diner cafe, with Tiffany-styled chandeliers, a massive wooden bar and a mishmash of antiques. Come for the stick-to-your-bones breakfasts and a Bloody Mary.

Drinking & Nightlife

The downtown Orlando drinking scene can be a crazy *Girls Gone Wild* meets Spring Break scene, particularly on the weekends and late at night,

Neighborhood bars in Celebration, Winter Park and Thornton Park (which is located just east of downtown Orlando's Lake Eola) offer an altogether different vibe, with wine bars, acoustic live music and outdoor cafes sporting water bowls for canine companions.

DOWNTOWN

Courtesy Bar Cocktail Bar

(Map p92; 407-450-2041; 114 N Orange Ave; drinks from $5; 5pm-2am, from 7pm Sat, from 3pm Sun) Housed in an historic Orlando space, with brick walls and Jefferson filament bulbs, this old-school cocktail bar serves up high-quality spirits with fresh and quirky artisan twists such as Himalayan pink salt, fresh honeydew juice and dandelion-eucalyptus tincture. We don't even know what all of it means, but what delights! There's also an excellent selection of beer and wine.

Woods Cocktail Bar

(Map p92; 407-203-1114; www.thewoodsorlando.com; 49 N Orange Ave, 2nd fl, Historic Rose Bldg; 5pm-2am Mon-Fri, from 7pm Sat) Craft cocktails hidden in a cozy smoke-free 2nd-floor setting, with exposed brick, a tree-trunk bar and an earthy feel.

Latitudes Bar

(Map p92; 407-649-4270; www.churchstreetbars.com; 33 W Church St; 4:30pm-2am) Island-inspired rooftop bar, with tiki lanterns and city views. There are two more thumping bars below.

On the Stage & Under the Stars

There's more to Orlando than theme parks and techno-club hopping. Walt Disney World® Resort, Universal Orlando Resort and SeaWorld also all have an island-inspired luau, Disney offers three dinner shows, and several Disney resorts screen classic Disney films outdoors (free).

There's also a free classic movie on the second Thursday of every month in Winter Park.

Cirque du Soleil La Nouba (p84) Get your Cirque du Soleil fix with Disney's best live show. Designed by Disney to specifically house La Nouba, there are no bad seats.

Blue Man Group (p130) Originally an off-Broadway phenomenon in 1991, Blue Man Group brings its shenanigans to Universal Orlando Resort.

Mad Cow Theatre (Map p92; ☎407-297-8788; www.madcowtheatre.com; 54 W Church, 2nd fl; tickets $18-30) A model of regional theater, with classic and modern performances in downtown space.

Theatre Downtown (Map p90; ☎407-841-0083; www.theatredowntown.net; 2113 N Orange Ave; tickets $16-22) Repertory theater featuring original works from local playwrights, regional actors and classic productions. Located two blocks west of Loch Haven Park.

SAK Comedy Lab (Map p92; ☎407-648-0001; www.sakcomedylab.com; 29 S Orange Ave, City Arts Factory, 2nd fl; tickets $15, Tue & Wed 9pm $3; ⏲Tue-Sat) Improv comedy in 200-seat downtown theater; 9pm shows Tuesday and Wednesday cost $3. Reservations recommended. Check the website for other show times.

John and Rita Lowndes Shakespeare Center (Map p90; ☎407-447-1700; www.orlandoshakes.org; 812 E Rollins St, Loch Haven Park; tickets $20-35) Set on the shores of Lake Estelle in grassy Loch Haven Park, this lovely theater includes three stages hosting classics like *Pride and Prejudice* and *Beowulf* and excellent children's theater.

Orlando Repertory Theater (Map p90; ☎407-896-7365; www.orlandorep.com; 1001 E Princeton St, Loch Haven Park; tickets $10-25) Performances for families and children run primarily in the afternoon or early evening. Shows stretch the gamut of styles and content, including *Anne Frank and Me, Hairspray* and *James and the Giant Peach.*

Bösendorfer Lounge — Lounge

(Map p92; ☎407-313-9000; www.grandbohemianhotel.com; 325 S Orange Ave, Westin Grand Bohemian; ⏲11am-2am) Zebra-fabric chairs, gilded mirrors, massive black pillars and marble floors ooze pomp and elegance. This hotel bar is popular for after-work drinks, and the lounge picks up with live jazz at 7pm. The name stems from the lounge's rare Bösendorfer piano.

GREATER ORLANDO

Wally's Mills Ave Liquors — Bar

(Map p90; ☎407-896-6975; www.wallysonmills.com; 1001 N Mills Ave; ⏲7:30am-1am) It's been around since the early '50s, before Orlando became Disney, and while its peeling naked-women wallpaper could use some updating, it wouldn't be Wally's without it. Nothing flashy, nothing loud, just a tiny, windowless, smoky bar with a jukebox and cheap, strong drinks – as much a dark dive as you'll find anywhere. And yes, it opens at 7:30*am*.

Matador Cocktail Bar
(Map p90; 407-872-0844; 724 Virginia Dr, Mills 50; 7pm-2am) Deep red walls, a pool table and furniture you'd expect in your grandmother's parlor. Low-key vibe perfect for sipping that Bulleit Rye.

Entertainment

Will's Pub Live Music
(Map p90; 407-898-5070; www.willspub.org; 1042 N Mills Ave; tickets $8-16; 4pm-2am Mon-Sat, from 6pm Sun) With $2 Pabst on tap, pinball and vintage pin-ups on the walls, this is Orlando's less-polished music scene but it enjoys a solid reputation as one of the best spots in town to catch local and nationally touring indie music. Smoke-free; beer and wine only.

Enzian Theater Cinema
(Map p90; 407-629-0054; www.enzian.org; 1300 S Orlando Ave, Maitland; adult/child $10/8; 5pm-midnight Tue-Fri, noon-midnight Sat & Sun) The envy of any college town, this clapboard-sided theater screens independent and classic films, and has the excellent **Eden Bar (407-629-1088; www.enzian.org; 1300 S Orlando Ave, Maitland; mains $10-16; 11am-11pm Sun-Thu, to 1am Fri & Sat;)** restaurant, featuring primarily local and organic fare. Have a veggie burger and a beer on the patio underneath the cypress tree, or opt for table service in the theater.

Beacham & the Social Live Music
(Map p92; 407-246-1419; www.thebeacham.com; 46 N Orange Ave; cover varies; 9pm-3am) Both the Beachum and the more intimate and recommended Social next door are cornerstones of Orlando's nightclub and live-music scene. They host bands from punk to reggae on the weekends and hop all week long with music and dancing. Shows are designated 'all ages,' '18 plus' or '21 plus.'

Tanqueray's Live Music
(Map p92; 407-649-8540; 100 S Orange Ave; 11am-2am Mon-Fri, 6pm-2am Sat & Sun) A former bank vault, this underground smoky dive bar draws folks looking to hang out with friends over a beer. There's Guinness on tap, and you can catch weekend local bands, usually reggae or blues.

Blue Man Group (p130) billboard

KEITH LEVIT/ALAMY ©

Shopping

Head to Celebration or Winter Park for pleasant browsing, small-town American style, or to Downtown Disney for shopping on steroids.

Orlando Farmers Market — Market

(Map p92; www.orlandofarmersmarket.com; Lake Eola; 10am-4pm Sun) Local produce and a beer and wine garden on the shores of downtown Orlando's Lake Eola.

Eli's Orange World — Food

(407-396-1306; www.orangeworld192.com; 5395 W Irlo Bronson Memorial Hwy/Hwy 192; 8am-9:45pm) Family-owned, friendly and plenty of samples of the iconic Florida fruit, as well as jams and kitschy souvenirs. Look for the half-an-orange-shaped building on the Kissimmee strip.

Information

Medical Services

Arnold Palmer Hospital for Children (407-649-9111; 1414 Kuhl Ave; 24hr) Orlando's primary children's hospital. Located just east of I-4 at exit 81.

Centra Care Walk-In Medical (407-934-2273; www.centracare.org; 8am-midnight Mon-Fri, to 8pm Sat & Sun) Walk-in medical center with more than 20 locations.

Doctors on Call Services (DOCS; 407-399-3627; www.doctorsoncallservice.com; 24hr) Twenty-four-hour doctors on-call to your hotel, including to Walt Disney World® Resort and Universal Orlando Resort.

Tourist Information

Official Visitor Center (407-363-5872; www.visitorlando.com; 8723 International Dr; 8:30am-6pm) Legitimate discount attraction tickets and best source for information on theme parks, accommodations, outdoor activities, performing arts and more.

Websites

Orlando Ballet (407-426-1739; http://orlandoballet.org) Performs primarily at downtown Orlando's Bob Carr Performing Arts Center (Map p90; 407-246-4262; www.orlandovenues.net; 401 W Livingston St). The **Family Series** productions (11am for 1 hour) include children-friendly classics such as *The Nutcracker*, *Beauty and the Beast* and *Snow White*.

Getting Around

To/From the Airport

Many hotels and motels run complimentary airport shuttles.

Legacy Towncar of Orlando (407-695-4413, 888-939-8227; www.legacytowncar.com) Prices include a 20-minute grocery-store stop.

Disney's Magical Express (866-599-0951; www.disneyworld.disney.go.com) If you're staying at a Walt Disney World® hotel and are arriving into the Orlando International Airport (as

Eli's Orange World

opposed to Sanford), arrange in advance for complimentary luggage handling and deluxe bus transportation.

Mears Transportation (**customer service 407-423-5566, reservations 855-463-2776; www.mearstransportation.com**)

Public Transportation

I-Ride Trolley (**407-354-5656; www.iridetrolley.com; rides adult/child 3-9yr $2/1, passes 1-/3-/5-/7-/14-days $5/7/9/12/18; 8am-10:30pm**) Services International Dr, from south of SeaWorld north to the Universal Orlando Resort area. Buses run at 20- to 30-minute intervals and exact change is required.

Lymmo (**www.golynx.com; 6am-10pm Mon-Thu, to midnight Fri, 10am-midnight Sat, to 10pm Sun**) Circles downtown Orlando for free.

Getting There & Away

Air

Orlando is serviced by two international airports: Orlando International Airport (www.orlandoairports.net), 12 miles east of downtown Orlando, and the much smaller Sanford International Airport (www.orlandosanfordairport.com), 30 miles north.

Car

Orlando is 285 miles from Miami; the fastest and most direct route is a 4½-hour road trip via the Florida Turnpike. From Tampa it is an easy 60 miles along I-4.

Universal Orlando Resort

Universal's got spunk, it's got spirit and it's got attitude. Universal Orlando Resort is Disney with a dash of hot sauce. Instead of the seven dwarfs, there's the Simpsons. Instead of Donald Duck and Mickey Mouse, there's Spider-Man and Shrek. While Universal can never replace Disney, and it certainly lacks the sentimental charm of Snow White, Peter Pan and Winnie the Pooh, it offers pure, unabashed, adrenaline-pumped, full-speed-ahead fun for the entire family. And we mean the *entire* family – yes, your children will enjoy it here, but in many ways, Universal is the theme-park version of the kid-oriented film that has enough adult humor to keep parents laughing throughout.

The Universal Orlando Resort consists of two theme parks – Islands of Adventure, with incredibly designed themed areas and the bulk of the thrill rides, and Universal Studios, with movie-based attractions and shows.

Dudley Do-Right's Ripsaw Falls (p119)

Diagon Alley, Wizarding World of Harry Potter (p122)

STEPHEN SEARLE/ALAMY ©

Universal Orlando Resort

1 Wizarding World of Harry Potter
2 Islands of Adventure
3 Universal Studios
4 Production Central
5 Springfield

Lake Cane
Vineland Rd
S Kirkman Rd
Universal Orlando Resort
Lake Marsha
Major Blvd
Florida's Turnpike (toll)
Millenia Rd
City Walk
P
P
Hollywood Way
Dr Phillips Blvd
Turkey Lake Rd
Sandy Lake
S Kirkman Rd
International Dr
Spring Lake
W Sand Lake Rd
W Sand Lake Rd
Universal Blvd
Little Sand Lake
Via Mercado
Turkey Lake Rd
Orlando's Official Visitor Center
Florida 400
Big Sand Lake
4
4
N
0 2 km
0 1 miles

Universal Orlando Resort's Highlights

Wizarding World of Harry Potter

The Wizarding World of Harry Potter (p122) is as close as any of us will get to Harry's universe (or at least, that universe as envisioned by the film franchise), barring a letter delivered by Owl Post. Hogwarts, Hogsmeade, Diagon Alley and other locations from the series are flawlessly re-created here, and experiences range from casual immersion to full or amusement-park-ride ridiculousness.

Islands of Adventure

Seven distinct islands (p118), each a fictional flight of fancy brought to theme-park life, means there is an experience for all comers in this corner of Universal Orlando Resort. As you wander you'll come across a children's village of Dr Seuss characters where the Lorax speaks for the trees, to the pages of Marvel comic books brought to whiz-bang-pow life, swinging superheroes and all. Cat in the Hat ride (p121)

TIM E WHITE/ALAMY ©

Universal Studios

3

Many people still refer to Universal Orlando Resort as Universal Studios (p121), which speaks to how iconic this portion of the park is to the resort's overall identity. Universal Studios is many things, but perhaps most notably, it is its name. This is a working film production studio combined with a series of attractions that bridge the gap between cinematic magic and lived-in experience.

4

RSBPHOTO1/ALAMY ©

5

Production Central

One of the mainstay centerpieces of the 'Studios' section of Universal Studios, Production Central (p123) takes you right into the imaginative wonderland of Hollywood filmmaking. There are a few ways this occurs; maybe you'll get to experience the sensory overload of the Hollywood Rip Ride Rockit roller coaster, or go on a wild chase after Princess Fiona with Shrek and Donkey at the Shrek 4-D show. Hollywood Rip Ride Rockit (p123)

Springfield

Some of us have been waiting our entire lives to step into the brightly colored, cartoon-eyed environs of Springfield (p121), USA, home of *The Simpsons* (the show), the Simpsons (the family) and their entire, enormous cast of supporting characters. Down a Duff beer (or a Flaming Moe) and marvel at a fantasy world recreation of imagined suburbia that rivals the sorcery at Hogwarts. The Simpsons Ride (p121)

Universal Orlando Resort's Best...

Hotels

Portofino Bay Hotel Luxurious, Italianate resort situated around a lagoon. (p125)

Royal Pacific Resort Pacific and Balinese themed, scattered with gardens and tropical flowers. (p125)

Hard Rock Hotel A bit cheesy, but lots of fun; caters to singles and families. (p125)

Cabana Bay Beach Resort One of Universal's newest resorts, with a retro Florida vibe. (p126)

Rides

Harry Potter & the Forbidden Journey Flying broomstick journey through Hogwarts. (p119)

Twister...Ride It Out Scary attraction puts you in a tornado path. (p123)

Incredible Hulk Coaster Roller coaster with great ride-narration synchronization. (p119)

Amazing Adventures of Spider-Man Help Spider-Man battle villains across New York. (p118)

The Simpsons Ride If you've ever wanted to visit the real Springfield, here's your chance. (p121)

Eating

Three Broomsticks Realize the dream of quaffing a Butterbeer. (p126)

Schwab's Pharmacy Lovely recreation of a Hollywood original. (p127)

Confisco Grille Outdoor dining and fresh pizza. (p126)

Emeril's Tchoup Chop Excellent sit-down dining in Universal Orlando. (p127)

Themed Areas

- **Springfield** The closest thing to living among *The Simpsons* without dyeing your skin yellow. (p121)

- **The Wizarding World of Harry Potter** You always knew, in your heart, you were a Hufflepuff. (p122)

- **Seuss Landing** Hang here for too much time and you'll only speak in rhyme...damn. (p121)

- **San Francisco** Oddly enjoy the experience of an earthquake. (p123)

Left: Portofino Bay Hotel (p125);
Above: Incredible Hulk Coaster (p119)

Need to Know

BE FOREWARNED

- **Wild About Harry** You haven't seen crowds and lines until you've seen Universal's Wizarding World of Harry Potter during high season. If it reaches capacity (it can), use Universal's 'return time' tickets, which allow you to enjoy other attractions and return for entry into the Wizarding World within a specific window of time.

ADVANCE PLANNING

- **Hotels** Book early to get grand deals and to cut the wait out of many of the parks' lines.

- **Express Pass** Highly recommended if you want to get the most out of the rides with the least amount of queuing.

- **Car Rentals** In Orlando, it's always best to book your rental vehicles as early as possible, especially in high tourist season (November to March).

- **Sunscreen** If you're going to be outside in the local waterparks, bring plenty of sunblock.

RESOURCES

- **Islands of Adventure** An unofficial site devoted to the most ride-heavy portion of Universal Studios: www.islandsofadventure.com.

- **Discover Universal** Another unofficial site devoted to the Universal Studios experience: www.discoveruniversal.com.

- **Theme Park Rangers** The reporting team for the *Orlando Sentinel* gives their insider, and sometimes investigative, perspective on the happenings in the region's theme parks: http://www.orlandosentinel.com/travel/attractions/theme-park-rangers-blog/

GETTING AROUND

- **Car** I-4 is your main road for getting between the region's parks.

- **Boat** Within Universal Studios, water taxis shuttle between the Universal Hotels and CityWalk.

- **Shuttle** Shuttle services exist between hotels, Universal Orlando Resort and in some cases, Walt Disney World® Resort.

- **Walking** All of Universal Studios' parks and hotels are linked by pedestrian walkways.

Universal Orlando Resort Itineraries

You're spoiled for choice here. You've got two main parks in Universal Orlando, each with sub-areas that span the world of film and television.

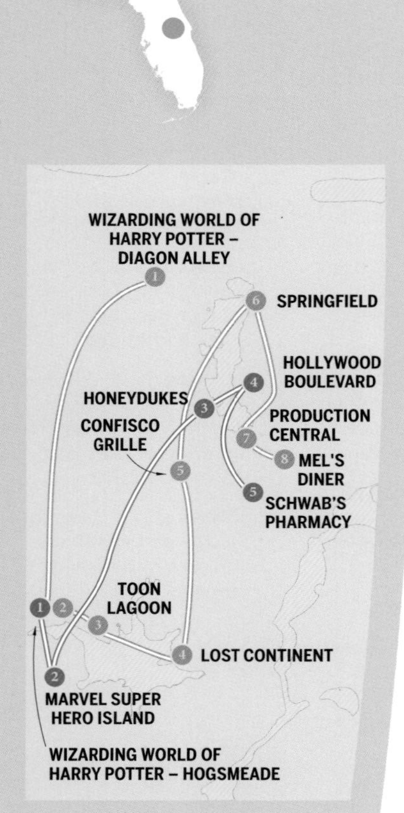

2 DAYS

BEST FOR TEENS

UNIVERSAL ORLANDO FOR TEENS

Head to Islands of Adventure early to get to the ❶ **Wizarding World of Harry Potter – Hogsmeade**. This is the Harry Potter universe realized in park form, and you could easily lose several days here; roller-coaster lovers won't want to miss the Dragon Challenge. If you can yank yourself away, head to ❷ **Marvel Super Hero Island**. Some of the rides you will encounter on this day count as among the very best in Orlando, including the twisty, speedy Incredible Hulk Coaster. Finish the day with dinner at ❸ **Honeydukes**.

On the next day, begin in the classic Hollywood backlot of Universal Studios, a park dedicated to realizing the magic of the movies. Wander up ❹ **Hollywood Boulevard** and ride on attractions that re-create special-effects wonders. Like disaster movies? Get tossed by a tornado and an earthquake in Twister...Ride It Out and Disaster!, respectively. Into action and adventure? Get your thrills on the Revenge of the Mummy roller coaster. At some stage, have a meal at ❺ **Schwab's Pharmacy**.

Top Left: Diagon Alley, Wizarding World of Harry Potter (p122); **Top Right:** Mel's Diner (p127)

2 DAYS

BEST FOR KIDS

UNIVERSAL ORLANDO FOR KIDS 10 & UNDER

As with the above itinerary, you'll want to head to the Wizarding World of Harry Potter early. This time, instead of roller coasters and faux pubs, you'll want to wander along ❶ **Diagon Alley** and through ❷ **Hogsmeade**, and enjoy rides like Escape from Gringotts. Afterwards, head into the rest of Islands of Adventure and dip your toes into ❸ **Toon Lagoon**, which has rides and a general theme more suited to younger kids, then swing by the Mystic Fountain at ❹ **Lost Continent**. Don't forget about the character buffet breakfast at ❺ **Confisco Grille**.

On the next day, at Universal Studios, venture into ❻ **Springfield**; this area, modeled after the hometown in *The Simpsons*, has sarcastic in-jokes for parents and cartoon-y vibe for kids. In ❼ **Production Central**, board Transformers the Ride 3-D, then add another 'D': Shrek 4-D is glorious family fun that parents and kids will appreciate. Don't forget to fuel up with a meal and a shake at ❽ **Mel's Diner**.

Discover Universal Orlando Resort

At a Glance

- **Islands of Adventure** (p118) You'll find the best theme-park rides in Florida here.
- **Universal Studios** (p121) Feel the magic of Hollywood, and watch out for *Jaws!*

Islands of Adventure
COLINSPICS/ALAMY ©

UNIVERSAL ORLANDO RESORT

Sights & Activities

The main attractions are the rides, movies and shows within **Islands of Adventure** (www.universalorlando.com; 6000 Universal Blvd, Universal Orlando Resort; adult 1/2 days $96/136, child $89/129, multiday & multipark tickets available; 9am-6pm, hours vary; Lynx 21, 37 or 40, Universal) and **Universal Studios** (407-363-8000; www.universalorlando.com; 1000 Universal Studios Plaza, Universal Orlando Resort; per 1/2 days adult $96/136, child $89/129, multiday & multipark tickets available; from 9am; Lynx 21, 37 or 40, Universal) theme parks. Across the canal from the two theme parks is CityWalk, Universal's entertainment district.

ISLANDS OF ADVENTURE

This place is just plain fun. Scream-it-from-the-rooftops, no-holds-barred, laugh-out-loud kind of fun. Superheroes zoom by on motorcycles, roller coasters whiz overhead, and plenty of rides will get you soaked.

Marvel Super Hero Island Ride
(www.universalorlando.com; Islands of Adventure; theme park admission required; 9am-6pm, hours vary; ; Lynx 21, 37 or 40) Bright, loud and fast moving, Marvel Super Hero Island is sensory overload and a thrill-lover's paradise. Don't miss the motion simulator **Amazing Adventures of Spider-Man** (Express Pass recommended), where super villains rendered in incredible 3-D are on the loose, jumping on your car and chasing you around the streets of New

York City, and the wild and crazy **Incredible Hulk Coaster** (Express Pass).

At **Dr Doom's Fearfall** (Express Pass), you rocket 150ft up in the air then free-fall down. Comic-book characters patrol this area, so keep an eye out for your favorites and check your map for scheduled Meet and Greet times with Spider-Man himself.

Toon Lagoon Ride

(www.universalorlando.com; Islands of Adventure; theme park admission required; 9am-6pm, hours vary; ; Lynx 21, 37 or 40) Island of Adventure's sparkly, lighthearted cartoon-themed Toon Lagoon transports visitors to the days when lazy weekends included nothing more than mornings watching Popeye and afternoons playing in the sprinkler. This is where you'll find most of Universal's water attractions, including **Popeye and Bluto's Bilge-Rat Barges** (Express Pass), a favorite that's short on thrills but high on silly soaking fun; and **Dudley Do-Right's Ripsaw Falls** (Express Pass), a classic with a short but steep fall. Be warned that you will get drenched, so protect phones and cameras, wear water-friendly shoes, and bring a change of clothes. If you forget, there are of course plenty of shops that sell towels, flip-flops and clothes.

Jurassic Park Ride

(www.universalorlando.com; Islands of Adventure; theme park admission required; 9am-6pm, hours vary; ; Lynx 21, 37 or 40) Oddly quiet, with no screams or loud music and no neon colors or hawking vendors, this oasis of palm trees, greenery and ferns offers a handful of attractions with a prehistoric twist. **Jurassic Park River Adventure** (Express Pass) floats you past friendly vegetarian dinosaurs, and all seems well and good until…things go wrong and those grass-munchin' cuties are replaced with the stuff of nightmares.

To escape the looming teeth of the giant T Rex, you plunge 85ft to the water below. Little children might be terrified by the creatures, the dark and the plunge, but if yours are tough-as-nails they'll love it. At **Pterandoon Flyers**, kids can float gently over the lush landscape and

Local Knowledge

Universal Orlando Resort Don't Miss List

KELLY TIMMINS, ORLANDO RESIDENT AND LEAD ADMISSIONS REPRESENTATIVE AT FULL SAIL UNIVERSITY.

1 INCREDIBLE HULK COASTER

This roller coaster is definitely for thrill-seekers only. After initially strapping in, you are inched forward before taking off on a zero-to-60 incline into tremendous loops and drops.

2 HARRY POTTER & THE FORBIDDEN JOURNEY

The Forbidden Journey is more than a ride; it's an experience. Upon entering the castle, you are surrounded by the world many of us have imagined from *Harry Potter*. The experience is peaked by a fast-paced 'broom ride' through the grounds of Hogwarts, the Forbidden Forest and the Quidditch pitch.

3 HONEYDUKES

This little shop brings the light-hearted, magical world of Harry Potter right into your hands. And stomachs! The shop is filled with candies and chocolates that avid readers of the series will be excited to get their hands on.

4 JURASSIC PARK RIVER ADVENTURE

Jurassic Park has been a classic ride since the '90s. Although it hasn't changed in years, it still stirs up thrills. As you journey on your boat through the forest, you are met with escaped raptors on the prowl. Finally, just when you think you'll fall victim to the jaws of the Tyrannosaurus Rex, you plunge to safety in a massive splash zone.

5 REVENGE OF THE MUMMY

This indoor coaster takes you through an Egyptian tomb as depicted in the movie series. You are met by countless menacing mummies intent on capturing you for sacrifice. At the end you come face-to-face with 'The Mummy,' and a hair-raising end to this fast-paced ride.

Universal Studios

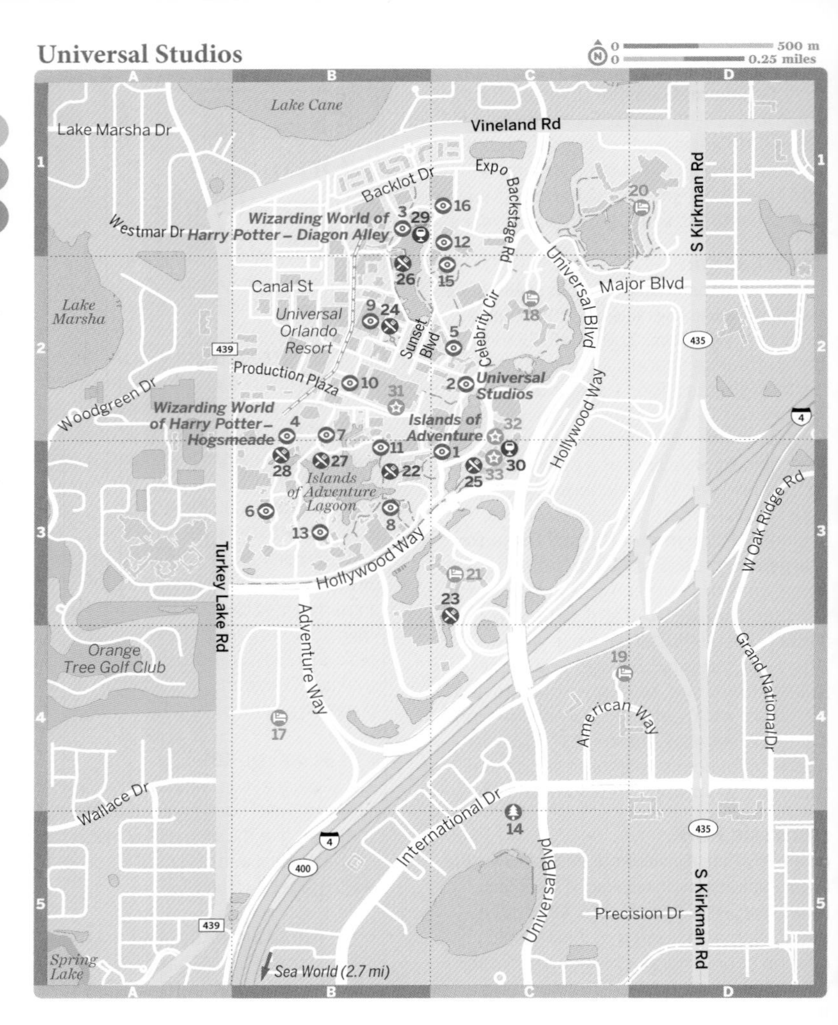

robotic dinosaurs of Jurassic Park. Note that you must be between 36in and 56in tall to fly, and adults can't fly without a kid. Waits can be upwards of an hour for the 80-second ride and there's no Express Pass.

Lost Continent — Show

(www.universalorlando.com; Islands of Adventure; theme park admission required; 9am-6pm, hours vary; ; Lynx 21, 37 or 40) Magic and myth from across the seas and the pages of fantasy books inspire this mystical corner of the park. Here you'll find dragons and unicorns, psychic readings and fortune-tellers. And don't be startled if that fountain talks to you as you walk past. The **Mystic Fountain** banters sassily, soaking children with its waterspouts when they least expect it and engaging them in silly conversation. And no, no one is hiding with a remote control. This is a talking fountain.

At the swashbuckling **Eighth Voyage of Sinbad Stunt Show** (Express Pass), Sinbad and his sidekick Kabob must

Universal Studios

Don't Miss Sights

1	Islands of Adventure	C3
2	Universal Studios	C2
3	Wizarding World of Harry Potter – Diagon Alley	B1
4	Wizarding World of Harry Potter – Hogsmeade	B2

Sights

5	Hollywood	C2
6	Jurassic Park	B3
7	Lost Continent	B2
8	Marvel Super Hero Island	B3
9	New York	B2
10	Production Central	B2
11	Seuss Landing	B3
12	Springfield	C1
13	Toon Lagoon	B3
14	Wet 'n Wild	C5
15	Woody Woodpecker's KidZone	C2
16	World Expo	C1

Sleeping

17	Cabana Bay Beach Resort	B4
18	Hard Rock Hotel	C2
19	Hilton Garden Inn International Drive North	C4
20	Portofino Bay Hotel	D1
21	Royal Pacific Resort	C3

Eating

22	Confisco Grille & Backwater Bar	B3
	Emack & Bolio's Marketplace	(see 18)
23	Emeril's Tchoup Chop	C3
24	Finnegan's Bar & Grill	B2
25	Jimmy Buffett's Margaritaville	C3
26	Lombard's Seafood Grille	B2
	Mama Della's Ristorante	(see 20)
	Mel's Diner	(see 5)
27	Mythos Restaurant	B3
	Orchid Court Sushi Bar	(see 21)
	Schwab's Pharmacy	(see 5)
28	Three Broomsticks	B3

Drinking & Nightlife

	Chez Alcatraz	(see 26)
29	Duff Brewery	B1
	Groove	(see 25)
	Hog's Head Pub	(see 28)
	Moe's Tavern	(see 12)
30	Pat O'Brien's	C3
	Red Coconut Club	(see 30)
	Velvet Bar	(see 18)

Entertainment

31	Blue Man Group	B2
32	CityWalk	C2
33	CityWalk's Rising Star	C3
	Wantilan Luau	(see 21)

rescue Princess Amoura from the terrible Miseria and, of course, Sinbad has to tumble and jump around to do it.

Seuss Landing Ride, Show

(www.universalorlando.com; Islands of Adventure; theme park admission required; 9am-6pm, hours vary; ; Lynx 21, 37 or 40) Anyone who has fallen asleep to the reading of *Green Eggs and Ham* or learned to read with *Sam I Am* knows the world of Dr Seuss: the fanciful creatures, the lyrical names, the rhyming stories. Here, realized in magnificently designed three-dimensional form, is Dr Seuss' imagination. The Lorax guards his truffula trees; Thing One and Thing Two make trouble; and creatures from all kinds of Dr Seuss favorites adorn the shops and the rides.

Drink Moose Juice or Goose Juice; eat Green Eggs and Ham; and peruse shelves of Dr Seuss books before riding through *The Cat in the Hat* or around and around on an elephant-bird from *Horton Hears a Who*. Seuss Landing is one of the best places for little ones in all of Orlando's theme parks, bringing the spirit and energy of Dr Seuss' vision to life. So come on in, walk into his world and take a spin on a fish.

UNIVERSAL STUDIOS

The silver screen inspired the majority of the rides at this quieter and more peaceful brother to the energy of Islands of Adventure (p118). The park features elaborate New York and San Francisco backdrops, motion-simulator rides and audience-participation shows.

Springfield Ride

(www.universalorlando.com; Universal Studios; theme park admission required; from 9am; ; Lynx 21, 37 or 40) In 2013 Universal opened *Simpsons*-themed Springfield, home to that iconic American TV family. Hang at Moe's Tavern, grab doughnuts at Lard Lad, and meet Krusty the Clown, Sideshow Bob and the Simpson family themselves. The child-friendly **Kang & Kodos' Twirl & Hurl** offers an interactive twist to whirling and don't miss **The Simpsons Ride** (Express Pass).

STEPHEN SEARLE/ALAMY ©

Don't Miss
Wizarding World of Harry Potter

Alan Gilmore and Stuart Craig, art director and production designer for the *Harry Potter* films, collaborated closely with the Universal Orlando Resort engineers to create what is, without exception, the most fantastically realized themed experience in Florida. The detail and authenticity tickle the fancy at every turn, from the screeches of the mandrakes in the shop windows to the groans of Moaning Myrtle in the bathroom; keep your eyes peeled for magical happenings.

The Wizarding World of Harry Potter is divided into two sections, each with rides and shows: **Hogsmeade** sits in Islands of Adventure and **Diagon Alley** (completed in 2014) is in Universal Studios. If you have a park-to-park ticket, hop on the Hogwarts Express from one section to the other.

In **Hogsmeade** (Islands of Adventure), you can poke along the cobbled streets and impossibly crooked buildings of the village of Hogsmeade, sip frothy Butter Beer, munch on Cauldron Cakes and mail a card via Owl Post, all in the shadow of Hogwarts Castle, and keep your eyes peeled for magical happenings. Highlights include:

- **Harry Potter and the Forbidden Journey** Wind through the corridors of Hogwarts, past talking portraits, Dumbledore's office and other well-known locations.
- **Dragon Challenge** Gut-churning dueling roller coasters twist and loop, narrowly avoiding each other.

THINGS YOU NEED TO KNOW

☎ 407-363-8000; www.universalorlando.com; Islands of Adventure & Universal Studios; theme park admission required; ⏲ theme park hours, one hour early admission for guests at Universal Orlando Resort hotels; 🚌 Lynx 21, 37 or 40

It's one of the best simulated experiences at Universal, a highlight even if you're not a *Simpsons* fan. Kids will want to try Springfield's signature drink, a bubbling and steaming **Flaming Moe** that rivals the theming fun of *Harry Potter*'s Butterbeer and tastes surprisingly good! Sure, it's just an orange soda, but it's a pretty cool orange soda, the cup makes a good souvenir, and in the eyes of an eight-year-old, it's worth every penny of that seven bucks.

Hollywood — Ride, Show

(www.universalstudios.com; Universal Studios; theme park admission required; from 9am; Lynx 21, 37 or 40) With glorious 3-D film footage, live action stunts and 4-D special effects, **Terminator 2: 3-D** (Express Pass) is complete sensory overload – delicious fun for some, overwhelming and scary for others. Fans of the famous redhead Lucille Ball will particularly enjoy **Lucy – A Tribute**, a biographical exhibit with *I Love Lucy* clips, costumes, photos and Lucy's letters.

If you're really into horror makeup, **Universal Horror Make-Up Show** (Express Pass) may be a little too short and thin on substance. It's humorous and full of silly antics, but optical illusions could freak out kids if they're not really clear from the get-go that it's not real.

Production Central — Ride, Show

(www.universalorlando.com; Universal Studios; theme park admission required; from 9am; ; Lynx 21, 37 or 40) Home to two of Universal's most talked-about rides, the incredible 3-D simulation **Transformers: The Ride 3-D** (Express Pass) and the high-thrill coaster **Hollywood Rip Ride Rockit** (Express Pass). This roller coaster is not for the faint of heart – you *Rip* up to 65mph, *Ride* 17 stories above the theme park, around a loop-dee-loop, and down a crazy-steep drop, and *Rockit* to customized music.

At **Shrek 4-D** (Express Pass), Shrek and Donkey try to save Princess Fiona from a dragon. And that dragon is indeed fierce, probably too fierce for tiny tots – it pops out at you with red eyes, spitting fire into your face. Unfortunately, the nonsensical preshow spiel goes on too long.

New York — Ride, Show

(www.universalorlando.com; Universal Studios; theme park admission required; from 9am; ; Lynx 21, 37 or 40) **Revenge of the Mummy** (Express Pass) combines roller-coaster speed and twists with in-your-face special effects. Head deep into ancient Egyptian catacombs in near pitch black, but don't anger Imhotep the mummy – in his wrath he flings you past fire, water and more.

The walk-through attraction **Twister... Ride It Out** (Express Pass) takes folks into a film set of a dilapidated Midwest American town, eerily quiet...until the storm rolls in. A radio announces a severe storm warning, and slowly you see and feel the change in weather. The sign rattles above the old gas station, and tumbleweed blows across the set. You see a tornado developing, far off in the distant sky, and it's coming, closer and closer, louder and louder. Anyone who has felt the fear of living through a real tornado, or children who already wake up scared of them thanks to sirens, hours in the basement and the eerie blanket of tornado-breeding green skies, should think twice before going to this attraction.

World Expo — Ride, Show

(www.universalorlando.com; Universal Studios; theme park admission required; from 9am; Lynx 21, 37 or 40) The main attraction here is **Men in Black Alien Attack** (Express Pass), a 3-D interactive video game that is a lot of fun but not at all scary. Your car swings and spins through a danger-laden downtown Manhattan, with all kinds of silly looking aliens all over the place, and you aim your lasers and shoot away to rack up points. Oddly, Universal is adamant that you put all bags in the complimentary locker before boarding.

San Francisco — Ride, Show

(www.universalorlando.com; Universal Studios; theme park admission required; from 9am; ; Lynx 21, 37 or 40) San Francisco, themed heavily around the city as the site of the massive 1906 earthquake

and the inspiration behind the 1974 film *Earthquake*, is home to Chez Alcatraz (p128), a tiny and pleasant outdoor bar in Fisherman's Wharf; Lombard's (p127), one of the park's two restaurants that accept reservations; and a couple of outdoor shows.

The only ride here is the mock-movie-making attraction **Disaster** (Express Pass), an unusual slow-moving ride that centers on narrative schtick and special effects rather than speed thrills. A fast-talking Hollywood agent casting a disaster movie chooses a handful of audience members and gives them directions ('give me terror like Britney Spears is your babysitter'), and then each volunteer is filmed for a second or so. Everyone then heads to the 'set' and boards a subway train in the incredibly authentic replica of a San Francisco BART (Bay Area Rapid Transit) station. Suddenly, the big one hits: tracks buckle, the place crumbles and general mayhem ensues. Hint: 65,000 gallons of water are released and recycled every six minutes, but you don't get wet. And yes, you do see the footage of those volunteers.

Woody Woodpecker's KidZone Ride, Show

(www.universalorlando.com; Universal Studios; theme park admission required; from 9am; Lynx 21, 37 or 40) Kid-friendly shows and rides, a fantastic water-play area and supercool foam-ball cannons – it rivals Islands of Adventure's Seuss Landing (p121) as a Universal favorite for the eight-and-under crowd.

Sleeping

Universal Orlando Resort boasts three excellent resorts. Generally less expensive than Walt Disney World® Resort's deluxe accommodations, they offer far superior service, food, decor, amenities and rooms. For reservations and package deals, call 888-273-1311.

Left: Men in Black Alien Attack (p123); **Below:** The Simpsons Ride (p121)
(LEFT) RSBPHOTO1/ALAMY ©; (BELOW) TIM E WHITE/ALAMY ©

Portofino Bay Hotel
Luxury Resort **$$$**
(☎407-503-1000; www.universalorlando.com; 5601 Universal Blvd, Universal Orlando Resort; r & ste value/regular/peak from $285/315/365, self-/valet parking per day $18/25; P ❄ @ ᯤ 🏊 🐾; 🚢 Universal) Sumptuous and elegant, with beautiful rooms, cobblestone streets and sidewalk cafes around a central lagoon, this resort evokes the relaxing charm of seaside Italy. There's a sandy zero-entrance family pool, the secluded Hillside pool, and the elegant Villa pool, as well as the Mandara Spa, evening waterside minstrel music and the excellent **Mama Della's (☎407-503-3463; www.universalorlando.com; 5601 Universal Blvd, Portofino Bay Hotel; mains $10-22; ⏰5:30-11pm; 🍷 👪; 🚢 Universal)**. Rates include one hour early entrance to Wizarding World of Harry Potter and Unlimited Express Pass.

Royal Pacific Resort Resort **$$$**
(☎407-503-3000; www.universalorlando.com; 6300 Hollywood Way, Universal Orlando Resort; r & ste value/regular/peak from $230/260/300, self-/valet parking per day $18/25; P ❄ @ ᯤ 🏊 🐾; 🚢 Universal) The glass-enclosed Orchid Court, with its reflecting pool, Balinese fountains and carved stone elephants splashing in the water, sits at the center of the airy lobby at this friendly South Pacific–inspired resort. The grounds are lovely, with lots of grass, tropical plantings, flowers, bamboo and palm trees, and the on-site restaurants are excellent. Rates include one hour early entrance to Wizarding World of Harry Potter and an Unlimited Express Pass.

Hard Rock Hotel Resort **$$$**
(☎407-503-2000; www.universalorlando.com; 5800 Universal Blvd, Universal Orlando Resort; r & ste value/regular/peak from $259/294/365, self-/valet parking per day $18/25; P ❄ @ ᯤ 🏊 🐾; 🚢 Universal) From the grand lawn with the massive guitar fountain at its entrance, to the pumped-in

Universal for Little Ones

The word on the street says that Universal Orlando Resort is great for teens and adults but doesn't offer much for kids under seven. This is simply not true. No, it doesn't have as much as Walt Disney World® Resort and you won't find Disney's nostalgic charm, but Universal Orlando Resort is a master at blending attractions for all ages into one easily digestible and navigable package of fun, fun, fun. Characters from *Scooby Doo, Shrek* and *The Simpsons* swing by restaurants at the three resort hotels on Wednesday, Friday and Saturday nights. CityWalk is very family-friendly, despite its many bars and live music, and the Wantilan Luau at Portofino Bay Hotel gives folks of all ages a taste of the Hawaiian islands.

underwater music at the pool, the modern and stylized Hard Rock embodies the pure essence and energy of rock-and-roll cool. Rates include one hour early entrance to Wizarding World of Harry Potter and an Unlimited Express Pass.

Cabana Bay Beach Resort Resort **$$**

(407-503-4000; www.universalorlando.com; 6550 Adventure Way, Universal Orlando Resort; r $115-150, ste $175-215, self-parking $18; P; Universal) Evoking the spirit of road trips c 1957, Universal's newest resort opened in March 2014 and has a beautifully themed hip retro-Florida vibe. It offers moderate and value-priced accommodations. Family suites have kitchenettes and sleep six; and there are two pools, a bowling alley, a food court and a lazy river.

While guests can enjoy early admission to Wizarding World of Harry Potter (a huge plus), they do not benefit from perks afforded to guests at the other three Universal Resorts, including Unlimted Express Pass, priority dining status and boat transportation to the parks. You must either walk the 20 minutes or take a Universal bus to the theme parks.

Eating

The dining options in Universal Orlando are about what you'd expect: a range of budgets are catered to, and everything is themed to the hilt.

ISLANDS OF ADVENTURE

Three Broomsticks British **$**

(www.universalorlando.com; Islands of Adventure; mains $11-16, theme park admission required; 8am-park closing; ; Lynx 21, 37 or 40) Fast-food styled British fare inspired by *Harry Potter*, with cottage pie and Cornish pasties, and rustic wooden bench seating. There's plenty of outdoor seating out back, too, by the river.

Confisco Grille & Backwater Bar American **$**

(407-224-4012; www.universalorlando.com; Islands of Adventure; mains $6-22, theme park admission required; 11am-park closing; ; Lynx 21, 37 or 40) Under-the-radar and often overlooked, the recommended Confisco Grille has outdoor seating, freshly made hummus, tasty wood-oven pizzas, and a full bar.

Mythos Restaurant Mediterranean **$$**

(407-224-4012, 407-224-4534; www.universalorlando.com; Islands of Adventure; mains $8-15, theme park admission required; 11am-5pm; ; Lynx 21, 37 or 40) Housed in an ornate underwater grotto with giant windows and running water.

UNIVERSAL STUDIOS

Finnegan's Bar & Grill Pub Food **$$**

(407-224-3613; www.universalorlando.com; Universal Studios; mains $8-20, theme park admission required; 11am-park closing; ;

Lynx 21, 37 or 40) An Irish pub with live acoustic music plopped into the streets of New York. Serves Cornish pasties and Scotch eggs, as well as Harp, Bass and Guinness on tap.

Schwab's Pharmacy Ice Cream $

(www.universalorlando.com; Universal Studios; theme park admission required; 11am-park closing; ; Lynx 21, 37 or 40) In the 1930s two brothers bought what would become a favorite lunch-counter hangout for struggling movie-star wannabes in Hollywood. They say Ava Gardner worked the soda fountain, Harold Arlin composed 'Over the Rainbow' here, and regulars included Marilyn Monroe, Clark Gable and Orson Welles. Grab some Ben and Jerry's at Universal's recreation of the famous original eatery.

Lombard's Seafood Grille Seafood $$

(407-224-3613, 407-224-6401; www.universalorlando.com; Universal Studios; mains $12-25, theme park admission required; 11am-park closing; ; Lynx 21, 37 or 40) Oriental rugs, a huge fish tank and a solid seafood menu make a calming respite from Universal Orlando's energy.

Mel's Diner Burgers $

(www.universalorlando.com; Universal Studios; mains $6-10, theme park admission required; 11am-park closing; ; Lynx 21, 37 or 40, Universal) Classic cars and rockin' bands outside, 1950s diner style inside. This is a fast-food eatery, not much different really than your standard McDonald's, but it's a lot more fun!

RESORT HOTELS

Call 407-503-3463 for reservations at other sit-down restaurants within the resort hotels.

Orchid Court Sushi Bar Japanese $$

(407-503-3000; www.universalorlando.com; 6300 Hollywood Way, Royal Pacific Resort; sushi $4-8, mains $12-20; 11am-11pm; ; Universal) This small, informal sushi bar oozes calm inside the light-and-airy, glass-enclosed lobby of the Royal Pacific Resort, decked out with cushioned couches and chairs. Try the cherry blossom saketini.

Emeril's Tchoup Chop Seafood $$$

(407-503-2467; www.emerilsrestaurants.com; 6300 Hollywood Way, Royal Pacific Resort; mains $15-30; 11:30am-2:30pm & 5-10pm; Universal) Island-inspired food, including plenty of seafood and Asian accents, prepared with the freshest ingredients. One of the best sit-down meals at the Universal Orlando Resort.

Emack & Bolio's Marketplace Ice Cream $

(407-503-2000; www.universalorlando.com; 5800 Universal Blvd, Hard Rock Hotel; ice cream $3-8; 6:30am-11pm; ; Universal)

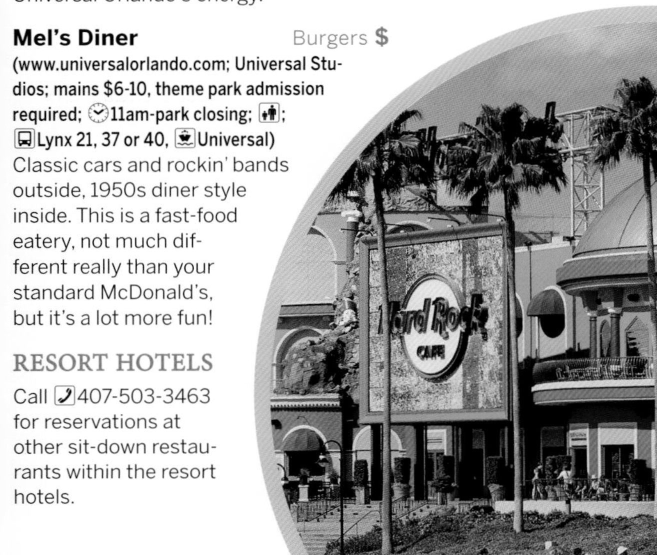

Hard Rock Cafe, near Orlando's Hard Rock Hotel (p125)

KEITH LEVIT/ALAMY ©

Originally from Boston, Emack and Bolio ice cream beats other national chains hands down. And of course, only at this bastion of rock and roll will you find Bye Bye Miss American Mud Pie.

Drinking & Nightlife

Moe's Tavern — Bar

(www.universalorlando.com; Universal Studios; drinks $3-9, theme park admission required; 11am-park closing; ; Lynx 21, 37 or 40) Brilliantly themed *Simpsons* bar with Isotopes memorabilia, the Love Tester and Bart Simpson crank-calling the red rotary phone; it's as if you walked straight into your TV to find yourself at Homer's favorite neighborhood joint. Buy a Krusty Burger from the neighboring food court and sidle up for a Duff Beer, Duff Lite or Duff Dry.

Duff Brewery — Bar

(www.universalorlando.com; Universal Studios; snacks $5-12, theme park admission required; 11am-park closing; ; Lynx 21, 37 or 40) Outdoor lagoonside bar serving Homer Simpson's beer of choice, on tap or by the bottle, and Springfield's signature Flaming Moe. Look for the topiary Seven Duffs out front.

Velvet Bar — Lounge

(407-504-2588, tickets & info 407-503-2401; www.hardrockhotelorlando.com; 5800 Universal Blvd, Hard Rock Hotel; 5pm-2am; Universal) Trendy and sleekly stylized, with hardwood floors, floor-to-ceiling windows, zebra-fabric chairs and excellent martinis. On the last Thursday of the month, the bar hosts **Velvet Sessions**, a rock-and-roll cocktail party with themed drinks, live music and finger food.

Hog's Head Pub — Pub

(www.universalorlando.com; Islands of Adventure; drinks $4-8, theme park admission required; 11am-park closing; Lynx 21, 37 or 40) Butterbeer, frozen or frothy, real beer on tap, pumpkin cider and more. Keep an eye on that hog over the bar – he's more real than you think! If the lines at the Butterbeer carts outside are too long, head inside. Same thing, same price.

Chez Alcatraz — Bar

(www.universalorlando.com; Universal Studios; theme park admission required; 11am-park closing; ; Lynx 21, 37 or 40) Frozen

Mel's Diner (p127)

Detour: CityWalk

Universal Studios and SeaWorld are connected by a pleasantly landscaped pedestrian **mall** (407-363-8000; www.universalorlando.com; 6000 Universal Studios Blvd, Universal Orlando Resort; 7am-2am, hours vary; Lynx 21, 37 or 40, Universal) lined with themed restaurants, bars, a multiplex movie theater, shops, a carousel and a fountain for kids to play in. Live music and mucho alcohol sums up the entertainment options here and though it can be packed with partying 20-somethings, particularly after the theme parks close, there's a distinct family-friendly vibe.

Individual bars charge nightly covers ($5 to $9), or purchase a CityWalk Party Pass ($12, free with multiday theme-park admission) for unlimited all-night club access. For a movie and clubbing, buy the CityWalk Party Pass and Movie Ticket ($15), and for dinner and a movie, purchase the Meal and Movie Deal ($15). Call or stop by CityWalk Guest Services Ticket Window or pick them up at any resort. For dinner reservations, call 407-224-3663. Expect changes here, including several new restaurants, as Universal rolls out a complete revamping of CityWalk.

Bob Marley – A Tribute to Freedom (407-224-3663; www.universalorlando.com; CityWalk; mains $8-16, cover after 9pm $7; restaurant 4-10pm Sun-Thu, to 11pm Fri & Sat, bar 9pm – 2am; Lynx 21, 37 or 40, Universal) Jamaica-inspired food and music.

CityWalk's Rising Star (407-224-4233; www.universalorlando.com; CityWalk; cover $7; 8pm-2am; Lynx 21, 37 or 40, Universal) Karaoke to live music and talent contests.

the groove (407-224-4233; www.universalorlando.com; CityWalk; cover $5; 9pm-2am; Lynx 21, 37 or 40, Universal) Dance club with sleek blue-neon walls and blaring music from the '70s and '80s. Look out for select 'teen nights.'

Jimmy Buffet's Margaritaville (407-224-2155; www.universalorlando.com; CityWalk; mains $8-15, cover after 10pm $10; 11:30am-2am; ; Lynx 21, 37 or 40, Universal) Three bars themed around Jimmy Buffet songs, a full menu and live music after 10pm.

Pat O'Brien's (407-224-2106; www.universalorlando.com; CityWalk; mains $8-17, cover after 9pm $7; 4pm-2am, piano bar from 5pm; Lynx 21, 37 or 40, Universal) A homogenized slice of New Orleans with Cajun food, cocktails with a punch and that strange Orlando obsession: dueling pianos.

Red Coconut Club (407-224-4233; www.universalorlando.com; CityWalk; cover $7; 8pm-2am Sun-Thu, from 6pm Fri & Sat; Lynx 21, 37 or 40, Universal) Live bands, martini bar and rooftop balcony.

Latin Quarter Latin American flair.

mojitos, flatbread and housemade potato chips on the waterfront at Fisherman's Wharf. With the sound of the boats jingling at the docks, views over the water to the *Simpsons*-themed Springfield and Bruce the infamous shark from *Jaws* dangling as a photo-op, this little outdoor bar makes a pleasant spot to kick back and relax.

Entertainment

Wantilan Luau Dinner Show
(407-503-3463; www.universalorlando.com; 6300 Hollywood Way, Royal Pacific Resort; adult

$63-70, child under 12yr $35-40; 6pm Tue & Sat May-Aug, 6pm Sat only Sep-Apr; Universal) Pacific Island fire dancers shimmy and shake on stage while guests enjoy a tasty buffet of roast suckling pig, guava-barbecued short ribs and other Polynesian-influenced fare. The atmosphere is wonderfully casual and, like everything at Universal Orlando, this is simple, unabashed silliness and fun. Unlimited mai tais, beer and wine are included in the price.

Blue Man Group Performing Arts

(407-363-8000, 407-258-3626; www.universalorlando.com; CityWalk; adult from $69, child 3-9yr from $29; times vary; Lynx 21, 37 or 40, Universal) Originally an off-Broadway phenomenon in 1991, this high-energy comedy theatrical troupe at Universal Orlando Resort features all kinds of multisensory craziness – percussion 'instruments,' paintballs, marshmallows, modern dancing and general mayhem.

Dive-In Movies Cinema

(Portofino Bay, Hard Rock & Royal Pacific Hotels, Universal Orlando Resort; dusk; Universal) Free family-friendly movies screened poolside at Universal Orlando's deluxe resort hotels. Details vary seasonally, and sometimes films are screened several nights a week.

Information

Child Care

Nursing facilities and companion bathrooms are located at the Health Services and First Aid facilities in each park. A baby-bottle icon next to select stores on the park map indicates which stores carry baby supplies (not on display). Each resort has a drop-off child-care center.

Lost & Found

Inside Guest Services at both parks.

Medical Services

Each theme park has medical facilities; see park maps for locations.

Park Hours

Theme park hours change not only by season, but day to day within any given month. Generally, parks open at 8 or 9am and close sometime between 6pm and 10pm. Guests at one of the three on-site hotels at Universal Orlando Resort can enter the Wizarding World of Harry Potter inside Islands of Adventure one hour before the park opens.

Blue Man Group poster

ZUMA PRESS, INC./ALAMY ©

Parking

Parking for both theme parks and CityWalk is available inside a giant garage structure (self/valet $17/30). Hotels charge per day for self-parking ($18) or valet ($25).

Stroller Rental

Single/double strollers cost $12/16 and are available at Guest Services inside both theme parks.

Tickets

A one-park one-/two-/three-/four-day ticket costs $96/136/146/156; a one-/two-/three-/four-day park-to-park ticket costs $136/176/186/196. Tickets for children three to nine cost about $12 less per day. Tickets are good for 14 consecutive days, and multiple-day tickets include admission to paid venues in CityWalk. Universal Orlando Resort participates in the Orlando Flex Ticket.

Express Plus

Avoid lines at designated Islands of Adventure and Universal Studios rides by flashing your Express Pass at the separate Express Pass line. The standard one-day pass (for one park $35 to $70; for two parks $40 to $90) allows one-time Express Pass access to each attraction. Alternatively, purchase the bundled two-day Park-to-Park Ticket Plus Unlimited Express ($135 to $180), which includes admission to both parks and unlimited access to Express Pass rides. With this, you can go to any ride, any time you like, as often as you like. If you are staying at one of Universal Orlando's three deluxe resort hotels – Portofino Bay, Hard Rock or Royal Pacific Resorts – up to five guests in each room automatically receive an Unlimited Express Pass. A limited number of passes per day are available online (www.universalorlando.com) or at the park gates.

Dining Plan

Universal offers two prepaid dining packages – **Dining Plan – Quick Service** (adult/child $20/13) and **Dining Plan** ($46/18), which include a broad selection of restaurants at Islands of Adventure, Universal Studios and CityWalk.

Wet 'n Wild

Package prices include admission to Wet 'n Wild, a water park a few miles away. See www.universalorlando.com for pricing.

Tourist Information

Guest Services inside each park and at CityWalk can help with anything you need, and there are concierge desks at the four on-site hotels. Furthermore, the front desk of just about any Orlando area hotel provides Universal Orlando Resort tourist information. ☎407-363-8000, toll-free 800-232-7827 is the central number for all things Universal.

Travelers with Disabilities

The free *Rider Safety and Guests With Disabilities* guidebook is available at Guest Services. Wheelchairs and Electric Convenience Vehicles (ECV) can be rented from the entrance to each park; ECVs can be reserved in advance (407-224-4423). Rent manual wheelchairs at the Rotunda section of the parking lot.

ℹ Getting There & Around

There are trains, planes and buses to Orlando.

Boat

Water taxis, which leave each point about every 20 minutes, shuttle regularly between the three Universal hotels and CityWalk, just outside the gates of the parks. Service usually begins at 8:30am and ends at 2am.

Car

From the I-4, take exit 74B or 75A and follow the signs. From International Drive, turn west at Wet 'n Wild onto Universal Blvd.

Shuttle

Most hotels just outside Universal Studios and along International Drive provide free shuttle service to the Universal Orlando Resort.

Walking

Universal Orlando's three resort hotels, two theme parks and CityWalk are linked by well-lit and landscaped pedestrian walkways.

Palm Beach & the Gold Coast

The Gold Coast lives up to its namesake on several levels.

With wealth. Luxury goods. Sunshine. The reflected allure of all of the above. Palm Beach is one of Florida's wealthiest enclaves – enjoy gawking at the castlelike beachfront mansions, but don't rear-end that $350,000 Bentley when parallel parking in front of the Gucci store.

And yet: all that glitters is not gold, and the 'Gold Coast' is more than glitz. Here you'll find an endearing collection of beach towns. From activity-packed, gay- and family-friendly Fort Lauderdale to laid-back Lauderdale-by-the-Sea to rugged Jupiter, you'll find more culture than you can handle.

Numerous natural gems – secluded islands, moss-draped mangrove swamps, wild rivers, empty dunes – will surely satisfy your demands for nonmaterial pleasures. So please, whatever you do, don't skip over this region on your journey from Miami to Disney World.

West Palm Beach (p146)

Breakers (p143)
JOHN COLETTI/GETTY IMAGES ©

Palm Beach & the Gold Coast

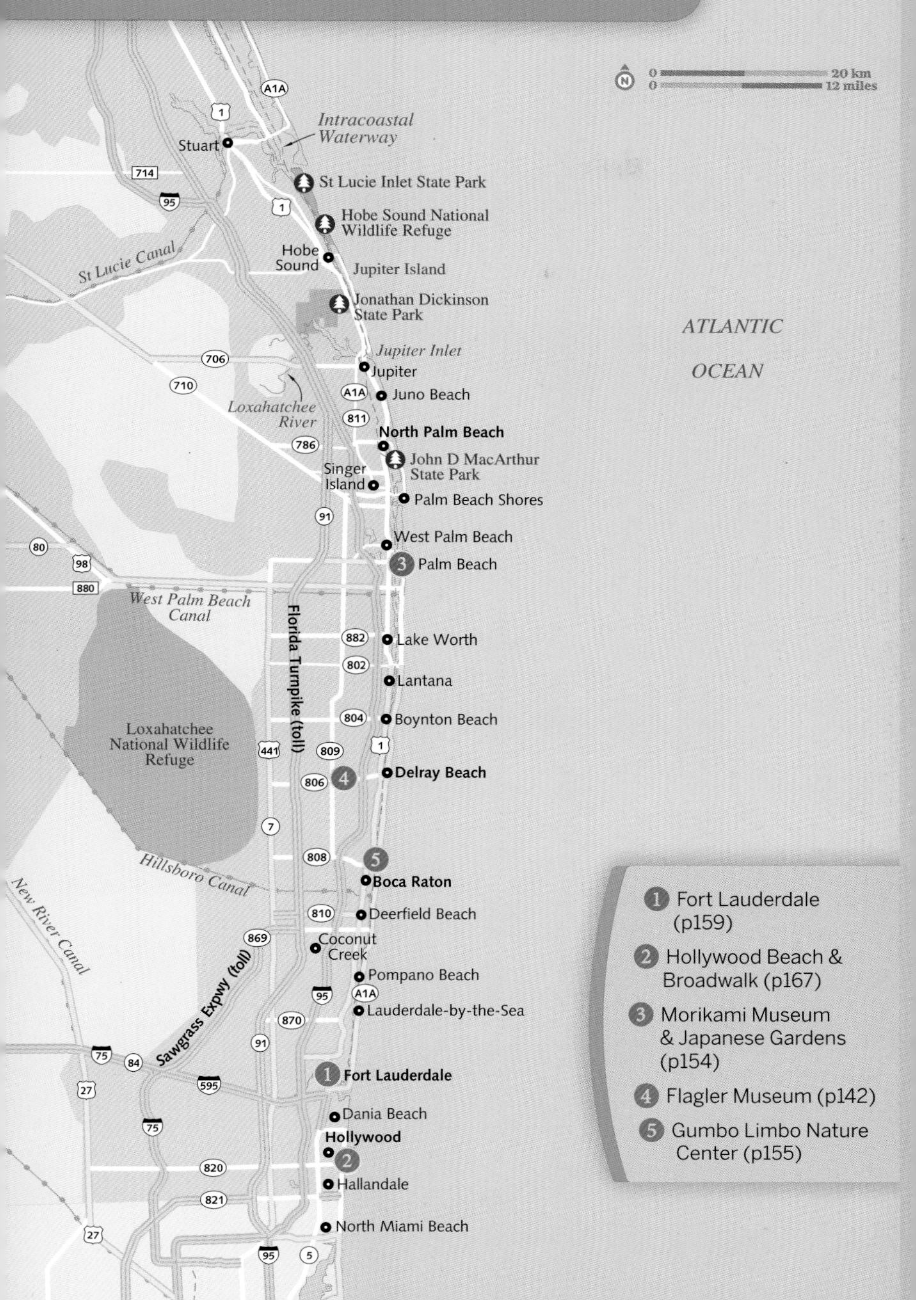

Palm Beach & the Gold Coast's Highlights

Fort Lauderdale

Although it's known as South Florida's second city, Fort Lauderdale doesn't deserve to take a backseat to anyone. This town has miles of canals, one of the loveliest beach promenades in the country and a busy cultural scene that will keep foodies, historians and nighthawks happy. Add a thriving gay and lesbian scene and you have a town for the ages.

1

2 Hollywood Beach & Broadwalk

While some beaches are grungy, and some are too up themselves, Hollywooc Beach, to quote the Three Bears, is Jus Right. There's a boardwalk that gets taken up with party animals, dog walkers, toned bodies and cruising teens and families out for the night. plus the quality of the sand and the sea is pretty fine as well.

RICHARD CUMMINGS/GETTY IMAGES ©

3 Flagler Museum

The original Palm Beach palace is the mansion that Henry Flagler, railroad baron and Florida tycoon, gifted to his wife in 1902. To say the house is opulent is to be guilty of gross understatement. Now a museum, the Flagler mansion is representative of both the heights of beaux-arts decor and the luxury (dare we say decadence) of old American aristocracy.

ZUMA PRESS, INC./ALAMY ©

4 Morikami Museum & Japanese Gardens

Delray Beach is probably not the first name that springs to mind when discussing Japanese art and aesthetics, but actually, one of the finest stateside collections of arts, crafts and sculpture from Nippon can be found here at the Morikami Museum. Make sure to stop in for tea at the on-site Seishin-An teahouse afterwards.

5 Gumbo Limbo Nature Center

Gumbo Limbo sounds like a dance invented in the back bayous of Louisiana to us, but the name actually applies to a singularly fine slice of nature preserve located near Boca Raton. You can hike on boardwalks between strands of wetland wilderness, and visit a host of oceanic animals, including sea turtles recovering in a rehabilitation center.

Loggerhead turtle

Palm Beach & the Gold Coast's Best...

Delicious Dining

- **Circle** Best brunch around, hands down. Plus: there's a harpsichordist. (p146)
- **Būccan** Pushing the limits of Modern American cuisine. (p145)
- **Rhythm Cafe** Bright, bouncy bistro with to-die-for chocolate cake. (p150)
- **Mediterranean Market & Deli** Fresh and delicious Middle Eastern and Mediterranean fare. (p150)
- **Gran Forno** Affordable, scrumptious Northern Italian cuisine; fantastic value for lunch. (p162)

Natural Beauty

- **Gumbo Limbo Nature Center** An awesome environmental education centre. (p155)
- **Blowing Rocks Preserve** Where waves, wind, tides and erosion combine to make something beautiful. (p158)
- **Lion Country Safari** Admittedly, an artificial environment – but one that lovingly re-creates the African bush. (p153)
- **Jonathan Dickinson State Park** A fine park that catalogs the natural beauty of Central Florida. (p158)

The Beaches

- **Lake Worth Beach** Simply one of the finest beaches on the Gold Coast. (p152)
- **Hollywood Beach** A good combination of natural prettiness and fun activities. (p167)
- **Fort Lauderdale Beach** The adjacent promenade is an exemplary boardwalk. (p159)
- **Palm Beach Municipal Beach** Lovely public beach that can get crowded in the high season. (p143)

Must-See Museums

- **Museum of Art** Fort Lauderdale's cultural cornerstone. (p160)
- **Boca Raton Museum of Art** Impressive collection of European masters. (p157)
- **Morikami Museum & Japanese Gardens** Japanese masterpieces presented in a tranquil atmosphere. (p154)
- **Flagler Museum** Lifestyles of the rich and famous (and historical). (p142)
- **Norton Museum of Art** A West Palm Beach gem for the arts. (p146)

Left: Blowing Rocks Preserve (p158); **Above:** Hollywood Beach (p167)

Need to Know

BE FOREWARNED

- **Dress up** If you're heading out in Palm Beach, dress to impress.
- **Humidity** It can get swampy and steamy in deep summer.
- **Spring Break** You may want to avoid Fort Lauderdale in Mar–Apr (unless you love partying with college kids).
- **Hurricanes** They can hit here, and hit hard; the season runs from Jun–Oct.

GETTING AROUND

- **Car** I-95 and the Florida Turnpike are the most direct roads between cities, but we recommend getting off the highways.
- **Bus** Greyhound connects major cities on the Gold Coast.
- **Train** The Miami Tri-Rail connects to Fort Lauderdale.
- **Air** For better ticket deals, try booking to any of the cities on the Gold Coast, as they're all fairly close to each other.

RESOURCES

- **Palm Beach County Convention & Visitors Bureau** Palm Beach resources, www.palmbeachfl.com.
- **South Florida Sun-Sentinel** Regional newspaper, www.sun-sentinel.com.
- **Fort Lauderdale Tourism** Includes information on Broward County, www.sunny.org.
- **Yachting** Go to www.saltwatertides.com for an excellent, searchable database of tide tables.

ADVANCE PLANNING

- **Hotels** During major festivals and events, hotels can get packed early.
- **Car rentals** Try to organize a month in advance.
- **Restaurants** You'll want reservations at the posher places we recommend.
- **Arts Calendar** If you want to know what's going on culturally in South Florida, visit www.artscalendar.com.

Palm Beach & the Gold Coast Itineraries

They call it the Gold Coast because the beaches shimmer, the sun is radiant and some of the houses are downright palatial. These itineraries will take in all of the above, plus lovely dining and treats for culture vultures.

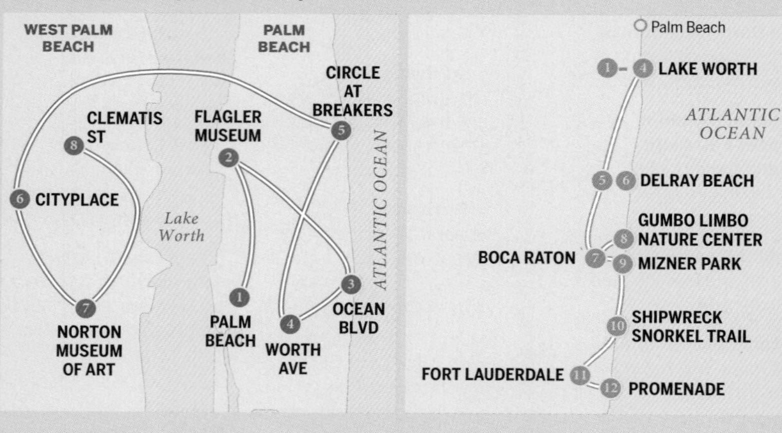

THE PALM BEACHES

PALM BEACH TO WEST PALM BEACH

We'll wake up in ❶ **Palm Beach**, one of the natural nerve centers for this region. When you're here you should check out the opulent homes folks have built up for themselves throughout the years, so we'll start on the historical end of things at the ❷ **Flagler Museum**. Built by South Florida founding father Henry Flagler, this museum is a monument to the man's wealth and beaux-arts decor. The on-site museum cafe is good for lunch.

Afterwards head up ❸ **Ocean Boulevard** (Hwy A1A) and goggle at the houses of the modern Palm Beach elite. These folks furnish their luxury on shopping streets like ❹ **Worth Avenue**; it's heavy on showy brand names, but that's kinda the point.

The next day head to West Palm Beach, but not before breakfast at the ❺ **Circle**. Wander around the shopping and dining district of ❻ **CityPlace** before balancing out all that consumerism with a dash of culture at the ❼ **Norton Museum of Art** and its attached sculpture garden. Finish your day in the historic revival cum dining and nightlife strip that is ❽ **Clematis Street**.

GOLD COAST CRUISING
LAKE WORTH TO HOLLYWOOD BEACH

Starts in ❶ **Lake Worth**, an artsy enclave located just south of the Palm Beaches. The beach here is simply outstanding. When you're done relaxing on it, grab dinner at ❷ **Paradiso** and enjoy a night at the ❸ **Havana Hideout** or Lake Worth Playhouse. The next day, check out the ❹ **Morikami Museum & Japanese Gardens** in Delray Beach for taste of Japanese aesthetics. Sip on some wine at ❺ **Joseph's Wine Bar** after. Spend the night in Delray, then go on to ❻ **Boca Raton**, where you'll discover the considerable natural beauty of Florida at the ❼ **Gumbo Limbo Nature Center**. When you've finished here, shop and dine in the Spanish villa-esque mall at ❽ **Mizner Park**.

On your fourth day drive to Lauderdale-by-the-Sea, where you can experience an underwater, treasure-hunting trail on the ❾ **Shipwreck Snorkel Trail**. If you have dinner in acclaimed ❿ **Gran Forno** you're already in Fort Lauderdale, where you can finish with a walk on the excellent beach ⓫ **Promenade**.

Norton Museum of Art (p146)

Discover Palm Beach & the Gold Coast

At a Glance

- **Palm Beach** (p142) Where the elite meet to sit on the beach, shop, dine and enjoy the good life.
- **West Palm Beach** (p146) Quiet community with diverse lifestyle offerings and surprisingly lively nightlife.
- **Delray Beach** (p154) A cultural haven in the tropics, perfect for a day's pottering about.
- **Fort Lauderdale** (p159) Fine dining, great beaches, vibrant nightlife.

West Palm Beach (p146)
DANITA DELIMONT/GETTY IMAGES ©

GOLD COAST

This coastline has a split personality. First, there's slow-going, ocean-fronting Rte 1, a pleasant drive revealing infinite vistas and unspoiled beaches...though occasionally it feels like driving through a high-rise condo-canyon. Second, there's wizened Dixie Hwy, running parallel to Rte 1 but further inland, past dive bars, hole-in-the-wall eateries and diverse, working-class communities. Drive both stretches; each is rich with divergent offerings.

Palm Beach

☎561 / POP 9600

The third-wealthiest city in America, Palm Beach looks every inch the playground for the rich and famous that it is. Though all the bling may feel a bit intimidating, fear not – much of Palm Beach is within the reach of even the brokest budget traveler.

Sights

Flagler Museum Museum

(Map p144; ☎561-655-2833; www.flaglermuseum.us; 1 Whitehall Way; adult/child $18/10; ⏰10am-5pm Tue-Sat, noon-5pm Sun) This museum is housed in the spectacular 1902 mansion built by Henry Flagler as a gift for his bride, Mary Lily Keenan. The beaux-arts-styled Whitehall was one of the most modern houses of its era and quickly became the locus of the winter season in Palm Beach. Designed by John Carrere and Thomas Hastings, both students of the Ecole des Beaux-Arts in Paris and collaborators on other Gilded Age landmarks such as the New York Public Library, the elaborate 75-room house was the first residential home to feature both a heating system and an air-con system. Its modish, pink aluminum-leaf wallpaper was more expensive, at the time, than gold.

Ocean Boulevard Scenic Drive

There are the rich, there are the super-rich, and then there are the denizens of Ocean Blvd. Driving along this seaside stretch of Hwy A1A is an eye-popping lesson in exactly how much money can buy – the road is lined with sprawling estates ranging from faux Greco-Roman temples to pink Spanish-style palaces as big as any hotel. And most of these houses are merely second (or third) homes for their owners! You may find the view inspirational, or it may make you want to start a proletarian uprising – either way, it's a gorgeous drive, with impeccably manicured lawns and snatches of cobalt sea visible through the hedgerows.

The most famous mansion overlooking this stretch of surf and sand is Donald Trump's predictably over-the-top **Mar-a-Lago (1100 S Ocean Blvd)**, purchased in 1985 for a paltry $8 million and soon turned into a private club. Best glimpsed driving over Southern Blvd Bridge from West Palm, it was the location of his most recent wedding reception.

Palm Beach Lake Trail Walking, Cycling

(Map p144; Royal Palm Way, at the Intracoastal Waterway) The first 'road' in Palm Beach ran along the Intracoastal Waterway, and provided a five-mile paved path stretching from Worth Ave (in the south) to Indian Rd (in the north) for Flagler's hotel guests to stretch their legs and scope out the social scene. Nicknamed 'The Trail of Conspicuous Consumption,' it is sandwiched between two amazing views: Lake Worth lagoon to the west, and an unending series of mansions to the east.

Palm Beach Municipal Beach Beach

(Map p144; Ocean Blvd, btwn Royal Palm Way & Hammon Ave; sunrise-sunset) This is one of Palm Beach's two beautiful public beaches, both of which are kept pleasantly seaweed-free by the town. Metered beachfront parking costs an absurd $5 per hour – head inland to snag free streetfront parking downtown. This beach can get crowded.

Sleeping

If you're looking for a deal, head west. Palm Beach properties aren't cheap.

Breakers Resort $$$

(Map p144; 561-655-6611; www.thebreakers.com; 1 S County Rd; r $329-1330; P @) Originally built by Henry Flagler (in 1904 rooms cost $4 per night, including meals), today this 550-room resort sprawls across 140 acres and boasts a staff of 2300, fluent in 56 languages. Just feet from the county's best snorkeling, this palace has two 18-hole golf courses, a mile of semiprivate beach, four pools, two croquet courts and the best brunch around. For opulence, elegance and old-world charm, there's no other choice. Green Lodging certified.

Palm Beach Historic Inn B&B $$

(Map p144; 561-832-4009; www.palmbeachhistoricinn.com; 365 S County Rd; r $159-239, ste $189-329;) Housed on the 2nd floor of a landmark building brimming with character, this intimate European-style hotel has airy, light-filled rooms with hardwood floors and period Palm Beach furnishings. Soak in enamel tubs and sleep like a baby beneath goose-down comforters. Stroll a block to the beach or two to Worth Ave. It's excellent value and the location can't be beaten.

Brazilian Court Hotel $$$

(Map p144; 561-655-7740; www.thebraziliancourt.com; 301 Australian Ave; r $199-422, ste $341-774; P) Built in 1926, this elegant resort is an excellent choice for those who want pampering but not obsequiousness. Trendy but timeless, it's got a lovely Mediterranean style, a romantic courtyard and fashionable suites that effortlessly blend sleek lines and soft comfort. The on-site Frédéric Fekkai salon and renowned (and ultraromantic) French Café Boulud (p145) are major draws, too.

Palm Beach

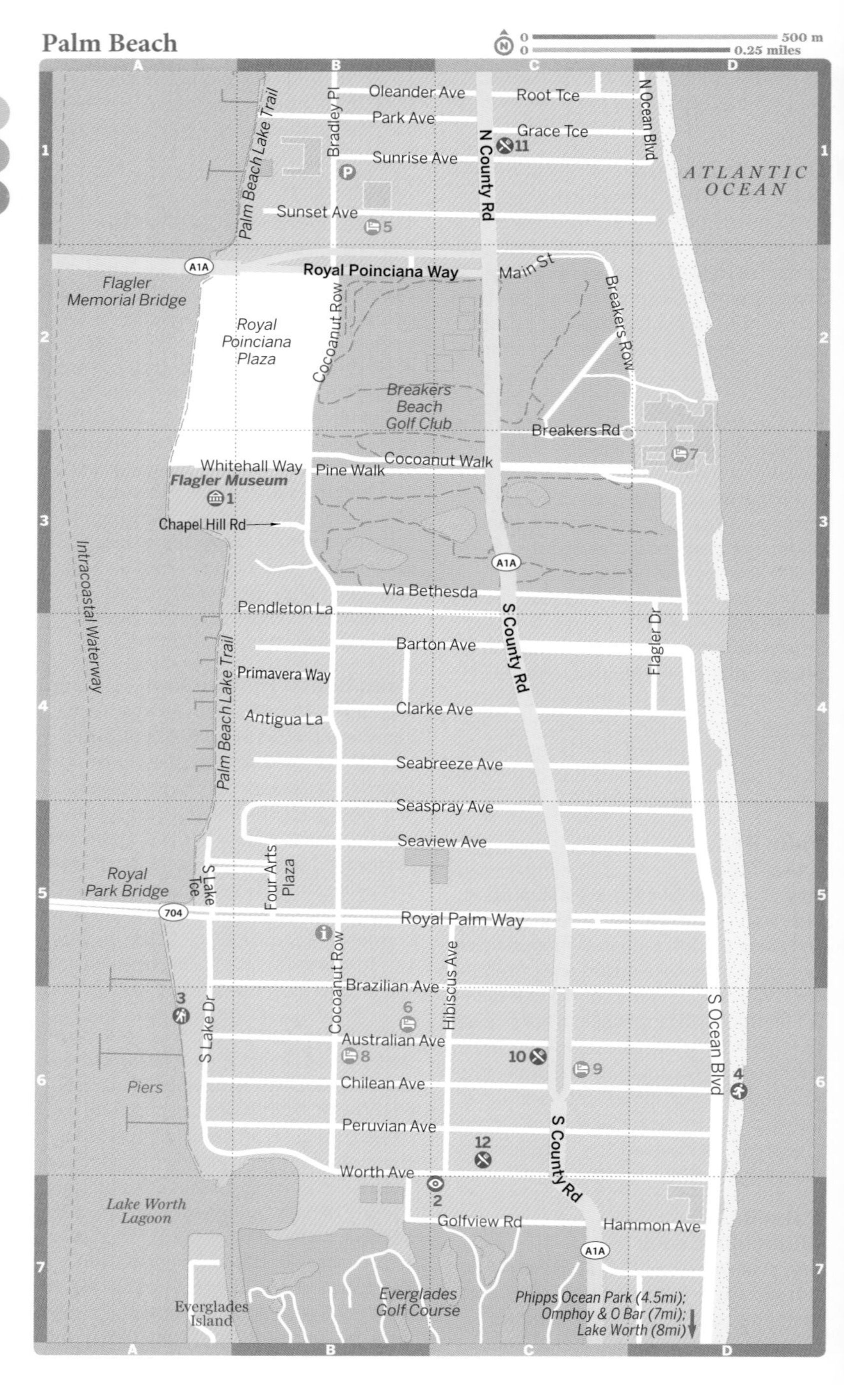

0 500 m
0 0.25 miles
A
B
C
D
1
2
3
4
5
6
7
Oleander Ave
Root Tce
Park Ave
Grace Tce
Sunrise Ave
Sunset Ave
Bradley Pl
N County Rd
N Ocean Blvd
Palm Beach Lake Trail
ATLANTIC OCEAN
A1A
Royal Poinciana Way
Main St
Flagler Memorial Bridge
Royal Poinciana Plaza
Cocoanut Row
Breakers Row
Breakers Beach Golf Club
Breakers Rd
Whitehall Way
Pine Walk
Cocoanut Walk
Flagler Museum
Chapel Hill Rd
Intracoastal Waterway
Via Bethesda
Pendleton La
S County Rd
Barton Ave
Flagler Dr
Primavera Way
Antigua La
Clarke Ave
Seabreeze Ave
Seaspray Ave
Seaview Ave
Royal Park Bridge
S Lake Tce
Four Arts Plaza
704
Royal Palm Way
Hibiscus Ave
Brazilian Ave
S Lake Dr
Australian Ave
Chilean Ave
Piers
S Ocean Blvd
Peruvian Ave
Worth Ave
Lake Worth Lagoon
Golfview Rd
Hammon Ave
Everglades Island
Everglades Golf Course
Phipps Ocean Park (4.5mi); Omphoy & O Bar (7mi); Lake Worth (8mi)

Palm Beach

Don't Miss Sights

Sights

Activities, Courses & Tours

Sleeping

Eating

Entertainment

Heading to the beach? Hitch a ride in the hotel's Jeep – your driver will supply you with chairs, umbrellas, towels, bottled water and magazines. Bliss.

Bradley Park Hotel Hotel $$
(Map p144; ☎561-832-7050; www.bradleyparkhotel.com; 2080 Sunset Ave; r $99-229, ste $129-575; P ❄ 🛜) The midrange Bradley offers large, gold-hued rooms, some with small kitchens and characterful furniture that looks like it's been bought at local estate sales. There's no lobby to speak of, but rooms with kitchens feel like mini-apartments, and it's located just a short walk from the shops and restaurants of Royal Poinciana Way.

Chesterfield Hotel $$$
(Map p144; ☎561-659-5800; www.chesterfieldpb.com; 363 Cocoanut Row; r $185-385, ste $410-735; P ❄ 🛜 ≋ 🐾) From its old-fashioned room keys to the cookie jar in the lobby, this hotel aims for an old-world elegance that's much appreciated by its loyal guests, many of whom have been returning for decades. Room decor is very 'Great White Hunter,' with English plaid wallpaper and murals of monkeys gamboling around the jungle. The hotel's **Leopard Lounge** **(Map p144; www.chesterfieldpb.com/dining/bar; 363 Cocoanut Row; ⏰6:30pm-1am)**, with its painted ceilings and tiger-print banquettes, is a perennial favorite for long lunches and evening piano music.

Eating

Dining out in Palm Beach is pretty much a high-end affair, though there is a pleasant selection of budget bites.

Green's Pharmacy Diner $
(Map p144; 151 N County Rd; mains $4-11; ⏰8am-6pm Mon-Fri, to 4pm Sat) Housed inside a working pharmacy, this place hasn't changed since John F Kennedy, looking to slip away from the Secret Service, would stroll across the mint-green linoleum to grab a bite. Choose between a table or a stool at the Formica counter and order from the paper menu just like everyone else, from trust-fund babies slumming it to college girls headed to the beach.

Būccan Modern American $$
(Map p144; ☎561-833-3450; www.buccanpalmbeach.com; 350 S County Rd; small plates $4.50-36; ⏰5pm-midnight Mon-Sat, to 11pm Sun) With its modern American menu and James Beard–nominated chef, Clay Conley, at the helm, Būccan is taking Palm Beach by storm. Flavor-hop with a selection of small plates, including exquisite short-rib empanadas, harissa and mint lamb sliders, and jumbo shrimp with housemade *tasso* (smoked, seasoned ham) and popcorn grits. Reservations recommended.

Café Boulud French $$$
(Map p144; ☎561-655-6060; www.thebraziliancourt.com; 301 Australian Ave; mains $16-46, prix-fixe menu lunch/dinner $25/45; ⏰7am-2:30pm daily, 5:30-10pm Sun-Thu) Created by renowned New York chef Daniel Boulud, the restaurant at the Brazilian Court is one of the few places in Palm Beach that truly justifies the sky-high prices. The warm gold-and-coral dining room and 60-seat terrace complements a rich menu of classic French and fusion dishes, all displaying Boulud's signature sophistication and subtlety.

Circle American, European $$$
(Map p144; ☎561-659-8440; www.thebreakers.com; 1 S County Rd; adult/child $95/45; ⏰11am-2:30pm Sun) Sure, it's steep, but brunch at the Breakers' storied restaurant will certainly rank among the most amazing you'll ever enjoy. Beneath soaring 30ft frescoed ceilings, surrounded by ocean views and entertained by a roving harpsichordist, guests begin their feast at the breakfast bar, which features homemade doughnuts, tropical fruits and on-demand omelets.

Ta-Boo Modern American $$$
(Map p144; ☎561-835-3500; www.taboorestaurant.com; 221 Worth Ave; mains $16-45; ⏰11:30am-10pm) If you believe the legend, the Bloody Mary was invented here, mixed to soothe the hangover of Woolworth heiress Barbara Hutton. Today the restaurant boasts the most coveted window seats on Worth Ave and competition to get in is as stiff as the heiress' drinks. But get past the intricate woodwork and jungle murals, and you'll enjoy a well-executed American bistro meal.

Shopping

The quarter-mile, palm-tree-lined strip along **Worth Avenue** (www.worth-avenue.com) is Florida's answer to Rodeo Dr. You'll find more than 200 shops, representing every exclusive brand known. Half the shops close for summer, but it's fun to stroll and window-shop (and celeb-spot), whether you want to lay down your plastic or not.

Information

Chamber of Commerce (Map p144; ☎561-655-3282; www.palmbeachchamber.com; 400 Royal Palm Way, Suite 106) Excellent maps, racks of pamphlets and a new android app of the *Palm Beach Guide*.

Getting There & Around

PalmTran (www.palmtran.org)

West Palm Beach

West Palm is a groovy place to explore, despite the seemingly never-ending condo construction. It's a community with a surprisingly diverse collection of restaurants, friendly inhabitants (including a strong gay community) and a gorgeous waterway that always seems to reflect the perfect amount of starlight.

Sights

Norton Museum of Art Museum
(Map p148; ☎561-832-5196; www.norton.org; 1451 S Olive Ave; adult/child $12/5; ⏰10am-5pm Tue-Sat, to 9pm Thu, 11am-5pm Sun) The largest art museum in Florida, the Norton opened in 1941 to display the enormous art collection of industrialist Ralph Hubbard Norton and his wife Elizabeth. The Nortons' permanent collection of more than 5000 pieces (including works by Matisse, Warhol and O'Keeffe) is displayed alongside important Chinese, pre-Columbian Mexican and US Southwestern artifacts, plus some wonderful contemporary photography and regular traveling exhibitions.

CityPlace Concert Venue
(Map p148; www.cityplace.com; 700 S Rosemary Ave; ⏰10am-10pm Mon-Sat, noon-6pm Sun) This massive entertainment and shopping complex is the crown jewel of West Palm Beach's urban-renewal initiative. At its center is the **Harriet Himmel Theater** (Map p148; ☎561-318-7136; www.cityplace.com; 600 S Rosemary Ave), a beautiful 1926 Colonial Revival structure that previously housed the Methodist Church, and now puts on an exhaustive round of exhibitions, fashion shows and concerts. Besides that there's a swanky new bowling alley, a 20-screen cinema theater, dozens of restaurants and a slew of stores.

National Croquet Center Croquet
(☎561-478-2300; www.nationalcroquetclub.com; 700 Florida Mango Rd; ⏰9am-5pm) FREE Get a real taste of the upper-crust Palm Beach lifestyle at the National Croquet Center, the largest croquet facility in the world.

JIM FAIRMAN ©

Don't Miss
Ann Norton Sculpture Garden

This serene collection of sculptures is a real West Palm gem. The historic house, verdant grounds and enormous sculptures are all the work of Ralph Norton's second wife, Ann. After establishing herself as an artist in New York in the mid-1930s, she became the first sculpture teacher at the Norton School of Art in West Palm, and created this luxurious garden as a place of repose.

After poking through Norton's antique-filled home, you can wander the grounds and uncover her soaring feats of granite, brick, marble and bronze. Perhaps most awe-inspiring is the 1965 *Cluster*, a collection of seven burka-clad women in pink granite. Before leaving, be sure to peek into Norton's light-filled studio, where dusty tools lie just as she left them.

Artists are free to bring their easels and indulge in a spot of plein air painting in the garden for $15.

THINGS YOU NEED TO KNOW

Map p148; www.ansg.org; 253 Barcelona Rd; adult/child $10/5; 10am-4pm Wed-Sun

Here, genteel sportspeople dressed in crisp whites hit balls through wickets on 12 of the world's biggest, greenest, most manicured lawns. It's members-only, but the public is invited to free lessons on Saturday mornings at 10am. The pro shop, inside the plantation-style clubhouse, has all the latest in mallets and croquet wear.

The center is about a 10-minute drive southwest of downtown West Palm.

Clematis Street Street

(Map p148) Long before CityPlace came along, there was Clematis St, a hip, bohemian strip bustling with locals doing their shopping, diners looking for a foodie scene, and scads of bar-hoppers come

West Palm Beach

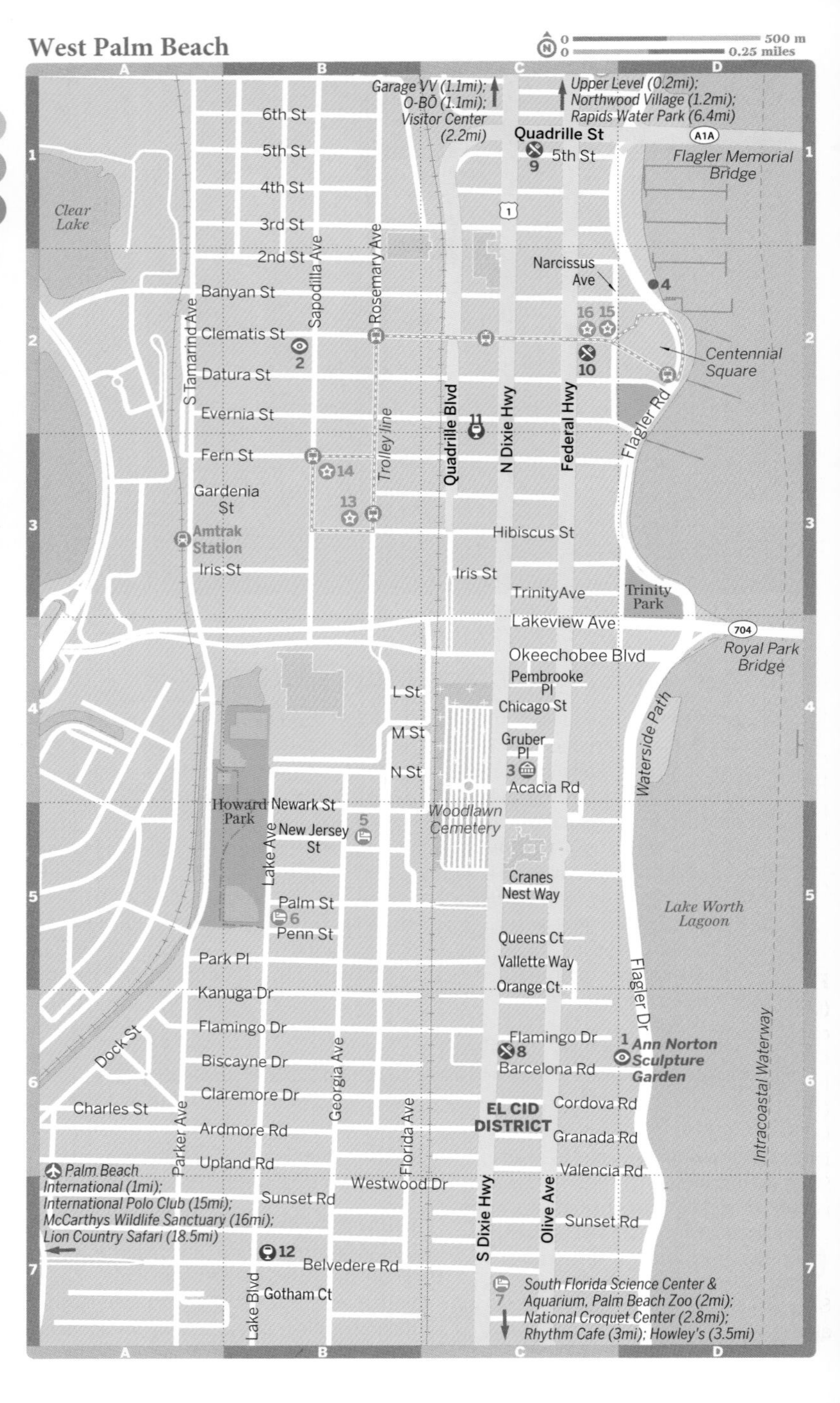

West Palm Beach

nightfall. In short, this stretch is the most eclectic strip in town – and much of it's also a historic district with a jumbled collection of architecture – Greek Revival, Venetian Revival, Mediterranean Revival and art deco. Every Thursday night, Clematis plays host to West Palm's signature event, **Clematis by Night** (**www.clematisbynight.net; 6-9:30pm Thu**).

Tours

Palm Beach Water Taxi Boat Tour
(**Map p148; 561-683-8294; www.sailfishmarina.com; 98 Lake Dr, Singer Island**) Water taxis run between downtown West Palm and Singer Island ($15), as well as to Peanut Island (round-trip $12), leaving from Singer Island. Additionally, the outfit offers guided tours along the Intracoastal, including 90-minute narrated tours of Palm Beach mansions (adult/child $30/15).

Sleeping

Skip the depressing chain hotels near the airport and try one of these cool spots.

Hotel Biba Motel $
(**Map p148; 561-832-0094; www.hotelbiba.com; 320 Belvedere Rd; r $75-149;**) Funky, retro Hotel Biba has injected an ordinary motel with pop-art flair. This groovy spot has lots going for it – spare-chic decor in vibrantly colored rooms; a leafy little courtyard with a hidden-away pool; and a hip, sexy bar where you'll find a thriving lounge scene at night. A block from the Intracoastal, the Biba is perched on the edge of the El Cid district.

Grandview Gardens B&B $$
(**Map p148; 561-833-9023; www.grandview-gardens.com; 1608 Lake Ave; r $125-209;** P) Book a room at this intimate resort and you'll feel like a local in no time. Hidden in a tropical garden on Howard Park, the enormous suites with their wrought-iron and four-poster beds access the pool patio through French doors. They're decorated to reflect the Spanish Mediterranean style that is so popular in these parts. The house is a period 1925 structure typical of the historic neighborhood and it sits opposite the Armory Art Center, so it's perfect for longer stays for the arts-inclined.

Casa Grandview B&B, Cottage $$$
(**Map p148; 561-313-9695; www.casagrandview.com; 1410 Georgia Ave; r $149-299;**) Hidden behind hedgerows in the historic Grandview Heights neighborhood, this intimate little compound has five B&B rooms, seven cottages and five suite apartments. B&B rooms are in the main house, which has a charming-if-odd medieval-Spanish feel, with a narrow stone staircase and elf-sized wooden doors in the walls. We love the cozy Library Suite – small but plush. Luxurious cottages have a stylized 1940s beach chic, with vintage signs and bright tiled kitchens – great for families.

Eating

The food scene here is an eclectic affair – ethnic eats mixed with quirky spaces and quaint tearooms – and lots of affordable options.

Detour: Kayaking the Loxahatchee River

One of two federally designated 'Wild and Scenic' rivers in the state, the free-flowing Loxahatchee River, about 23 miles north of downtown West Palm, is home to a wide range of habitats, from tidal marsh riverines and dense mangrove communities to tidal flats and oyster bars. Translated as 'River of Turtles,' the coffee-colored river is home to shelled reptiles, as well as herons, ospreys, otters, raccoons, the occasional bobcat – and lots of alligators. For a great day exploring the various aquatic preserves here, no one beats Riverbend Park's **Canoe Outfitters** (561-746-7053; www.canoeoutfittersofflorida.com; 9060 W Indiantown Rd, Jupiter; double canoes/single kayaks per day $42.50/37), which provides access to this waterway. This terrific day out is gentle enough to be kid-friendly but eye-popping enough to appeal to the discerning adventurer.

Mediterranean Market & Deli Middle Eastern $
(Map p148; 561-659-7322; www.mediterraneanmarketandbakery.com; 327 5th St; mains $2-11.50) Don't be put off by the nondescript warehouse exterior – this Middle Eastern deli serves up some of the most flavorful lunches in town. Fresh baked pita is stuffed with homemade hummus, feta and kefta accompanied by zingy lima bean salad and tabbouleh. You can then order honey-drenched baklava or lady fingers to go.

Curbside Gourmet Food Truck $
(Map p148; 561-371-6565; http://curbsidegourmet.com; 2000 S Dixie Hwy) This bright, peppermint truck is Palm Beach's first mobile food truck dedicated to bringing good, seasonal staples to resident gourmands. The short, sweet menu includes a breakfast burrito, BLT's, crabcake sliders, fresh fish and pork tacos, and a daily panini or frittata. Fries are hand cut; add-ons include heritage tomatoes and Applewood smoked bacon; and dessert is caramelized grapefruit. Yum.

On Mondays, Wednesdays and Fridays the truck parks at South Dixie; on Tuesdays and Thursdays at Trinity Park.

Garage VV Modern American $$
(561-802-4441; www.garagevv.com; 409 Northwood Rd; mains $12-25.50; 11am-11pm Mon-Thu, to midnight Fri & Sat, to 4pm Sun) You can tell Northwood is on the up by this latest addition to its culinary landscape. The brainchild of Vivian Bordieri Moir, partner to Mike Moir of Jupiter's famous **Little Moir's Food Shack** (www.littlemoirsfoodshack.com; 103 S US 1; mains $9-24; 11am-9pm Mon-Sat), and partners Nina Wasserman and Kimberly Levine, industrial-styled Garage focuses on inventive fish dishes crusted and marinated with an array of interesting spices, nuts and herbs. Fresh baked breads and pastas made on the premises are also available to buy from the small market inside the restaurant.

Rocco's Tacos & Tequila Bar Mexican $$
(Map p148; www.roccostacos.com; 224 Clematis St; mains $12-23; 11:30am-11pm Sun-Wed, to midnight Thu-Sat) This saucy Nuevo Mexican restaurant, in the heart of West Palm's Clematis St, is not your typical taqueria. Under the warm twinkle of funky chandeliers, you can enjoy guacamole prepared tableside, fresh-made ceviche, or a range of tacos from pork to mushroom to cactus paddle. And, oh yeah, there are 175 different kinds of tequila to choose from.

Rhythm Cafe Fusion $$$
(561-833-3406; www.rhythmcafe.cc; 3800 S Dixie Hwy; mains $17-30; 5:30-10pm Tue-Sat, to 9pm Sun) There's no lack of flair at this colorful, upbeat bistro set in a converted drugstore in West Palm's antiques district.

It's strung with Christmas lights and hung with bright, bobbing paper lanterns. The menu is equally vibrant, bopping happily from goat's cheese pie to 'the best tuna tartar ever' to the pomegranate-infused catch of the day. Dessert's a star – the chocolate butter-cream cake is advertized as 'so good you'll slap your momma!' We don't advise that, but do taste the cake.

O-BŌ Modern American **$$$**

(☎561-366-1185; 422 Northwood Rd; plates $8-32; ⏲5pm-12:30am Tue-Sat) At O-BŌ art gallerist Jeffery Thompson and chef Bob Reilly have come up with a perfect combination of retro-cool interior, delectable small plates, a carefully curated wine and beer list and soulful live music. House specials include black-and-white lobster ravioli, spicy short rib spring rolls and the unique Saketini – a white-hot sake martini. Check out the Facebook page for live acts and events.

Drinking & Nightlife

Clematis St and CityPlace have a revolving door of ultrachic bar-lounges and late-night dance clubs; they're also home to a couple of great, casual, stalwart hangouts.

Blind Monk
Wine Bar

(Map p148; ☎561-833-3605; http://theblindmonk.com; 410 Evernia St #107; ⏲4pm-late) With a team of knowledgeable sommeliers behind it, the Blind Monk is arguably the best wine bar in West Palm. It offers an extensive list of wines by the glass, including international labels and local craft beers. Small plates of cheese, salami, grapes, pickles and nuts soak up the vino, while silent old movies play on the wall.

HG Roosters Gay

(Map p148; http://roosterswpb.com; 823 Belvedere Rd; ⏲3pm-3am Mon-Sat, noon-3am Sun) A mainstay of West Palm's thriving gay community, this bar has been offering wings, bingo and hot young male dancers since 1984.

Entertainment

Palm Beach Dramaworks Theater

(Map p148; ☎561-514-4042; www.palmbeachdramaworks.org; 201 Clematis St) 'Theatre to Think About' is the tagline of this award-winning resident theater, which is committed to presenting underrated classic and contemporary plays from the likes of Lorca, Steinbeck, Pinter, Lorraine Hansberry and Horton Foote.

Pawnshop Club

(Map p148; http://pawnshopwpb.com; 219 Clematis St; cover $10; ⏲5pm-3am Tue-Thu, to 4am Fri & Sat) This former Miami dance club and celebrity haunt opened with a knock-out party in March 2014. Situated in the previous Dr Feelgood venue, it features the

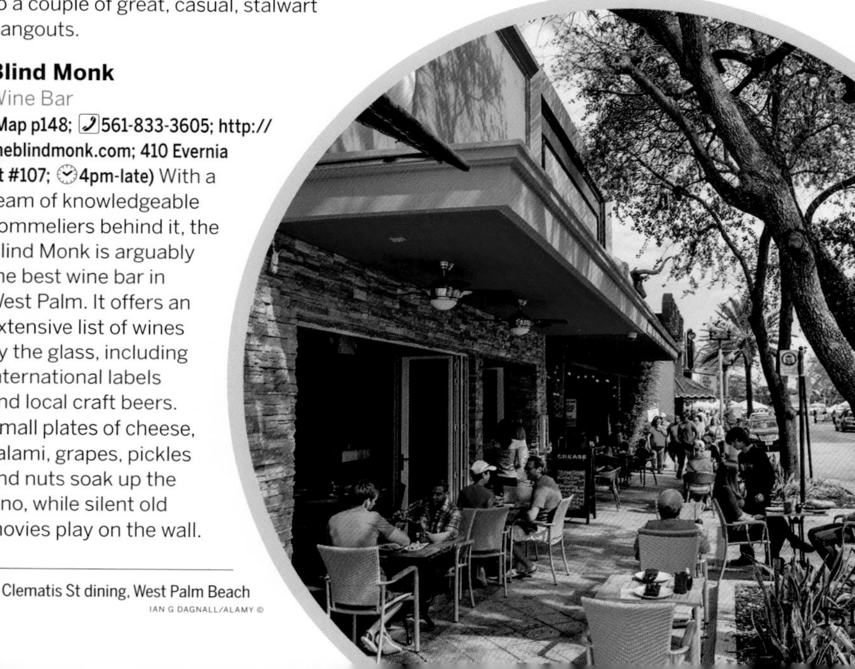

Clematis St dining, West Palm Beach
IAN G DAGNALL/ALAMY ©

familiar pawn shop trappings along with a life-sized vintage Ferris wheel and a DJ booth designed out of a Mack truck. DJs, dancers and light shows keep the party going til 3am while rivers of alcohol flow from the 175ft bar.

Information

Visitor Center (☎561-233-3000; www.palmbeachfl.com; 1555 Palm Beach Lakes Blvd) Extensive area information, maps and online guides.

Getting There & Around

Palm Beach International Airport (PBI; ☎561-471-7420; www.pbia.org; 1000 Palm Beach) **Palm Beach International Airport** is 2.5 miles west of downtown West Palm Beach. Can be a good alternative gateway to the south Florida region.

Lake Worth

☎561 / POP 36,000

Billing itself as 'Where the tropics begin', this bohemian community has an artsy vibe and a cool collection of eateries and nightspots.

Sights & Activities

Snook Islands Natural Area Park

(www.lakeworth.org/visitors/parks; Lake Avenue Bridge) Twenty-mile long Lake Worth lagoon is the largest estuary in Palm Beach county and is an important warm-water refuge for manatees. Years of development have surrounded the lagoon with premium property, resulting in some lamentable environmental degradation. To reverse some of the damage the $18 million Snook Islands Natural Area was created in a biologically dead zone, stretching 1.2 miles north from Lake Avenue into the lagoon. Restoring miles of mangroves and laying down new oyster beds to encourage the growth of sea grasses, a favorite manatee snack, has enabled the return of a startling number of birds and marine life.

Lake Worth Beach Beach

This stretch of sand is universally agreed to be the finest between Fort Lauderdale and Daytona. Surfers come from miles to tame the waves; everyone else comes to enjoy the fine white sand.

Paradiso Ristorante

Detour: Lion Country Safari

A half an hour's drive west of West Palm, you'll find the first cageless drive-through safari in the country: **Lion Country Safari** (561-793-1084; www.lioncountrysafari.com; 2003 Lion Country Safari Rd; adult/child $29.95/21.95; 9:30am-5:30pm;) This incredible animal park puts you in the cage (ie your car) as 900 creatures roam freely, staring at *you*. Equal parts conservation area and safari, the park's 500 acres are home to bison, zebra, white rhinos, chimpanzees and, of course, lions. You tour the safari section in your car (unless it's a convertible; short-term rentals are available), driving slowly, hoping the animals approach the vehicle. The best time to go is when it rains, because the animals are more active when it's cool.

Eating

Mother Earth Sanctuary Café American, Cafe $

(561-460-8647; www.motherearthsanctuarycafe.com; 410 2nd Ave N; mains $4.50-10; 8:30am-4pm Tue-Sat, 10am-2pm Sun;) Since when do you have option-paralysis over *which* veggie burger to eat? At the Sanctuary Café you can feed your body and soul on hearty yamburgers, black-bean burgers and sweet-potato chakra burgers. These are served alongside an array of organic salads topped with locally grown micro-greens, and chicken dishes. This cafe is also the only purveyor of fair-trade Larry's Beans, and the homemade Mighty Leaf Chai is heavenly.

Pelican Diner, Indian $

(610 Lake Ave; mains $3-10; 6:30am-2pm;) This early-risers' place offers hearty portions of perfectly prepared breakfast, plus a carnival of vegetarian-friendly specials, many with Mediterranean or Middle Eastern flavors (the owners are Pakistani). It also offers divine Indian dinners on Fridays from 6pm to 10pm, including a range of potent curries and masalas.

Paradiso Ristorante Italian $$$

(561-547-2500; www.paradisolakeworth.com; 625 Lucerne Ave; 3-course lunch menu $21, mains $32-56; 11:30am-3pm & 5:30-10pm) From the elegant interiors to the exquisitely presented dishes of homemade pasta, sheep ricotta gnocchi and succulent veal fillet, this is a dining experience to savor. Seasonal delights such as truffles, chestnuts and huckleberries call for specialty menu. Scheduled wine dinners and theatre packages are arranged in conjunction with the Lake Worth Playhouse (p154).

Reservations are recommended.

Drinking & Nightlife

Nightlife is where Lake Worth shines. It offers an outsized wealth of great bars and music venues.

Havana Hideout Bar

(www.havanahideout.com; 509 Lake Ave; 11-2am) The most happening place in town, open-air, palm-fringed Havana has live music most nights, a thoughtful draft-beer selection and an on-site taqueria. Countless stomachs get filled on Taco Tuesdays, when tacos are $1.50 apiece.

Entertainment

Bamboo Room Live Music

(561-585-2583; www.bamboorm.com; 25 S J St; 7pm-3am Thu-Sat) This favorite spot has an intimate roadhouse feel and features regional and internationally known blues, rockabilly, alt-country and jam bands, drawing music-lovers from miles around.

Lake Worth Playhouse Theater
(☎561-586-6410; www.lakeworthplayhouse.org; 713 Lake Ave; tickets $15-32) Housed in a restored 1924 vaudeville venue, this intimate spot stages classic community theater. The attached **Stonzek Studio Theatre** screens independent films (tickets cost from $6 to $8). The Dinner + Theater package with Paradiso Ristorante (p153) is an absolute bargain at $55.

Lake Worth Drive-In Cinema
(☎561-965-4517; 3438 Lake Worth Rd) When was the last time you went to the drive-in? Screening first-run movies under the stars seven nights a week – drive in, tune in and sit back. Coolers are welcome; dogs are not.

Information

Chamber of Commerce (☎561-790-6200; www.cpbchamber.com; 501 Lake Ave; ⏲9am-5pm)

Getting There & Around

The **Tri-Rail Station** (www.tri-rail.com; 1703 Lake Worth Rd) is at the intersection of A St. PalmTran bus 61 connects the station to downtown.

Delray Beach

☎561 / POP 65,000

Delray effortlessly juggles casual seaside vibe, suave urban sophistication and wide-ranging restaurant options.

Sights & Activities

Morikami Museum & Japanese Gardens Museum, Gardens
(☎561-495-0233; www.morikami.org; 4000 Morikami Park Rd; adult/child $14/9; ⏲10am-5pm Tue-Sun) Japanese immigrant and pineapple farmer Sukeji 'George' Morikami, a member of the original Yamato settlement of Delray, donated his spectacularly landscaped 200-acre property for the establishment of a museum showcasing Japanese culture. Today you can wander more than a mile of pine-lined nature trails around koi-filled ponds, experiencing different Japanese gardens from bonsai to a 12th-century *shinden* (pleasure) garden modelled on a noble estate. To complement the gardens, the outstanding museum showcases more than 5000 Japanese antiques, objects and works of fine art.

Bamboo Room (p153)

BRANDON KRUSE/THE PALM BEACH POST/ZUMA PRESS, INC/ALAMY ©

Beaches Beaches

Among the best sandy spits are the **Atlantic Dunes Beach** (1600 Ocean Blvd), with 7 acres of shorefront sporting clean restroom facilities, volleyball courts and picnic areas, and the **public beach** (Ocean Blvd, at Atlantic), a hip gathering spot for young locals and visitors, with excellent surf for swimming. Coin-operated parking meters charge $1.25 per hour.

Cornell Museum of Art & History Museum

(adult/child $10/3; 10am-4:30pm Tue-Sat, from 1pm Sun) Housed in the restored 1913 Delray Elementary building, this charming museum hosts rotating exhibits featuring an eclectic mix of local, national and international fine art, crafts and pop culture.

Eating

Delray's got one of the area's best eating scenes, with everything from Parisian-style cafes to funky lunch counters to swanky seafood bistros.

Doc's All-American Burgers, American $

(10 N Swinton Ave; mains $6-15; 11am-11pm Sun-Thu, to 1am Fri & Sat;) Great, greasy burgers and thick, frosty shakes are summertime classics at this beloved open-air '50s-style walk-up counter.

Bamboo Fire Caribbean $$

(www.bamboofirecafe.com; 149 NE 4th Ave; mains $9-15; 6:30-11pm Wed-Thu, to 11:30pm Fri, noon-11:30pm Sat;) On a quiet shopping street a few blocks from the main Delray action, this arty little hole-in-the-wall is a cult favorite for authentic Caribbean fare such as conch fritters, jerk chicken and oxtail stew. Veggies and vegans will be in tofu heaven – try it curried, grilled or fried.

Joseph's Wine Bar Mediterranean $$$

(561-272-6100; www.josephswinebar.com; 200 NE 2nd Ave #107; lunch mains $9-14, dinner mains $21-36; 11am-10pm) Hosted by the gregarious Joseph, lunch or dinner at this friendly eatery is an elegant and convivial affair. Everything is made fresh to order so relax, take a wine recommendation from Joseph and await a vibrant selection of dips (including a deliciously smokey baba ghanoush), salads and wraps at lunchtime, and a sophisticated selection of mains in the evening. The baked rack of lamb in an unctuous Chianti sauce is a particular highlight.

Information

Chamber of Commerce (561-279-1380; www.delraybeach.com; 140 NE 1st St; 9am-5pm) For maps, guides and local advice.

Getting There & Around

Delray Beach is about 20 miles south of West Palm Beach and 45 miles north of Miami on I-95, US Hwy 1 or Hwy A1A.

Boca Raton

561 / POP 86,000

The name Boca Raton may mean 'mouth of the rat', but there's nothing ratty about this proud-to-be-posh coastal town especially not its alfresco mall, Mizner Park.

Sights & Activities

Gumbo Limbo Nature Center Park

(561-544-8605; www.gumbolimbo.org; 1801 N Ocean Blvd; suggested $5 donation; 9am-4pm Mon-Sat, noon-4pm Sun;) Boca's best asset is this stretch of waterfront parkland. It's a preserve of tropical hammock and dunes ecosystems, and a haven for all manner of sea creatures and birds. Dedicated to educating the public about sea turtles and other local fauna, the natural-history displays include saltwater tanks full of critters. The highlight is the brand-new sea-turtle rehabilitation center, which is open for 90-minute tours (10am and 1pm from Monday to Saturday; 1pm Sundays).

Mizner Park Plaza

(www.miznerpark.com) This Spanish-style outdoor shopping mall, bookended on one side by the Boca Raton Museum of Art, has valet parking and a slew of

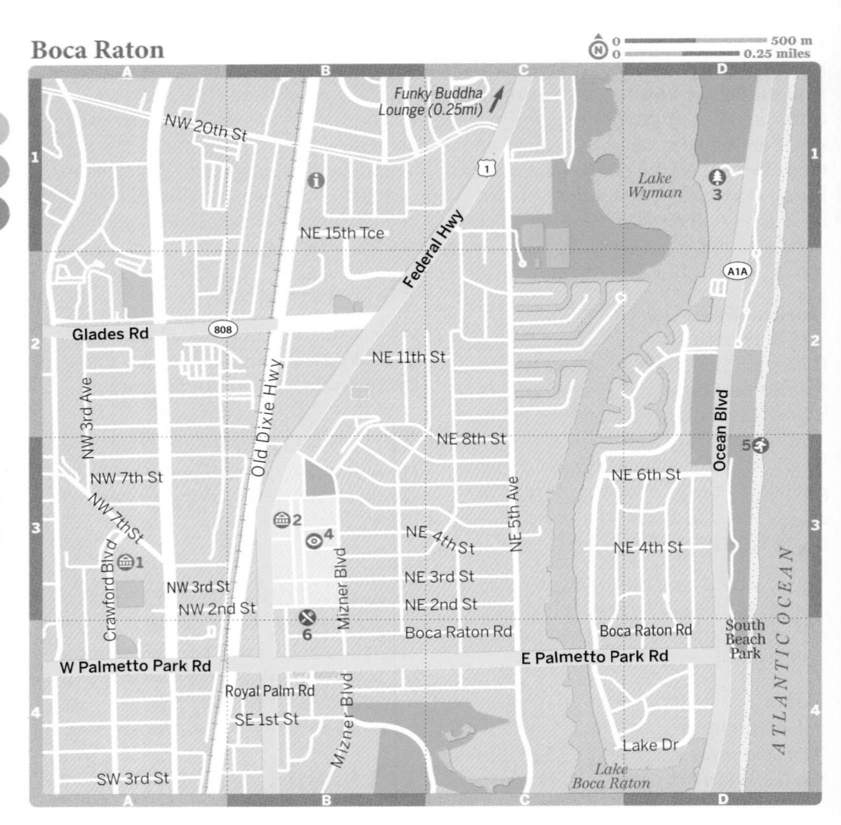

Boca Raton

Sights
1 Boca Raton Children's Museum A3
2 Boca Raton Museum of Art B3
3 Gumbo Limbo Nature Center D1
4 Mizner Park..B3

Activities, Courses & Tours
5 Red Reef Beach.....................................D3

Eating
6 Six Tables..B3

chichi restaurants and upscale chain stores. At the north end, the Count de Hoernle Amphitheater accommodates more than 4000 people for symphonies, ballet, rock concerts and other cultural events. Since Boca lacks a cohesive downtown, Mizner Park generally serves as the city's center.

Eating & Drinking

Mizner Park has a half dozen or so upscale restaurants with outdoor seating and a see-and-be-seen vibe.

Ben's Kosher Deli Deli **$**
(www.bensdeli.net; 9942 Clint Moore Rd; mains $5-12; 11am-9pm) The Florida outpost of a well-loved New York–based deli, Ben's sprawling menu covers all the Jewish classics – corned-beef sandwiches, knishes (potato-stuffed pastries), sweet-and-sour beef tongue and eggs with smoked salmon. The deli is about 20 minutes' drive northwest of Mizner Park.

Six Tables Modern American **$$$**
(561-347-6260; www.sixtablesbocaraton.com; Mizner Plaza, 112 NE 2nd St; menu $79; 7-10pm Wed-Sat) Chef Jonathan Fyhrie offers an

elegant and romantic dining experience for just six lucky tables. The evening starts with the chef drawing the curtains and locking the door, then a shared glass of bubbles, some cheese puffs and a presentation. Settle in for a flavorful five-course fixed-price menu, which often includes a peerless lobster bisque and chateaubriand. Book weeks in advance.

Information

Chamber of Commerce (**561-395-4433; www.bocaratonchamber.com; 1800 N Dixie Hwy; 8:30am-5pm**) Helpful, with racks of pamphlets and a map.

Getting There & Around

Boca Raton is about 50 miles north of Miami and sprawls several miles east and west of I-95. You can also get there from points north and south on Hwy A1A or US 1.

Boca Taxi (**561-392-2727; www.bocaratontaxi.com**) serves the area. Cabs to the Fort Lauderdale or West Palm airports are $55; the Miami airport is $95.

Lauderdale-by-the-Sea & Deerfield Beach

954 / POP LAUDERDALE-BY-THE-SEA 5900 / POP DEERFIELD BEACH 75,000

Just north of Fort Lauderdale, the high-rises and mega-hotels thin out, giving way to these two sleepy, family-oriented vacation communities.

Sights & Activities

Quiet Waters Park Water Park

(**www.broward.org/parks/quietwaterspark; 401 S Powerline Rd, Deerfield Beach; admission per person/car $1.50/8;**) Hardly quiet, this 430-acre county park rings with the squeals of kids (and grown-ups) enjoying all kinds of wet 'n' wild fun. There's **Splash Adventure** ($5 per person), a water playground with a shallow pool and fountains spraying every which way. Then there's the **Ski Rixen** (**www.skirixenusa.com; cable pass per hr/half-day $25/40; noon-8pm Tue-Sun**), a super-cool cable water-ski system. Using an innovative cabling

If You Like... Museums

For a relatively small town, Boca Raton has a surprising amount of excellent museums. They tend to cater to adults and children, and in that vein, we present two exemplars of each genre.

1 **BOCA RATON MUSEUM OF ART**

(**561-392-2500; www.bocamuseum.org; 501 Plaza Real; adult/student $14/6; 10am-5pm Tue-Fri, noon-5pm Sat & Sun**) In Mizner Park, this elegant museum showcases the minor works of modern masters such as Picasso, Chagall and Modigliani. It also has a genuinely worthwhile collection of pieces by 20th- and 21st-century American and European painters, sculptors and photographers.

2 **BOCA RATON CHILDREN'S MUSEUM**

(**561-368-6875; www.cmboca.org; 498 Crawford Blvd; admission $5; 10am-5pm Mon-Sat;**) Housed in the 1925 'Singing Pines' home, one of the oldest wooden structures in town, this children's museum has rooms with various themes, like Oscar's Post Office, KidsCent's banking and FACES Multicultural Room (with musical instruments, try-on clothing and crafts from around the world).

3 **LOXAHATCHEE EVERGLADES TOURS**

(**561-482-6107; www.evergladesairboattours.com; 15490 Loxahatchee Rd; adult/child under 12yr $55/24.50; 9:30am-4pm**) Ten miles west of downtown, Wild Lyle's **Loxahatchee Everglades Tours** offers hourly ecoexplorations of the Everglades on one of eight custom airboats (a boat using a fan instead of a propeller to push it over the water). Guests enjoy an adventure ride through swampy marsh, around papyrus and hurricane grass, past long-winged birds and turtles and gators sunning themselves.

4 **RED REEF BEACH**

(**1 N Ocean Blvd; per vehicle Mon-Fri $16, Sat & Sun $18; 8am-sunset;**) Sadly hurricane Sandy buried most of the artificial reef, but this beach is still tops for water-lovers. There are lifeguards and great shallow pools for beginner snorkelers.

If You Like... Nature Preserves

The Treasure Coast encompasses a series of fine nature and wildlife preserves.

1 JOHN D MACARTHUR STATE PARK

(**561-624-6952; www.macarthurbeach.org; 10900 Jack Nicklaus Dr; per vehicle/bicycle $5/2; 8am-sunset**) While this state park is one of the smallest in the region, it has among the best turtle-watching programs around, as loggerhead, green and leatherback turtles nest along the beach in June and July. The on-site nature center offers guided (single/double $26.50/42.40) and unguided (single/double $12/18 per hour) kayak trips.

2 JONATHAN DICKINSON STATE PARK

(**772-546-2771; www.floridastateparks.org/jonathandickinson; 16450 SE Federal Hwy; per vehicle/bicycle $6/2; 8am-sunset**) With almost 11,500 acres to explore, this is an excellent state park between US Hwy 1 and the Loxahatchee River. There's no ocean access in the park, but its attraction lies in its several habitats: pine flatwoods, cypress stands, swamp and increasingly endangered coastal sand-pine scrub. Ranger-led nature walks leave at 9am Sundays from the Cypress Creek Pavilion.

3 HOBE SOUND NATIONAL WILDLIFE REFUGE

(**www.fws.gov/hobesound; US 1**) A 1035-acre federally protected nature sanctuary, Hobe Sound has two sections: a small slice on the mainland, opposite the Jonathan Dickinson State Park; and the main refuge grounds at the northern end of Jupiter Island. In June and July, nighttime turtle-watching walks occur on Tuesdays and Thursdays (reservations necessary), and birding trips can be arranged through the Hawley Education Center at Blowing Rocks Preserve.

4 BLOWING ROCKS PRESERVE

(**574 S Beach Rd; admission $2; 9am-4:30pm**) This preserve encompasses a mile-long limestone outcrop riddled with holes, cracks and fissures. Bring a tripod and an empty memory card. Even when seas are calm, you can hike through four coastal biomes: shifting dune, coastal strand, interior mangrove wetlands and tropical coastal hammock.

system suspended from towers surrounding a half-mile course, water-skiers (and wake-boarders) are pulled over a wake-free watercourse. For lower-octane adventures, the park has fishing, kayak rental, hiking and a mountain-bike trails.

Butterfly World — Nature Reserve

(**www.butterflyworld.com; 3600 W Sample Rd, Coconut Creek; adult/child $25/20; 9am-5pm Mon-Sat, from 11am Sun;**) The first indoor butterfly park in the US is also one of the largest butterfly exhibits anywhere. It features thousands of live, exotic species, such as the bright-blue morphos or camouflaged owl butterfly. Various exhibits highlight different creatures – from butterflies to hummingbirds. Butterfly World is an excellent place to spend the better part of a day, especially with wide-eyed children or trigger-happy shutterbugs.

Eating & Drinking

Tucker Duke's Lunchbox — Burgers $

(**954-708-2035; www.tuckerdukeslunchbox.com; 1101 S Powerline Rd, Deerfield Beach; mains $4-11; 10:30am-10pm Sun-Wed, to 11pm Thu-Sat**) Superior burgers and southern comfort food made from local, seasonal ingredients. The brain behind the brand is Florida native and 'Cutthroat Kitchen' winner chef Brian Cartenuto, who is passionate about getting back to basics in the kitchen. Check out the website for blogged recipes, including the invaluable 'Hangover Breakfast Tacos.' You'll find it just south of Quiet Waters Park.

Sea — Seafood $$$

(**954-533-2580; www.seatherestaurant.com; 235 Commercial Blvd, Lauderdale-by-the-Sea; menu $25-45; noon-2:30pm & 5-10pm Tue-Fri**) See if you can squeeze into Sea for a perfectly executed three-course fixed-price menu featuring succulent blackened grouper, tender conch, Florida snapper or hummus-encrusted sea bass. Chef Tony Sindaco has Michelin-starred pedigree and presides over the kitchen with a fanatical attention to detail. If it's on the menu, don't miss his signature whiskey cake in a starburst of raspberry coulis.

Information

Deerfield Beach Chamber of Commerce (☎954-427-1050; www.deerfieldchamber.com; 1601 E Hillsboro Blvd; ⏰9am-3pm Mon-Fri Apr-Dec, 9am-3pm Mon-Sat & noon-4pm Sun Jan-Mar)

Lauderdale-by-the-Sea Chamber of Commerce (☎954-776-1000; www.lbts.com; 4201 N Ocean Dr; ⏰9am-5pm) Info on businesses throughout the area.

Getting There & Around

Tri-Rail (www.tri-rail.com) heads north from Fort Lauderdale. If you're driving, try to take A1A (sometimes called Ocean Blvd): the drive's glorious.

Fort Lauderdale

☎954 / POP 185,000

After years of building a reputation as *the* destination for Spring Break, Fort Lauderdale now angles for a slightly more mature and sophisticated crowd – think martinis rather than tequila shots, There's still plenty of carrying-on within the confines of area bars and nightclubs. But there's also beautiful beaches, a system of Venice-like waterways, an international yachting scene, spiffy new hotels, top-notch restaurants and gay hot spots.

Beach, Fort Lauderdale

RICHARD CUMMINGS/GETTY IMAGES ©

Sights

Fort Lauderdale Beach & Promenade — Beach

Fort Lauderdale's promenade – a wide, brick, palm-tree-dotted pathway swooping along the beach and the A1A – is a magnet for runners, in-line skaters, walkers and cyclists. The white-sand beach, meanwhile, is one of the nation's cleanest and best. Stretching 7 miles to Lauderdale-by-the-Sea, it has dedicated family-, gay- and dog-friendly sections. Boating, diving, snorkeling and fishing are all extremely popular.

Riverwalk & Las Olas Riverfront — Waterfront

Curving along the New River, the meandering **Riverwalk** (Map p160; www.goriverwalk.com) runs from Stranahan House to the Broward Center for the Performing Arts. Host to culinary tastings and other events, the walk connects a number of sights, restaurants and shops. **Las Olas Riverfront** (Map p160; cnr SW 1st Ave & Las Olas Blvd) is basically a giant alfresco

Fort Lauderdale

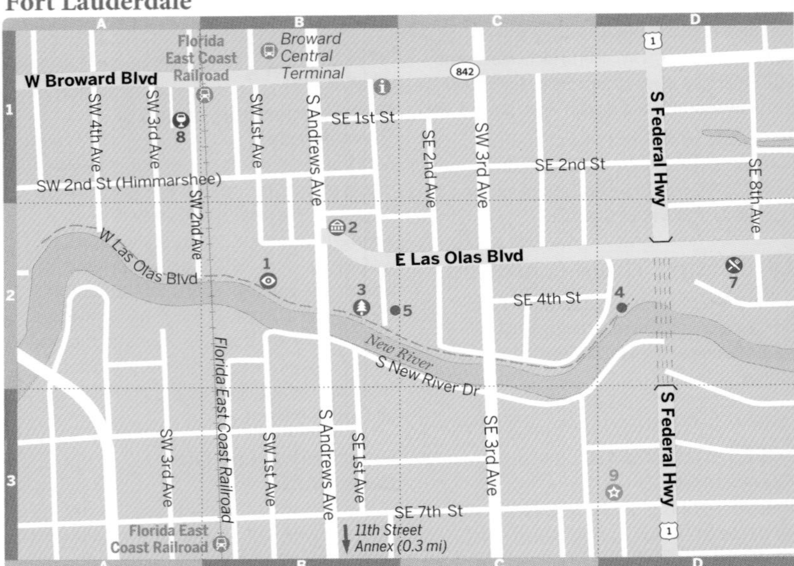

shopping mall with stores, restaurants and live entertainment nightly; it's also the place to catch many river cruises.

Bonnet House Historic Building

(Map p162; ☎954-563-5393; www.bonnethouse.org; 900 N Birch Rd; adult/child $20/16, grounds only $10; ⏲10am-4pm Tue-Sat, from 11am Sun) This pretty plantation-style property was once the home of artists and collectors Frederic and Evelyn Bartlett. It is now open to guided tours that swing through its art-filled rooms and studios. Beyond the house, 35 acres of lush, subtropical gardens protect a pristine barrier-island ecosystem, including one of the finest orchid collections in the country.

Museum of Art Museum

(Map p160; www.moafl.org; 1 E Las Olas Blvd; adult/student/child $10/5/free; ⏲11am-5pm Mon-Sat, noon-5pm Sun) A curvaceous Florida standout known for its William Glackens collection (among Glackens fans) and its exhibitions on wide-ranging themes from northern European art to contemporary Cuban art, American pop art and contemporary photography. On Thursday evenings, the museum stays open late and hosts lectures, films and performances, as well as a happy hour in the museum cafe. Day courses and workshops are also available. Check the website for details.

Activities

Fort Lauderdale Parasail Parasailing

(Map p162; ☎954-462-7266; www.ftlauderdaleparasail.com; 1005 Seabreeze Blvd; flights $70-95) If you're curious how the mansions along Millionaires' Row look from above, sign up for a parasailing trip. You'll soar between 600ft and 1000ft above the waves while strapped securely to an enormous smiley-face parachute.

Sea Experience Boating, Snorkeling

(Map p162; ☎954-770-3483; www.seaxp.com; 801 Seabreeze Blvd; snorkeling adult/child $35/21; ⏲10:15am & 2:15pm daily; 👪) Takes guests in a 40ft glass-bottom boat along the Intracoastal and into the ocean to snorkel on a natural reef, thriving with marine life, in 10ft to 20ft of water. Also

offers scuba trips to multiple wreck sites and the Tenneco Towers from $55.

Tours

Fort Lauderdale's miles of canals make it one of the top spots in Florida for boat tours.

Carrie B Boat Tour
(Map p160; ☎954-642-1601; www.carriebcruises.com; 440 N New River Dr E; tours adult/child $23/13; tours 11am, 1pm & 3pm) Hop aboard this replica 19th-century riverboat for a narrated 90-minute 'lifestyles of the rich and famous' tour of the ginormous mansions along the Intracoastal and New River. Tours depart from Las Olas at SE 5th Ave.

Gondola Man Boat Tour
(Map p160; ☎201-919-1999; www.gondolaman.com; SE 1st Ave; tour $150) Explore the 'Venice of America' with a romantic ride in an original Venetian gondola, accompanied by Italian music. The tour lasts roughly 75 minutes and takes you past the homes of the rich and famous.

Fort Lauderdale

Sights
1 Las Olas Riverfront B2
2 Museum of Art B2
3 Riverwalk B2

Activities, Courses & Tours
4 Carrie B D2
5 Gondola Man B2

Eating
6 Floridian F2
7 Gran Forno D2

Drinking & Nightlife
8 Stache A1

Entertainment
9 Cinema Paradiso D3

Sleeping

The splashiest (and priciest) hotels are found along the beach. Go inland and you'll discover wonderful inns with Old Florida charm.

Pillars B&B **$$$**
(Map p162; ☎954-467-9639; www.pillarshotel.com; 111 N Birch Rd; r $199-569; P) From the harp in the sitting area to the private balconies and the intimate prearranged dinners for two, this tiny boutique B&B radiates hushed good taste and is often booked months in advance. A block from the beach, it faces one of the best sunsets in town.

Pineapple Point Guesthouse **$$$**
(☎888-844-7295; www.pineapplepoint.com; 315 NE 16th Tce; r $298, ste $429-449; P) Tucked away in a quiet residential neighborhood, this guesthouse caters exclusively to a loyal gay male clientele. Suites and apartments are bright and beachy, all clustered around a handful of pools, hot tubs and tree-shaded sitting areas. Daily happy hours ensure mingling, and the super-friendly staff know all the best restaurants and gay bars in town. Located six blocks north of E Las Olas Blvd, east off SE 16th Ave.

Alhambra Beach Resort Hotel **$$**
(Map p162; ☎954-525-7601; www.alhambrabeachresort.com; 3021 Alhambra St; r $119-199;

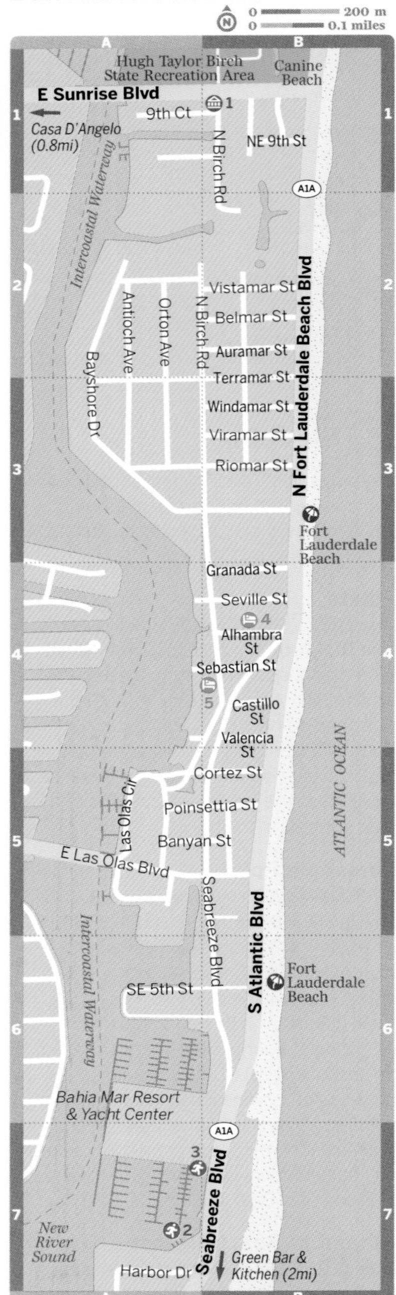

Fort Lauderdale Beach

Sights

Activities, Courses & Tours

Sleeping

P ❄ ☎ ≈) Beloved for its reasonable prices and warm-hearted owners, this charming 1930s-era inn has modest-but-immaculate rooms and suites painted in cheerful buttercup yellow, and a pleasant pool deck amid a manicured garden of palms and hibiscus. A gate adds a private feel, though the beach is only half a block away. Lots of return-guests means the place books up quickly.

Island Sands Inn B&B $$

(954-990-6499; www.islandsandsinn.com; 2409 NE 7th Ave, Wilton Manors; r $129-209; P ❄ ☎ ≈) It's hard to say whether it's the ultrathick beach towels, the luxurious bed and bedding, the thoughtful attention to details (tissues, bath products, mini-bar, microwave – you name it, they've thought about it) or the utterly unpretentious *ease* of the place that makes Island Sands Inn so comfortable and accommodating.

Eating

Fort Lauderdale's got a great food scene; Las Olas Blvd in downtown Fort Lauderdale has the bulk of nicer spots.

Gran Forno Italian $

(Map p160; http://gran-forno.com; 1235 E Las Olas Blvd; mains $6-12; 7am-6pm Tue-Sun) This delightfully old-school Milanese-style bakery and cafe is the best lunch spot in downtown Fort Lauderdale: warm crusty pastries, bubbling pizzas, and fat golden loaves of ciabatta, sliced and stuffed with ham, roast peppers, pesto and other delicacies.

Floridian Diner $

(Map p160; 954-463-4041; 1410 E Las Olas Blvd; mains $5-12; 5:30-10pm Tue-Sun) 'The

Flo' satisfies with good diner food including outstanding breakfasts served round the clock. A 1930s classic diner, it keeps up with the times by offering free wi-fi.

Green Bar & Kitchen Vegan **$$**

(☎954-533-7507; www.greenbarkitchen.com; 1075 SE 17th St; mains $8-14; ⊙11am-9pm Mon-Sat, 9am-3pm Sun;) Discover bright flavors and innovative dishes at this cult vegan eatery. Instead of pasta-layered lasagna, slithers of zucchini are layered with macadamia ricotta and sundried tomatoes. Almond milk replaces dairy in cold-pressed fruit smoothies, and the delectable cashew cup gives Reese's a run for its money. To reach it from the beach continue south on A1A and cross the Intracoastal Waterway to Southport. After two miles turn right into the shopping mall.

Rustic Inn Seafood **$$**

(☎954-584-1637; www.rusticinn.com; 4331 Ravenswood Rd; mains $9.50-30; ⊙11:30am-10:30pm Mon-Sat, noon-9:30pm Sun) Hungry locals at this messy, noisy crab house use wooden mallets at long, newspaper-covered tables to get at the Dungeness, blue and golden crabs drenched in garlic. The Inn is located on the Dania Cut-Off Canal on the west side of the airport. To reach it take I-95 S and exit 23 onto Ravenswood Rd.

Casa D'Angelo Italian **$$$**

(☎954-564-1234; http://casa-d-angelo.com; 1201 N Federal Hwy; mains $25-50; ⊙5:30-10:30pm) Chef Angelo Elia presides over an impressive kitchen specializing in Tuscan and southern Italian dishes, many handed down by his mother. Seasonality and quality translate into intense flavors and delightful textures: the sunburst taste of just-ripe tomatoes, peppery arugula, silken sea bass and surprisingly spicy cinnamon gelato. The restaurant stocks one of the finest wine lists in the state. The restaurant sits canal-side on North Federal Hwy, 1.4 miles north of East Sunrise Blvd.

Eduardo de San Angel Mexican **$$$**

(☎954-772-4731; www.eduardodesanangel.com; 2822 E Commercial Blvd; mains $24-34;

Local Knowledge

Fort Lauderdale Don't Miss List

ANDREA RICHARD IS AN EDITOR, AUTHOR AND NATIVE OF FORT LAUDERDALE.

1 **BONNETT HOUSE**
Bonnet House (p160) and gardens is a historical oasis of art, nature and eclectic architecture. The estate, which boasts rooms portraying different architecture styles, was built in 1920. It sits atop 35 acres of preserved land and gardens composed of Fort Lauderdale's native ecosystem and foreign plants.

2 **LASER WOLF**
Excellent Laser Wolf (p164) is operated and owned by natives. The space has a courtyard where indie bands perform, and an extensive menu of craft brews, sake and wine. A 'no jerks' policy caters to Lauderdale's artsy, intellectual folks.

3 **HIMMARSHEE NIGHTLIFE DISTRICT**
Most nightlife districts in the US don't offer what Fort Lauderdale's Himmarshee does: bars that open until 4am and an open-container allowance. Yes, within the confines of Himmarshee, it is legal to bar-hop with an open container.

4 **LAUDERDALE-BY-THE-SEA/ SHIPWRECK SNORKEL TRAIL**
Quaint Lauderdale-by-the-Sea has a code restricting buildings to two stories. Aside from charming restaurants, bars and a sandy beach, what's truly worth visiting about this spot is an artificial reef built to resemble a shipwreck a short distance offshore.

5 **THE FLORIDIAN**
Whether late-night munchies or traditional breakfast cause your hunger pangs, 'The Flo' is there, 24/7. Located on chic Las Olas, The Floridian (p162) is anything but upscale. Ideal for people-watching – oddballs sometimes frequent here late nights.

⌚5:30am-10pm Mon-Sat) Dreamy upscale Mexican food full of romantic ingredients – squash blossoms! Chocolate-chili! Guava syrup! – served in a warmly elegant dining room full of Mexican folk art. The restaurant is located north of downtown, nearly in Lauderdale-by-the-Sea.

Drinking & Nightlife

The best variety of bars in Fort Lauderdale can be found in the **Himmarshee Nightlife District** area. These places run the gamut from mellow wine bars to more raucous frat-pack spots. The beach offers plenty of open-air boozing.

Stache Cocktail Bar
(Map p160; ☎954-449-1044; http://stacheftl.com; 109 SW 2nd Ave; ⌚5pm-4am) Stache is a sexy 1920s drinking den serving crafted cocktails and rocking a crossover classic rock/funk/soul/R&B blend. At weekends there's live music, dancing and burlesque. Dress up; this is where the cool cats come to play.

Laser Wolf Bar
(www.laserwolf.com; 901 Progresso Dr, Suite 101) We don't want to call Laser Wolf sophisticated, but its extensive booze menu and pop-art styling definitely attracts Fort Lauderdale's cerebral set. But they're a cerebral set that *loves* to party, so if this wolf is sophisticated, it knows how to let its hair down. To run with the pack, head 2 miles west along Sunrise Blvd before turning left onto NE 4th Ave, which merges with Progresso Dr.

Entertainment

Cinema Paradiso Cinema
(Map p160; ☎954-525-3456; www.fliff.com/Cinema_Paradiso; 503 SE 6th St) This funky church-turned-cinema offers plush velvet seats, film festival entries, independent and European films, and plenty of kid-friendly programs. It's a great rainy-day standby. Events and films are posted on its Facebook page.

Shopping

Fort Lauderdale Beach Blvd has T-shirt shops and sunglass huts, while Las Olas is lined with swanky boutiques and antiques shops.

Swap Shop Market
(www.floridaswapshop.com; 3291 W Sunrise Blvd; ⌚9am-5pm) Perhaps the most fun shopping in town, the state's biggest flea market has acres of stalls selling everything from underwear to antique cookie jars to pink lawn flamingos, and a carnival atmosphere of mariachi music, hot-dog trucks and a 14-screen drive-in movie theater. The flea market is slightly northwest of downtown.

Gay & Lesbian Fort Lauderdale

Compared to South Beach, Fort Lauderdale is a little more rainbow-flag oriented and a little less exclusive. The city is home to several dozen gay bars and clubs, as many gay guesthouses, and a couple of way-gay residential areas including **Victoria Park**, the established gay hub just northeast of downtown Fort Lauderdale. A bit further north is **Wilton Manors**, more recently gay-gentrified and boasting endless nightlife options, including **Bill's Filling Station** (www.billsfillingstation.com; 2209 Wilton Dr; ⌚4pm-2am), a friendly 'bear' bar, and **Georgie's Alibi** (www.georgiesalibi.com; 2266 Wilton Dr; ⌚11-2am), which is best known for its Wednesday comedy night with Cashetta, a fabulous female impersonator.

For more information, see www.gayftlauderdale.com and the glossy weekly rag *Hot Spots* (www.hotspotsmagazine.com).

CHRIS GUG/ALAMY ©

Don't Miss
Shipwreck Snorkel Trail

Head to Datura Ave in Lauderdale-by-the-Sea (it intersects N Ocean Blvd and El Mar Dr), then go east till you hit water. Now head *under* water and you'll find the Shipwreck Snorkel Trail, an artificial reef that has been designed to resemble a sunken Spanish galleon. There are over 300 recorded species of fish here, and the area is regarded as having some of the best underwater wildlife viewing in the Western Atlantic Ocean. With a pair of flippers and a snorkel or some SUBA gear (easily rented by businesses within walking distance of Datura), you can live out your underwater archaeology fantasies; keep an eye out for an authentic anchor and replica cannons.

Information

Convention & Visitors Bureau (Map p160; ☎954-765-4466; www.sunny.org; 100 E Broward Blvd, Suite 200; ⏰8:30-5pm Mon-Fri) Has an excellent array of visitor information about the greater Fort Lauderdale region.

Getting There & Away

Air

Fort Lauderdale-Hollywood International Airport (FLL; ☎866-435-9355; www.broward.org/airport; 320 Terminal Dr) A viable gateway airport to the Florida region, located 21 miles north of Downtown Miami.

Boat

The Port Everglades Authority (www.porteverglades.org) runs the enormous Port Everglades cruise port. From the port, walk to SE 17th St and take bus 40 to the beach or to Broward Central Terminal.

Train

Tri-Rail (☎954-783-6030; www.tri-rail.com; 6151 N Andrews Ave) Tri-Rail runs between Miami and Fort Lauderdale (one way $5, 45 minutes). A feeder system of buses has connections at no charge. Free parking is provided at most stations.

JEFF GREENBERG/ALAMY ©

Don't Miss
Whiskey Creek

Once an important stop for Prohibition-era bootleggers, lush Whiskey Creek (get it?), nestled inside John U Lloyd Beach State Park, is now a kayaking hot spot. The dense mangrove-lined route, roughly 2.5 miles long, is shallow, calm, ideal for beginners and just 15 minutes from downtown Dania.

THINGS YOU NEED TO KNOW

John U Lloyd Beach State Park www.floridastateparks.org/lloydbeach; 6503 North Ocean Dr, Dania Beach; per vehicle/cyclist $6/2; 8am-sundown

Getting Around

Broward County Transit (BCT; www.broward.org/bct; single fare/day pass $1.75/4) operates between downtown, the beach and Port Everglades.

From **Broward Central Terminal** (Map p160; 101 NW 1st Ave), take bus 11 to upper Fort Lauderdale Beach and Lauderdale-by-the-Sea; bus 4 to Port Everglades; and bus 40 to 17th St and the beaches.

Water Taxi (954-467-6677; www.watertaxi.com; all-day pass adult/child $22/11) travels the canals and waterways between 17th St to the south, Atlantic Blvd/Pompano Beach to the north, the Riverfront to the west and the Atlantic Ocean to the east.

Sun Trolley (www.suntrolley.com; single fare/day pass $1/3) Runs between Las Olas and the beaches between 9:30am and 6:30pm Friday to Monday.

Hollywood & Dania Beach

954 / POP HOLLYWOOD 143,000 / POP DANIA BEACH 28,000

Hollywood is a bustling, varied waterfront town that positions itself as a gateway to Fort Lauderdale. Dania (*dane*-ya) remains a mellow little town, with a fledgling antiques district and a breezy fishing pier.

Sights & Activities

Hollywood Beach & Broadwalk — Beach

Reminiscent of California's famed Venice Beach, this beach and adjacent promenade teem with scantily clad Rollerbladers and fanny-pack-wearing tourists. The Broadwalk itself is a 2.2-mile, six-person-wide path, extending from pretty **North Beach Park** (3601 N Ocean Dr; 11am-5pm) FREE, where the route is lined with seagrapes, all the way to **South Surf Road**. It's regularly clogged with skaters, strollers and entire families pedaling enormous group bikes. The latter like to stop at **Charnow Park** (300 Garfield St), where there's shaded seating and a popular interactive fountain.

Eating & Drinking

Give most of the Boardwalk restaurants a miss – they're overpriced, overcrowded and mediocre. There are better eats to be found along Ocean Dr, or inland in downtown Hollywood.

Tarks of Dania Beach — Seafood $

(954-925-8275; www.tarks.com; 1317 S Federal Hwy, Dania Beach; mains $2-9) This jaunty clam stand has been going strong since 1966 and is now a local landmark. Most of the tiny interior is taken up with the cooking counter, where they broil, fry and steam daily specials.

Taco Beach Shack — Mexican $

(www.tacobeachshack.com; 334 Arizona St, Hollywood; tacos $4-10; 11:30am-10pm Mon-Thu, to midnight Fri & Sat) Hipsters and hangers-on lounge around on wicker chaises at this open-air taqueria. The menu has a very of-the-moment mix of ethnic flavors – try the Korean short rib and kimchi tacos. You'll feel cooler just by eating one.

Jaxson's Ice Cream Parlor — Ice Cream $

(www.jaxsonsicecream.com; 128 S Federal Hwy, Dania; ice cream from $4; 11:30am-11pm Sun-Thu, to midnight Fri & Sat;) Established in 1956, this place has 80-plus flavors of homemade ice cream.

Getting There & Around

An old-fashioned trolley travels between downtown Hollywood and the beach from 10am to 10pm Wednesday through Sunday. Fares are $1; bright-colored signs mark the stops.

Parking at the beach in Hollywood is hellacious – if you can't find on-street parking, try the parking deck on Johnson St.

CONCH REPUBLIC

Miami & the Keys

You're still technically in the USA. But you're also somewhere…different.

Florida's edge is the state at her most cosmopolitan and endearingly funky. Spanish and Haitian Creole are as common as English. Miami's nickname is the 'Magic City,' as if to underscore it's shimmering beauty, which stretches from the sexy sand and deco design of South Beach to the Mediterranean mansions of Coral Gables; from the glass skyline of Downtown to quiet, family-friendly beaches on Key Biscayne.

Meanwhile, in Key West, fishermen on brightly painted boats and artists who dress up as gossamer fairies sit on planning committees with doctors and police. And in the other 'Keys' (islands), villages are tucked away, connected by causeway, bridge and boat, not boulevards.

There's a different rhythm in the air here. Listen to the beat of Miami salsa and the Keys Caribbean parades, and get ready to dance.

Nightlife, Key West (p229)

Miami & the Keys

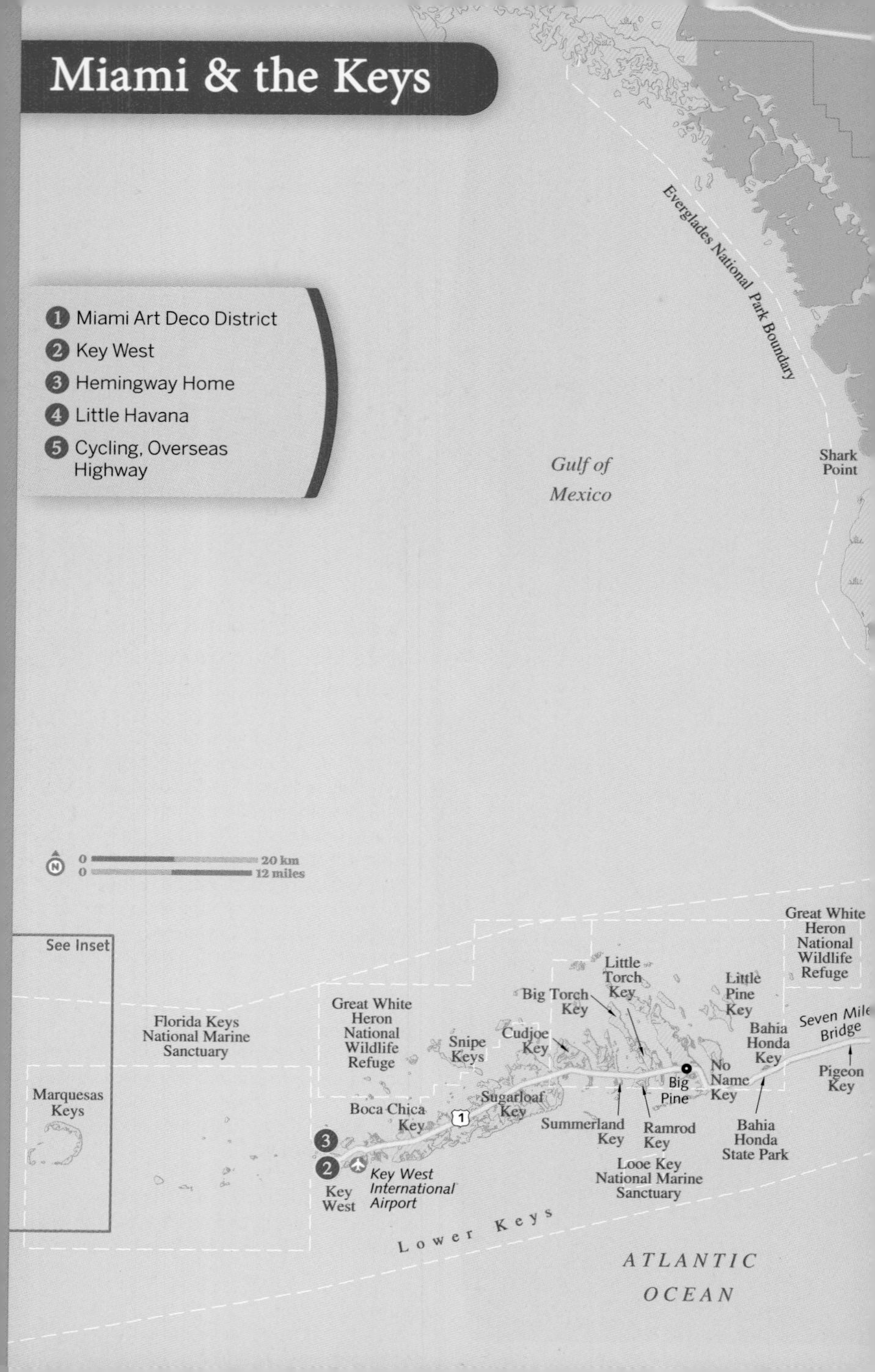

1. Miami Art Deco District
2. Key West
3. Hemingway Home
4. Little Havana
5. Cycling, Overseas Highway

Everglades National Park Boundary

Shark Point

Gulf of Mexico

See Inset

Marquesas Keys

Florida Keys National Marine Sanctuary

Great White Heron National Wildlife Refuge

Snipe Keys

Cudjoe Key

Big Torch Key

Little Torch Key

Little Pine Key

Great White Heron National Wildlife Refuge

Seven Mile Bridge

Pigeon Key

Bahia Honda Key

No Name Key

Big Pine

Sugarloaf Key

Boca Chica Key

1

3

2

Key West

Key West International Airport

Summerland Key

Ramrod Key

Bahia Honda State Park

Looe Key National Marine Sanctuary

Lower Keys

ATLANTIC OCEAN

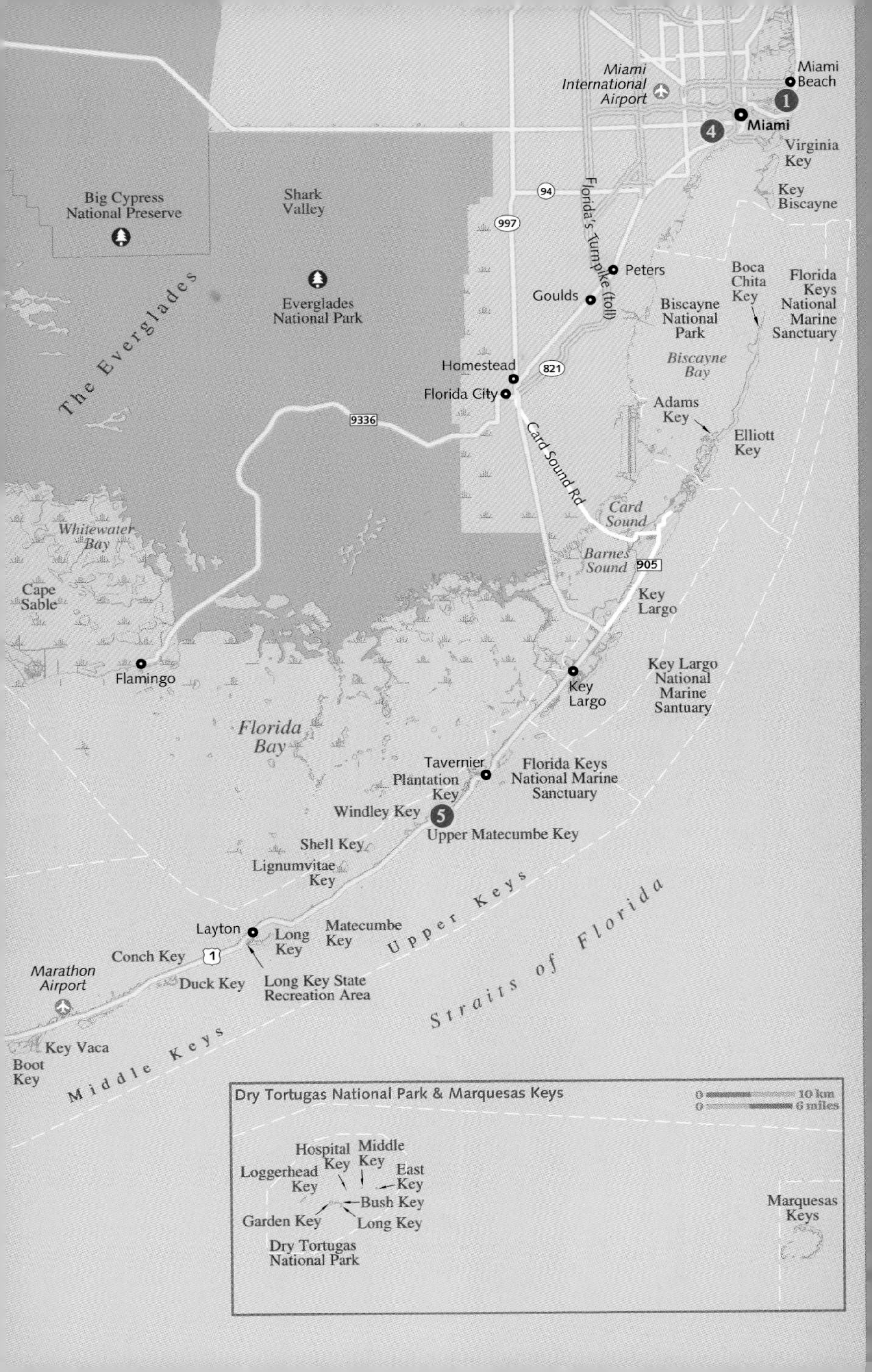

Miami Beach
Miami International Airport
Miami
Virginia Key
Key Biscayne
Big Cypress National Preserve
Shark Valley
94
997
Florida's Turnpike (toll)
Peters
Goulds
Boca Chita Key
Florida Keys National Marine Sanctuary
Biscayne National Park
Biscayne Bay
The Everglades
Everglades National Park
Homestead
821
Florida City
9336
Card Sound Rd
Adams Key
Elliott Key
Card Sound
Whitewater Bay
Barnes Sound
905
Cape Sable
Key Largo
Flamingo
Key Largo
Key Largo National Marine Santuary
Florida Bay
Tavernier
Plantation Key
Florida Keys National Marine Sanctuary
Windley Key
Upper Matecumbe Key
Shell Key
Lignumvitae Key
Upper Keys
Straits of Florida
Layton
Long Key
Matecumbe Key
Conch Key
1
Marathon Airport
Duck Key
Long Key State Recreation Area
Key Vaca
Boot Key
Middle Keys
Dry Tortugas National Park & Marquesas Keys
0 10 km
0 6 miles
Hospital Key
Middle Key
Loggerhead Key
East Key
Bush Key
Garden Key
Long Key
Dry Tortugas National Park
Marquesas Keys

Miami & the Keys' Highlights

Miami Art Deco Historic District

Miami's indigenous deco design, which melds an early 20th century conception of the future with pastel shades and beach-y brightness, is without a doubt the architectural highlight of South Florida. Greater Miami's deco can be found amid hotels, housing projects, restaurants bars and other assorted buildings. The area can easily be explored by foot or on a bicycle. Mainly concentrated in South Beach. Art Deco hotels, Miami

1

2

Key West

This Caribbean-colonial gem marks the very end of the road, which in this case means the Overseas Highway, that sea-bound span that arches across the Florida Keys. You'll likely spend most of your time exploring Old Town, where there are rows and rows of preserved historical homes, cute cafes, fine restaurants and enough bars to keep several universities partying for a year.

Colonial cottages, Key West

PETER PTSCHELINZEW/GETTY IMAGES ©

Hemingway House

3

Besides being the digs of one of the masters of 20th-century fiction and arguably the father of literary modernism, the Hemingway Home is also a great example of Keys' Caribbean colonial architecture. Note the six-toed cats that wander about, the author's writing desk, photos of Papa throughout his storied life, and the pool that broke Hemingway's bank, where the author famously left behind his 'last penny.'

AURORA PHOTOS / ALAMY ©

Little Havana

While it's officially the heart of South Florida's Cuban community, the fact is Latin South Florida extends far beyond the boundaries of Little Havana. With that said, much of the key arts, food, social scene and history of Miami's Cubans can be found here. Máximo Gómez Park is a fantastically atmospheric space where older Caribbean men battle it out on the chess board and dominoes table. Dominoes, Máximo Gómez Park (p195)

Overseas Highway Cycling

The sea salt breeze, the presence of two beautiful bodies of water – one dark blue, the other a shimmering turquoise – a wealth of bridges, mangrove orchards, swaying palmettos and the flat topography of the Keys make the Overseas Hwy one of the finest places in Florida for getting on board two wheels. Nothing compliments a road trip like the sea extending to either horizon.

Miami & the Keys' Best...

Cultural Encounters

- **Wynwood** Studio central and arts walks. (p191)
- **New World Center** Stunning stage and concert hall. (p183)
- **Adrienne Arsht Center for the Performing Arts** Miami's premier performing-arts venue. (p187)
- **Viernes Culturales** Little Havana's Friday fiesta. (p197)
- **Pérez Art Museum Miami** Art of the Americas overlooking Biscyane Bay. (p190)

Foodie Finds

- **Key West** Great food variety on this small island. (p228)
- **South Beach** Four-star elegance and tiny cafes. (p209)
- **Wynwood** The best of new Miami cuisine. (p211)
- **Coral Gables** A magnet for foodies. (p213)
- **Little Havana** Cuban cuisine done right. (p212)

When Night Falls...

- **Green Parrot** Key West's locals' hideaway, with crazy art and live music. (p231)
- **Coconut Grove** Down-to-earth, student-y scene. (p215)
- **Design District** New bars, clubs and concert halls in Miami's fastest-growing 'hood. (p214)
- **Islamorada** Beach bars and sunsets. (p219)
- **South Beach** Chic clubs, grungy dives and neighborhood pubs. (p213)

Family-Friendly Fun

- **Bill Baggs Cape Florida State Park** Short trails, family-friendly beach and nature center. (p193)
- **Key West** Historic homes and walkable shady streets. (p223)
- **Crane Point Museum** A walkable exploration of the environment of the Florida Keys. (p220)
- **Marjory Stoneman Douglas Biscayne Nature Center** Hands-on introduction to South Floridian ecology. (p193)
- **Metrozoo** Playful otters gambol next to mysterious monitor lizards. (p198)

Left: Pérez Art Museum Miami (p190);
Above: Art Deco buildings, Ocean Drive (p183)

Need to Know

RESOURCES

- **Miami & the Beaches** (www.miamiandbeaches.com) Official tourism website for Miami and Miami Beach.
- **Florida Keys** (www.fla-keys.com) Official online resource for the Florida Keys and Key West.
- **Art of Miami** (http://artofmiami.com/) Comprehensive Miami gallery and arts walking guide.

ADVANCE PLANNING

- **Hotels** Book at least a month in advance if visiting during winter, and a week in advance even in low season.
- **Restaurants** Make reservations a week before at pricier places.
- **Excursions** Boat trips, walking tours and the like can usually be booked the day before.
- **Traffic** If driving to the Keys, keep in mind one accident can jam the entire Overseas Highway.

GETTING AROUND

- **Car** Convenient for distances, but annoying for parking. Book rentals early for the best rates.
- **Bicycle** Highly recommended for Key West and Miami Beach. Other areas are flat, but bicycle infrastructure isn't nearly as well developed.
- **Bus** Miami has a decent city bus system; Key West's is easier to navigate. The Keys are connected to the mainland by commuter buses.
- **Train** The Tri-Rail system connects Miami to its suburbs.

BE FOREWARNED

- **Traffic** Miami traffic is some of the worst in Florida. If you have a good GPS system, you can use backroads to avoid the inevitable jams on the main highways.
- **Crime** Avoid Overtown and Downtown Miami at night.
- **Sun** Even on cloudy days you can get badly burnt.
- **Language** In much of Miami, especially Little Havana and Downtown, it really helps to know a little Spanish.

Miami & the Keys Itineraries

From the mangrove-fringed beaches of the Florida Keys to the shiny towers of Miami, from dark-blue oceans to aquamarine lagoons in Florida Bay, we take in some of the best schedules for exploring South Florida.

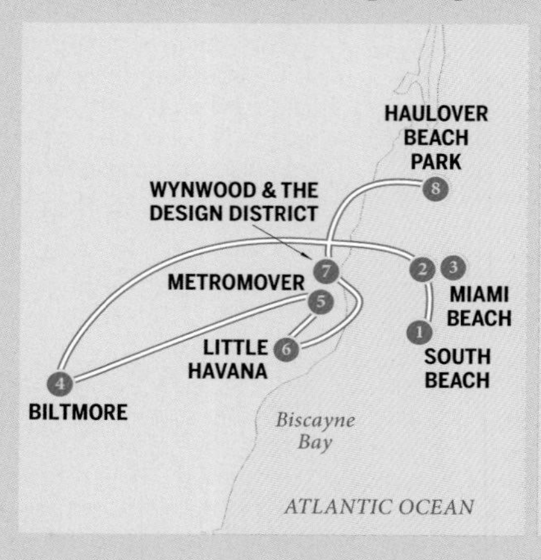

BEST OF MIAMI

SOUTH BEACH TO NORTH BEACH

Start your days exploring ❶ **South Beach**, making sure to stop by the headquarters of the ❷ **Miami Design & Preservation League** (MDPL), the facades of the hotels on Ocean Dr and the exhibits that put local architecture in context at the ❸ **Wolfsonian-FIU Museum**. On your second day in the city, head to Coral Gables to take in the opulence of the ❹ **Biltmore** and go shopping along the Miracle Mile.

On your third day in the city take the ❺ **Metromover**, a free commuter train, around town to get a great view of the Miami skyline. When you're done, you're not far from 8th St, better known as Calle Ocho, in ❻ **Little Havana**. On the final day, take in some of the art galleries of ❼ **Wynwood and the Design District**, then relax on the quiet beaches in North Miami Beach. We like ❽ **Haulover Beach Park** – just keep in mind one of its beaches is a nude beach!

THE KEYS QUEST

KEY LARGO TO KEY WEST

In Key Largo, spend a day snorkeling, diving or on board a glass-bottom boat at the lovely ❶ **John Pennekamp Coral Reef State Park**. For dinner, make sure to have a fish taco at the ❷ **Key Largo Conch House**. The next day, drive down to Islamorada, making sure to see the giant tarpon fish at ❸ **Robbie's Marina**. Continue to Marathon, where there's excellent lobster reubens at ❹ **Keys Fisheries**, and have a walk around pretty ❺ **Crane Point**.

On your third day, you'll make the one-hour drive to Key West, where you can take a tour of the ❻ **Hemingway Home** and potter around leafy Old Town. Make sure to head to ❼ **Mallory Square** for the sunset celebrations. Enjoy a night out on ❽ **Duvall St** or have an elegant dinner at ❾ **Café Sole**.

Mallory Square (p223)

JIM WEST/ALAMY ©

Discover Miami & the Keys

At a Glance

- **Miami** (p178) Startling contrasts, sparkling skylines.
- **Miami Beach** (p185) White sands hug a celebrity-studded shoreline.
- **The Keys** (p218) A smattering of quirky islands that march to their own beat.
- **Key West** (p223) A historical, funky fantasy town at the end of the road.

Ocean Drive (p183), South Beach

RUSSELL KORD/ALAMY ©

MIAMI

☎305 / POP 362,500

Miami is so many things, but to most visitors it's glamour, condensed into urban form.

Well, the archaic definition of 'glamour' is a kind of spell that mystifies a victim. And they call Miami the Magic City. And it is mystifying. In its beauty, certainly: the clack of a model's high heels on Lincoln Rd; the teal sweep of Biscayne Bay, flowing cool into the wide South Florida sky; the blood-orange of the sunset setting the Downtown skyline aflame.

Then there's less conventional beauty: a Haitian dance party in the ghetto attended by University of Miami literature students, or a Venezuelan singing Metallica *en español* in a Coral Gables karaoke bar, or the passing *shalom/buenos días* traded between Orthodox Jews and Cuban exiles.

Miami is so many things. All glamorous, in every sense of the word. You could spend a fun lifetime trying to escape its spell.

When to Go

January to March Warm and dry, with lots of tourists, snowbirds from the northeast and Europeans.

April to June Not as muggy as deep summer, but lusher and greener than winter.

July to October Prices plummet, but when it's not as hot as an oven, there are storms: it's hurricane season.

Sights

Miami's major sights aren't concentrated in one neighborhood; there is something for everyone just about everywhere.

SOUTH BEACH

South Beach, the most iconic neighborhood in Greater Miami, encompasses the region south of 21st St in the city of Miami Beach.

Art Deco Historic District Neighborhood

(Map p180) South Beach's heart is its Art Deco Historic District, from 18th St and south along Ocean Dr and Collins Ave. It's ironic that in a city built on speculative real estate, the main engine for urban renewal was the preservation of a unique architectural heritage. See, all those beautiful hotels, with their tropical-Americana facades, scream 'Miami.' They screamed it so loud when they were preserved they gave this city a brand, and this neighborhood a new lease on life. Back in the day, South Beach was a ghetto of vagrants, druggies and retirees. Then it became one of the largest areas in the USA on the National Register of Historic Places, and then it attracted models, photographers, hoteliers, chefs and...well, today it's a pastel medina of cruisers, Euro-fashionistas, the occasionally glimpsed celebrity and tourists from Middle America.

Your first stop here should be the Art Deco Welcome Center (p217), run by the **Miami Design Preservation League** (MDPL). To be honest, it's a bit of a tatty gift shop, but it's located in the old beach-patrol headquarters, one of the best deco buildings out there. You can book excellent $20 guided walking tours (plus audio and private tours), which are some of the best introductions to the layout and history of South Beach on offer. Tours depart at 10:30am daily, except on Thursday when they leave at 6:30pm. No advance reservations required; just show up and smile. Call ahead for information on walking tours of Lincoln Rd and Collins Park, the area that encompasses upper South Beach.

Wolfsonian-FIU Museum

(Map p180; ☎305-531-1001; www.wolfsonian.org; 1001 Washington Ave; adult/child 6-12 $7/5; ⏲noon-6pm Thu & Sat-Tue, to 9pm Fri) Visit

Local Knowledge

Miami Beach Don't Miss List

BY JEFF DONNELLY, PUBLIC HISTORIAN & TOUR GUIDE, MIAMI DESIGN & PRESERVATION LEAGUE

1 ART DECO WELCOME CENTER
Come here for information on everything to do and see in the art deco district. Daily Miami Design Preservation League (MDPL) walking tours start here. The MDPL website has information about MDPL-sponsored festivals, film and lecture series and exhibitions.

2 WOLFSONIAN-FIU MUSEUM
Mickey Wolfson donated his collection of art, artifacts, and day-to-day materials from the 1885–1945 period. A tour of the Wolfsonian's permanent and touring exhibits makes an excellent counterpoint to the District's buildings, which document the same transition from romanticism to modernism.

3 MAC'S CLUB DEUCE
Don't be put off by Mac's Club Deuce (p213) listing in Playboy's *Guide to America's Greatest Bars*. The Deuce, which has been around since 1926 and survived Prohibition, will always resist trendiness.

4 TAP TAP
In Haiti, the jitney buses that navigate the back roads are called tap-taps. Food here (p208) is simple but good, and Haitian art fills tabletops and walls. Many artists were exiles who supported former President Aristide's Fanmi Lavalas party, and previous owners gave them employment both as waitstaff and artists.

5 PARK CENTRAL HOTEL
This 1937 art-deco building was fully restored 50 years later in 1987 at the beginning of the South Beach Renaissance. Listed with the National Trust for Historic Preservation among the Historic Hotels of America, the Park Central preserves and presents the work of both Henry Hohauser and Leonard Horowitz.

South Beach

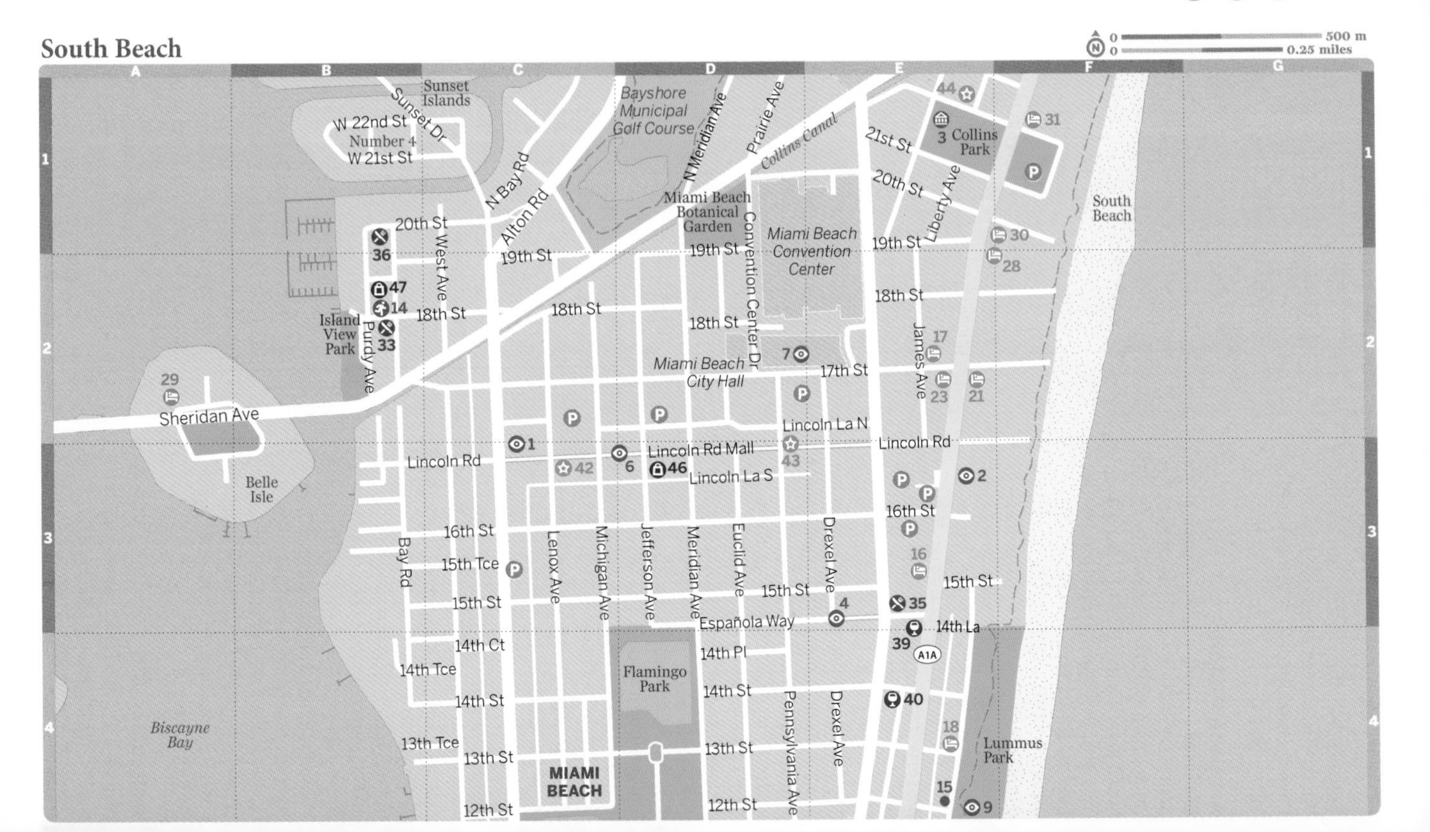
0 500 m
0 0.25 miles
A
B
C
D
E
F
G
1
2
3
4
Sunset Islands
Sunset Dr
W 22nd St
Number 4
W 21st St
N Bay Rd
Alton Rd
Bayshore Municipal Golf Course
N Meridian Ave
Prairie Ave
Collins Canal
Miami Beach Botanical Garden
Convention Center Dr
Miami Beach Convention Center
21st St
20th St
19th St
18th St
17th St
Liberty Ave
James Ave
Collins Park
South Beach
West Ave
Purdy Ave
Island View Park
Sheridan Ave
Belle Isle
Miami Beach City Hall
Lincoln Rd
Lincoln Rd Mall
Lincoln La N
Lincoln La S
16th St
15th Tce
15th St
Española Way
14th La
14th Ct
14th Pl
14th Tce
14th St
13th Tce
13th St
12th St
Bay Rd
Lenox Ave
Michigan Ave
Jefferson Ave
Meridian Ave
Euclid Ave
Pennsylvania Ave
Drexel Ave
Flamingo Park
MIAMI BEACH
Lummus Park
Biscayne Bay
A1A
1
2
3
4
6
7
9
14
15
16
17
18
21
23
28
29
30
31
33
35
36
39
40
42
43
44
46
47

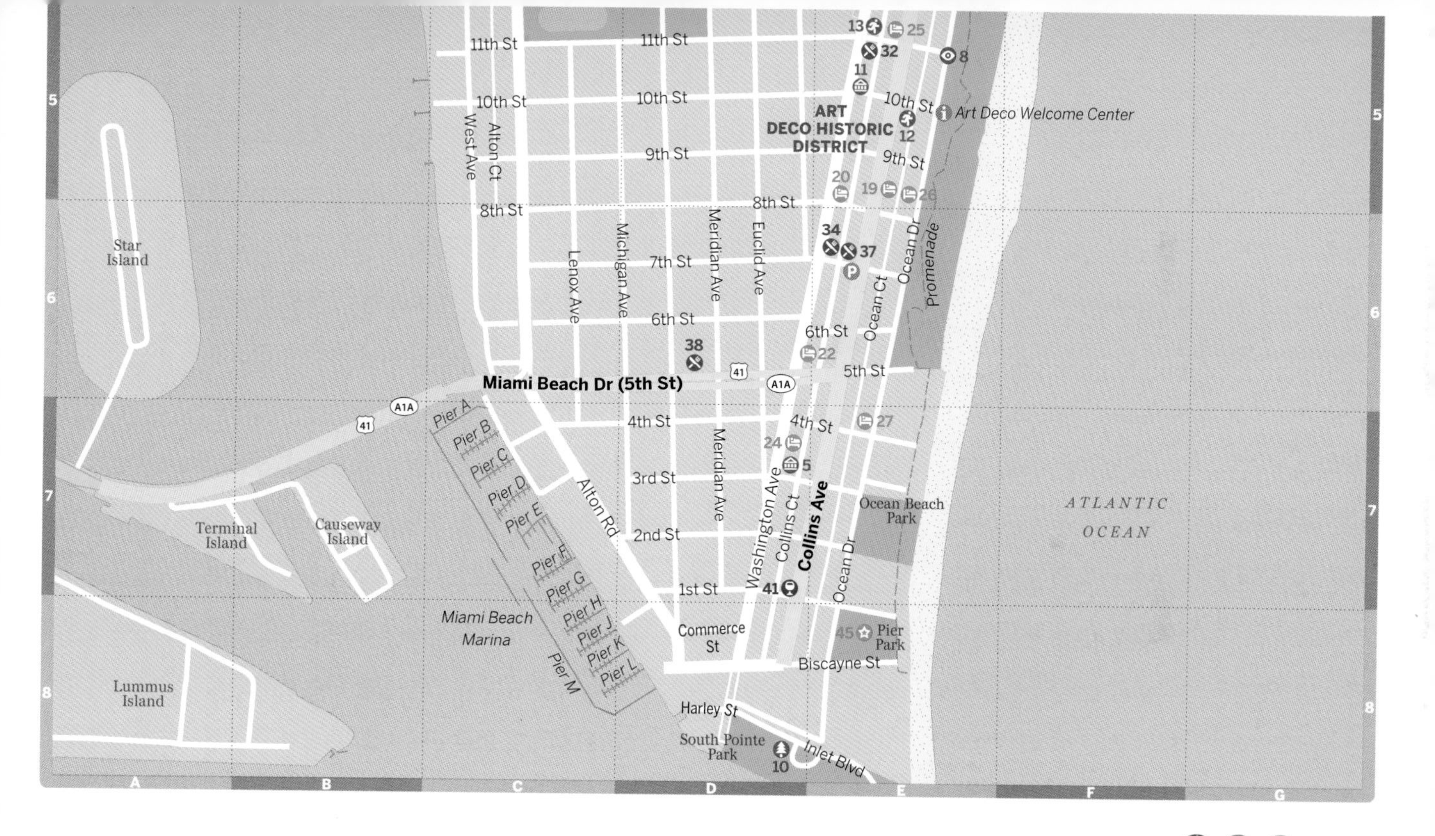
11th St
10th St
9th St
8th St
7th St
6th St
5th St
4th St
3rd St
2nd St
1st St
West Ave
Alton Ct
Lenox Ave
Michigan Ave
Meridian Ave
Euclid Ave
Washington Ave
Collins Ct
Collins Ave
Ocean Ct
Ocean Dr
Promenade
Alton Rd
Miami Beach Dr (5th St)
Commerce St
Biscayne St
Harley St
Inlet Blvd
ART
DECO HISTORIC
DISTRICT
Art Deco Welcome Center
Ocean Beach Park
Pier Park
South Pointe Park
Miami Beach Marina
Pier A
Pier B
Pier C
Pier D
Pier E
Pier F
Pier G
Pier H
Pier J
Pier K
Pier L
Pier M
Star Island
Terminal Island
Causeway Island
Lummus Island
ATLANTIC
OCEAN
A1A
41
13
25
32
8
11
12
20
19
26
34
37
22
38
27
24
5
41
45
10
A
B
C
D
E
F
G
5
6
7
8

South Beach

Sights

1	1111 Lincoln Rd	C3
2	Art Deco Historic District	E3
3	Bass Museum of Art	E1
4	Española Way Promenade	E3
5	Jewish Museum of Florida	D7
6	Lincoln Road Mall	D3
7	New World Center	D2
8	Ocean Drive	E5
9	Promenade	E4
10	South Pointe Park	D8
11	Wolfsonian-FIU	E5

Activities, Courses & Tours

12	BikeAndRoll	E5
13	Bikram Yoga Miami Beach	E5
14	Green Monkey Yoga	B2
15	Miami Design Preservation League	E4

Sleeping

16	Aqua Hotel	E3
17	Cadet Hotel	E2
18	Cardozo Hotel	E4
19	Chesterfield Hotel	E5
20	Clinton Hotel	E5
21	Delano Hotel	E2
22	Fashionhaus	D6
23	Gale South Beach	E2
24	Hotel St Augustine	D7
25	Nash Hotel	E5
26	Pelican Hotel	E5
27	Sense South Beach	E7
28	Shore Club	E2
29	The Standard	A2
30	Townhouse Hotel	F1
31	W Hotel	F1

Eating

32	11th St Diner	E5
33	Burger & Beer Joint	B2
34	Grazie	E6
35	Osteria del Teatro	E3
36	Pubbelly	B1
37	Puerto Sagua	E6
38	Tap Tap	D6

Drinking & Nightlife

39	Kill Your Idol	E3
	Lost Weekend	(see 39)
40	Mac's Club Deuce Bar	E4
41	Room	D7

Entertainment

42	Colony Theater	C3
43	Lincoln Theatre	D3
44	Miami City Ballet	E1
	New World Symphony	(see 7)
45	Nikki Beach Club	E8

Shopping

46	Consign of the Times	D3
47	Metta Boutique	B2

this excellent design museum early in your stay to put the aesthetics of Miami Beach into fascinating context. It's one thing to see how wealth, leisure and the pursuit of beauty manifests in Miami Beach, it's another to understand the roots and shadings of local artistic movements. By chronicling the interior evolution of everyday life, the Wolfsonian reveals how these trends were architecturally manifested in SoBe's exterior deco. Which reminds us of the Wolfsonian's own noteworthy facade – remember the Gothic-futurist apartment-complex-cum-temple-of-evil in *Ghostbusters*? Well, this imposing structure, with its grandiose 'frozen fountain' and lion-head-studded grand elevator, could serve as a stand-in for that set.

Lincoln Road Mall — Road

(Map p180; farmers market 9am-6:30pm Sun)
Calling Lincoln Rd a mall, which many do, is like calling Big Ben a clock: it's technically accurate but misses the point. Yes, you can shop, and shop very well here. But this outdoor pedestrian thoroughfare between Alton Rd and Washington Ave is really about seeing and being seen; there are times when Lincoln feels less like a road and more like a runway. We wouldn't be surprised if you developed a slight crick in your neck from whipping around to check out all the fabulously gorgeous creatures that call 'the road' their natural environment. Carl Fisher, the father of Miami Beach, envisioned the road as a '5th Ave of the South.' Morris Lapidus, one of the founders of the loopy, neo-Baroque Miami Beach style, designed much of the mall, including several shady overhangs, waterfall structures and traffic barriers that look like the marbles a giant might play with. Other architectural icons of note include the **Lincoln Theatre (Map p180; 541 Lincoln Rd)**, designed by renowned theater and cinema architect Thomas W Lamb (now an H&M), and the wonderfully deco **Colony Theater (Map p180; 305-434-7091; www.colonytheatre**

miamibeach.com; 1040 Lincoln Rd). There's also an excellent **farmers market** and the **Antique & Collectible Market** (www.antiquecollectiblemarket.com; 8am-6pm, fortnightly 2nd Sun Oct-May), both held along Lincoln.

1111 Lincoln Rd Building

(Map p180; www.1111lincolnroad.com; P) The West Side of Lincoln Rd is anchored by what may be the most impressive parking garage you'll ever lay eyes on, a geometric pastiche of sharp angles, winding corridors and incongruous corners that looks like a lucid fantasy dreamed up by Pythagoras after a long night out. In fact, the building was designed by Swiss architecture firm Herzog & de Meuron, who describe the structure as 'all muscle without cloth.' Besides parking, 1111 Lincoln Rd is filled with retail shops and residential units.

New World Center Building

(Map p180; 305-673-3331; www.newworldcenter.com; 500 17th St; tours $5; tours 4pm Tue & Thu, noon Fri & Sat) Miami has a penchant for sumptuous performing-arts venues and the New World Center is certainly competing with the Arsht Center for most-impressive concert hall in the city. Designed by Frank Gehry, the Center rises majestically out of a manicured lawn just above Lincoln Rd, looking somewhat like a tissue box from the year 3000 with a glass facade; note the 'fluttering' stone waves that pop out of the exterior. The grounds form a 2½-acre public park; performances inside the center are projected to those outside via a 7000-sq-ft projection wall (like you're in the classiest drive-in movie theater in the universe). Inside, the folded layers of white walls feel somewhere between organic and origami. Tours are led by docents; call ahead to book, as space is limited.

Ocean Drive Road

(Map p180; from 1st to 11th St) This is the great cruising strip of Miami; an endless parade of classic cars, testosterone-sweating young men, peacocklike young women, street performers, vendors, those guys who yell unintelligible crap at everyone, celebrities pretending to be tourists, tourists who want to play celebrity, beautiful people, ugly people, people people and the best ribbon of art-deco preservation on the beach. Say 'Miami.' That image in your head? Probably Ocean Dr.

Miami for Children

Well really, it's Florida, folks; your kids will be catered to. Many of the attractions run toward animal experiences, starting with the Metrozoo (p198), a 740-acre zoo with plenty of natural habitats (thank you, tropical weather). Should your little ones like colorful animal shows, the outdoors and the smell of animal poo in all its myriad varieties, Miami shall not disappoint. Monkey Jungle (p199) acts as a habitat for endangered species and is everything you'd expect: screeching primates, covered pathways and a grand finale show of crab monkeys diving for fruit. Jungle Island (p199), on the other hand, tends to entertain with brilliant bird shows. Next door is the Miami Children's Museum (p200), an indoor playland where youngsters can try out the roles of TV anchor, banker and supermarket customer, among others.

For a natural, hands on eco-educational experience, take your kids to Crandon Park (p193) and the nearby Marjory Stoneman Douglas Biscayne Nature Center (p193). Crandon Park is simply a nice beach and a generally laid-back place for youngsters to stretch their legs, while the educational facilities at the Marjory Stoneman Douglas center are an excellent introduction to South Florida's unique environment.

WALTER BIBIKOW/GETTY IMAGES ©

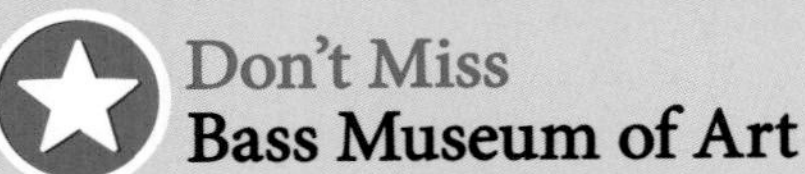

Don't Miss
Bass Museum of Art

The best art museum in Miami Beach has a playfully futuristic facade, a crisp interplay of lines and bright, white wall space – like an Orthodox church on a space-age Greek isle. All designed, by the way, in 1930 by Russell Pancoast (grandson of John A Collins, who lent his name to Collins Ave). The collection isn't shabby either: permanent highlights range from 16th-century European religious works to northern European and Renaissance paintings. The Bass forms one point of the **Collins Park Cultural Center** triangle, which also includes the three-story **Miami City Ballet** and the lovingly inviting **Miami Beach Regional Library**, which is a great place for free wi-fi.

THINGS YOU NEED TO KNOW

Map p180; ☎305-673-7530; www.bassmuseum.org; 2121 Park Ave; adult/child $8/6; ⏰noon-5pm Wed, Thu, Sat, Sun, to 9pm Fri

Promenade Promenade
(Map p180; Ocean Dr) This beach promenade, a wavy ribbon sandwiched between the beach and Ocean Dr, extends from 5th St to 15th St. A popular location for photo shoots, especially during crowd-free early mornings, it's also a breezy, palm-tree-lined conduit for in-line skaters, cyclists, volleyball players (there's a net at 11th St), dog walkers, yahoos, locals and tourists. The beach that it edges, called Lummus Park, sports six floridly colored lifeguard stands. There's a public bathroom at 11th St; the sinks are a popular place for homeless bathing.

Española Way Promenade Promenade
(Map p180; btwn 14th & 15th Sts) Española Way is an 'authentic' Spanish promenade...in the Florida theme-park spirit of authenticity. Oh, whatever; it's a lovely,

terra-cotta and cobbled arcade of rose-pink and Spanish-cream architecture, perfect for browsing art (it was an arts colony in the 1920s and today houses the studios of several local artists), window-shopping, people-watching and coffee-sipping. A craft market operates here on weekend afternoons.

South Pointe Park Park
(Map p180; 1 Washington Ave; ⌚sunrise-10pm) The very southern tip of Miami Beach has been converted into a lovely park, replete with manicured grass for lounging; views over a remarkably teal-colored fresh ocean; a restaurant; a refreshment stand; warm, scrubbed-stone walkways; and lots of folks who want to enjoy the great weather and views sans the South Beach strutting. That said, we saw two model photo shoots here in under an hour, so it's not all casual relaxation.

Jewish Museum of Florida Museum
(Map p180; ☎305-672-5044; http://jmof.fiu.edu; 301 Washington Ave; adult/student & senior $6/5, Sat admission free; ⌚10am-5pm Tue-Sun, closed Jewish holidays) Housed in a 1936 Orthodox synagogue that served Miami's first congregation, this small museum chronicles the rather large contribution Jews have made to the state of Florida. After all, it could be said that while Cubans made Miami, Jews made Miami Beach, both physically and culturally. Yet there were times when Jews were barred from the American Riviera they carved out of the sand, and this museum tells that story, along with some amusing anecdotes (like seashell Purim dresses).

NORTHERN MIAMI BEACH

Mid-Beach is located around the 40th streets, while North Beach extends from 70th St and above. Indian Creek waterway separates the luxury hotels and high-rise condos from the residential districts in the west.

Boardwalk Beach
(21st St to 46th St) What's trendy in beach-wear this season? Seventeenth-century Polish gabardine coats, apparently. There are plenty of skimpily dressed hotties on the Mid-Beach boardwalk, but there are also Orthodox Jews going about their business in the midst of gay joggers, strolling tourists and sunbathers. Nearby are numerous condo buildings occupied

Jewish Museum of Florida

RADHARC IMAGES/ALAMY ©

Northern Miami Beach

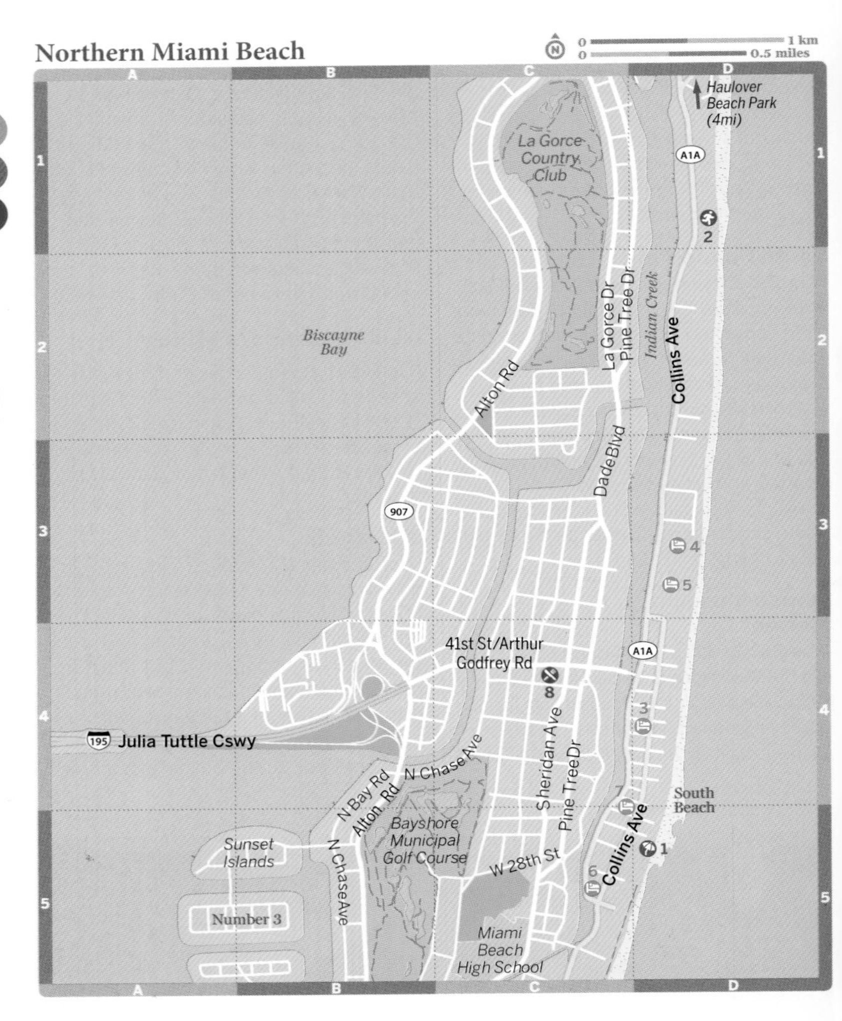

by middle-class Latinos and Jews, who walk their dogs and play with their kids here, giving the entire place a laid-back, real-world vibe that contrasts with the nonstop glamour of South Beach.

Haulover Beach Park Park

(www.miamidade.gov/parks/parks/haulover_park.asp; 10800 Collins Ave; per car weekday/weekend $5/7; sunrise-sunset; P) Where are all those tanned men in gold chains and Speedos going? That would be the clothing-optional beach in this 40-acre park hidden from condos, highways and prying eyes by vegetation. There's more to do here than get in the buff, though; most of the beach is 'normal' (there's even a dog park) and it's one of the nicer spots for sand in the area (also note the colorful deco-ish shower 'cones'). The park is located on Collins Ave about 4.5 miles north of 71st St.

Oleta River State Park Park

(www.floridastateparks.org/oletariver; 3400 NE 163rd St; per person/car $2/6; 8am-sunset;

Northern Miami Beach

P) Tequesta people were boating the Oleta River estuary as early as 500 BC, so you're just following in a long tradition if you canoe or kayak in this park. At almost 1000 acres, this is the largest urban park in the state and one of the best places in Miami to escape the maddening throng. Boat out to the local mangrove island, watch the eagles fly by, or just chill on the pretension-free beach. On-site Blue Moon Outdoor Center (p200) offers single kayaks ($18 per 1½ hours, $25 per three hours), tandem kayaks ($25.50 per 1½ hours, $40 per three hours) and bike rental ($18 per 1½ hours, $25 per three hours). The park is off 163rd St NE/FL-826 in Sunny Isles, about 8 miles north of North Miami Beach.

DOWNTOWN MIAMI

Adrienne Arsht Center for the Performing Arts — Building

(Map p188; www.arshtcenter.com; 1300 N Biscayne Blvd) The largest performing-arts center in Florida (and second largest, by area, in the USA) is Miami's beautiful, beloved baby. It is also a major component of downtown's urban equivalent of a face-lift and several regimens of Botox. Designed by Cesar Pelli (the man who brought you Kuala Lumpur's Petronas Towers), the center has two main components: the Ziff Ballet Opera House and Knight Concert Hall, which span both sides of Biscayne Blvd. The venues are connected by a thin, elegant pedestrian bridge, while inside the theaters there's a sense of ocean and land sculpted by wind; the rounded balconies rise up in spirals that resemble a sliced-open seashell. If you have the chance, catch a show here; the interior alone is easily a highlight of any Miami trip.

Metromover — Monorail

(www.miamidade.gov/transit/metromover.asp) This elevated, electric monorail is hardly big enough to serve the mass-transit needs of the city, and has become something of a tourist attraction. Whatever its virtues as a commuting tool, the Metromover is a really great (and free!) way to see central Miami from a height

Metromover
MITCHELL FUNK/GETTY IMAGES ©

Downtown Miami

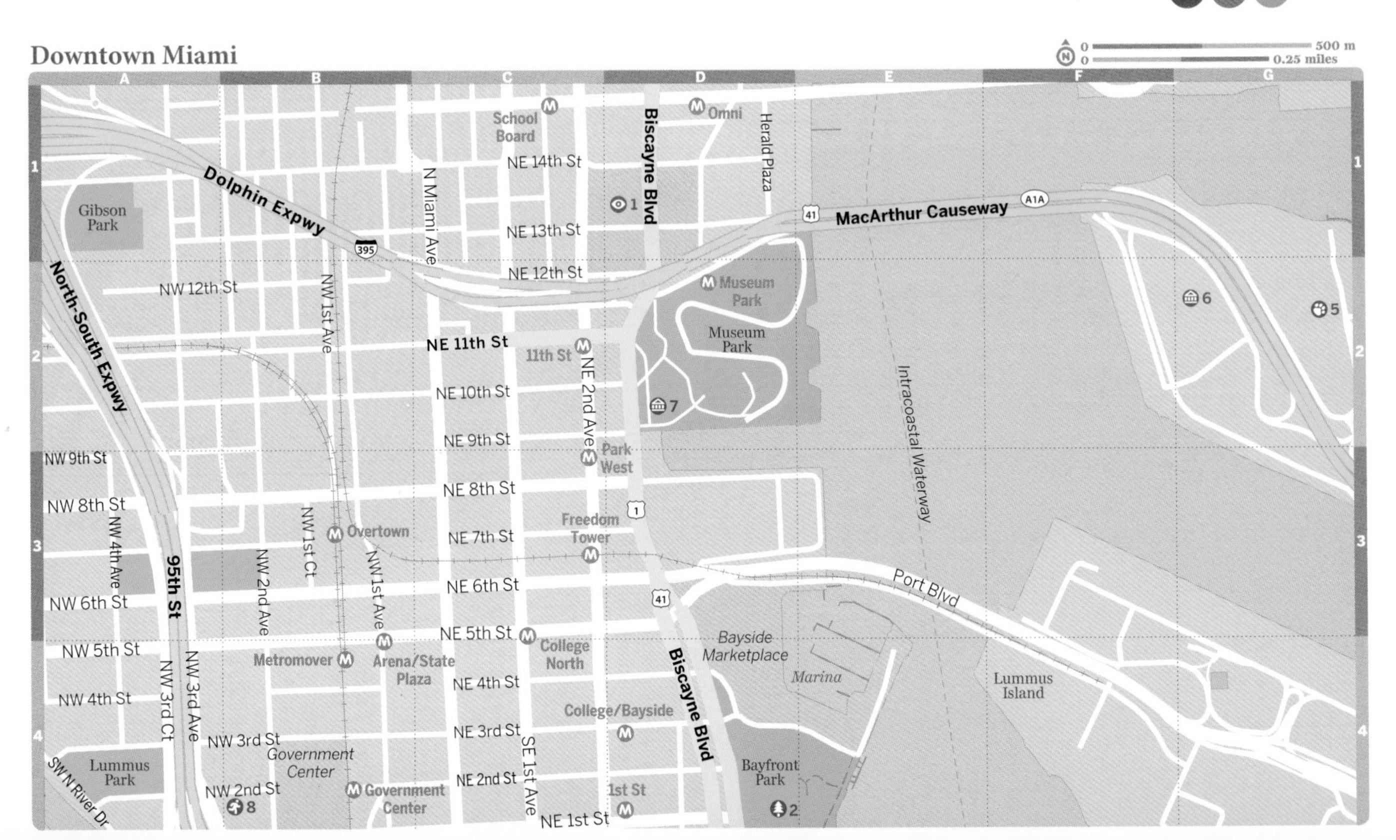

Miami-Dade Cultural Center
4
W Flagler St
E Flagler St
3
9
SW 4th Ave
968
SW 1st St
Miami Ave
SE 1st St
Chopin Plaza
SW 2nd St
SE 2nd St
Bayfront Park
Third St
Knight Center
SE 3rd St
SW 4th St
José Martí Riverfront Park
SW 3rd St
Riverwalk
Biscayne Blvd Way
10
Metrorail
Miami River
Brickell Ave Bridge
Miami River Bridges
5th St
SW 5th St
SE 5th St
SE 6th St
Brickell Park
SW 6th St
12
Brickell Key Dr
Biscayne Bay
SW 7th St
14
8th St
Brickell Key
SW 8th St (Calle Ocho)
SW 5th Ave
SW 1st Ave
SW 9th St
S Miami Ave
Brickell Ave
Brickell Bay Dr
SW 10th St
SW 3rd Ave
SW 2nd Ave
SW 1st Ct
Intracoastal Waterway
SW 11th St
13
10th St Promenade
Brickell
SW 12th St
SW 13th St (Coral Way)
Sailboards Miami (1.3mi); Vizcaya Museum & Gardens (1.4mi)
El Carajo (1.7mi)
Financial District
11

Downtown Miami

Sights
1 Adrienne Arsht Center for the Performing Arts ... D1
2 Bayfront Park ... D4
3 Gusman Center for the Performing Arts ... C5
4 HistoryMiami ... B5
5 Jungle Island ... G2
6 Miami Children's Museum ... G2
7 Pérez Art Museum Miami ... D2

Activities, Courses & Tours
8 Miami-Dade County Parks & Recreation Dept ... B4
9 Urban Tour Host ... D5

Sleeping
10 Epic ... D6
11 Four Seasons Miami ... C8

Eating
12 Bonding ... C6
13 Choices ... A8

Drinking & Nightlife
14 Blackbird Ordinary ... C7

Entertainment
Adrienne Arsht Center for the Performing Arts ... (see 1)
Gusman Center for the Performing Arts ... (see 3)

(which helps, given the skyscraper-canyon nature of downtown). Because it's gratis, Metromover has a reputation as a hangout for the homeless, but commuters use it as well.

Pérez Art Museum Miami — Museum

(PAMM; Map p188; ☎305-375-3000; www.pamm.org; 1103 Biscayne Blvd; $12/8 adult/seniors & students; ⏰10am-6pm Tue, Wed & Fri-Sun, to 9pm Thu) The Pérez can claim fine rotating exhibits that concentrate on post-WWII international art, but just as impressive are its location and exterior. This art institution inaugurated Museum Park, a patch of land that oversees the broad blue swathe of Biscyane Bay. Swiss architects Herzog & de Meuron designed the structure, which integrates tropical foliage, glass and metal – a melding of tropical vitality and fresh modernism that is a nice architectural analogy for Miami itself.

Bayfront Park — Park

(Map p188; www.bayfrontparkmiami.com; 301 N Biscayne Blvd) Few American parks can claim to front such a lovely stretch of turquoise (Biscayne Bay), but Miamians are lucky like that. Lots of office workers catch quick naps under the palms at a little beach that does you the favor of setting out 'sit and chill' chairs. Notable park features are two performance venues: the **Klipsch Amphitheater**, which boasts excellent views over Biscayne Bay, is a good spot for live-music shows, while the smaller 200-seat (lawn seating can accommodate 800 more) **Tina Hills Pavilion** hosts free springtime performances. Look north for the **JFK Torch of Friendship**, and a fountain recognizing the accomplishments of longtime US congressman Claude Pepper. There's a huge variety of activities here, including yoga classes, trapeze classes and, we hear, flying-trapeze yoga classes (seriously).

Noted artist and landscape architect Isamu Noguchi redesigned much of Bayfront Park in the 1980s and dotted the grounds with three **sculptures**. In the southwest corner is the **Challenger Memorial**, a monument designed for the astronauts killed in the 1986 space-shuttle explosion, built to resemble both the twisting helix of a human DNA chain and the shuttle itself. The **Light Tower** is a 40ft, somewhat abstract allusion to Japanese lanterns and moonlight over Miami. Our favorite is the **Mantra Slide**, a twisting spiral of marble that doubles as a playground piece for the kids.

Gusman Center for the Performing Arts — Building

(Map p188; ☎305-374-2444; www.gusmancenter.org; 174 E Flagler St) Miami loves modern, but the Olympia Theater at the Gusman Center for the Performing Arts is vintage-classic beautiful. The ceiling, which features 246 twinkling stars and clouds cast over an indigo-deep night, frosted with classical Greek sculpture and Vienna Opera House–style embellishment, will melt your heart. The theater opened in 1925; today the lobby serves as the Downtown Miami Welcome Center, doling out visitor information and organizing tours of the historic district; at night you can still catch theater and music performances.

WYNWOOD, DESIGN DISTRICT & LITTLE HAITI

Now rebranded as 'Midtown,' Wynwood and the Design District are Miami's official arts neighborhoods, plus the focal points of new art, food and nightlife in Greater Miami. Little Haiti sits above the Design District.

Little Haiti Cultural Center
Gallery

(Map p192; ☎305-960-2969; www.miamigov.com/LHCulturalcenter; 212 NE 59th Tce; ⏰9am-5pm) Miami has the largest community of Ayisyens (Haitians) in the world outside Haiti, and this is the place to learn their story. The cultural center is a study in playful island designs and motifs that houses a small but vibrant art gallery, crafts center and activities space – dance classes, drama productions and similar events are held here year-round. The best time to visit is for the **Big Night in Little Haiti** (www.rhythmfoundation.com/series/big-night-in-little-haiti), a street party held on the third Friday of every month from 6pm to 10pm. The celebration is rife with music, mouth-watering Caribbean food and beer, and is one of the safest, easiest ways of accessing the culture of Haiti outside of that island.

Wynwood Walls
Public Art

(Map p192; www.thewynwoodwalls.com; NW 2nd Ave btwn 25th & 26th Sts; ⏰noon-8pm Wed-Sat) In the midst of rusted warehouses and concrete blah, there's a pastel-and-graffiti explosion of urban art. Wynwood Walls is a collection of murals and paintings laid out over an open courtyard that invariably bowls people over with its sheer color profile and unexpected location. What's on offer tends to change with the coming and going of major arts events such as Art Basel, but it's always interesting stuff.

KEY BISCAYNE

The scenic drive along the Rickenbacker Causeway leads to Key Biscayne, an island just 7 miles long. The road turns into Crandon Blvd, the key's only real main road, which runs to the Cape Florida Lighthouse at the island's southernmost tip.

Miami Seaquarium
Aquarium

(Map p194; ☎305-361-5705; www.miamiseaquarium.com; 4400 Rickenbacker Causeway; adult/child $40/30; ⏰9:30am-6pm, last entry 4:30pm; P 👪) The Seaquarium was one of the country's first facilities dedicated to marine life, and its mission remains one of protecting aquatic creatures and educating the public about their charges. There are dozens of shows

Gusman Center for the Performing Arts
JEFF GREENBERG/ALAMY ©

Wynwood, Design District & Little Haiti

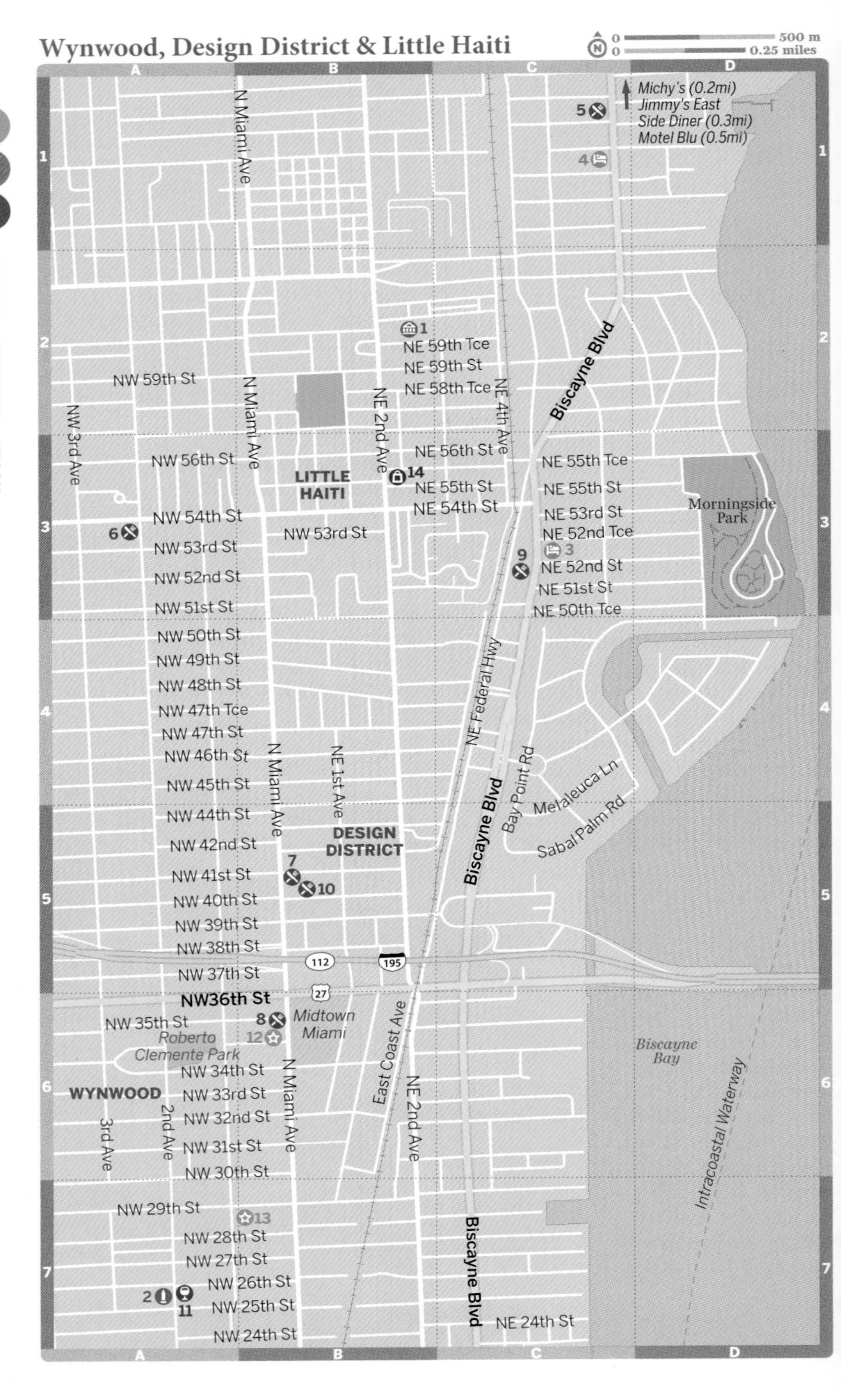

Wynwood, Design District & Little Haiti

Sights
1 Little Haiti Cultural Center ... B2
2 Wynwood Walls ... A7

Sleeping
3 Motel Bianco ... C3
4 New Yorker ... C1

Eating
5 Blue Collar ... C1
6 Chef Creole ... A3
7 Egg & Dart ... B5
8 Gigi ... B6
9 Honey Tree ... C3
10 Oak Tavern ... B5

Drinking & Nightlife
11 Wood Tavern ... A7

Entertainment
12 Bardot ... B6
13 O Cinema ... B7

Shopping
GO! Shop ... (see 2)
14 Sweat Records ... B3

and exhibits, including a tropical reef; the Shark Channel, with feeding presentations; and Discovery Bay, a natural mangrove habitat that serves as a refuge for rehabilitating rescued sea turtles. Check out the Pacific white-sided dolphins or West Indian manatees being nursed back to health; some are released into the wild.

With that said, the big attraction at the Seaquarium is also its most controversial: dolphin and whale shows, including swim with the dolphin programs. While the Seaquarium say they are protecting cetaceans (sea mammals) and educating the public about them, animal welfare organizations claim any form of captivity and human interaction is debilitating to dolphins and whales. If you decide you want to swim with dolphins, note that people under 5ft 2in cannot participate and children under three cannot enter the observation area. Last entry is at 4:30pm.

Crandon Park — Park

(Map p194; 305-361-5421; www.miamidade.gov/parks/parks/crandon_beach.asp; 6747 Crandon Blvd; per car $5; sunrise-sunset; P) This 1200-acre park boasts Crandon Park Beach, a glorious but crowded beach that stretches for 3 miles. Much of the park consists of a dense coastal hammock (hardwood forest) and mangrove swamps. Pretty cabanas at the south end of the park can be rented by the day ($37.45). The 2-mile-long beach here is clean, uncluttered with tourists, faces a lovely sweep of teal goodness and is regularly named one of the best beaches in the USA.

Bill Baggs Cape Florida State Park — Park

(Map p194; 305-361-5811; www.floridastateparks.org/capeflorida; 1200 S Crandon Blvd; per car/person $8/2; 8am-sunset; P) If you don't make it to the Florida Keys, come to this park for a taste of their unique island ecosystems. The 494-acre space is a tangled clot of tropical fauna and dark mangroves – look for the 'snorkel' roots that provide air for half-submerged mangrove trees – all interconnected by sandy trails and wooden boardwalks, and surrounded by miles of pale ocean. A concession shack rents kayaks, bikes, in-line skates, beach chairs and umbrellas.

At the state recreation area's southernmost tip, the 1845 brick **Cape Florida Lighthouse** is the oldest structure in Florida (it replaced another lighthouse that was severely damaged in 1836 during the Second Seminole War). Free tours run at 10am and 1pm Monday to Thursday.

Marjory Stoneman Douglas Biscayne Nature Center — Museum

(Map p194; 305-361-6767; www.biscaynenaturecenter.org; Crandon Park, 6767 Crandon Blvd; 10am-4pm; P) FREE Marjory Stoneman Douglas was a beloved environmental crusader and worthy namesake of this child-friendly nature center. The structure is a perfect introduction and exploration of the continental USA's own subtropical ecosystem: South Florida. There are weekend hikes and nature lessons that let kids wade into the

Key Biscayne

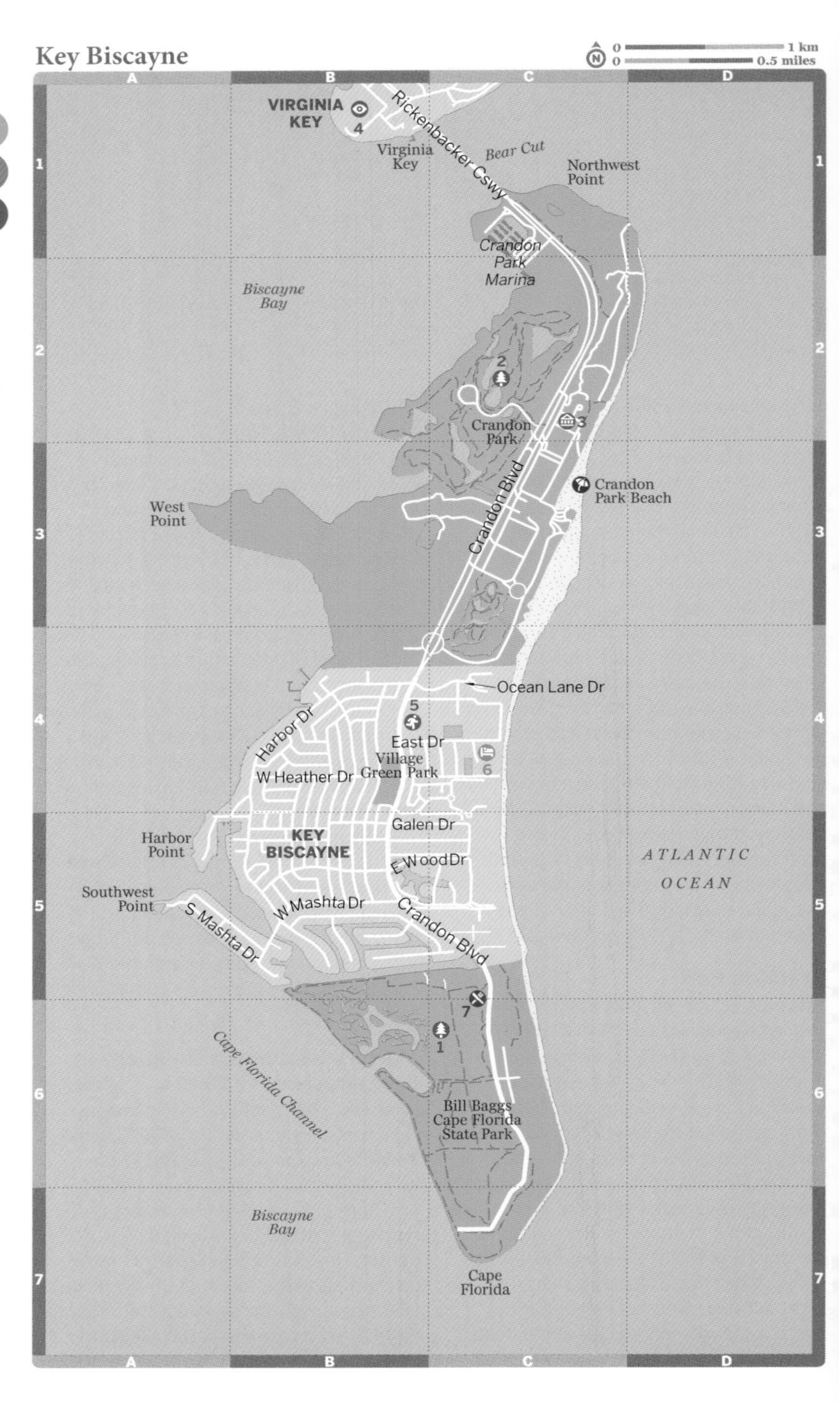

Key Biscayne

water in search of marine wildlife; check the website for a full breakdown of the many activities on offer, most of which cost $12 per person.

LITTLE HAVANA

Little Havana's main thoroughfare is Calle Ocho (8th St).

Máximo Gómez Park — Park

(Map p196; SW 8th St at SW 15th Ave; 9am-6pm) Little Havana's most evocative reminder of Old Cuba is Máximo Gómez Park, or 'Domino Park,' where the sound of elderly men trash-talking over games of chess is harmonized by the quick clack-clack of slapping dominoes. The jarring back-track, plus the heavy smell of cigars and a sunrise-bright mural of the 1993 Summit of the Americas, combine to make Máximo Gómez one of the most sensory sites in Miami (although it is admittedly one of the most tourist-heavy ones as well).

Cuban Memorials — Monument

(Map p196) The two blocks of SW 13th Ave south of Calle Ocho contain a series of monuments to Cuban and Cuban American heroes, including those that died in the Cuban War of Independence and anti-Castro conflicts. The memorials include the **Eternal Torch in Honor of the 2506th Brigade**, for the exiles who died during the Bay of Pigs Invasion; a huge **Cuba brass relief** depicting a map of Cuba, dedicated to the 'ideals of people who will never forget the pledge of making their Fatherland free'; a **José Martí memorial**; and a **Madonna statue**, which is supposedly illuminated by a shaft of holy light every afternoon. Bursting out of the island in the center of the boulevard is a massive ceiba tree, revered by followers of Santeria. The tree is an unofficial reminder of the poorer *Marielitos* (those who fled Cuba in the 1980 Mariel Boatlift) and successive waves of desperate-for-work Cubans, many of whom are *santeros* (Santeria practitioners) who have come to Miami since the 1980s.

Just away from the main drag are a fountain and monument, collectively entitled **La Plaza de la Cubanidad**

Máximo Gómez Park

Little Havana

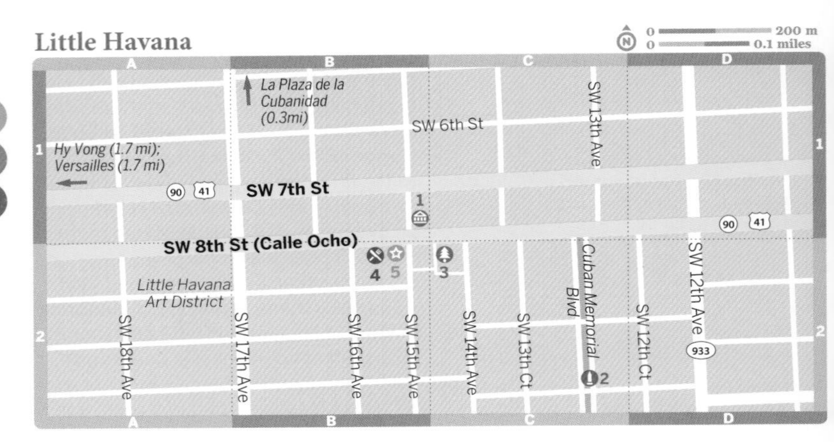

Little Havana

Sights

1 Cuba Ocho B1
2 Cuban Memorials C2
3 Máximo Gómez Park C2

Eating

4 Exquisito Restaurant B2

Entertainment

5 Tower Theater B2

(cnr W Flagler St & NW 17th Ave), which is a tribute both to the Cuban provinces and to migrants who drowned in 1994 while trying to leave Cuba on a ship, *13 de Marzo,* which was sunk by Castro's forces just off the coast.

Cuba Ocho Gallery

(Map p196; ☎305-285-5880; cubaocho.com; 1465 SW 8th St; ⏰11:30am-3am Tue-Sat) The jewel of the Little Havana Art District, Cuba Ocho functions as a community center, art gallery and research outpost for all things Cuban. The interior resembles a cool old Havana cigar bar, yet the walls are decked out in artwork that references both the classical past of Cuban art and its avant-garde future. Frequent live music, films, drama performances, readings and other events go off every week. The center opens during the evening for these events; check online for more information.

COCONUT GROVE

Coconut Grove, which attracts a mix of old hippies, middle-class and mall-going Miami, and college students, unfolds along S Bayshore Dr as it hugs the shoreline.

Vizcaya Museum & Gardens Historic Building

(☎305-250-9133; www.vizcayamuseum.org; 3251 S Miami Ave; adult/6-12yr/student & senior $18/6/10; ⏰9:30am-4:30pm Wed-Mon; P) They call Miami the Magic City, and if it is, this Italian villa – the housing equivalent of a Fabergé egg – is its most fairy-tale residence. In 1916, industrialist James Deering started a long and storied Miami tradition by making a ton of money and building ridiculously grandiose digs. He employed 1000 people (then 10% of the local population) for four years to fulfill his desire for a home that looked centuries old. He was so obsessed with creating an atmosphere of old money that he had the house stuffed with 15th- to 19th-century furniture, tapestries, paintings and decorative arts; had a monogram fashioned for himself; and even had paintings of fake ancestors commissioned. The 30-acre grounds are full of splendid gardens and Florentine gazebos, and both the house and gardens are used for the display of rotating contemporary-art exhibitions.

Barnacle Historic State Park Park

(www.floridastateparks.org/thebarnacle; 3485 Main Hwy; admission $2, house tours $3; park 9am-4pm Fri-Mon, house tours 10am, 11:30am, 1pm, 2:30pm Fri-Mon;) In the center of the village is the 1891, 5-acre pioneer residence of Ralph Monroe, Miami's first honorable snowbird. The house is open for guided tours, and the park it's located on is a lovely, shady oasis for strolling. Barnacle hosts frequent (and lovely) moonlight concerts, from jazz to classical. A little way down Main Hwy, on the other side of the road, there's a small Buddhist temple shaded by large groves of banyan trees.

Kampong Historic Site, Gardens

(305-442-7169; www.ntbg.org/gardens/kampong.php; 4013 Douglas Rd; tours by appointment only 9am-4pm Mon-Fri) David Fairchild, Indiana Jones of the botanical world and founder of Fairchild Tropical Gardens, would rest at the Kampong (Malay/Indonesian for 'village') in between journeys in search of beautiful and economically viable plant life. Today this lush garden is listed on the National Register of Historic Places and the lovely grounds serve as a classroom for the National Tropical Botanical Garden. Free self-guided tours (allow at least an hour) are available by appointment, as are $20 two-hour guided tours.

CORAL GABLES

The lovely city of Coral Gables, filled with Mediterranean-style buildings, is bordered by Calle Ocho to the north, Sunset Dr to the south, Ponce de León Blvd to the east and Red Rd to the west.

Biltmore Hotel Historic Building

(855-311-6903; www.biltmorehotel.com; 1200 Anastasia Ave; P) In the most opulent neighborhood of one of the showiest cities in the world, the Biltmore peers down her nose and says, 'hrmph.' It's one of the greatest of the grand hotels of the American Jazz Age, and if this joint were a fictional character from a novel, it'd be, without question, Jay Gatsby. Al Capone had a speakeasy on-site, and the Capone Suite is still haunted by the spirit of Fats Walsh, who was murdered here (for more ghost details, join in the weekly storytelling in the lobby, 7pm Thursday). Back in the day, imported gondolas transported celebrity guests like Judy Garland and the Vanderbilts around because, of course, there was a private canal system out back. It's gone now, but the largest hotel pool in the continental USA, which resembles a sultan's water garden from *A Thousand & One Arabian Nights,* is still here.

Lowe Art Museum Museum

(www.lowemuseum.org; 1301 Stanford Dr; adult/student $10/5; 10am-4pm Tue-Sat, noon-4pm Sun) Your love of the Lowe, located on

Viernes Culturales (Cultural Fridays)

The Little Havana Arts District may not be Wynwood, but it does constitute an energetic little strip of galleries and studios (concentrated on 8th St between SW 15th Ave & SW 17th Ave) that house some of the best Latin American art in Miami. Rather than pop into each gallery, look around and feel pressure to buy, why not visit on the last Friday of each month for **Viernes Culturales** (www.viernesculturales.org). No mere wine-sipping art walk this; Cultural Fridays in Little Havana are like little carnival seasons, with music, old men in *guayaberas* (Cuban dress shirts) crooning to the stars and more booty-shaking than brie. Although there is also brie, and plenty of time to appreciate local art as all the Little Havana galleries throw open their doors.

Right: El Pub, Calle Ocho, Little Havana; **Below:** Vizcaya Museum (p196)

the campus of the University of Miami, depends on your taste in art. If you're into modern and contemporary works, it's good. If you're into the art and archaeology of cultures from Asia, Africa and the South Pacific, it's great. And if you're into pre-Columbian and Mesoamerican art, it's fantastic. That isn't to discount the lovely permanent collection of Renaissance and baroque art, Western sculpture from the 18th to 20th centuries, and paintings by Gauguin, Picasso and Monet.

Venetian Pool Outdoors
(**305-460-5306; www.coralgablesvenetianpool.com; 2701 De Soto Blvd; adult/child $11.50/7.70; hours vary;**) Just imagine: it's 1923, tons of rock have been quarried for one of the most beautiful neighborhoods in Miami, and now an ugly gash sits in the middle of the village. What to do? How about pump the irregular hole full of water, mosaic and tile up the whole affair, and make it look like a Roman emperor's aquatic playground? Result: one of the few pools listed on the National Register of Historic Places, a wonderland of coral rock caves, cascading waterfalls, a palm-fringed island and Venetian-style moorings. Take a swim and follow in the footsteps (fin-steps?) of stars like Esther Williams and Johnny 'Tarzan' Weissmuller. Opening hours vary depending on the season; call or check the website for details.

GREATER MIAMI – SOUTH

Zoo Miami Zoo
(**Miami Metrozoo; 305-251-0400; www.miamimetrozoo.com; 12400 SW 152nd St; adult/child $16/12; 9:30am-5:30pm, last entry 4pm; P**) Miami's tropical weather makes strolling around the Metrozoo almost feel like a day in the wild. Look for Asian and African elephants, rare and regal Bengal tigers prowling an evocative Hindu temple, and a pair of Komodo dragons from Indonesia. For a quick overview (and because the zoo is so big), hop on the

Safari Monorail; it departs every 20 minutes. There's a glut of grounds tours, and kids will love feeding the Samburu giraffes ($2). Last admission at 4pm.

Jungle Island Zoo

(Map p188; ☎305-400-7000; www.jungleisland.com; 1111 Parrot Jungle Trail, off MacArthur Causeway; adult/child/senior $35/27/33; ⏰10am-5pm; P 👪) Jungle Island, packed with tropical birds, alligators, orangutans, chimps, lemurs, a – wait for it, *Napoleon Dynamite* fans – liger (a cross between a lion and a tiger) and a Noah's Ark of other animals, is a ton of fun. It's one of those places kids (justifiably) beg to go, so just give up and prepare for some bright-feathered, bird-poopie-scented fun in this artificial, self-contained jungle.

Fairchild Tropical Garden Gardens

(www.fairchildgarden.org; 10901 Old Cutler Rd; adult/child/senior $25/12/18; ⏰7:30am-4:30pm; P 👪) If you need to escape Miami's madness, consider a green day in the country's largest tropical botanical garden. A butterfly grove, jungle biospheres, and gentle vistas of marsh and keys habitats, plus frequent art installations from folks like Roy Lichtenstein, are all stunning. In addition to easy-to-follow, self-guided walking tours, a free 40-minute tram tours the entire park on the hour from 10am to 3pm. Located 5 miles south of Coral Gables.

Monkey Jungle Zoo

(☎305-235-1611; www.monkeyjungle.com; 14805 SW 216th St; adult/child $30/24; ⏰9:30am-5pm, last entry 4pm; P 👪) The Monkey Jungle tag line is: 'Where humans are caged and monkeys run free.' Indeed, you'll be walking through screened-in trails, with primates swinging, screeching and chattering all around you. It's incredibly fun, and just a bit odorous. The big show of the day takes place at feeding time, when crab-eating monkeys and Southeast Asian macaques dive into the pool for fruit and other treats. There's a lovely aviary with clouds of beautiful rescued parrots.

Miami Children's Museum Museum

(Map p188; ☎305-373-5437; www.miamichildrensmuseum.org; 980 MacArthur Causeway; admission $18; ⏰10am-6pm; 👪) This museum, located between South Beach and downtown Miami, isn't exactly a museum. It feels more like an uberplayhouse, with areas for kids to practice all sorts of adult activities – banking and food shopping, caring for pets, reporting scoops as a TV news anchor in a studio, and acting as a local cop or firefighter.

Activities

BIKING

Miami-Dade County Parks & Recreation Department Cycling (Map p188; ☎305-755-7800; www.miamidade.gov/parksmasterplan/bike_trails_map.asp) 🍃 leads frequent eco-bike tours through parklands and along waterfront paths, and offers a list of traffic-free cycling paths on its website. For less strenuous rides, try the side roads of South Beach or the shady streets of Coral Gables and Coconut Grove. Some good trails include the Old Cutler Bike Path, which starts at the end of Sunset Dr in Coral Gables, the ride over the Rickenbacker Causeway to Key Biscayne, and a series of paths in Oleta River State Park (p186).

KAYAKING & WINDSURFING

Kayaking through mangroves, one of the coolest ecosystems on Earth, is magical: all those slender roots kiss the water while the ocean breeze cools your flanks.

Also, try these places:

Blue Moon Outdoor Center Water Sports

(☎305-957-3040; http://bluemoonoutdoor.com; 3400 NE 163rd St; ⏰9am-sunset Mon-Fri, from 8am Sat & Sun) Offers single kayaks ($23 per 1½ hours, $41 per three hours), tandem kayaks ($33 per 1½ hours, $51 per three hours) and bike rental ($18 per 1½ hours, $26 per three hours).

Sailboards Miami Water Sports

(☎305-892-8992; www.sailboardsmiami.com; 1 Rickenbacker Causeway; ⏰10am-6pm Fri-Tue) Also rents kayaks. You can purchase 10 hours' worth of kayaking for $90. This is also a good spot to rent (and learn how to

Pineapple, Fairchild Tropical Garden (p199)

Doing the DecoBike

Miami Beach is flat, warm, and covered in concrete. In other words, it's about perfect for cycling. Yet cycling infrastructure has been slow to develop on the beach, leading to traffic snarls, gridlock and the inevitable slow roll of a Hummer blasting EDM at every stop light on Collins Ave. Well no more (although the cars blasting EDM will probably be with us for a long time).

DecoBike (p217) saves the day, sort of. This bike-sharing program, modeled after similar initiatives in New York, London and Paris, makes cycling from South Beach to Surfside a relative breeze. Just rock up to a solar-powered DecoBike station (a handy dandy map can be found at www.decobike.com/map-location), insert a credit card and ride away. You can return your bike at any DecoBike location.

Pricing varies; you'll pay $4 for 30 minutes, $6 for an hour, $10 for two hours, or $24 for a whole day's riding. If you keep your bicycle past the allotted time, you're charged $4 per half-hour. So get out there! Bike away! Get in shape while biking around South Beach so you don't feel self-conscious on South Beach. Winning all around.

operate) windsurfing gear (lessons from $35, gear per hour $30).

Haulover Beach Park Surfing
(10800 Collins Ave, Bal Harbour)

Bill Baggs Cape Florida State Park
(Map p194; www.floridastateparks.org/cape florida; 1200 S Crandon Blvd)

YOGA

A few studios offer a large range of classes; bring your own mats.

Green Monkey Yoga Yoga
(Map p180; ☎305-397-8566; www.greenmonkey.net; 1827 Purdy Ave; classes from $20) Miami Beach; also has a branch in South Miami.

Prana Yoga Center Yoga
(☎305-567-9812; www.pranayogamiami.com; 247 Malaga Ave, Coral Gables; 1-/5-/10-class pass $20/99/169) In Coral Gables.

Bikram Yoga Miami Beach Yoga
(Map p180; ☎305-534-2727; www.bikramyogamiami.com; 235 11th St, Miami Beach; per day/week $25/50) South Beach.

Tours

Miami Design Preservation League Tour
(Map p180; ☎305-531-3484; www.mdpl.org; 1001 Ocean Dr, South Beach; guided tour per adult/senior & students $20/15; ⏲tours 10:30am Fri-Wed, 6:30pm Thu) Tells the stories and history behind the art-deco buildings in South Beach, either with a lively guide from the Miami Design Preservation League, or a well-presented recording and map for self-guided walks (try the guides). Tours last 90 minutes. Also offers tours of Jewish Miami Beach, Gay & Lesbian Miami beach and other themed walks; check website for details.

Dr Paul George Tour
(☎305-375-1492; www.historymiami.org/tours/walking-tours; tours from $30) For great historical perspective, call the lively Dr George, a historian for **HistoryMiami (Map p188; www.historymiami.org; 101 W Flagler St; adult/child $8/5; ⏲10am-5pm Tue-Fri, from noon Sat & Sun)**. George leads several popular tours – including those that focus on Stiltsville, Miami crime, Little Havana and Coral Gables at twilight – between September and late June; hours vary.

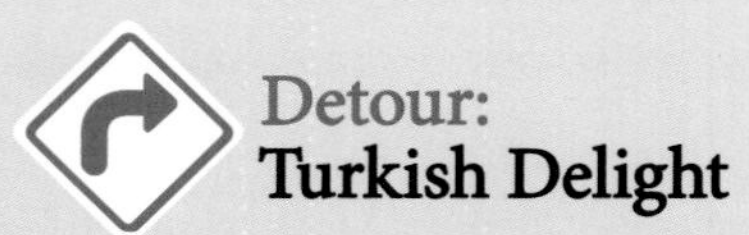

Detour: Turkish Delight

Just because you enjoy a good back rub doesn't mean you need to go to some glitzy spa where they constantly play soft house music on a repetitive loop. Right? Why not head to a favorite 'hot' spot among folks who want a spa experience without the glamor, the **Russian & Turkish Baths** (**☎305-867-8316; www.russianandturkishbaths.com; 5445 Collins Ave; ⏰noon-midnight**). Enter this little labyrinth of *banyas* (steam rooms) and there's a plethora of spa choices. You can be casually beaten with oak leaf brooms (for $40) called *venik* in a lava-hot spa (it's actually really relaxing...well, interesting anyway). There's Dead Sea salt and mud exfoliation ($50), plus the on-site cafe serves delicious borscht, blintzes, dark bread with smoked fish and, of course, beer.

Dr George also offers private tours by appointment.

EcoAdventure Bike Tours Cycling
(**☎305-365-3018; www.miamidade.gov/ecoadventures; from $28**) The Dade County parks system leads excellent bike tours through peaceful areas of Miami and Miami Beach, including along beaches, on Key Biscayne and into the Everglades.

Urban Tour Host Walking
(**Map p188; ☎305-416-6868; www.miamiculturaltours.com; 25 SE 2nd Ave, Suite 1048; tours from $20**) Has a rich program of custom tours that provides face-to-face interaction in all of Miami's neighborhoods. A deluxe city tour includes Coral Gables, South Beach, downtown Miami and Coconut Grove.

Sleeping

What sets South Beach apart – what defines it as a travel destination – is the deco district, and the deco district's backbone is hotels. This is one of the largest concentrations of boutique hotels in the country.

SOUTH BEACH (1ST TO 11TH STREETS)

Clinton Hotel Boutique Hotel $$
(**Map p180; ☎305-938-4040; www.clintonsouthbeach.com; 825 Washington Ave; r $150-180, ste from $205; P ❄ 📶 🏊**) Washington Ave is the quietest of the three main drags in SoBe, but the Clinton doesn't mind. This joint knows it would be the hottest girl in the most crowded party, with her velveteen banquettes and Zen sun porches. Balcony rooms offer a nice view onto the hip courtyard.

Hotel St Augustine Boutique Hotel $$
(**Map p180; ☎305-532-0570; www.hotelstaugustine.com; 347 Washington Ave; r $155-289; P ❄ 📶**) Wood that's blonder than Barbie and a crisp-and-clean deco theme combine to create one of SoFi's most elegant yet stunningly modern sleeps. Color schemes blend beige, caramel, white and cream – the sense is the hues are flowing into one eye-smoothing palette. The familiar, warm service is the cherry on top for this hip-and-homey standout, although the soothing lighting and glass showers – that turn into personal steam rooms at the flick of a switch – are pretty appealing, too.

Pelican Hotel Boutique Hotel $$$
(**Map p180; ☎305-673-3373; www.pelicanhotel.com; 826 Ocean Dr; r $165-425, ste $295-555; ❄ 📶**) When the owners of Diesel jeans purchased the Pelican in 1999, they started scouring garage sales for just the right ingredients to fuel a mad experiment: 30 themed rooms that come off like a fantasy-suite hotel dipped in hip. From

the cowboy-hipster chic of 'High Corral, OK Chaparral' to the jungly electric tiger stripes of 'Me Tarzan, You Vain,' all the rooms are completely different (although all have beautiful recycled-oak floors), fun and even come with their own 'suggested soundtrack.'

Sense South Beach Boutique Hotel **$$$**
(Map p180; ☎305-538-5529; www.sensesobe.com; 400 Ocean Dr; r $300; P ❄ ≋ ≋) The Sense is fantastically atmospheric – smooth white walls disappearing behind melting blue views of South Beach, wooden paneling arranged around lovely sharp angles that feel inviting, rather than imposing, and rooms that contrast whites and dark grays into straight duochromatic cool. Pop art hangings and slender furnishings round out the MacBook-esque air.

Nash Hotel Boutique Hotel **$$**
(Map p180; ☎305-674-7800; www.nashsouthbeach.com; 1120 Collins Ave; r $164-204, ste from $360; P ❄ ≋ ≋) This used to be the Lords Hotel, an epicenter of South Beach's gay scene. Today the Nash is still a pretty cream puff of a hotel, with rooms decked out in lemony yellow and whites offset by graphic and pop art. At time of writing, it seemed less GLBT-focused than in the past, if still popular with the boys.

Fashionhaus Boutique Hotel **$$**
(Map p180; ☎305-673-2550; www.fashionhaushotel.com; 534 Washington Ave; r $130-250; P ❄ ≋ ≋) The Fashionhaus doesn't just sound like a Berlin avant-garde theater; it kinda feels like one, with its smooth geometric furnishings, 48 individualized rooms decked out in original artwork – from abstract expressionism to washed-out photography – and its general blending of comfort, technology and design. Popular with Europeans, fashionistas, artists (and European fashionista artists) and those who just want to emulate that lifestyle.

Chesterfield Hotel Boutique Hotel **$$$**
(Map p180; ☎305-531-5831; www.thechesterfieldhotel.com; 855 Collins Ave; r $200-250, ste $300-600; P ❄ ≋) Hip-hop gets funky with zebra-stripe curtains and cushions in the small lobby, which hosts a chill happy hour when the sun goes down at the in-house Safari Bar. Rooms mix up dark

Clinton Hotel

INGOLF POMPE/ALAMY ©

wood furniture overlaid with bright-white beds and vaguely tropical colors swathed throughout. Make sure to enoy the view from the roof deck.

SOUTH BEACH (11TH TO 23RD STREETS)

Townhouse Hotel Boutique Hotel **$$**
(Map p180; ☎305-534-3800; www.townhousehotel.com; 150 20th St at Collins Ave; r $145-195, ste from $350;) You'd think the Townhouse was designed by the guy who styled the iPod but no, it was Jonathan Morr and India Mahdavi who fashioned a cool white lobby and igloo-like rooms with random scarlet accents and a breezy, white rooftop lounge. Who needs mints on pillows when the Townhouse provides beach balls? One of the better value hotels on South Beach.

Aqua Hotel Boutique Hotel **$$**
(Map p180; ☎305-538-4361; www.aquamiami.com; 1530 Collins Ave; r $150-180, ste from $200; P) A front desk made of shiny surfboard sets the mellow tone at this former motel – the retro, family kind where the rooms are set around a pool. That old-school vibe barely survives under the soft glare of aqua spotlights and an alfresco lounging area. The sleekness of the rooms is offset by quirky furniture and deep sea-blue bathrooms.

Shore Club Boutique Hotel **$$$**
(Map p180; ☎305-695-3100; www.shoreclub.com; 1901 Collins Ave; r/ste from $348/455; P@) Imagine a Zen ink-brush painting; what's beautiful isn't what's there, but what gets left out. If you could turn that sort of art into a hotel room, it might look like the stripped-down yet serene digs of the Shore Club. Yeah, yeah: it has the 400-thread-count Egyptian cotton sheets, Mexican sandstone floors etc, but what the Shore Club does like no other hotel is arrange these elements into a greater whole that's impressive in its understatement; the aesthetic is compelling because it comes across as an afterthought.

Gale South Beach Hotel **$$$**
(Map p180; ☎855-532-2212; galehotel.com; 1690 Collins Ave; r from $310; P) The Gale's exterior is an admirable re-creation of classic boxy deco aesthetic expanded to the grand dimensions of a modern

Cardozo Hotel

ANDY SELINGER/ALAMY©

SoBe super resort. This blend of classic and haute South Beach carries on indoors, where you'll find bright rooms with clean colors and sharp lines and a retro-chic vibe inspired by the Mid Century Modern movement.

The Standard Boutique Hotel **$$$**
(Map p180; ☎305-673-1717; www.standardhotels.com/miami; 40 Island Ave; r/ste from $240/480; P ❄ 🛜 🏊) Look for the upside-down 'Standard' sign on the old Lido building on Belle Island (between South Beach and downtown Miami) and you'll find the Standard – which is anything but. This excellent boutique blends a bevy of spa services, hipster funk and South Beach sex, and the result is a '50s motel gone glam. There are organic wooden floors, raised white beds, and gossamer curtains, which open onto a courtyard of earthly delights, including a heated *hammam* (Turkish bath).

Cardozo Hotel Boutique Hotel **$$$**
(Map p180; ☎305-535-6500, 800-782-6500; www.cardozohotel.com; 1300 Ocean Dr; r $230-290, ste $320-460; P ❄ 🛜) The Cardozo and its neighbor, the Carlyle, were the first deco hotels saved by the Miami Design Preservation League, and in the case of the Cardozo, we think they saved the best first. It's the combination of the usual contemporary sexiness (white walls, hardwood floors, high-thread-count sheets) and playful embellishments: leopard-print details, handmade furniture and a general sense that, yes, you are cool if you stay here, but you don't have to flaunt it. Oh – remember the 'hair gel' scene in *There's Something About Mary*? Filmed here.

Cadet Hotel Boutique Hotel **$$$**
(Map p180; ☎305-672-6688; www.cadethotel.com; 1701 James Ave; r from $209; ❄ 🛜 🏊) From paper lanterns hanging from ceilings to furry throw rugs; from clamshell designs encapsulating large mirrors to classical Asian furniture and, as always, a great art-deco facade, the Cadet has the aesthetics right. Check out the shaded verandah at the back, lifted from a fantasy idea of what a plantation should feel like.

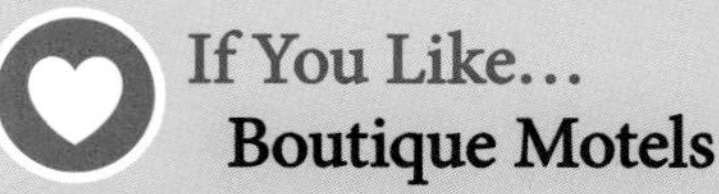

If You Like... Boutique Motels

'Mimo on Bibo' is a hideously precocious phrase, but it's clever, too. It's an abbreviation for 'Miami Modern on Biscayne Boulevard.' and refers to the architectural style of buildings on north Biscayne Blvd past 55th Street. Specifically, there are some great roadside motels here with lovely, Rat Pack–era '50s neon beckoning visitors in. This area was neglected for a long time, but today north BiBo is one of Miami's rapidly gentrifying areas, and savvy motel owners are cleaning up their act and looking to attract the hipsters, artists and gay population flocking to the area.

1 **NEW YORKER**
(Map p192; ☎305-759-5823; www.hotelnewyorkermiami.com; 6500 Biscayne Blvd; r $75-130; P ❄ 🛜) This hotel has been around since the 1950s and it shows – in a good way. If you could turn a classic Cadillac into a hotel with a modern interior and hipster cred, then bam, there's the New Yorker in a nutshell. Staff are friendly and rooms – done up with pop art, geometric designs and solid colors – would make Andy Warhol proud.

2 **MOTEL BLU**
(off Map p192; ☎877-784-6835; www.motelblumiami.com; 7700 Biscayne Blvd; r $52-150; P ❄ 🛜 🏊) Situated above Miami's Little River, the Blu may not look like much from the outside, but inside you'll find freshly done-up rooms with a host of modern amenities. Rooms are comfortable and have a soothing lime-and-lemon interior.

3 **MOTEL BIANCO**
(Map p192; ☎305-751-8696; www.motelbianco.com; 5255 Biscayne Blvd; r $80-110; P ❄ 🛜) The Bianco situates several orange-and-milky-white rooms around a glittery courtyard where coffee is served and guests can get to know each other. Contemporary art designs swirl through the larger rooms and wicker furniture abounds throughout.

W Hotel Resort **$$$**
(Map p180; ☎305-938-3000; www.wsouthbeach.com; 2201 Collins Ave; r from $470, ste $700-5700; P ❄ 📶 🏊) There's an astounding variety of rooms available at the South Beach outpost of the W chain, which brings the whole W-brand mix of luxury, hipness and overblown cool to Miami Beach in a big way. The 'spectacular studios' balance long panels of reflective glass with cool tablets of cipollino marble; the Oasis suite lets in so much light you'd think the sun had risen in your room; the Penthouse may as well be the setting of an MTV video (and given the sort of celebrities who stay here, that assessment might not be far off). The attendant bars, restaurants, clubs and pool built into this complex are some of the most well-regarded on the beach.

Delano Hotel Boutique Hotel **$$$**
(Map p180; ☎305-672-2000; www.delano-hotel.com; 1685 Collins Ave; r $430-650, ste from $899; P ❄ 📶 🏊) The Delano opened in the 1990s and immediately started ruling the South Beach roost. If there's a quintessential 'I'm too sexy for this song' South Beach moment, it's when you walk into the Delano's lobby, which has all the excess of an overbudgeted theater set. 'Magic mirrors' in the halls disclose weather info, tide charts and inspirational quotes. The pool area resembles the courtyard of a Disney princess's palace and includes a giant chess set; there are floor-to-ridiculously-high-ceiling curtains in the two-story waterfront rooms; and the bedouin tent cabanas are outfitted with flat-screen TVs. Rooms are almost painfully white and bright; all long, smooth lines, reflective surfaces and sexy, modern, luxurious amenities.

NORTHERN MIAMI BEACH

Circa 39 Boutique Hotel **$$**
(☎305-538-4900; www.circa39.com; 3900 Collins Ave; r $130-170; P ❄ @ 🏊) If you love South Beach style but loathe South Beach attitude, Circa has got your back. The lobby, with its molded furniture and wacky embellishments, is one of the funkiest in Miami. Chic rooms, bursting with tropical lime green and subtle earth tones, are hip enough for the design-obsessed scenesters.

Freehand Miami Boutique Hotel **$$**
(☎305-531-2727; http://thefreehand.com; 2727 Indian Creek Dr; dm/r from $50/220; ❄ 📶 🏊) The Freehand is the brilliant re-imagining of the old Indian Creek Hotel, a classic of the Miami Beach scene. Rooms are comfortably minimalist, with just the right amount of local artwork and wooden tones to strike a nice balance between warm funky and cool hip. Dorms serve the hostel crowd, and the on-site Broken Shaker (p214) is one of the best bars in town.

Red South Beach Boutique Hotel **$$**
(☎800-528-0823; www.redsouthbeach.com; 3010 Collins Ave; r $130-200; ❄ 📶 🏊) Red is indeed the name of the game, from the cushions on the sleek chairs in the lobby to the flashes dancing around the marble pool to deep, blood-crimson headboards and walls wrapping you in warm sexiness in the small but beautiful guest rooms. The Red is excellent value for money and come evening the pool-bar complex is a great place to unwind and meet fellow guests.

Fontainebleau Resort **$$$**
(☎800-548-8886, 305-535-3283; www.fontainebleau.com; 4441 Collins Ave; r $344-461, ste from $550; P ❄ 📶 🏊) The grand Fontainebleau opened in 1954, when it became a celeb sunning spot. Numerous renovations have added beachside cabanas, seven tennis courts, a grand ballroom, a shopping mall and a fabulous swimming pool. The rooms are surprisingly bright and cheerful – we expected more hard-edged attempts to be cool, but the sunny disposition of these chambers is a welcome surprise.

Eden Roc Renaissance Resort **$$$**
(☎855-433-3676, 305-531-0000; www.edenrocmiami.com; 4525 Collins Ave; r/ste from $305/440; P ❄ 📶 🏊) The Roc's immense inner lobby draws inspiration from the Rat

Pack glory days of Miami Beach cool, and rooms in the Ocean Tower boast lovely views over the Intracoastal Waterway. All the digs here have smooth, modern embellishments and amenities ranging from MP3 players to HDTV, ergonomic furniture and turndown service, among others.

DOWNTOWN MIAMI

Epic Hotel **$$$**

(Map p188; ☎866-760-3742, 305-424-5226; www.epichotel.com; 270 Biscayne Blvd; r $240-510, ste from $570; P ❄ 📶 🏊) Epic indeed! This massive Kimpton hotel is one of the more attractive options downtown and it possesses a coolness cred that could match any spot on Miami Beach. Of particular note is the outdoor pool and sun deck, which overlook a gorgeous sweep of Brickell and the surrounding condo canyons. The rooms are outfitted in designer-chic furnishings and some have similarly beautiful views of greater Miami-Dade. There's a youthful energy throughout that's lacking in other corporate-style downtown hotels.

Four Seasons Miami Hotel **$$$**

(Map p188; ☎305-358-3535; www.fourseasons.com/miami; 1435 Brickell Ave; r/ste from $330/450; P ❄ 📶 🏊) The marble common areas double as art galleries, a massive spa caters to corporate types and there are sweeping, could-have-been-a-panning-shot-from-*Miami-Vice* views over Biscayne Bay in some rooms. The 7th-floor terrace bar, Bahia, is pure *mojito*-laced, Latin-loved swankiness, especially on Thursdays and Fridays from 6pm to 8pm, when ladies drink free.

KEY BISCAYNE

Silver Sands Beach Resort Resort **$$**

(Map p194; ☎305-361-5441; www.silversandsbeachresort.com; 301 Ocean Dr; r $169-189, cottages $279-349; P ❄ 🏊) Silver Sands: aren't you cute, with your one-story, stucco tropical tweeness? How this little, Old Florida–style independent resort has survived amid the corporate competition is beyond us, but it's definitely a warm, homey spot for those seeking some intimate, individual attention – to say nothing of the sunny courtyard, garden area and outdoor pool.

Collins Ave hotels, Miami Beach

CORAL GABLES

Hotel St Michel Hotel $$

(**305-444-1666; www.hotelstmichel.com; 162 Alcazar Ave; r $120-225;**) The Michel is more Metropole than Miami, and we mean that as a compliment. The old-world wooden fixtures, refined sense of tweedy style and dinner-jacket ambience don't get in the way of friendly service. The lovely restaurant and cool bar-lounge are as elegant as the hotel they occupy.

Biltmore Hotel Historic Hotel $$$

(**855-311-6903; www.biltmorehotel.com; 1200 Anastasia Ave; r from $209;**) Though the Biltmore's standard rooms can be small, a stay here is a chance to sleep in one of the great laps of US luxury. The grounds are so palatial it would take a solid week to explore everything the Biltmore has to offer – we highly recommend reading a book in the Romanesque/Arabian Nights opulent lobby, sunning underneath enormous columns and taking a dip in the largest hotel pool in the continental USA.

Eating

Miami is a major immigrant entrepôt and a place that loves showing off its wealth. Thus you get a good mix of cheap ethnic eateries and high-quality top-end cuisine here.

SOUTH BEACH (1ST TO 11TH STREETS)

Puerto Sagua Cuban $

(**Map p180; 305-673-1115; 700 Collins Ave; mains $6-20; 7:30am-2am**) There's a secret colony of older working-class Cubans and construction workers hidden among South Beach's sex-and-flash, and evidently, they eat here (next to a Benetton). Puerto Sagua challenges the US diner with this reminder: Cubans can greasy-spoon with the best of them. Portions of favorites such as *picadillo* (spiced ground beef with rice, beans and plantains) are stupidly enormous. The Cuban coffee here is not for the faint of heart – strong stuff.

11th St Diner Diner $

(**Map p180; 1065 Washington Ave; mains $9-18; 24hr except midnight-7am Wed**) You've seen the art-deco landmarks. Now eat in one: a Pullman-car diner trucked down from Wilkes-Barre, Pennsylvania – as sure a slice of Americana as a *Leave It to Beaver* marathon. If you've been drinking all night, we'll split a three-egg omelet with you and the other drunkies at 6am – if there's a diner where you can replicate Edward Hopper's *Nighthawks*, it's here.

Tap Tap Haitian $$

(**Map p180; 305-672-2898; www.taptaprestaurant.com; 819 5th St; mains $9-20; noon-11:30pm**) In Haiti, tap-taps are brightly colored pickup trucks turned public taxis,

Puerto Sagua
JEFF GREENBERG/ALAMY©

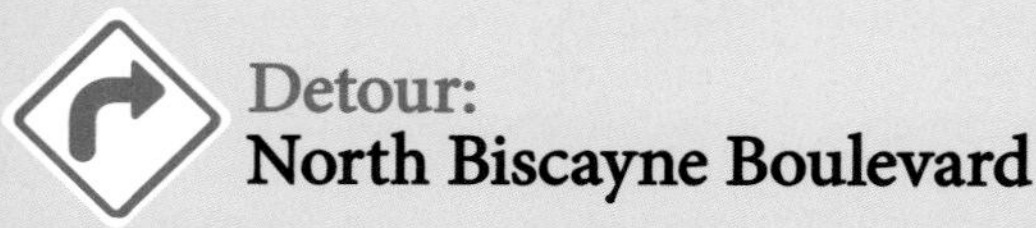

Detour: North Biscayne Boulevard

As North Biscayne Blvd continues to gentrify, better and better restaurants are opening up. Here are some winners from this foodie find:

Michy's (305-759-2001; http://michysmiami.com; 6927 Biscayne Blvd; meals $29-38; 6-10:30pm Tue-Thu, to 11pm Fri & Sat, to 10pm Sun;) Blue-and-white pop-decor. Organic, locally sourced ingredients. A stylish, fantastical bar where Alice could drink before painting Wonderland red. Welcome to Michelle 'Michy' Bernstein's culinary lovechild – one of the brightest stars in Miami's culinary constellation. The emphasis is on good food and fun. The 'half plates' concept lets you halve an order and mix up delicious gastronomic fare, such as foie gras on corn cakes, chicken pot pie with wild mushrooms, white almond gazpacho, and blue-cheese *croquettes*.

Honey Tree (Map p192; 305-756-1696; 5138 Biscayne Blvd; mains under $10; 8am-8pm Mon-Thu, to 7pm Fri, 9am-6pm Sat;) The Honey Tree is a health-food store that happens to serve excellent juices, smoothies and what many consider to be Miami's best vegan lunch. What's on offer varies day by day, but rest assured it will be cheap (it's priced by weight) and delicious. Lunch is usually served from noon to 2pm, but keep in mind that food often runs out due to high demand.

Jimmy's East Side Diner (305-754-3692; 7201 Biscayne Blvd; mains $5-13; 6:30am-4pm) Come to Jimmy's, a classic greasy spoon (that happens to be very gay-friendly; note the rainbow flag out front), for big cheap breakfasts of omelets, French toast or pancakes, and turkey clubs and burgers later in the day.

and their tropi-psychedelic paint schemes inspire the decor at this excellent Haitian eatery. This is no Manhattan-style South Beach lounge – here you dine under bright murals of Papa Legba, guardian of the dead, emerging from a Port-au-Prince cemetery. Meals are a happy marriage of West African, French and Caribbean: spicy pumpkin soup, snapper in a scotch-bonnet lime sauce, curried goat and charcoal-grilled Turks and Caicos conch. Make sure you try the *mayi moulen*, a signature side of cornmeal smothered in a rich bean sauce – bloody delicious! If you need some liquid courage, shoot some Barbancourt rum, available in several grades (all strong).

Grazie Italian $$$
(Map p180; 305-673-1312; www.grazieitaliancuisine.com; 702 Washington Ave; mains $19-34; noon-3pm Mon-Fri, 6pm-midnight daily) Thanks indeed; Grazie is top class and comfortably old-school Northern Italian. There's a distinct lack of gorgeous, clueless waitstaff and unwise menu experimentation. Instead there's attentive service, solid and delicious mains, and extremely decent prices given the quality of the dining and high-end nature of the location. The porcini risotto is simple in construction yet deeply complex in execution – one of the best Italian dishes on the beach.

SOUTH BEACH (11TH TO 23RD STREETS)

Burger & Beer Joint Burgers $
(Map p180; 305-672-3287; www.bnbjoint.com; 1766 Bay Rd; mains $5.50-9; 11:30am-midnight Sun-Thu, to 2am Fri & Sat;) Gourmet burgers. Microbrew beer. Clearly, the folks at B&B did their marketing research. Because who doesn't love both? Oh yes, vegetarians, you're catered to as well: the

'Dear Prudence', a mix of portobello, red pepper, walnut pesto and zucchini fries will keep herbivores happy. Oh, there's a turkey and stuffing burger with gravy served *between turkey patties,* an ahi tuna burger, a patty of wagyu beef with foie gras...you get the idea. Did we mention the microbrew beer?

Pubbelly Fusion $$

(Map p180; ☎305-532-7555; 1418 20th Street; mains $11-26; ⏲6pm-midnight Tue-Thu & Sun, to midnight Fri & Sat) Pubbelly's dining genre is hard to pinpoint, besides delicious. It skews between Asian, North American and Latin American, gleaning the best from all cuisines. Examples? Try duck and scallion dumplings, or the mouth watering udon 'carbonara' with pork belly, poached eggs and parmesan. Hand-crafted cocktails wash down the dishes a treat.

Osteria del Teatro Italian $$$

(Map p180; ☎305-538-7850; 1443 Washington Ave; mains $17-45; ⏲6-11pm Mon-Thu, to 1am Fri-Sun) There are few things to swear by but the specials board of Osteria, one of the oldest and best Italian restaurants in Greater Miami, ought to be one. When you get here, let the gracious Italian waiters seat you, coddle you and then basically order for you off the board. They never pick wrong.

NORTHERN MIAMI BEACH

Roasters' n Toasters Deli $

(☎305-531-7691; 525 Arthur Godfrey Rd; mains $8-16; ⏲6:30am-3:30pm) Given the crowds and the satisfied smiles of customers, Roasters' n Toasters meets the demanding standards of Miami Beach's large Jewish demographic, thanks to juicy deli meat, fresh bread, crispy bagels and warm *latkes*. Sliders (mini-sandwiches) are served on *challah* bread, an innovation that's as charming as it is tasty.

Shuckers American $

(☎305-866-1570; 1819 79th St Causeway; mains $8-19; ⏲11am-late) With excellent views overlooking the waters from the 79th St Causeway, Shuckers has to be one of the best-positioned restaurants around. The food is pub grub: burgers, fried fish and the like. We come here for one reason: the chicken wings. They're basted in several mouthwatering sauces, deep-fried and grilled again. We could sit here and devour a flock of poultry if our willpower was low.

Steve's Pizza Pizzeria $$

(☎305-891-0202; www.stevespizzas.net; 12101 Biscayne Blvd; slices $3, pizzas $10-16; ⏲11am-3am Sun-Wed, to 4am Thu & Fri, to 2am Sat) So many pizza chains compete for the attention of tourists in South Beach, but ask a Miami Beach local where to get the best pizza and they'll tell you about Steve's. This is New York–style pizza, thin crust and handmade with care and good ingredients. New branches of Steve's are opening elsewhere in Miami, all in decidedly nontouristy areas, which preserves that feeling of authenticity. Steve's flagship is in South Miami; the closer North Miami outpost listed here caters to nighthawks, and is located about 6 miles (15 minutes' drive) north of the Design District.

DOWNTOWN MIAMI

Choices Vegetarian $$

(Map p188; ☎305-400-8895; 379 SW 15th Rd; mains $10-16; ⏲8am-9pm Mon-Fri, to 9pm Sat; 🖉 👪) The description everyone writes when vegan food tastes good is that you're not missing the meat. This trope actually holds true at Choices. With clever ingredient combinations like walnut 'meat' and daiya cheese, this restaurant lives up to its name, offering burgers, tacos and pizza – all 100% vegan, and all delicious.

Bonding Fusion $$

(Map p188; ☎786-409-4796; 638 S Miami Ave; mains $12-28; ⏲noon-11pm Mon-Fri, to midnight Sat, 5pm-midnight Sun; 🖉) Multiple Asian cuisines, including Thai, Japanese and Korean, come together into an excellent whole at Bonding. Chicken is expertly tossed with chilis and basil, red curry is deliciously fiery and sushi rolls are given a South Florida splash with ingredients like mango salsa and spicy mayo. The bar here keeps some excellent sake under the counter.

WYNWOOD, DESIGN DISTRICT & LITTLE HAITI

Chef Creole — Haitian $

(Map p192; ☎305-754-2223; 200 NW 54th St; mains $7-20; ⊙11am-11pm Mon-Sat) When you need Caribbean food on the cheap, head to the edge of Little Haiti and this excellent take-out shack. Order up fried conch, oxtail or fish, ladle rice and beans on the side, and you'll be full for a week. Enjoy the food on nearby picnic benches while Haitian music blasts out of tinny speakers – as island an experience as they come.

Blue Collar — American $$

(Map p192; ☎305-756-0366; www.bluecollarmiami.com; 6730 Biscayne Blvd; mains $15-22; ⊙11:30am-3:30pm Mon-Fri, 11am-3:30pm Sat & Sun, 6-10pm Sun-Thu, 6-11pm Fri & Sat; **)** It's not easy striking a balance between laid back and delicious in a city like Miami, where even 'casual' eateries can feel like nightclubs, but Blue Collar has the formula nailed. Friendly staff serve All-American fare sexied the hell up, from crispy snapper to smoky ribs to a superlatively good cheeseburger. A well-curated veg board keeps non-carnivores happy.

Egg & Dart — Greek $$

(Map p192; ☎786-431-1022; 4029 N Miami Ave; small plates $4-16, mains $15-36; ⊙4-11:30pm Tue-Thu, to midnight Fri, 11am-11:30pm Sat & Sun; P) Miami has a habit of sexing up the presentation of most ethnic cuisines, but we have to admit, we hadn't seen Greek done with glam till Egg & Dart. The effort is marvelous. Crafted cocktails (try the orange *mojito*) loosen up the palette for small plates like grilled *halloumi* and zucchini croquettes, and big mains like lovingly grilled lamb and a delicious beet-and-cheese stack.

Oak Tavern — American $$

(Map p192; ☎786-391-1818; 35 NE 40th St; mains $12-26; ⊙noon-10:30pm Mon-Thu, to midnight Fri, 6pm-midnight Sat, 11am-9:30pm Sun;) Oak is a fine addition to the burgeoning dining scene in leafy Buena Vista. Grilled grouper sandwiches, wood-fired pizzas, farm-fresh vegetables, mushroom-crusted strip steaks and some great burgers are ostensibly hearty, but presented with sleek Miami attitude in a dining room that successfully pulls off sexy and rustic simultaneously.

Cuban buffet

JEFF GREENBERG/ALAMY ©

Gigi Asian **$$**

(Map p192; ☎305-573-1520; 3470 North Miami Ave; mains $14-28; ⏰noon-midnight Sun & Mon, to 3am Tue-Thu, to 5am Fri & Sat; P) Gigi does Asian cuisine, but it's the sort of Asian you'd expect to find on the border of the ultra-hip Design District. Ribs come glazed in hoisin and South American aji, the sweet-and-savory cornbread is an excellent complement and the pad Thai is divine. Does sushi go with country chicken? Surprisingly well.

KEY BISCAYNE

Boater's Grill Seafood **$$**

(Map p194; ☎305-361-0080; 1200 S Crandon Blvd; mains $12-29; ⏰9am-9pm) Located in Crandon Park, this waterfront restaurant (actually there's water below and all around) feels like a Chesapeake Bay sea house from up north, except the menu is packed with South Florida maritime goodness: stone crabs, mahimahi and lobster paella.

LITTLE HAVANA

Exquisito Restaurant Cuban **$**

(Map p196; ☎305-643-0227; 1510 SW 8th St; mains $7-13; ⏰7am-11pm) For great Cuban cuisine in the heart of Little Havana, this place is exquisite (ha ha). The roast pork has a tangy citrus kick and the *ropa vieja* is wonderfully rich and filling. Even standard sides like beans and rice and roasted plantains are executed with a little more care and tastiness. Prices are a steal, too.

Islas Canarias Cuban **$**

(☎305-559-6666; 285 NW 27th Ave; mains $8-19; ⏰7am-11pm) Islas may not look like much, sitting in a strip mall, but it serves some of the best Cuban in Miami. The *ropa vieja* is delicious and there are nice Spanish touches on the menu (the owner's father is from the Canary Islands, hence the restaurant's name). Don't pass up the signature homemade chips, especially the ones cut from plantains.

Versailles Cuban **$$**

(☎305-444-0240; 3555 SW 8th St; mains $5-26; ⏰8am-1am) Versailles (ver-*sigh*-yay) is an institution,one of the mainstays of Miami's Cuban gastronomic scene. Try the ground beef in a gratin sauce or chicken breast cooked in creamy garlic sauce. Older Cubans and Miami's Latin political elite still love coming here, so you've got a real chance to rub elbows with a who's who of Miami's most prominent Latin citizens.

COCONUT GROVE

Coral Bagels Deli **$**

(☎305-854-0336; 2750 SW 26th Ave; mains $3.75-9; ⏰6:30am-3pm Mon-Fri, 7am-4pm Sat & Sun; P ✍) At the risk of engaging in hyperbole, we can't imagine a better way of starting the day than a garlic bagel at this little deli. Breakfast (bagels and more traditional eggs, meat and potatoes) is the way to go;

Pastries, Versailles

you'll be hard pressed to spend double digits, and you'll leave satisfied.

LoKal — American $

(☎305-442-3377; 3190 Commodore Plaza; burgers $11-14; ⏰noon-10pm Sun-Thu, to 11pm Fri & Sat;) This little Coconut Grove joint does two things very well: burgers and smart ingredient sourcing. The former come in several variations, all utilizing excellent beef (bar the oat-bran-based veggie version); we love the frita, which adds in guava sauce. The latter comes in the form of genuine farm-to-table relationships: there's a reason the avocado slices are so beautiful.

CORAL GABLES

Matsuri — Japanese $

(☎305-663-1615; 5759 Bird Rd; mains $7-23; ⏰11:30am-2:30pm Tue-Fri, 5:30-10:30pm Tue-Sat) Note the customers here: Matsuri, tucked into a nondescript shopping center, is consistently packed with Japanese customers. They don't want scene; they want a taste of home, although many of the diners are actually South American Japanese who order *unagi* (eels) in Spanish. Spicy *toro* (fatty tuna) and scallions, grilled mackerel with natural salt, and an ocean of raw fish are all *oishii* (delicious).

El Carajo — Spanish $$

(☎305-856-2424; www.el-carajo.com; 2465 SW 17th Avenue; tapas $4.50-17; ⏰noon-10pm Mon-Wed, to 11pm Thu-Sat, 1-9pm Sun) Pass the Penzoil, please. We know it is cool to tuck restaurants into unassuming spots, but the Citgo station on SW 17th Ave? Really? Really. Walk past the motor oil into a Granadan wine cellar and try not to act too fazed. And now the food, which is absolutely incredible: chorizo in cider blends burn, smoke and juice; frittatas are comfortably filling; and *sardinas* and *boquerones*...wow. These sardines and anchovies cooked with a bit of salt and olive oil are dizzyingly delicious.

Drinking & Nightlife

Miami has an intense variety of bars to pick from, that range from grotty dives to beautiful – but still laid-back – lounges and nightclubs. Not to say you can't spot celebrities if you want to...

SOUTH BEACH

Room — Bar

(Map p180; www.theotheroom.com; 100 Collins Ave; ⏰7pm-5am) The Room's a gem: a crowded, dimly lit boutique beer bar where you can guzzle the best (brew) Miami has to offer and gawk at the best (hotties) South Beach has to show off. It's hip as hell, but the attitude is as low-key as the sexy mood lighting. Just beware, it gets crowded and it can be tough to find seats as the night goes on.

Kill Your Idol — Bar

(Map p180; ☎305-672-1852; 222 Española Way; ⏰8pm-5am) Kill Your Idol is a self-conscious dive that aims snooty condescension at South Beach's celebrity scene with one hand (see: the name of the place) while sipping a PBR with the other. Precocious? But it does have sweet post-modern art, graffiti and undeniably cute hipsters, and it's adjoined to that most unselfconscious of dives, **Lost Weekend** (Map p180; 218 Española Way; ⏰noon-5am).

Mac's Club Deuce Bar — Bar

(Map p180; 222 14th St; ⏰8am-5am) The oldest bar in Miami Beach (established in 1926), the Deuce is a real neighborhood bar and hype-free zone. It's just straight-up seediness, which depending on your outlook can be quite refreshing. Plan to see everyone from transgendered ladies to construction workers – some hooking up, some talking rough, all having a good time.

Nikki Beach Club — Club

(Map p180; ☎305-538-1111; www.nikkibeach.com; 1 Ocean Dr; cover from $25; ⏰noon-6pm Mon-Thu, noon-11pm Fri & Sat, 11am-11pm Sun) Get your groove on outdoors, wandering from immaculate gossamer beach cabana to cabana at Nikki's, which feels like an incredibly upscale full-moon party. On Sunday (Sunday?!), starting around 4pm, it's the hottest party in town, as folks clamor to get in and re-live whatever it was they did the night before.

NORTHERN MIAMI BEACH

Broken Shaker Bar

(☎305-531-2727; 2727 Indian Creek Dr; ⏰6pm-2am Sun-Thu, 2pm-2am Fri & Sat) Craft cocktails are having their moment in Miami, and if mixology is in the spotlight, you can bet Broken Shaker is sharing the glare. Expert bartenders run this spot, located in the back of the Freehand Miami hotel (p206), which takes up one closet-sized indoor niche and a sprawling outdoor courtyard of excellent drinks and beautiful people.

DOWNTOWN MIAMI

Blackbird Ordinary Bar

(Map p188; ☎305-671-3307; 729 SW 1st Ave; ⏰3pm-5am Mon-Fri, 6pm-5am Sat & Sun) The Ordinary is almost that...well, no. It isn't ordinary at all – this is an excellent bar, with great cocktails (the London Sparrow, with gin, cayenne, lemon juice and passion fruit, goes down well) and an enormous courtyard. But it is 'ordinary' in the sense that it's a come as you are joint that eschews judgment for easy camaraderie.

WYNWOOD, DESIGN DISTRICT & LITTLE HAITI

Wood Tavern Bar

(Map p192; ☎305-748-2828; 2531 NW 2nd Ave; ⏰5pm-2am Tue-Sun) So many new bars in Miami want to be casual but cool; Wood is one of the few locales achieving this Golden Mean of atmosphere and aesthetic. The crowd is local Miami kids who don't want a dive, but don't want the long lines and attitude of South Beach. Ergo: Anglo kids joking with Latinos in an outdoor space that includes picnic benches, a wooden stage complete with bleachers and giant Jenga game, and an attached art gallery with rotating exhibits. Food specials are cheap, the beer selection is excellent and the crowd is friendly – this Wood's got the right grain.

Bardot Club

(Map p192; ☎305-576-5570; 3456 N Miami Ave; ⏰8pm-3am Tue & Wed, to 5am Thu-Sat) You really should see the interior of Bardot before you leave the city. It's all sexy French vintage posters and furniture seemingly plucked from a private club that serves millionaires by day, and becomes a scene of decadent excess by night. The entrance

Nightlife, South Beach

Art Walks: the New Clubbing?

It's hipsters gone wild! Or to put it another way: it's free wine! And artsy types, and galleries open till late, and the eye candy of a club, and the drunken momentum of a pub crawl and – best of all – no red ropes. The free Wynwood and Design District Art Walk is one of the best nightlife experiences in Miami. And we're not (just) being cheapskates. The experience of strolling from gallery to gallery ('That piece is *gorgeous*. Pour me another'), perusing the paintings ('No, I don't think there's a bathroom behind the performance artist') and delving into the nuances of aesthetic styles ('The wine's run out? Let's bounce') is as genuinely innovative as...well, the best contemporary art. Just be careful, as a lot of galleries in Wynwood are separated by short drives (the Design District is more walkable). Art Walks take place on the second Saturday of each month, from 7pm to 10pm (some galleries stretch to 11pm); when it's all over, lots of folks repair to Electric Pickle or Bardot. Visit www.artcircuits.com for information on participating galleries.

looks to be on N Miami Ave, but it's actually in a parking lot behind the building.

COCONUT GROVE

Everything here closes at 3am.

Taurus Bar

(☎305-529-6523; 3540 Main Hwy; ⏲4pm-3am) The oldest bar in Coconut Grove is a cool mix of wood paneling, smoky leather chairs, about 100 beers to choose from and a convivial vibe – as neighborhood bars go in Miami, this is one of the best.

CORAL GABLES

Seven Seas Bar

(☎305-266-6071; 2200 SW 57th Ave; ⏲noon-1am Sun-Thu, to late Fri & Sat) Seven Seas is a genuine Miami neighborhood dive, decorated on the inside like a nautical theme park and filled with University of Miami students, Cuban workers, gays, straights, lesbians and folks from around the way. Come for the best karaoke in Miami on Tuesday, Thursday and Saturday – there's plenty of Spanish-language music, which adds Latin spice.

The Bar Bar

(☎305-442-2730; 172 Giralda Ave; ⏲11:30am-3am) All in a name, right? Probably the best watering hole in the Gables, The Bar is just what the title says (which is unusual in this neighborhood of extravagant embellishment). If you're in the 'hood on Friday, come here for happy hour (5pm to 8pm), when young Gables professionals take their ties off and let loose long into the night.

Entertainment

Miami's artistic merits are obvious: homegrown talent, migratory snowbirds bringing the funding and attention of northeastern galleries, and immigrants from across the Americas.

PERFORMING ARTS

Gusman Center for the Performing Arts Performing Arts

(Map p188; ☎305-374-2444; www.gusmancenter.org; 174 E Flagler St) This elegantly renovated 1920s movie palace services a huge variety of performing arts including film festivals, symphonies, ballets and touring shows. The acoustics are excellent.

THEATER

Jerry Herman Ring Theatre Theater

(☎305-284-3355; www.miami.edu/ring; University of Miami, 1321 Miller Dr; tickets $8-15) This

If You Like... Independent Cinemas

Miami has a glut of art-house cinemas showing first-run, independent and foreign films. Here are some of our favorites:

1 **COSFORD CINEMA**
(305-284-4861; www.cosfordcinema.com; Memorial Classroom Bldg, 5030 Brunson Dr, University of Miami) On the University of Miami campus, this renovated art house was launched in memory of the *Miami Herald* film critic, Bill Cosford.

2 **CORAL GABLES ART CINEMA**
(786-385-9689; www.gablescinema.com; 260 Aragon Ave) Indie and foreign films in a 144-seat cinema.

3 **TOWER THEATER**
(Map p196; 305-643-8706; www.mdc.edu/culture/tower; 1508 SW 8th St) In a gem of a deco building, managed by Miami Dade College.

4 **O CINEMA**
(Map p192; 305-571-9970; www.o-cinema.org; 90 NW 29th St) Indie screenings in Wynwood.

University of Miami troupe stages musicals, dramas and comedies, with recent productions including *Falsettos* and *Baby*. Alumni actors include Sylvester Stallone, Steven Bauer, Saundra Santiago and Ray Liotta.

Miami City Ballet Dance
(Map p180; 305-929-7000; www.miamicityballet.org; 2200 Liberty Ave) Formed in 1985, this troupe is based out of a lovely three-story headquarters designed by famed local architectural firm Arquitectonica. The facade allows passers-by to watch the dancers rehearsing through big picture windows, which makes you feel like you're in a scene from *Fame*, except the weather is better and people don't spontaneously break into song.

CLASSICAL

New World Symphony Classical Music
(NWS; Map p180; 305-673-3330; www.nws.edu; 500 17th St) Housed in the New World Center – a funky explosion of cubist lines and geometric curves, fresh white against the blue Miami sky – the acclaimed New World Symphony holds performances from October to May. The deservedly heralded NWS serves as a three- to four-year preparatory program for talented musicians from prestigious music schools.

Shopping

GO! Shop Arts & Crafts
(Map p192; 305-576-8205; 2516 NW 2nd Ave; noon-8pm Thu-Sat) If you fancy the art at the Wynwood Walls (p191), make sure to pop into the GO! shop, located within the street art complex. Original artwork, prints and other arts accoutrements are presented on a rotating basis; the stuff for sale is either produced by or related to the works created by the current crop of Wynwood Walls artists.

Consign of the Times Vintage
(Map p180; 305-535-0811; www.consignofthetimes.com; 1635 Jefferson Ave; 11am-9pm) Cute vintage boutique that carries labels as lovely as Gucci (patent-leather shoes!), Von Furstenberg (leather sling-backs!) and Versace (silver bustier!).

Books and Books Books
(305-442-4408; 265 Aragon Ave; 9am-11pm Sun-Thu, to midnight Fri & Sat) The best indie bookstore in South Florida is a massive emporium of all things literary. Hosts frequent readings and is generally just a fantastic place to hang out. Has other outposts on **Lincoln Rd (305-532-3222; 927 Lincoln Rd)** and at the Bal Harbour shops.

Metta Boutique Gifts
(Map p180; 305-763-8230; 1845 Purdy Ave; 9am-8pm Mon-Thu, to 9pm Fri & Sat, 11am-6pm Sun) A cute store that brings some sustainability to South Beach.

All of the goodies – clothes, journals, accessories, gifts and tchotchkes – are decidedly green/organic/sustainable/fair trade.

Sweat Records Music
(Map p192; ☎786-693-9309; 5505 NE 2nd Ave; ⏲noon-10pm Tue-Sat, to 5pm Sun) Sweat's almost a stereotypical indie record store – there's funky art and graffiti on the walls, it has big purple couches, it sells weird Japanese toys and there are skinny guys with thick glasses arguing over LPs and EPs you've never heard of, and of course, there's coffee and vegan snacks.

Information

Dangers & Annoyances

At night, avoid Liberty City, in northwest Miami; Overtown, from 14th St to 20th St; Little Haiti; and stretches of the Miami riverfront.

Emergency

Ambulance **(☎911)**

Beach Patrol **(☎305-673-7714)**

Hurricane Hotline **(☎305-468-5400)**

Poison Information Center **(☎305-585-5250)**

Rape Hotline **(☎305-585-7273)**

Suicide Intervention **(☎305-358-4357)**

Medical Services

Miami Beach Community Health Center **(Stanley C Meyers Center; ☎305-538-8835; 710 Alton Rd, South Beach)** Walk-in clinic with long lines.

Mount Sinai Medical Center **(☎305-674-2121, emergency room 305-674-2200; 4300 Alton Rd)** The area's best emergency room. Beware that you must eventually pay, and fees are high.

Visitor's Medical Line **(☎305-674-2222; ⏲24hr)** For physician referrals.

Tourist Information

Art Deco Welcome Center **(Map p180; ☎305-672-2014; www.mdpl.org; 1001 Ocean Dr, South Beach; ⏲9:30am-5pm Fri-Wed, to 7pm Thu)** Run by the Miami Design Preservation League (MDPL); has tons of art-deco district information and organizes excellent walking tours.

Websites

Art Circuits **(www.artcircuits.com)** The best insider info on art events; includes excellent neighborhood-by-neighborhood gallery maps.

Short Order **(http://blogs.miaminewtimes.com/shortorder)** The *New Times* food blog that always seems ahead of the curve on eating events in the Magic City.

Meatless Miami **(www.meatlessmiami.com)** Vegetarians in need of an eating guide, look no further.

Miami Beach 411 **(www.miamibeach411.com)** A great guide for Miami Beach visitors, covering just about all concerns.

Miami Nights **(www.miaminights.com)** Get a good, opinionated lowdown on Miami's ever-shifting after-dark scene.

Beached Miami **(www.beachedmiami.com)** The best independent arts website in Miami.

Getting There & Away

Air

Miami is served by all major carriers via two main airports: Miami International Airport (MIA) and the Fort Lauderdale-Hollywood International Airport (FLL), half an hour north of MIA. **MIA** **(☎305-876-7000; www.miami-airport.com)** is the third-busiest airport in the country. Just 6 miles west of downtown Miami, the airport is open 24 hours and is laid out in a horseshoe design. There are left-luggage facilities on two concourses at MIA, between B and C, and on G; prices vary according to bag size.

Getting Around

To/From the Airport

Miami International Airport

If you're driving, follow Rte 112 from the airport, then head east on the Julia Tuttle Causeway or the I-195 to get to South Beach. Other options include free shuttles offered by most hotels or a taxi ($38 flat rate from the airport to South Beach). Alternatively, catch the Airport Owl night-only public bus, or the **SuperShuttle** **(☎305-871-8210; www.supershuttle.com)** shared-van service, which will cost about $26 to South Beach.

Bicycle

The city of Miami Beach offers the **DecoBike** **(☎305-532-9494; www.decobike.com)** bike-share

program. Bike stations are located in dozens of spots around Miami Beach (there's a map on the website, plus an iPhone app that tells you where the nearest station is).

Places that rent bicycles:

BikeAndRoll (Map p180; ☎305-604-0001; www.bikeandroll.com; 210 10th St; per hr/day from $5/15; ⏰9am-7pm) Also does bike tours.

Mangrove Cycles (Map p194; ☎305-361-5555; 260 Crandon Blvd, Key Biscayne; per 2hr/day/week from $20/25/75; ⏰10am-6pm Tue-Sun) Rents bicycles.

Bus

The local bus system is called **Metrobus** (☎305-891-3131; www.miamidade.gov/transit/routes.asp; tickets $2). An easy-to-read route map is available online. You may spend more time waiting for a bus than riding on one.

In South Beach, an excellent option is the **South Beach Local Circulator** (☎305-891-3131; 25¢), a looping shuttle bus with disabled-rider access that operates along Washington between South Pointe Dr and 17th St and loops back around on Alton Rd on the west side of the beach. Rides come along every 10 to 15 minutes.

Taxi

Central Cabs (☎305-532-5555)

Flamingo Taxis (☎305-759-8100)

Metro (☎305-888-8888)

Miami Taxi Service (☎305-525-2455)

Sunshine (☎305-445-3333)

Yellow (☎305-400-0000)

FLORIDA KEYS

The Keys are physically and culturally separate from the mainland. They march to the beat of their own drum, or Alabama country band, or Jimmy Buffet single, or Bahamanian steel calypso set...whatever. The point is, this is a place where those who reject everyday life in the Lower 48 escape to. What do they find? About 113 mangrove-and-sandbar islands where the white sun melts over tight fists of deep-green mangroves, long, gloriously soft mudflats and tidal bars, and water as teal as Arizona turquoise.

Upper Keys

No, really, you're in the islands!

It's a bit hard to tell when you first arrive, as the huge, rooty blanket of mangrove forest that forms the South Florida coastline spreads like a woody morass into Key Largo. In fact, the mangroves become Key Largo, which is more famous for its underwater than above-ground views. If you want to avoid traffic on US Hwy 1, you can try the less trafficked FL 997 and Card Sound Rd to FL 905 (toll $1), which passes Alabama Jack's.

KEY LARGO & TAVERNIER

Sights & Activities

John Pennekamp Coral Reef State Park Park

(☎305-451-6300; www.pennekamppark.com; MM 102.6 oceanside; car/motorcycle/cyclist or pedestrian $8/4/2; ⏰8am-sunset, aquarium to 5pm; 👪) 🍃 John Pennekamp has the singular distinction of being the first underwater park in the USA. There's 170 acres of dry parkland here and over 48,000 acres (ie 75 sq miles) of wet: the vast majority of the protected area is the ocean. Before you get out in that water, make sure to dig around some pleasant beaches and stroll over the nature trails.

Florida Keys Wild Bird Rehabilitation Center Wildlife Reserve

(www.fkwbc.org; 93600 Overseas Hwy, MM 93.6; suggested donation $5; ⏰sunrise-sunset; P 👪) 🍃 This sanctuary is the first of many animal hospitals you'll come across that is built by critter-loving Samaritans throughout the Keys. You'll find an alfresco bird hospital that cares for birds that have swallowed fish hooks, had wings clipped in accidents, been shot by BB pellets etc. A pretty trail leads back to a nice vista of Florida Bay and a wading bird pond. Just be warned, it does smell like bird doo back here.

Eating

Key Largo Conch House Fusion $$

(☎305-453-4844; www.keylargoconchhouse.com; MM 100.2 oceanside; mains $8-26; ⌚8am-10pm; P 📶 👪) This wi-fi hotspot, coffee-house and innovative kitchen likes to sex up local classics (conch in a lime and white-wine sauce, or in a vinegar sauce with capers). Set in a restored old-school Keys mansion wrapped in a *Gone With the Wind* veranda, it's hard not to love the way the period architecture blends in seamlessly with the local tropical fauna.

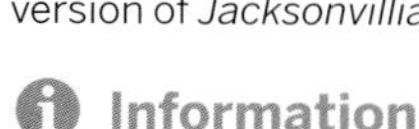

Drinking

Alabama Jack's Bar

(58000 Card Sound Rd; ⌚11am-7pm) Welcome to your first taste of the Keys: zonked-out fishermen, exiles from the mainland and Harley heads getting drunk on a mangrove bay. This is the line where Miami-esque South Florida gives way to the country-fried American South. Wildlife-lovers: you may spot the rare mulleted version of *Jacksonvillia Redneckus*!

Information

Mariner Hospital (☎305-434-3000; www.baptisthealth.net; Tavernier, MM 91.5 bayside)

Getting There & Away

The Greyhound bus stops at MM 99.6 oceanside.

ISLAMORADA

Islamorada (eye-luh-murr-*ah*-da) is also known as 'the Village of Islands.' Doesn't that sound pretty? Well, it really is. This little string of pearls (well, keys) – Plantation, Upper and Lower Matecumbe, Shell and Lignumvitae (lignum-*vite*-ee) – shimmers as one of the prettiest stretches of the islands.

Sights & Activities

Robbie's Marina Marina

(☎305-664-8070; www.robbies.com; MM 77.5 bayside; kayak & SUP rentals $40-75; ⌚9am-8pm; 👪) More than a boat launch, Robbie's is a local flea market, tacky tourist shop (all the shells you ever wanted), sea pen for tarpons (very big-ass fish) and jump-off for fishing expeditions, all wrapped into one driftwood-laced compound. Boat-rental and tour options are also available. The party boat (half-day/night trips $40/45) is just that: a chance to drink, fish and basically achieve Keys Zen.

Anne's Beach Beach

(MM 73.5 oceanside) Anne's is one of the best beaches in these parts. The small ribbon of sand opens upon a sky-bright stretch of tidal flats and a green tunnel of hammock and wetland. Nearby mudflats are a joy to get stuck in, and will be much loved by the kids.

Coral, Islamorada

Indian Key Historic State Park — Island

(☎305-664-2540; www.floridastateparks.org/indiankey; MM 78.5 oceanside; $2.50; ⏰8am-sunset) This quiet island was once a thriving city, complete with a warehouse, docks, streets, a hotel and about 40 to 50 permanent residents. There's not much left at the historic site – just the foundation, some cisterns and jungly tangle. Robbie's (p219) used to bring boats this way, and still does boat rentals (around $30 for a kayak or canoe). You can also see the island from the water on an eco-tour with Robbie's ($37.50).

Eating

Midway Cafe — Cafe $

(☎305-664-2622; 80499 Overseas Hwy; dishes $2-11; ⏰7am-3pm Thu-Tue, to 2pm Sun; P 👪) The lovely folks who run this cafe, which is stuffed with every variety of heart-warming art the coffee-shop trope can muster, roast their own beans, make baked goods that we would swim across the Gulf for, and are friendly as hell. You're almost in the Middle Keys: celebrate making it this far with a cup of joe.

Information

Chamber of Commerce (☎305-664-4503; www.islamoradachamber.com; MM 83.2 bayside; ⏰9am-5pm Mon-Fri, to 4pm Sat, to 3pm Sun) Located in an old caboose.

Getting There & Away

The Greyhound bus stops at the Burger King at MM 82.5 oceanside.

Middle Keys

MARATHON

Marathon is at the halfway point between Key Largo and Key West, and is a good place to stop on a road trip across the islands.

Sights & Activities

Crane Point Museum — Museum

(☎305-743-9100; www.cranepoint.net; MM 50.5 bayside; adult/child $12.50/8.50; ⏰9am-5pm Mon-Sat, from noon Sun; P 👪) 🍃 This is one of the nicest spots on the island to stop and smell the roses. And the pinelands. And the palm hammock – a sort of palm jungle (imagine walking under giant, organic Japanese fans) that only grows between MM 47 and MM 60. There's also Adderly House, a preserved example of a Bahamian immigrant cabin (which must have *baked* in summer) and 63 acres of green goodness to stomp through.

Turtle Hospital — Wildlife Reserve

(☎305-743-2552; www.theturtlehospital.org; 2396 Overseas Hwy; adult/child $15/7.50; ⏰9am-6pm; P 👪) 🍃 Be it a victim of disease, boat propeller strike, flipper entanglement with fishing lines or any other danger, an injured sea turtle in the Keys will hopefully end up in this motel-cum-sanctuary. We know we shouldn't anthropomorphize animals, but these turtles just seem so sweet. It's sad to see the injured and sick ones, but heartening to see them so well looked after. Tours are educational, fun and offered on the hour from 10am-4pm.

Eating

Keys Fisheries — Seafood $

(☎305-743-4353; www.keysfisheries.com; 3502 Louisa St; mains $7-16; ⏰8am-9pm; P 👪) The lobster Reuben is the stuff of legend here. Sweet, chunky, creamy, so good it'll make you leave unsightly drool all over the place mat. But you can't go wrong with any of the excellent seafood here, all served with sass. Expect pleasant levels of seagull harassment as you dine on a working waterfront.

Drinking

Hurricane — Bar

(☎305-743-2200; MM 49.5 bayside; ⏰11am-midnight) The staff is sassy and warm. The

AMAR AND ISABELLE GUILLEN - GUILLEN PHOTO LLC/ALAMY ©

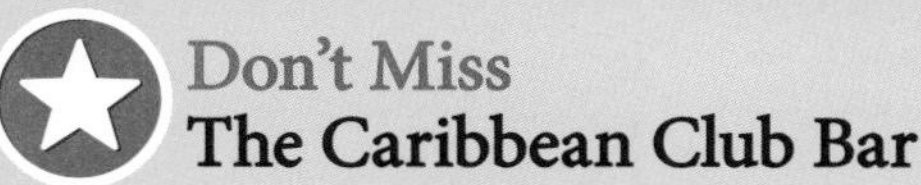

Don't Miss
The Caribbean Club Bar

Here's one for the movie fans, particularly Bogie buffs: the Caribbean Club Bar (open 7am to 4am), located at MM 104 bayside is, in fact, the only place in Key Largo where *Key Largo,* starring Humphrey Bogart and Lauren Bacall, was filmed (the rest of the island was a Hollywood soundstage). If that's not enough, the original African Queen, of the same-titled movie, is docked in a channel at the Holiday Inn at MM 100 – just walk around the back and there she is.

drinks will kick your ass out the door and have you back begging for more. The clientele: locals, tourists, mad fishermen, rednecks and the odd journalist saddling up for endless Jägerbombs before dancing the night away to any number of consistently good live acts. It's the best bar before Key West, and it deserves a visit.

Information

Fisherman's Hospital (**305-743-5533; www.fishermanshospital.com; 3301 Overseas Hwy**) Has a major emergency room.

Lower Keys

The Lower Keys are fierce bastions of conch culture. Some local families have been Keys castaways for generations, and there are bits of Big Pine that feel more Florida Panhandle than Overseas Hwy.

BIG PINE, BAHIA HONDA & LOOE KEY

Big Pine is home to stretches of quiet roads, Key West employees who found a way around astronomical real-estate rates, and packs of wandering Key deer.

Keys for Children

Check out some of the following options to entertain the kids:

Florida Keys Eco-Discovery Center (p223) Get an understanding of the region's environment.

Glass-bottom boat tours at John Pennekamp Coral Reef State Park (305-451-6300; adult/child $24/17; 9:15am, 12:15pm & 3:15pm) Your own window to the underwater world.

Turtle Hospital (p220) Save (or watch) the turtles.

Conch Tour Train (p227) Kitschy, corny, enjoyable tour.

Robbie's Marina (p219) All sorts of activities, including the ever-popular tarpon (giant fish) feeding frenzy.

Sights & Activities

Bahia Honda State Park Park

(305-872-3210; www.bahiahondapark.com; MM 36.8; car/motorcycle/cyclist $5/4/2; 8am-sunset;) This park, with its long, white-sand (and seaweed-strewn) beach, named Sandspur Beach by locals, is the big attraction in these parts. As Keys beaches go, this one is probably the best natural stretch of sand in the island chain, but we wouldn't vote it best beach in the continental USA (although Condé Nast did...in 1992). As a tourist, the more novel experience is walking on the **old Bahia Honda Rail Bridge**, which offers nice views of the surrounding islands.

National Key Deer Refuge Headquarters Wildlife Reserve

(305-872-2239; www.fws.gov/nationalkeydeer; Big Pine Shopping Center, MM 30.5 bayside; 8am-5pm Mon-Fri;) What would make Bambi cuter? Mini Bambi. Introducing: the Key deer, an endangered subspecies of white-tailed deer that prance about primarily on Big Pine and No Name Keys. The folks here are an incredibly helpful source of information on the deer and all things Keys. The refuge sprawls over several islands, but the sections open to the public are on Big Pine and No Name.

Sleeping

Deer Run Bed & Breakfast B&B $$$

(305-872-2015; www.deerrunfloridabb.com; 1997 Long Beach Dr, Big Pine Key, off MM 33 oceanside; r $255-375;) This state-certified green lodge and vegetarian B&B is isolated on a lovely stretch of Long Beach Dr. It's a garden of quirky delights, complemented by love-the-earth paraphernalia, street signs and four simple but cozy rooms. The helpful owners will get you out on a boat or into the heated pool for relaxation while they whip up delicious vegetarian meals.

Eating

No Name Pub Pizzeria $

(305-872-9115; N Watson Blvd, Big Pine Key, off MM 30.5 bayside; mains $7-18; 11am-11pm; P) The No Name's one of those off-the-track places that everyone seems to know about. It feels isolated, it looks isolated, yet somehow, the tourists are all here – and this doesn't detract in the slightest from the kooky ambience, friendly service, excellent locally brewed beer and primo pizzas served up at this colorful semidive.

KEY WEST

Key West is still defined by its motto, which we love – One Human Family – an ideal that equals a tolerant, accepting ethos where anything goes and life is always a party (or at least a hangover the day after). The color scheme: watercolor pastels cooled by breezes on a sunset-kissed Bahamian porch. Welcome to the End of the USA.

Sights

Mallory Square Square

() Take all those energies, subcultures and oddities of Keys life and focus them into one torchlit, family-friendly (but playfully edgy), sunset-enriched street party. The child of all these raucous forces is Mallory Sq, one of the greatest shows on Earth. It all begins as the sun starts to set, a sign for the madness that it's OK to break out. Watch a dog walk a tightrope, a man swallow fire, and British acrobats tumble and sass each other.

Duval Street Street

Key West locals have a love-hate relationship with the most famous road in Key West (if not the Keys). Duval, Old Town Key West's main drag, is a miracle mile of booze, tacky everything and awful behavior. But it's fun. The 'Duval Crawl' is one of the wildest pub crawls in the country. The mix of neon drink, drag shows, T-shirt kitsch, local theaters, art studios and boutiques is more charming than jarring.

Hemingway House House

(**305-294-1136; www.hemingwayhome.com; 907 Whitehead St; adult/child $13/6; 9am-5pm**) Key West's biggest darling, Ernest Hemingway, lived in this gorgeous Spanish colonial house from 1931 to 1940. Papa moved here in his early 30s with wife No 2, a Vogue fashion editor and (former) friend of wife No 1 (he left the house when he ran off with wife No. 3). *The Short Happy Life of Francis Macomber* and *The Green Hills of Africa* were produced here, as well as many six-toed cats, whose descendants basically run the grounds.

Florida Keys Eco-Discovery Center Museum

(**305-809-4750; http://eco-discovery.com/ecokw.html; 35 East Quay Rd; 9am-4pm Tue-Sat; P**) FREE So, you've been making your way down the Keys, thinking, Gosh, could there be a place that ties all the knowledge of this unique ecological phenomenon into one fun, well-put-together educational exhibit? OK, maybe those weren't your exact thoughts, but this is exactly what you get at this excellent center. This place does a marvelous job of filling in all the wild details of the natural Keys. The kids love it.

Key West Cemetery Cemetery

(**cnr Margaret & Angela Sts; 7am-6pm;**) A darkly alluring Gothic labyrinth beckons at the center of this pastel town. Built in 1847, the cemetery crowns Solares Hill, the highest point on the island (with an elevation of 16ft). Some of the oldest families in the Keys rest in peace – and close proximity – here. With body space at a premium, mausoleums stand pretty much shoulder to shoulder. Island quirkiness penetrates the gloom: seashells and macramé adorn headstones with inscriptions like, 'I told you I was sick.'

Studios of Key West Gallery

(**TSKW; 305-296-0458; www.tskw.org; 600 White St; 10am-6pm**) This nonprofit showcases about a dozen artists' studios in a gallery space located in the old Armory building, which includes a lovely sculpture garden. Besides its public visual-arts displays, TSKW hosts readings, literary and visual workshops, concerts, lectures and community discussion groups. Essentially, it has become the accessible heart of this city's enormous arts movement, and offers a good point-of-entry for visitors who want to engage in Key West's creative scene but don't have a clue where to start.

Key West

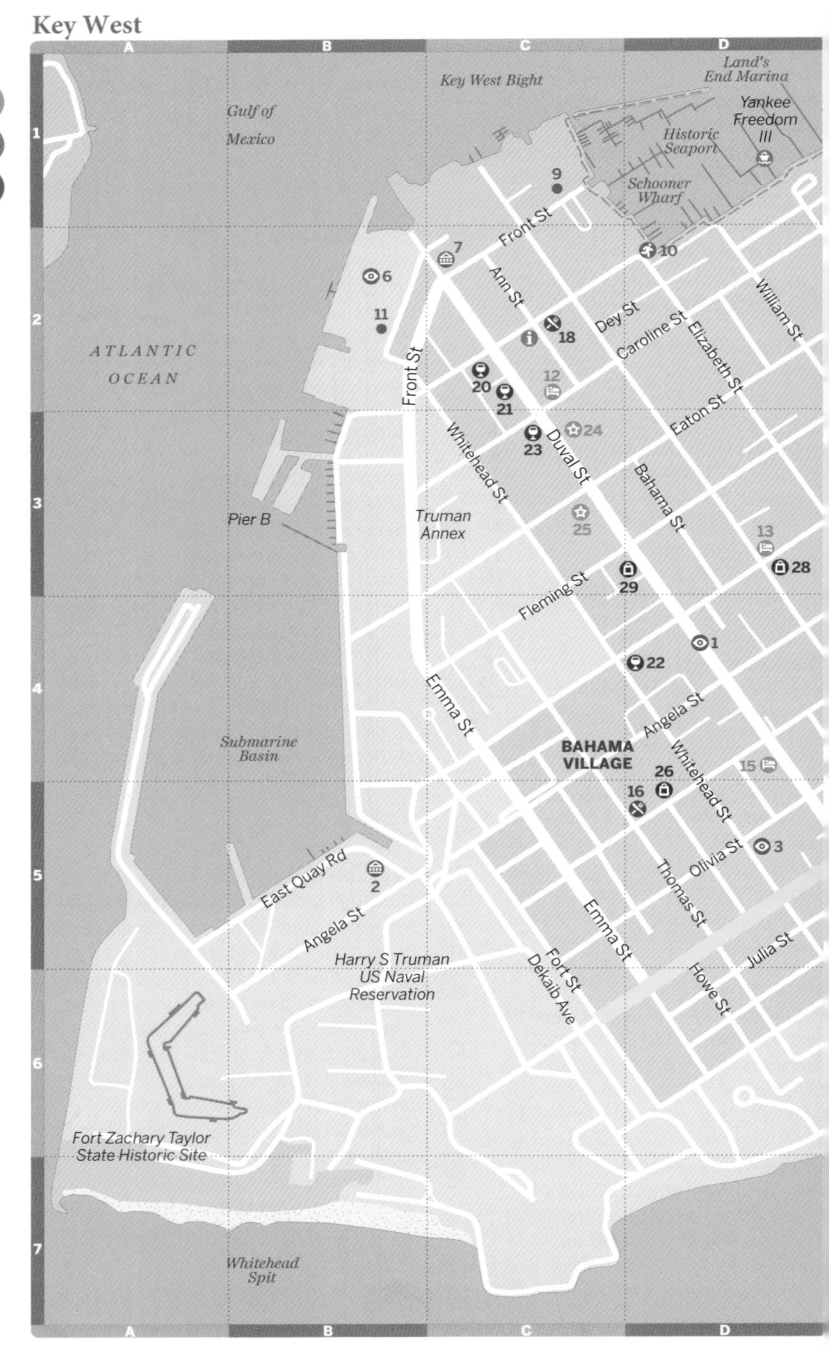

Key West Bight
Land's End Marina
Gulf of Mexico
Yankee Freedom III
Historic Seaport
Schooner Wharf
Front St
Ann St
Dey St
Caroline St
Elizabeth St
William St
ATLANTIC OCEAN
Front St
Eaton St
Whitehead St
Duval St
Bahama St
Pier B
Truman Annex
Fleming St
Emma St
Angela St
BAHAMA VILLAGE
Whitehead St
Submarine Basin
East Quay Rd
Olivia St
Angela St
Thomas St
Harry S Truman US Naval Reservation
Fort St
Dekalb Ave
Emma St
Howe St
Julia St
Fort Zachary Taylor State Historic Site
Whitehead Spit

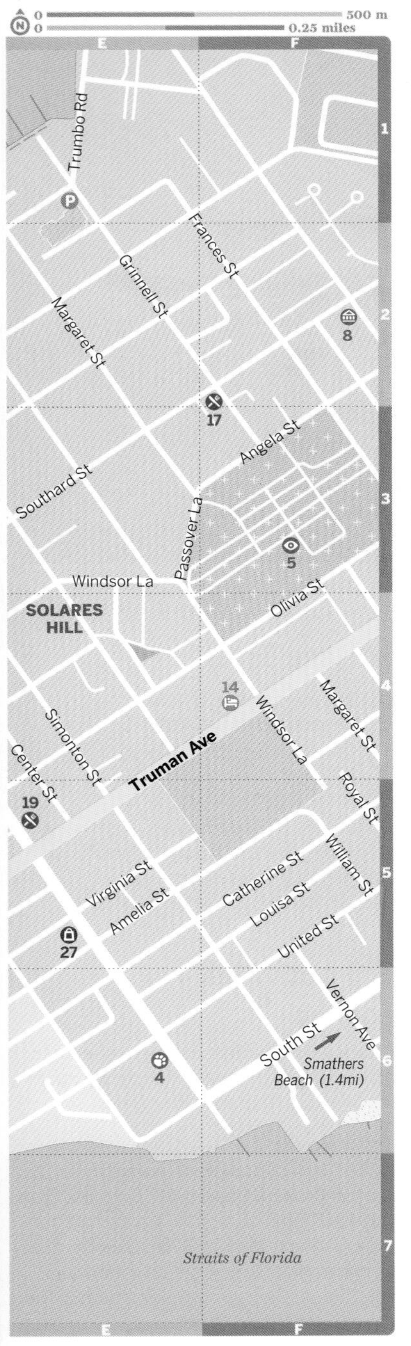

Key West

Sights

Activities, Courses & Tours

Sleeping

Eating

Drinking & Nightlife

Entertainment

Shopping

Museum of Art & History at the Custom House — Museum

(**305-295-6616; www.kwahs.com/custom-house; 281 Front St; adult/child $9/5; 9:30am-4:30pm**) There is art at the end of the road, and you'll find the best at this museum, which is worth a look-see if only for its gorgeous home – the grand Customs House, long abandoned until its impressive renovation in the '90s. The permanent display includes massive portraits and some

DURAVITSKI/ALAMY ©

Don't Miss
Florida Keys Overseas Heritage Trail

One of the best ways to see the Keys is by bicycle. The flat elevation and ocean breezes are perfect for cycling, and the **Florida Keys Overseas Heritage Trail** (FKOHT; www.dep.state.fl.us/gwt/state/keystrail) will connect all the islands from Key Largo to Key West.

If you are keen to ride, it's currently possible to bike through the Keys by shoulder riding (it takes three days at a good clip). There are particularly pleasant rides around Islamorada, and if you're uncomfortable riding on the shoulder, you can contact the FKOHT through its website for recommended bike excursions.

of the best showcases of international (particularly Caribbean) art in the region.

Key West Butterfly & Nature Conservatory Animal Sanctuary

(**☎305-296-2988; www.keywestbutterfly.com; 1316 Duval St; adult/4-12yr $12/8.50; ⏰9am-5pm; 👪**) This vast domed conservatory allows you to stroll through a magic garden of flowering plants, colorful birds and up to 1800 fluttering butterflies of various species, all live imports from around the globe.

Activities

BOATING

Check www.charterboatkeywest.com for a directory of the many fishing and cruising charters offered in Key West.

Jolly Rover Cruise

(**☎305-304-2235; www.schoonerjollyrover.com; cnr Greene & Elizabeth Sts, Schooner Wharf; cruise $45**) This outfit has a gorgeous, tanbark (reddish-brown) 80ft schooner that embarks on daily sunset cruises under sail. It looks like a pirate ship and has the cannons to back the image up.

Tours

Worth noting is *Sharon Wells' Walking & Biking Guide to Historic Key West*, a booklet of self-guided walks available for free at inns and businesses around town, written by a local. See www.seekeywest.com.

Old Town Trolley Tours Tour
(**☎888-910-8687; www.trolleytours.com/key-west; adult/child under 13yr/senior $30/free/27; ⏲tours 9am-4:30pm;**) These tours are a great introduction to the city. The 90-minute, hop-on, hop-off narrated tram tour starts at Mallory Sq and makes a loop around the whole city, with nine stops along the way. Trolleys depart every 15 to 30 minutes from 9am to 4:30pm daily. The narration is hokey, but you'll get a good overview of Key West history.

Conch Tour Train Tour
(**☎305-294-5161; www.conchtourtrain.com; adult/child under 13yr/senior $30/free/27; ⏲tours 9am-4:30pm;**) Run by the same company as Trolley Tours, this one seats you in breezy linked train cars with no on/off option. Offers discounted admission to sights like the Hemingway House.

Historic Key West Walking Tour Tour
(**☎800-844-7601; www.trustedtours.com; 1 Whitehead St; adult/child $18/9)** A walking tour that takes in some of the major architecture and historical sights of the island. Takes about two hours. You need to book in advance.

Sleeping

There's a glut of boutique hotels, cozy B&Bs and four-star resorts here at the end of the USA. Any hotel in Old Town will put you within walking distance of all the action.

Tropical Inn Boutique Hotel $$$
(**☎888-651-6510; www.tropicalinn.com; 812 Duval St; r $175-360;**) The Tropical Inn has excellent service and a host of individualized rooms spread out over a historic home property. Each room comes decked out in bright pastels and shades of mango, lime and seafoam. A delicious breakfast is included and can be enjoyed in the jungly courtyard next to a lovely sunken pool. Two attached cottages offer romance and privacy for couples.

Curry Mansion Inn Hotel $$$
(**☎305-294-5349; www.currymansion.com; 511 Caroline St; r winter $240-365, summer $205-310;**) In a city full of stately 19th-century homes, the Curry Mansion is especially handsome. All the elements of an aristocratic American home come together here, from plantation-era Southern colonnades to a New England–style widow's walk and, of course, bright Floridian rooms with canopied beds.

Local Knowledge

Key West Don't Miss List

BY JULIET GRAY, KEY WEST CONCH (NATIVE), BOX OFFICE DIRECTOR, RED BARN THEATRE

1 KEY WEST ON TWO WHEELS
To truly experience Key West like a local, you must ride like a local. Rent a bike (or 'conch cruiser' as locals call it) to really get to know the southernmost city. A car is just not necessary in Key West.

2 RED BARN THEATRE
'The Barn' (p231) is Key West's longest-running professional theatre. Shows start most nights at 8pm and range from classic musicals to Broadway hits. In addition to local writers and performers, Shel Silverstein, Jimmy Buffett and Tennessee Williams have all made the Barn a part of their cultural experience in Key West.

3 THE PORCH
Best place on the island to get craft beer (and root beer!) on tap as well as wine by the glass or bottle. In addition to fabulous libations, also on tap at The Porch (p229) you'll find wine tastings, local art installations, jewelry shows, mustache parties or even a zombie jamboree.

Enjoy bougainvillea and breezes on the veranda.

Mermaid & the Alligator Guesthouse **$$$**
(305-294-1894; www.kwmermaid.com; 729 Truman Ave; r winter $278-348, summer $188-248;) It takes a real gem to stand out amid the jewels of Keys hotels, but this place, located in a 1904 mansion, more than pulls off the job. Each of the nine rooms is individually designed with a great mix of modern comfort, Keys Colonial ambience and playful laughs.

Mango Tree Inn B&B **$$**
(305-293-1177; www.mangotree-inn.com; 603 Southard St; $150-200;) This down-to-earth B&B offers a courtyard pool and elegant accommodation in a number of airy rooms, each decorated with swathes of tropical-chic accoutrement, from rattan furniture to flowering hibiscus. Rates are a deal for this kind of downtown proximity.

Eating

Key West has delicious neighborhood joints-in-the-wall and top-end purveyors of haute cuisine that could easily compete with the best restaurants in Miami.

Café Solé French **$$$**
(305-294-0230; www.cafesole.com; 1029 Southard St; dinner $20-34; 5:30-10pm) Conch carpaccio with capers? Yellowtail fillet and foie gras? Oh yes. This locally and critically acclaimed venue is known for its cozy back-porch ambience and innovative menus, cobbled together by a chef trained in southern French techniques who works with island ingredients. The memory of the anchovies on crostini makes us smile as we type.

Nine One Five Fusion **$$$**
(305-296-0669; www.915duval.com; 915 Duval St; mains $18-34; 6pm-midnight;) Classy Nine One Five certainly stands out from the nearby Duval detritus of alcoholic aggression and tribal band tattoos. Ignore all that and enter this immaculate, modern and elegant space, which serves a creative, New American-dips-into-Asia menu. It's all quite rich – imagine a butternut squash and almond risotto, or local lobster accompanied by duck confit potatoes.

Blue Heaven American **$$$**
(305-296-8666; http://blueheavenkw.homestead.com; 729 Thomas St; dinner $17-35; 8am-4pm, until 2pm Sun & 5-10:30pm daily;) Proof that location is *nearly* everything, this is one of the quirkiest venues on an island of oddities. Customers (and a local chicken) flock to dine in the spacious courtyard where Hemingway once officiated boxing matches. This place gets packed with customers

Bar, Key West

Detour: Dry Tortugas National Park

Ponce de León named these islands Las Tortugas (The Turtles) for the sea turtles that roamed here. A lack of fresh water led sailors to add a 'dry.' Today the Dry Tortugas are a national park under the control of the **National Park Service** (NPS; ☎305-242-7700; www.nps.gov/drto; admission $5) and are accessible by boat or plane.

The park is open for day trips and overnight camping. Garden Key has 13 campsites ($3 per person, per night), which are given out on a first-come, first-served basis. Reserve early by calling the National Park office. There are toilets, but no freshwater showers or drinking water; bring everything you'll need. The sparkling waters offer excellent snorkeling and diving opportunities. A **visitor center** is located within fascinating Fort Jefferson.

If you're hungry, watch for Cuban-American fishing boats trolling the waters. They'll happily trade for lobster, crab and shrimp; you'll have the most leverage trading beverages. Just paddle up and bargain for your supper. In March and April, there is stupendous bird-watching, including aerial fighting. Star-gazing is mind-blowing any time of the year

GETTING THERE

The **Yankee Freedom II** (☎800-634-0939; www.drytortugas.com/; Historic Seaport) operates a fast ferry between Garden Key and the Historic Seaport (at the northern end of Margaret St). Round-trip fares cost $170/125 per adult/child. Reservations are recommended. Continental breakfast, a picnic lunch, snorkeling gear and a 45-minute tour of the fort are all included.

Key West Seaplanes (☎305-294-0709; www.seaplanesofkeywest.com) can take up to 10 passengers (flight time 40 minutes each way). A four-hour trip costs per adult/child 12 years or under/child under two $295/236/free; an eight-hour trip costs $515/412/free. Again, reserve at least a week in advance.

The $5 park admission fees are included in the above prices.

who wolf down Southern-fried takes on Keys cuisine.

Duetto Pizza & Gelato Italian $

(☎305-848-4981; 540 Greene St; mains under $10; ⏰8am-11pm;) This little pizza and gelato stand is a good-value stop for a quick slice or scoop, especially compared to the greasy cardboard pie served elsewhere in town.

Green Parrot Bar

(www.greenparrot.com; 601 Whitehead St; ⏰10am-4am) The oldest bar on an island of bars, this rogues' cantina opened in the late 19th century and hasn't closed yet. The owner tells you the parachute on the ceiling is 'weighed down with termite turds,' while defunct business signs and local artwork litter the walls and the city attorney shows off her new tattoo at the pool table.

Porch Bar

(www.theporchkw.com; 429 Caroline St; ⏰10am-2am Mon-Sat, noon-2am Sun) If you're getting tired of the frat-boy bars on the Duval St strip, head to the Porch. It's a friendly little artisan beer bar that's more laid back (but hardly civilized) than your average Keys watering hole. The knowledgeable bartenders will trade jokes with you and point you in the right direction for some truly excellent brew.

Should You Swim with Dolphins?

There are four swim-with-the-dolphin (SWTD) centers in the Keys, and many more arguments for and against the practice.

FOR

- While SWTD sites are commercial, they are also research entities devoted to learning more about their charges.
- The dolphins raised on-site are legally obtained and have not been captured from the wild.
- The dolphins are used to humans and pose a negligible danger to swimmers, especially when overseen by expert trainers.
- Dolphin-swim programs increase our knowledge of dolphins and promote conservation.
- At places such as the Dolphin Research Center, the dolphins can actually swim out of their pens into the open water, but choose not to.

AGAINST

- Dolphins are social creatures that require interaction, which is impossible to provide in captivity.
- SWTD tourism encourages the capture of wild dolphins in other parts of the world.
- Dolphin behavior is never 100% predictable. Dolphins can seriously injure a human, even while playing.
- SWTD centers encourage customers to think of dolphins as anthropomorphized 'friends,' rather than wild animals.
- Dolphins never appreciate captivity. Those that voluntarily remain in SWTD sites do so to remain close to food.

SWTD CENTERS

If you decide to swim or see dolphins in the Keys, you can contact one of the following:

Theater of the Sea (305-664-2431; www.theaterofthesea.com; MM 84.7 bayside; adult/child 3-10 $30/21; 9:30am-5pm) Has been here since 1946. Structured dolphin-swims and sea-lion programs ($135) include 30 minutes of instruction and a 30-minute supervised swim. You can also swim with stingrays ($55).

Dolphins Plus (305-451-1993, 866-860-7946; www.dolphinsplus.com; off MM 99.5 bayside; swim programs $135-220) Key Largo center that specializes in recreational and educational unstructured swims. They expect you know a good deal before embarking upon the swim, even though a classroom session is included.

Dolphin Research Centre (305-289-0002; www.dolphins.org; MM 59 bayside; adult/under 4yr/4-12yr/senior $20/free/15/17.50, swim program $120-675; 9am-4pm;) Here the dolphins are free to leave the grounds and a lot of marine-biology research goes on behind the (still pretty commercial) tourist activities, such as getting a dolphin to paint your T-shirt or playing 'trainer for a day' ($650).

Garden of Eden Bar
(224 Duval St; 12pm-4am) Go to the top of this building and discover Key West's own clothing-optional drinking patio. Lest you get too excited, cameras aren't allowed, most people come clothed, and those who do elect to flaunt their birthday suits are often…erm…older.

Captain Tony's Saloon Bar
(www.capttonyssaloon.com; 428 Greene St; 10am-2am) Propagandists would have you believe the nearby megabar complex of Sloppy Joe's was Hemingway's original bar, but the physical place where the old man drank was right here, the original Sloppy Joe's location (before it was moved onto Duval St and into frat-boy hell).

Entertainment

Red Barn Theatre Theater
(305-296-9911; www.redbarntheatre.org; 319 Duval St) An occasionally edgy and always fun, cozy little local playhouse.

Tropic Cinema Cinema
(877-761-3456; www.tropiccinema.org; 416 Eaton St) Great art-house movie theater.

Shopping

Bright and breezy art galleries, excellent cigars, leather fetish gear and offensive T-shirts – Key West, what don't you sell?

Montage Souvenirs
(512 Duval St; 9am-10pm) Had a great meal or wild night at some bar or restaurant in the Keys? Well, this store probably sells the sign for the place, which makes for a nice souvenir.

Bésame Mucho Gifts
(315 Petronia St; 10am-6pm, to 4pm Sun) This place is well stocked with high-end beauty products, eclectic jewelry, clothing and housewares.

Frangipani Gallery Arts & Crafts
(1102 Duval St; 10am-6pm) One of the best galleries of local artists' work.

Haitian Art Co Arts & Crafts
(305-296-8932; 605 Simonton St; 10am-7pm) Haitian arts and crafts.

Information

Medical Services

Key West's most accessible medical services:

Lower Keys Medical Center (305-294-5531, 800-233-3119; www.lkmc.com; 5900 College Rd, Stock Island, MM 5) Has 24-hour emergency room.

South Med (305-295-3838; www.southmed.us; 3138 Northside Dr) Dr Scott Hall caters especially to the gay community, but serves all visitors.

Tourist Information

Key West Chamber of Commerce (305-294-2587; www.keywestchamber.org; 510 Greene St; 8:30am-6:30pm Mon-Sat, to 6pm Sun) An excellent source of information.

Getting There & Around

Key West International Airport (EYW) is off S Roosevelt Blvd on the east side of the island. You can fly into Key West from some major US cities such as Miami or New York.

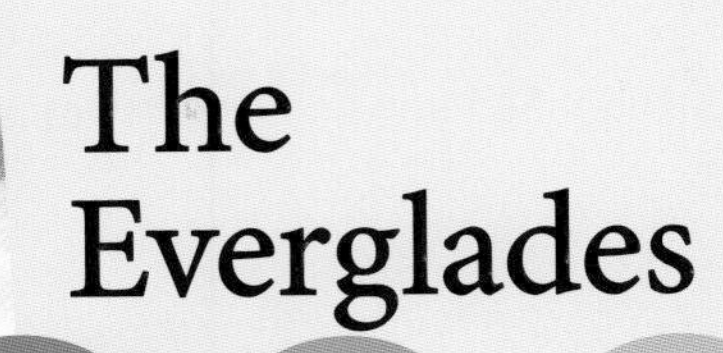

The Everglades

More than Miami, the Everglades make South Florida truly unique. Called the 'River of Grass' by Native Americans, this is not just a wetland, or a swamp, or a lake, or a river or a prairie – it is all of the above, twisted together into a series of soft horizons, long vistas, sunsets that stretch across your entire field of vision and the creeping grin of a large population of dinosaur-era reptiles.

When you watch anhinga flex their wings before breaking into corkscrew dives, or the slow, Jurassic flap of a great blue heron gliding over its domain, or the sun kissing miles of unbroken sawgrass as it sets behind humps of skeletal cypress domes, you'll have an idea of what we're speaking of. In a nation where natural beauty is measured by its capacity for drama, the Everglades subtly, contentedly flows on.

Anhinga Trail (p245), Everglades National Park
DANITA DELIMONT/GETTY IMAGES ©

The Everglades
Everglades Parkway (Alligator Alley) (toll)
75
29
Turner River Rd
Big Cypress Swamp
Tamiami Trail
951
Big Cypress
National Preserve
2
Fakahatchee Strand
Preserve Park
92
Collier-
Seminole
State Park
Marco
Island
839
29
Ochopee
Monroe
Station
Everglades
City
41
Chokoloskee
Cape
Romano
Loop Rd
94
Chevalier
Bay
Ferry
Big
Lostmans
Bay
The Everglades
Everglades National Park Boundary
Gulf of
Mexico
Tarpon
Bay
Shark
Point
Whitewater
Bay
4
3
Cape
Sable
Flamingo
1 Everglades
National Park
2 Big Cypress
National Preserve
3 Hell's Bay
4 Chickee Camping
5 Everglades
International Hostel

Lauderdale-by-the-Sea
Fort Lauderdale
Dania Beach
Hollywood
North Miami Beach
Miami Beach
Miami
Hialeah
Florida's Turnpike (toll)
Miami Canal
Miccosukee Indian Reservation
The Everglades
Miccosukee Village
Tram tour
ATLANTIC OCEAN
Key Biscayne
Bill Baggs Cape Florida Florida State Park
Peters
Goulds
Homestead
Florida City
Everglades National Park
Biscayne National Park
Boca Chita Key
Florida Keys National Marine Sanctuary
Black Point
Biscayne Bay
Coon Point
Sands Cut
Elliott Key
Turkey Point
Adams Key
Card Sound
Barnes Sound
Key Largo
John Pennekamp Coral Reef State Park
Key Largo National Marine Santuary
Florida Bay
Florida Keys National Marine Sanctuary
Islamorada
30 km
20 miles

The Everglades' Highlights

Everglades National Park

The third-largest national park in the lower 48 states is an odd, compelling place, a wilderness where elevation is recorded in inches and beauty is measured by subtlety rather than showy majesty. Yet beautiful the Everglades are, and visiting them, along with their population of clouds of waterfowl, thrashing fish and grinning gators, is a highlight of many Florida trips. Baby alligator

2 Big Cypress National Preserve

This preserve both abuts and is partially encompassed by Everglades National Park. The portion of the Florida Scenic Trail that runs through the Big Cypress Preserve is a muddy yet absolutely gorgeous slog across the flooded forests and plains that spread across Florida's interior shelf. Hiking out here is not for novices, but if you have the experience, don't pass Big Cypress up.

Hell's Bay

3

The Everglades is truly the Wet Wild, and as such, to appreciate this landscape you need to get into the water. And not just any water, but the water that flows into and becomes a part of the land. There are countless creeks, streams and watercourses here, but our favorite is Hell's Bay, a bracken tunnel that snakes through the dense vegetation of the River of Grass.

4

Chickee Camping

Just as you should get on the water via a boat to explore the far reaches of the Everglades, you may want to consider sleeping on the water via a chickee to get a sense of living in the Everglades. What's a chickee? Essentially, a raised, shaded platform. Chickee camping down here is incredibly romantic and serene, but you best bring some bug spray.

5

Everglades International Hostel

This spot deserves a shout out for being one of the best hostels in America, bar none. How can you not love a lodging that collects travelers from every country, of every age group and every race, and unites them under one funky roof? Take excellent guided tours of the park with local staff, or chill out in the wonderfully weird backyard garden.

The Everglades' Best...

Wildlife

- **Shark Valley Tram Tour** This asphalt path goes past loads of wading birds and sunbathing alligators. (p244)
- **Royal Palm Visitor Center** The boardwalk trails lead over literally dozens of alligators. (p245)
- **Pa-hay-okee Overlook** From this 'elevation' you can see plenty of birds at dawn and dusk. (p246)
- **Wilderness Waterway** Paddle about and spot jumping dolphins and fish-eating raptors. (p247)

Hiking

- **West Lake Trail** A boardwalk trail that goes through a protected mangrove forest. (p247)
- **Florida National Scenic Trail** A long slog, but you'll see the best of the Everglades. (p247)
- **Christian Point** This winding path leads through forest and fields to Florida Bay. (p247)
- **Mahogany Hammock** 'Island-hop' across the Sea of Grass to copses of hardwood trees. (p247)

Boating

- **Hell's Bay** Take a canoe or kayak through this overgrown watery labyrinth. (p248)
- **10,000 Islands** Can you count them all as you paddle across the teal Gulf? (p247)
- **Biscayne National Park** Practically the entire park is protected waters! (p2521)
- **Graveyard Creek** A beautiful series of tidal flats and exposed mangroves. (p248)

Only in the Everglades

- **Robert is Here** Fun food stand and farmer's market. (p251)
- **Coral Castle** An oddly appealing monument to unrequited love and idiosyncrasy. (p250)
- **Skunk Ape Research Center** Reptile petting zoo meets 'research' outpost into Florida's Bigfoot. (p245)
- **Wet Walks** Via Everglades Hostel, you can wade deep into a watery Cypress Dome. (p243)

Left: Hiking, Ocala National Forest (p326); **Above:** Anhinga Trail, Royal Palm Visitor Center (p245)

Need to Know

RESOURCES

- **Everglades National Park (www.nps.gov/ever)** Official NPS website for Everglades National Park.
- **Biscayne National Park (www.nps.gov/bisc)** Official NPS website for Biscayne National Park.

ADVANCE PLANNING

- **Camping** If you're planning on camping within the park, contact the National Park Service (www.nps.gov/ever) and consult about what is the best campsite for your needs.
- **Weather** It's very important to check up on weather conditions before hiking or boating: the wind and rain here can be furious.
- **Maps** Again, contact the National Park Service to request the best maps if you intend to get into the bush.
- **Bug Spray** Bring it. Lots of it.

GETTING AROUND

- **Car** You need a car to explore the three main areas of this enormous park in under a week.
- **Boat** Kayaking and canoeing is a great means of exploring interior waterways, while any kind of boat can be used to shoot up and down the gorgeous Gulf Coast.
- **Bicycle** The flat roads of the Everglades, especially in the Ernest Coe section, are great for cycling, but bring lots of food and water.
- **Foot** Hikes here are great; make sure to supply the National Park Service with your contact details and itineraries.

BE FOREWARNED

- **Storms** From July to September is prime hurricane season, and bad thunderstorms can strike anytime.
- **Tides** If camping on the beach, pitch in designated, signed areas. Tides can wash in with no warning.
- **Wildlife** The main annoyance is bugs, but avoid snakes and, please, don't be foolish and feed the alligators.
- **Speed Limits** Obey them! It's tempting to speed, especially on US 41, but this is panther territory, and the endangered cats' biggest threat is cars.

The Everglades Itineraries

While the Everglades have shrunk considerably since the beginning of the 20th century, they still take up a sizable chunk of South Florida. Everglades National Park is divided into three areas; we will explore all of them in these itineraries.

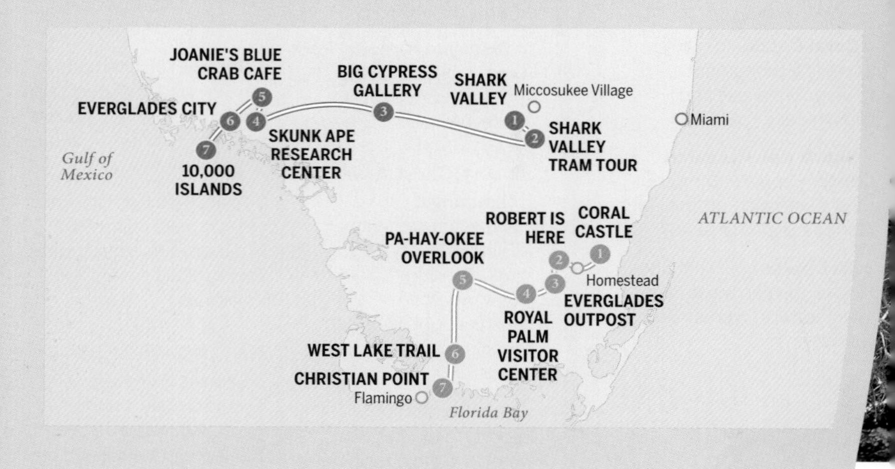

TAMIAMI TRAIL & THE GULF COAST

MIAMI TO EVERGLADES CITY

We assume you'll be coming from Miami when you start this itinerary, but if you come from Fort Myers you can take this entire trip in reverse.

From Miami, head west on US 41/ Tamiami Trail, and feel free to stop for an airboat tour along the way. Our first mandatory stop is ❶ **Shark Valley**. Don't forget to rent a bicycle or book a ticket onto the ❷ **Shark Valley Tram Tour**, which winds its way past wildlife to a watchtower where you can look over the horizon.

Head out of Shark Valley and continue west, making sure to peep in on the photographic exhibits on display in the ❸ **Big Cypress Gallery** and the general eccentricity of the ❹ **Skunk Ape Research Center**. You may also want to grab a bite to eat at ❺ **Joanie's Blue Crab Cafe**, which fries up seafood like nobody else can. In Everglades City, stop by the ❻ **Gulf Coast Visitor Center** and either take a guided boat tour, or rent a boat and paddle along the ❼ **10,000 Islands**.

CREEKS & PRAIRIES

HOMESTEAD TO FLAMINGO POINT

In the southeast corner of the park, you'll explore the Ernest Coe section. You'll have to come through Homestead to get here, where there is a triumvirate of roadside attractions: 1 **Coral Castle**, a ruin of blocks of stone made by a lovestruck Latvian; 2 **Robert Is Here**, a farmer's stand that sells fresh produce and is a family favorite; and the 3 **Everglades Outpost**, a volunteer-run refuge for rescued animals.

At Homestead, head to the 4 **Royal Palm Visitor Center**, where boardwalks stretch over what is likely the most alligators you'll ever spot in your life. We recommend waiting for night to fall and doing a guided tour of the boardwalks with a ranger: the nocturnal experience at Royal Palm is something special. Head from here to the 5 **Pa-hay-okee Overlook**, which affords fantastic views over the grasslands and 'domes' of hardwood trees that characterize this part of the park. As you proceed to Flamingo Point, stop for side hikes down the boardwalk on the 6 **West Lake Trail** or wind your way to Florida Bay via beautiful 7 **Christian Point**.

Cypress trees, Pa-hay-okee Overlook (p246)

Discover the Everglades

At a Glance

- **Shark Valley** (p243) Bicycle trails and alligator tails.
- **Gulf Coast** (p244) Ten thousand islands sparkle in the sun.
- **Ernest Coe** (p244) The long, low prairie of the 'River of Grass.'
- **Biscayne National Park** (p251) Dive into this almost-all-underwater park.

Boardwalk, Shark Valley
WALTER BIBIKOW/GETTY IMAGES ©

THE EVERGLADES NATIONAL PARK

Everglades National Park was formed in the mid-20th century to protect the largest subtropical wilderness in the USA. The park boundaries cover some 25% of the fragile Everglades ecosystem, which ranges from mangrove islands to blackwater cypress forests to cyclically inundated grasslands. There are three primary 'regions' in the park: Shark Valley, Gulf Coast and Ernest Coe.

History

It's tempting to think of the Everglades as a swamp, but 'prairie' may be a more apt description. The Glades (Colonial cartographer Gerard de Brahm named the region 'River Glades,' which became Everglades on later English maps) are grasslands that are flooded for most of the year. Run-off water from central Florida flows down the peninsula via streams and rivers, over and through the Glades, and into Florida Bay. Small wonder the Calusa Indians called the area Pa-hay-okee (grassy water). Conservationist Marjory Stoneman Douglas called the Everglades the River of Grass.

Starting in 1905, Floridians cut hundreds of canals to separate the Glades from the state's natural flow of water. The idea was to 'reclaim' the land and turn it into farmland. Unfortunately, this has actually upset the natural water cycle and replenishment of the Florida aquifer (the state's freshwater supply).

In 2011, the water levels in Okeechobee were almost 2.7 inches below normal levels. The number of wading birds nesting has declined by 90% to 95% since the 1930s.

Currently, there are 67 threatened and endangered plant and animal species in the park. At this stage, scientists estimate the wetlands have been reduced by 50 to 75% of their original size.

The **Comprehensive Everglades Restoration Project** (CERP; www.evergladesplan.org), a partnership between several federal, state and local government agencies, is designed to address the root issue of water, but political battles over funding have intensified. Opponents of CERP say the program is low-priority during an economic recession. Old anti-Everglades arguments – that CERP curtails agriculture and development – have significantly slowed CERP's implementation.

When to Go

December to March Dry season means optimum wildlife viewing along watercourses, but some kayaking will be difficult.

April to June Although the weather gets pretty hot, there's a good mix of water and wildlife.

July to November Lots of heat, lots of bugs and (except October and November) chances of hurricanes.

Orientation

There are three main entrances and three main areas of the park: one along the southeast edge near Homestead and Florida City (Ernest Coe section); at the central-north side on the Tamiami Trail (Shark Valley section); and a third at the northwest shore (Gulf Coast section), past Everglades City.

Sights

SHARK VALLEY SECTION

The northern and western portion of the park hugs the Tamiami Trail/US 41. Here you'll find flooded forests and swampy bottomlands.

Shark Valley Park
(☎305-221-8776; www.nps.gov/ever/planyourvisit/svdirections.htm; 36000 SW 8th St, GPS 25°45'27.60; car/cyclist $10/5; ⏲9:15am-5:15pm; P 👪) Shark Valley

Local Knowledge

Everglades National Park Don't Miss List

LINDA FRIAR, PARK RANGER, EVERGLADES NATIONAL PARK

1 HIKING PINE ISLANDS

Go on the Anhinga Amble at Royal Palm (p245) where you'll see wading birds, alligators, and maybe a few turtles, otters, and different fish. From Anhinga head to Mahogany Hammock, where you'll experience one of the most beautiful tree islands in the Everglades!

2 SLOUGH SLOG/WET WALK INTO CYPRESS DOMES

A wet walk (or slough slog) should be done the first time with a ranger guide. Once you're ready to go – you will get wet – either ankle- or hip-deep, the deeper the more exciting! Wading through the river of grass into the shadows of a 'gator hole' or cypress dome just can't be beat. (☎305-248-1122, 800-372-3874; www.evergladeshostel.com; 20 SW 2nd Ave; half-day/full-day tours from $65/120)

3 SHARK VALLEY TRAM TOUR

The tram road (p244), a remnant of oil exploration days, is a 15-mile loop through Everglades habitats. A naturalist provides an interpretive tour during the ride. There are opportunities to hop off the tram along the way to take photos and get a better look at the wildlife.

4 SHARK VALLEY SUNSET BIKE TOUR

Enjoy the kaleidoscope of colors and the movement of wildlife as the sun sets over the sawgrass prairie. Join a ranger for a 15-mile bike ride (p243). Bring your own bike or rent one.

5 CANOE/KAYAK, GULF COAST

Paddle through the 10,000 Islands (p244) with a ranger as your guide. You'll look for wildlife, paddle through mangroves and learn about the park's natural and cultural history. Reservations required.

sounds like it should be the headquarters for the villain in a James Bond movie, but it is in fact a slice of National Park Service grounds, heavy with informative signs and knowledgeable rangers. Shark Valley is located in the cypress-and-hardwood-and-riverine section of the Everglades, a more traditionally jungly section of the park than the grassy fields and forest domes surrounding the Ernest Coe visitor center. A 15-mile/24km paved trail takes you past small creeks, tropical forest and 'borrow pits' (manmade holes that are now basking spots for gators, turtles and birdlife). The pancake-flat trail is perfect for bicycles, which can be rented at the entrance for $7.50 per hour. Bring water with you.

Shark Valley Tram Tour Tram

(305-221-8455; www.sharkvalleytramtours.com; adult/child under 12yr/senior $22/19/12.75; departures May-Dec 9:30am, 11am, 2pm, 4pm, Jan-Apr 9am-4pm every hr on the hr)

If you don't feel like exerting yourself, the most popular and painless way to immerse yourself in the Everglades is via the two-hour tram tour that runs along Shark Valley's entire 15-mile trail. If you only have time for one Everglades activity, this should be it, as guides are informative and witty, and you'll likely see gators sunning themselves on the road. Halfway along the trail is the 50ft-high Shark Valley Observation Tower, an ugly concrete tower that offers dramatically beautiful views of the park.

Big Cypress Gallery Gallery

(941-695-2428; www.clydebutcher.com; Tamiami Trail; swamp walk 1.5hr adult/child $50/35, 45min adult/child $35/25; 10am-5pm; P) The highlight of many Everglades trips, this gallery showcases the work of Clyde Butcher, an American photographer who follows in the great tradition of Ansel Adams. His large-format black-and-white images elevate the swamps to a higher level. Butcher has found a quiet spirituality in the brackish waters and you might, too, with the help of his photos. Every Labor Day (first weekend in September), the gallery holds a gala event, which includes a fun $20 swamp walk onto his 30-acre property; the party attracts swamp-stompers from across the state.

GULF COAST SECTION

The northwest corner of the park rubs up against Everglades City, an old Florida fishing village of raised houses, turquoise water and scattershot emerald-green mangrove islands. Hwy 29 runs south through town into the peaceful residential island of Chokoloskee, past a great psychedelic mural of a gator on a shed. This is the sort of town where you can easily lose yourself for a day.

Gulf Coast Visitor Center Boating

(239-695-3311, 239-695-2591; http://evergladesnationalparkboattoursgulfcoast.com; 815 Oyster Bar Lane, off Hwy 29; per day canoe/single kayak/tandem kayak $24/45/55; 9am-4:30pm mid-Apr–mid-Nov, 8am-4:30pm mid-Nov–mid-Apr;) This is the northwestern-most ranger station for Everglades National Park, and provides access to the 10,000 Islands area. Boat tours depart from the downstairs marina into the mangrove flats and green islands – if you're lucky you may see dolphins springing up beside your craft. This tangled off-shore archipelago was a major smuggling point for drugs into the mainland USA during the late 1970s and early '80s; bales of marijuana were nicknamed 'square grouper' by local fishermen.

ERNEST COE SECTION

The southern and eastern portions of the park can be accessed from Homestead, an hour south of Miami. This part of the park consists of grassy prairies, small creeks and small wooded copses.

Ernest Coe Visitor Center Park

(305-242-7700; www.nps.gov/ever; State Rd 9336; 9am-5pm) As you go past Homestead and Florida City, the farmland loses its uniformity and the flat land becomes more tangled, wild and studded with pine and cypress. After a few more miles you'll enter Everglades National Park at this friendly visitor center. Have a look at the excellent exhibits, including a diorama of

JEFF GREENBERG/ALAMY ©

Don't Miss
Skunk Ape Research Headquarters

This only-in-Florida roadside attraction is dedicated to tracking down Southeastern USA's version of Bigfoot, the eponymous Skunk Ape (a large gorilla-man who supposedly stinks to high heaven). We never saw a Skunk Ape, but you can see a corny gift shop and, in the back, a reptile-and-bird zoo run by a true Florida eccentric, the sort of guy who wraps albino pythons around his neck for fun. Donate a few bucks at the entrance.

THINGS YOU NEED TO KNOW

239-695-2275; www.skunkape.info; 40904 Tamiami Trail E; 7am-7pm, 'zoo' closes around 4pm; P

'typical' Floridians (the fisherman looks like he should join ZZ Top).

Royal Palm Visitor Center Park
(239-305-242-7700; State Rd 9336; 8am-4:15pm) Four miles past Ernest Coe Visitor Center, Royal Palm offers the easiest access to the Glades in these parts. Two trails, the **Anhinga** and **Gumbo Limbo** (the latter named for the gumbo-limbo tree, also known as the 'tourist tree' because its bark peels like a sunburned Brit), take all of an hour to walk and put you face to face with a panoply of Everglades wildlife. Gators sun on the shoreline, anhinga spear their prey and wading birds stalk haughtily through the reeds. Come at night for a ranger walk on the boardwalk and shine a flashlight into the water to see one of the coolest sights of your life: the glittering eyes of dozens of alligators prowling the waterways.

Flamingo Visitor Center Park
(239-695-3101, 239-695-2945; marina 7am-7pm, from 6am Sat & Sun) The most isolated portion of the park is a squat **marina** (239-696-3101, 239-695-2591)

where you can go on a backcountry boat tour or rent boats. Due to its isolation, this area is subject to closure during bad weather. Boat tours to Florida Bay or into the swampy backcountry run for $32.25/16.13 per adult/child, while canoes (two hours/four hours/full day $16/22/40) and sea kayaks (half-/full day $35/45) are available for rental; if you do rent, you're largely left to explore the channels and islands of Florida Bay on your own. During rough weather be cautious, even when on land, as storm surges can turn an attractive spread of beach into a watery stretch of danger fairly quickly.

Hell's Bay Lake

(Royal Palm Visitor Center) The real joy of the Everglades is canoeing into the bracken heart of the swamp. There are plenty of push-off points, all with names that sound like they were read off Frodo's map to Mordor, including Hell's Bay (our favorite).

'Hell to get into and hell to get out of,' was how this sheltered launch was described by old Gladesmen, but damn if it isn't heaven inside: a capillary network of mangrove creeks, sawgrass islands and shifting mudflats, where the brambles form a green tunnel and all you can smell is sea salt and the dark, organic breath of the swamp. Three chickee sites (wooden platforms built above the waterline) are spaced along the trail.

Pa-hay-okee Overlook Viewpoint

Rte 9336 cuts through the soft heart of the park, past long fields of marsh prairie, white, skeletal forests of bald cypress and dark clumps of mahogany hammock. Further on the Pa-hay-okee Overlook is a raised platform that peeks over one of the prettiest bends in the River of Grass.

Activities

Be it by boat, bicycle or your own feet, there are plenty of ways to explore the wet wild of the Everglades.

SHARK VALLEY

HIKING

At the park entrance, the easy **Bobcat Boardwalk** makes a loop through a thick copse of tropical hardwoods before emptying you out right back into the Shark Valley parking lot. A little ways past

Bald cypress trees, Pa-hay-okee Overlook

VICKI BEAVER/ALAMY ©

Detour: Big Cypress National Preserve

The 1139-sq-mile Big Cypress Preserve (named for the size of the park, not its trees) is the result of a compromise between environmentalists, cattle ranchers and oil-and-gas explorers. The rains that flood the Preserve's prairies and wetlands slowly filter down through the Glades. About 45% of the cypress swamp (actually a group of mangrove islands, hardwood hammocks, slash pine, prairies and marshes) is protected. Great bald cypress trees are nearly gone, thanks to pre-Preserve lumbering, but dwarf pond cypress trees are plentiful. The **Oasis Visitor Center** (941-695-1201; 8am-4:30pm Mon-Fri;), about 20 miles west of Shark Valley, has great exhibits for the kids and an outdoor, water-filled ditch popular with alligators.

is the **Otter Cave Trail**, which heads over a limestone shelf that has been Swiss-cheesed into a porous sponge by rainwater. Animals now live in the eroded holes (although it's not likely you'll spot any) and Native Americans used to live on top of the shelf.

There are some 31 miles of the **Florida National Scenic Trail** (www.nps.gov/bicy/planyourvisit/florida-trail.htm) within Big Cypress National Preserve. From the southern terminus, which can be accessed via Loop Rd, the trail runs 8.3 miles north to US 41. The way is flat, but it's hard going: you'll almost certainly be wading through water, and you'll have to pick your way through a series of solution holes (small sinkholes) and thick hardwood hammocks. There is often no shelter from the sun, and the bugs are...*plentiful*. There are (free) primitive campsites with water wells along the trail; pick up a map at the visitor center. **Monument Lake** (May-Dec 14 free, Dec 15-Apr $16) has water and toilets.

ERNEST COE TO FLAMINGO POINT

State Rd 9336 cuts through the soft heart of the park; all of the following are half a mile (800m) long. **Mahogany Hammock** leads into an 'island' of hardwood forest floating on the waterlogged prairie, while the **Pinelands** takes you through a copse of rare spindly swamp pine and palmetto forest; further on you'll find the Pa-hay-okee Overlook (p246).The **West Lake Trail** runs through the largest protected mangrove forest in the Northern Hemisphere. Further down you can take a good two-hour, 1.8-mile (2.9km) hike to **Christian Point**, which ends with a dramatic view of the windswept shores of Florida Bay.

GULF COAST

KAYAKING & CANOEING

The **10,000 Islands** consist of many (but not really 10,000) tiny islands and a mangrove swamp that hugs the southwestern-most border of Florida. The **Wilderness Waterway**, a 99-mile path between Everglades City and Flamingo, is the longest canoe trail in the area, but there are shorter trails near Flamingo. Most islands are fringed by narrow beaches with sugar-white sand, but note that the water is brackish, and very shallow most of the time. It's not Tahiti, but it's fascinating. You can camp on your own island for up to a week.

Getting around the 10,000 Islands is pretty straightforward if you religiously adhere to National Oceanic & Atmospheric Administration (NOAA) tide and nautical charts. Going against the tides is the fastest way to make a miserable trip. The Gulf Coast Visitor Center sells nautical charts and gives out free tidal charts. You can also purchase

charts prior to your visit – ask for chart Nos 11430, 11432 and 11433.

ERNEST COE TO FLAMINGO POINT

There are plenty of spots in the southeast part of the park, all with names that sound like they were read off *Lord of the Rings*, including **Hell's Bay**, the **Nightmare**, **Snake Bight** and **Graveyard Creek**. The guys at **North American Canoe Tours** (NACT; 239-695-3299, 877-567-0679; www.evergladesadventures.com; Ivey House Bed & Breakfast, 107 Camellia St; tours $99, rentals from $35; Nov–mid-Apr) rent out camping equipment and canoes for full/half days ($35) and touring kayaks ($45 to $99).

Sleeping

If you don't feel like camping in the park, there are good hotels in Everglades City (near the Gulf Coast section of the park) and Homestead (near the Homestead section of the park).

INSIDE THE PARK

National Park Service Campsites Campground $
(NPS; 800-365-2267; www.nps.gov/ever/planyourvisit/camping; sites May-Oct free, Nov-Apr $16) There are campgrounds run by the NPS located throughout the park. Sites are primitive and do not have hookups. Depending on the time of year, cold-water showers are either bracing or a welcome relief. The NPS information office at Royal Palm can provide a map of all campsites, as does the park website.

Swamp Cottage Cottage $$
(239-695-2428; www.clydebutchersbigcypressgallery.com/swamp-cottage; cottage $275; P) Want to get as close to the swamp as possible without giving up on the amenities? This two-bedroom cottage, which sits behind the Big Cypress Gallery (p244), may be the answer you're seeking. It's like a beach cottage, except the 'beach' is one of America's great wetlands. It's comfortably appointed, and if not luxurious, it's certainly cozy.

Left: Royal Palm Visitor Center (p245);
Below: Kayaking, Big Cypress National Preserve (p247)
(LEFT) JEFF GREENBERG/ALAMY ©; (BELOW) FRANZ MARC FREI/GETTY IMAGES ©

EVERGLADES CITY

Everglades City Motel Motel $
(☎800-695-8353, 239-695-4224; www.evergladescitymotel.com; 310 Collier Ave; r from $80; P ❄ 📶) With large renovated rooms that have flat-screen TVs, arctic air-conditioning and a fantastically friendly staff that will hook you up with whatever tours your heart desires, this is an exceptionally good-value lodge for those looking to spend some time near the 10,000 Islands.

Ivey House Bed & Breakfast B&B $$
(☎239-695-3299, 877-567-0679; www.iveyhouse.com; 107 Camellia St; lodge $89-120, inn $99-219; P ❄ 📶) This family-run tropical inn serves good breakfasts in its small Ghost Orchid Grill. Plus it operates some of the best nature trips around (North American Canoe Tours (p248)). Ivey offers an entire range of package vacations (see the website), from day trips to six-day excursions including lodging, tours and some meals; trips run from $300 to $2290.

Rod & Gun Club Lodge B&B $$
(☎239-695-2101; www.evergladesrodandgun.com; 200 Riverside Dr; r Jul–mid-Oct $95, mid-Oct–Jun $110-140; P ❄) Built in the 1920s as a hunting lodge by Barron Collier (who needed a place to chill after watching workers dig his Tamiami Trail), this masculine place, fronted by a lovely porch, has a restaurant that serves anything that moves in them thar waters.

HOMESTEAD

Everglades International Hostel Hostel $
(☎305-248-1122, 800-372-3874; www.evergladeshostel.com; 20 SW 2nd Ave, Florida City; camping $18, dm $28, d $61-75, ste $125-225; P ❄ 📶 🏊) Located in a cluttered, comfy 1930s boarding house, this friendly hostel has good-value dorms, private rooms and

If You Like... Roadside Attractions

Homestead, for all her sprawl, houses two great attractions of the Florida roadside.

1 **CORAL CASTLE**

(☎305-248-6345; www.coralcastle.com; 28655 S Dixie Hwy; adult/senior/child $15/12/7; ⏲8am-6pm Sun-Thu, to 8pm Fri & Sat) 'You will be seeing unusual accomplishment,' reads the inscription on the rough-hewn quarried wall. That's an understatement. There is no greater temple to all that is weird and wacky about South Florida. The legend: a Latvian gets snubbed at the altar. Comes to the US. Moves to Florida. Hand carves, unseen, in the dead of night, a monument to unrequited love: a rock compound that includes a 'throne room,' a sun dial, a stone stockade (his intended's 'timeout area') and a revolving boulder gate that engineers around the world, to this day, cannot explain. Oh, and there are audio stations situated around the place that explain the site in a replicated Latvian accent, so it feels like you're getting a narrated tour by Borat.

2 **EVERGLADES OUTPOST**

(☎305-247-8000; 305-247-8000; www.evergladesoutpost.org; 35601 SW 192nd Ave; recommended donation $20; ⏲10am-5pm Mon, Tue & Fri-Sun, by appointment Wed & Thu) The Everglades Outpost houses, feeds and cares for wild animals that have been seized from illegal traders, abused, neglected or donated by people who could not care for them. Residents of the outpost include gibbons, a lemur, wolves, cobras, alligators and a pair of majestic tigers (one of whom was bought by an exotic dancer who thought she could incorporate it into her act). Your money goes into helping the outpost's mission.

'semi-privates' (you have an enclosed room within the dorms and share a bathroom with dorm residents). But what they've done with their backyard – wow. It's a serious garden of earthly delights. There's a tree house; a natural rock-cut pool with a waterfall; a Bedouin pavilion that doubles as a dancehall; a gazebo; an open-air tented 'bed room'; an oven built to resemble a tail-molting tadpole. It all needs to be seen to be believed, and best of all you can sleep anywhere in the back for $18. Sleep in a treehouse! We think that's an amazing deal. We should add the crowd is made up of all those funky international traveler types that made you fall in love with backpacking in the first place, and the hostel conducts some of the best tours into the Everglades around.

Eating

Old Florida fare, rich produce, fresh seafood and Southern cuisine are the name of the game.

EVERGLADES CITY

Joannie's Blue Crab Café American $$

(☎239-695-2682; Tamiami Trail; mains $9-17; ⏲9am-5pm) This quintessential shack, east of Ochopee, with open rafters, shellacked picnic tables and alligator kitsch, serves delicious food of the 'fried everything' variety on paper plates. There's live music most days.

JT's Island Grill & Gallery American $

(238 Mamie St, Chokoloskee; mains $5-16; ⏲11am-3pm late Oct-May; 🥕) Just a mile or so past the edge of town, this awesome cafe-cum-art-gallery sits in a restored 1890 general store. It's outfitted with bright retro furniture and piles of kitschy books, pottery, clothing and maps (all for sale). But the best part is the food (lunch only) – fresh crab cakes, salads, fish platters and veggie wraps, made with locally grown organic vegetables.

HOMESTEAD

Robert Is Here Market $

(www.robertishere.com; 19200 SW 344th St, Homestead; mains $3-8; ⏲8am-7pm Nov-Aug) More than a farmers' stand, Robert's is an institution. This is Old Florida at its kitschy best, in love with the Glades and the agriculture that surrounds it. There's a petting zoo for the kids, live music at night, plenty of homemade preserves and sauces, and while everyone goes crazy for the milkshakes – as they should – do not leave without having the fresh orange juice. It's the best in the world.

Information

Ernest Coe Visitor Center (☎305-242-7700; www.nps.gov/ever; 40001 State Rd 9336; 8am-5pm)

Getting There & Away

8th St SW in Miami becomes US 41/Tamiami Trail. Shark Valley is about an hour west of Miami. The Ernest Coe entrance is an hour south of Miami. There are no buses into the park.

BISCAYNE NATIONAL PARK

Just to the east of the Everglades is Biscayne National Park, or the 5% of it that isn't underwater. A portion of the world's third-largest reef sits here off the coast of Florida, along with mangrove forests and the northernmost Florida Keys. Fortunately this unique 300-sq-mile park is easy to explore independently with a canoe, via a glass-bottom boat tour or a snorkeling or diving trip.

Sights

Biscayne National Park Park

(☎786-335-3612, 305-230-7275; www.nps.gov/bisc; 9700 SW 328th St) The park itself offers canoe rentals, transportation to the offshore keys, snorkeling and scuba-diving trips, and glass-bottom boat viewing of the exceptional reefs. All tours require a minimum of six people, so call to make reservations. Three-hour glass-bottom boat trips ($45) depart at 10am and are very popular; if you're lucky you may spot some dolphins or manatees. Canoe rentals cost $12 per hour and kayaks $16; they're rented from 9am to 3pm. Three-hour snorkeling trips ($45) depart at 1:15pm daily; you'll have about 1½ hours in the water. Scuba trips ($99) depart at 8:30am Friday to Sunday. You can also arrange a private charter boat tour around the park for $300.

Maritime Heritage Trail Dive Site

The Maritime Heritage Trail takes 'hikers' through one of the only trails of its kind in the USA. If you've ever wanted to explore a sunken ship, this may well be the best opportunity in the country. Six are located within the park grounds; the trail experience involves taking visitors out, by boat, to the site of the wrecks, where they can swim and explore among derelict vessels and clouds of fish – there are even

Manatee, Biscayne National Park

Wilderness Camping

Three types of backcountry campsites are available: beach sites, on coastal shell beaches and in the 10,000 Islands; ground sites (mounds of dirt built up above the mangroves) and 'chickees,' wooden platforms built above the water line where you can pitch a free-standing (no spikes) tent. Chickees, which have toilets, are the most civilized – there's a serenity found in sleeping on what feels like a raft levitating above the water.

Warning: if you're paddling around and see an island that looks pleasant for camping but isn't a designated campsite, beware – you may end up submerged when tides change.

From November to April, camping permits cost $10, plus $2 per person per night; from May to October sites are free, but you must still self-register at Flamingo and Gulf Coast Visitor Centers or call ☎239-695-2945.

Some backcountry tips:

- Store food in a hand-sized, raccoon-proof container (available at gear stores).
- Bury your waste at least 10 inches below ground, but keep in mind some ground sites have hard turf.
- Use a backcountry stove to cook. Ground fires are only permitted at beach sites, and you can only burn dead or drowned wood.

waterproof information site cards placed among the ships. Five of the vessels are suited for scuba divers, but one, the *Mandalay,* a lovely two-masted schooner that sank in 1966, can be accessed by snorkelers.

Activities

Boating and **fishing** are naturally popular and often go hand in hand, but to do either you'll need to get some paperwork in order. Boaters will want to get tide charts from the park (or from www.nps.gov/bisc/planyourvisit/tide-predictions.htm). And make sure you comply with local slow-speed zones, designed to protect the endangered manatee.

The slow zones currently extend 1000ft out from the mainland, from Black Point south to Turkey Point, and include the marinas at Black Point and Homestead Bayfront Parks. Another slow zone extends from Sands Cut to Coon Point; maps of all of the above can be obtained from rangers, and are needed for navigation purposes in any case.

For information on boat tours and rental, contact **Biscayne Underwater** (www.biscayneunderwater.com), which can help arrange logistics.

Sleeping

Primitive camping on Elliott and Boca Chita Keys costs $15 per tent, per night; you pay on a trust system with exact change on the harbor (rangers cruise the Keys to check your receipt). There is potable water on the island, but it always pays to be prepared. It costs $20 to moor your boat overnight at Elliott or Boca Chita harbors, but that fee covers the use of one campsite for up to six people and two tents.

Information

Dante Fascell Visitor Center (☎305-230-7275; www.nps.gov/bisc; 9700 SW 328th St; ⏲8:30am-5pm) Located at Convoy Point, this center shows a great introductory film for an

overview of the park, and has maps, information and excellent ranger activities. The grounds around the center are a popular picnic spot on weekends and holidays, especially for families from Homestead. Also showcases local artwork.

Getting There & Away

To get here, you'll have to drive about 9 miles east of Homestead (the way is pretty well signposted) on SW 328th St (North Canal Dr) into a long series of green-and-gold flat fields and marsh.

Tampa Bay & the Gulf Coast

The Gulf Coast is muddled color. Slow tides. Soft wind.

To drive along the water in southwest Florida is to enter an impressionistic watercolor painting. First, there is the white-quartz sand of the barrier-island beaches, whose illuminated turquoise waters darken to silver-mantled indigo as the sun lowers to the horizon. Later, seen from the causeways, those same islands become a phosphorescent smear beneath the inky-black, star-flecked night sky.

The Gulf Coast's beauty is surely its main attraction, but variety is a close second: from Tampa to St Petersburg to Sarasota to Naples, there is urban sophistication, passionate artistry and exquisite cuisine. There are secluded islands, family-friendly resorts and Spring Break–style parties.

Here, Ringling's circus and Salvador Dalí's melting canvases fit perfectly – both are bright, bold, surreal entertainments to match manatees, roseate spoonbills, open-mouthed alligators and earthy Ybor City cigars.

Downtown Tampa Bay (p264)
RIDDHISH CHAKRABORTY/GETTY IMAGES ©

Spoonbills feeding
STEVEN BLANDIN / BIRD-WILDLIFEPHOTOGRAPHY.COM/GETTY IMAGES ©

Tampa Bay & the Gulf Coast

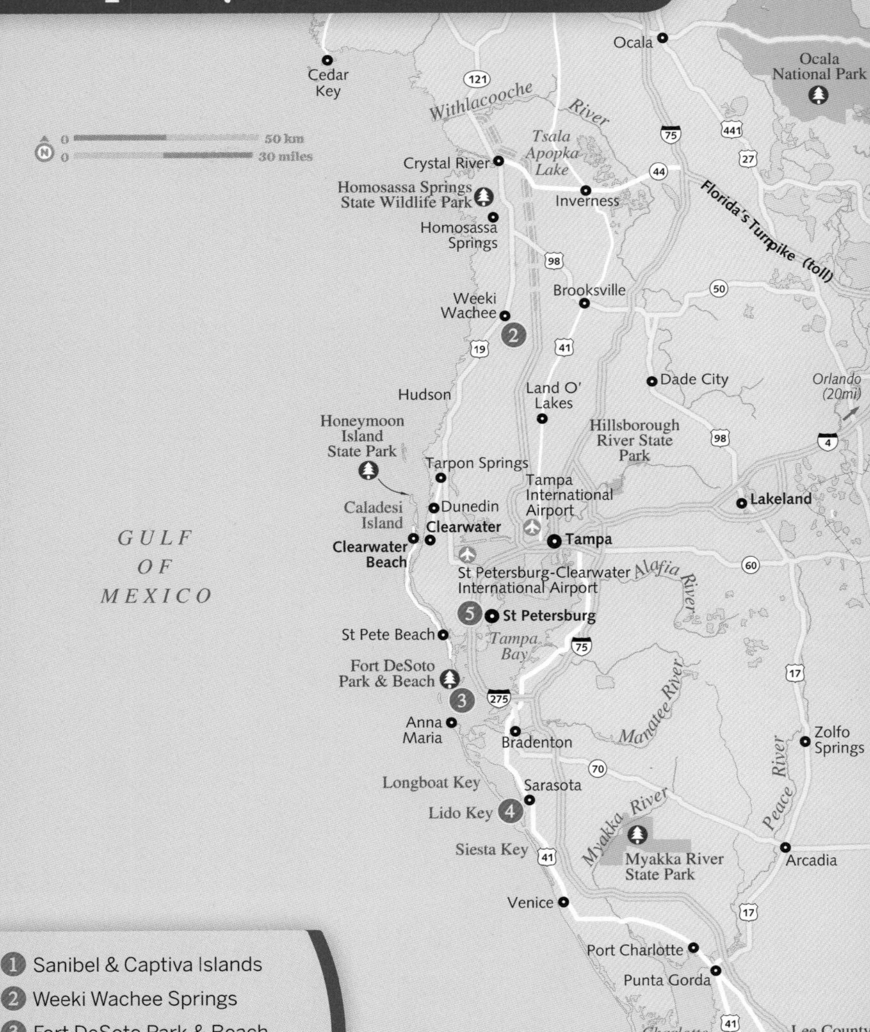

1. Sanibel & Captiva Islands
2. Weeki Wachee Springs
3. Fort DeSoto Park & Beach
4. Mote Marine Laboratory
5. Salvador Dalí Museum

Tampa Bay & the Gulf Coast's Highlights

Sanibel & Captiva Islands

This pair of barrier islands, connected to Fort Myers by a long causeway, is a prime example of Florida development done right. Businesses and residences are built low to the ground so as to minimize their visual presence, and the gentle physical beauty of the islands constantly shines through. Sanibel Island

1

2 Weeki Wachee Springs

Seriously, God bless Weeki Wachee Springs for keeping the greatest in Old Florida nostalgia alive and well. Grandparents take grandchildren here and the parents in the middle get teary, remembering their own first time marveling at beautiful mermaids dancing their graceful underwater acrobatics. Weeki Wachee is more than ballet. It's our memories of what makes Florida fun.

IMAGES-USA/ALAMY ©

Mote Marine Laboratory

3

We're tempted to say the Mote Marine Laboratory is the best aquarium in Florida, but it's not just an aquarium. It's a respected research facility that regularly breaks new ground in marine biological research. At the same time, the Mote is very much open to visitors, who can marvel at stingrays, sharks, sea turtles and manatees. OK: it's the best aquarium in Florida.

ILENE MACDONALD/ALAMY ©

4

Fort DeSoto Park & Beach

There are so many beaches stretching south of St Petersburg we're hard pressed to elevate any one above the others. But then along comes Fort DeSoto beach. The sand and sea alone don't make this place great (although they are great). It's the mix of the beach and the accompanying park, with its canoe trails, nature trails, dog park and complex interplay of Gulf Coast ecosystems.

5

Salvador Dalí Museum

Salvador Dalí was an exciting artist who should be known for more than pictures of clocks melting in the desert. If you want to know more about the man and his genius, visit this museum in St Petersburg. It's not just an art gallery: it's a building whose layout, design and exhibits lead you into an exploration of one of the psyches behind surrealism.

Tampa Bay & the Gulf Coast's Best...

Beach Bumming

- **Fort DeSoto Park & Beach** Natural beauty and a sense of comfortable isolation south of St Petersburg. (p280)
- **Bowman's Beach** White sand and long horizons on Sanibel Island. (p289)
- **St Pete Beach** Not just beautiful – stacked with food and drinking options. (p280)
- **Caladesi Island State Park** Practically pristine barrier island beach north of Tampa. (p281)

Arts & Culture

- **Straz Center for the Performing Arts** This enormous Tampa concert hall hosts symphonies, Broadway, ballet and opera. (p272)
- **Salvador Dalí Museum** The finest modern-art museum in Florida. (p275)
- **Arcade Theatre** Home base for the fantastic Florida Repertory Theatre. (p289)
- **Ringling Museum Complex** Encompasses arts, local history and the institution of the American circus. (p284)

Quirky Delights

- **Weeki Wachee Springs** Mermaids performing underwater ballet? Sign us up! (p290)
- **Sanibel Shelling** Pluck a huge assortment of enamel off these shell-studded beaches. (p289)
- **Coffee Pot Bayou & Old Northeast** St Petersburg's most attractive neighborhood is also her oldest. (p274)
- **Mote Marine Laboratory** Part research center, part amazing Gulf Coast aquarium. (p283)

Wildlife-Watching

- **Myakka River State Park** Hundreds of alligators call these wetlands home. (p288)
- **Homosassa Springs Wildlife State Park** See all the great birds, reptiles and mammals of the Florida menagerie. (p293)
- **Crystal River National Wildlife Refuge** Excellent area for manatee sightings. (p294)
- **JN 'Ding' Darling National Wildlife Refuge** A drive-through 'safari' takes you past clouds of birdlife. (p289)

Left: Shells, Sanibel Island (p289); **Above:** JN 'Ding' Darling National Wildlife Refuge (p289)

Need to Know

ADVANCE PLANNING

- **Rentals** The Gulf Coast is studded with vacation properties: see www.gulfcoastrentals.com for a directory on short-term rentals.
- **Events** There's a packed cultural calendar out here: see www.artstampabay.com for more information.
- **Restaurants** Dining is pretty casual, but it's still best to make reservations in cities like Tampa Bay and St Petersburg.
- **Shelling** Beaches here (especially in Sanibel) are studded with shells; print this guide before you visit: www.sanibel-captiva.org/play/shelling_center.

RESOURCES

- **Lee County Visitor & Convention Bureau** Information and resources for Fort Myers, Sanibel Island and the surrounding area: www.leevcb.com.
- **Visit St Petersburg & Clearwater** Tourism website for St Pete and its beaches; www.visitstpeteclearwater.com.
- **Ybor.org** Ybor City Chamber of Commerce, with information on galleries, nightlife and food: www.ybor.org.
- **Visit Tampa Bay** Clearing house on tourism information for Tampa Bay: www.visittampabay.com.

GETTING AROUND

- **Car** I-75 is the main highway that connects this area of the Gulf Coast
- **Bus** Greyhound buses connect Tampa Bay, St Petersburg, Bradenton (Sarasota) and Fort Myers.
- **Air** Major airlines fly directly to St Petersburg, Tampa Bay, Sarasota and Fort Myers.
- **Boat** Make sure to check out ferry schedules for information on services to various barrier islands.

BE FOREWARNED

- **Crime** Tampa has big-city problems with homelessness, panhandlers and crime. Both downtown and Ybor City are safe in themselves, but they are bordered by tough neighborhoods; don't wander aimlessly.

Tampa Bay & the Gulf Coast Itineraries

The Gulf Coast is Florida's quiet, family-friendly alternative to the glamor and Spring Break partying of the Atlantic Coast. We'll explore gentle nature preserves, cerebral art museums and miles of soft beach.

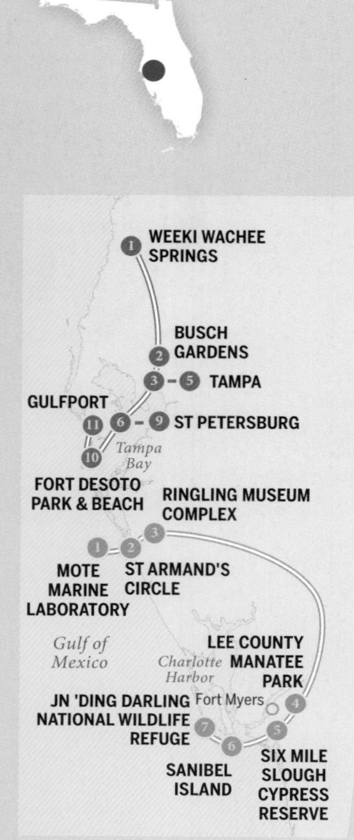

4 DAYS

BAY BLITZ

WEEKI WACHEE TO ST PETERSBURG & TAMPA

❶ **Weeki Wachee Springs**, where mermaids dance underwater and kids and their grandparents laugh at the un-ironic joy of it all, is a slice of Old Florida that's a bit of a rarity these days. Head from here to ❷ **Busch Gardens**, an African-themed amusement park that improves its rides and attractions every day. From here you'll head down to ❸ **Tampa Bay**, where you'll find the ❹ **Museum of Art** and excellent shows at the ❺ **Straz Center for the Performing Arts**.

Head to ❻ **St Petersburg** the next day and take in the ❼ **Salvador Dalí Museum**. In the historical neighborhood of ❽ **Coffee Pot Bayou** walk the cobbled streets, or inject your day with greenery at the ❾ **Gizella Kopsick Palm Arboretum**. Day four, take advantage of some of the beaches south of St Petersburg: we recommend ❿ **Fort DeSoto Park & Beach**. Once you've gotten your fill of all the sun, sand and calm surf that is the Gulf Coast, get dinner in the artsy enclave/village of ⓫ **Gulfport**.

Top Left: Tampa Museum of Art (p265), designed by architect Stanley Saitowitz;
Top Right: Otter, Six Mile Cypress Slough Preserve (p286)

3 DAYS

BEST OF FLORIDA'S SOUTHWEST
SARASOTA TO FORT MYERS

Sarasota is the home of some of Florida's quirkier attractions, including the 1 **Mote Marine Laboratory**, one of the nation's foremost marine research centers and a highly recommended aquarium that is open to the public. You'll want to spend a part of your day (and night) wandering around 2 **St Armand's Circle**, a lovely alfresco mall. Also visit the 3 **Ringling Museum Complex**, a sort of museum that has a hard time figuring out if it wants to showcase art, historical design and architecture, or the history of the circus. It does all three well.

Spend the next day driving down to Fort Myers; if it's anytime between November and March, head to the 4 **Lee County Manatee Park** and see if you can spot one of these gentle, cute 'sea cows.' Otherwise go to 5 **Six Mile Slough Cypress Preserve** and walk along the boardwalk into the heart of Florida's remaining wild wetlands. On your third day, grab breakfast in the historic downtown district of Ft Myers, then drive out to 6 **Sanibel Island**, for a 'safari' through the 7 **JN 'Ding' Darling National Wildlife Refuge**.

Discover Tampa Bay & the Gulf Coast

At a Glance

- **Tampa Bay** (p264) Family-friendly, culture capital of the Gulf Coast.
- **St Petersburg** (p274) A party town turned arts enclave.
- **Sarasota** (p283) Circuses, sea life and surf.
- **Sanibel & Captiva Islands** (p289) Laid-back beaches and low-key development.

Tampa Riverwalk
DENNIS MACDONALD/GETTY IMAGES ©

TAMPA BAY AREA

Tampa Bay

813 / POP 335,700

Tampa may be sprawling and businesslike, but it's also more fun than meets the eye. New museums, parks and gourmet restaurants are popping up on a monthly basis, so much so we'd happily say the Gulf Coast capital is finally a bit stylish.

Sights

Downtown, the attractive **Tampa Riverwalk** (www.thetampariverwalk.com) connects most sights. The Franklin St Mall is a pedestrian-only corridor between Kennedy Blvd and Zack St that's lined with food carts and lunchtime eateries.

Lowry Park Zoo Zoo

(**813-935-8552; www.lowryparkzoo.com; 1101 W Sligh Ave; adult/child $25/20; 9:30am-5pm; P**) North of downtown, Tampa's zoo gets you as close to the animals as possible, with several free-flight aviaries, a camel ride, giraffe feeding, wallaby enclosure and rhino 'encounter.'

Florida Aquarium Aquarium

(**813-273-4000; www.flaquarium.org; 701 Channelside Dr; adult/child $24/19; 9:30am-5pm;**) Tampa's excellent aquarium is among the state's best. Cleverly designed, the re-created swamp lets you walk among herons and ibis as they prowl the mangroves. Programs let you swim with the fishes (and the sharks) or take a catamaran ecotour in Tampa Bay.

Glazer Children's Museum
Museum

(813-443-3861; www.glazermuseum.org; 110 W Gasparilla Plaza; adult/child $15/9.50; 10am-5pm Mon-Fri, to 6pm Sat, 1-6pm Sun;) This crayon-bright, interactive museum provides a creative play space for under 10s. Eager staff and tons of coolio fun; adjacent Curtis Hixon Park is picnic- and playground-friendly.

Tampa Museum of Art
Museum

(813-274-8130; www.tampamuseum.org; 120 W Gasparilla Plaza; adult/student $10/5; 11am-7pm Mon-Thu, to 8pm Fri, to 5pm Sat & Sun) Architect Stanley Saitowitz's dramatically cantilevered museum building appears to float above Curtis Hixon Park overlooking the Hillsborough River. Inside its sculptural shell six galleries house a permanent collection of Greek and Roman antiquities beside contemporary exhibitions of photography and new media. Its most recent show exhibited the work from Tampa's cutting-edge Graphicstudio, showcasing 110 printworks by 45 artists including Robert Rauschenberg, Louise Bourgeois, Chuck Close and Christian Marclay.

Manatee Viewing Center
Wildlife Reserve

(813-228-4289; www.tampaelectric.com/manatee; Big Bend Rd, Apollo Beach; 10am-5pm 1 Nov–15 Apr) FREE One of Florida's more surreal wildlife encounters is spotting manatees in the warm-water discharge canals of coal-fired power plants. Yet these placid mammals show up here so reliably from November through April that this is now a protected sanctuary. Look for tarpon, rays and sharks, too. A snack bar, small exhibit, bathrooms and picnic tables round out the sight.

Ybor City
Neighbourhood

Like the illicit love child of Key West and Miami's Little Havana, Ybor City is a multiethnic, nostalgia-rich neighborhood that hosts the Tampa Bay area's hippest party scene. The cobblestone 19th-century historic district is a redolent mix of wrought-iron balconies and rustling palm trees, of globe streetlamps and brick buildings, that preserves its strong Cuban, Spanish and Italian heritage.

For a guided, 90-minute walking tour, reserve ahead with **Ybor City Historic Walking Tours** (813-505-6779; www.yborwalkingtours.com; adult/child $15/5); they typically run twice daily.

Museum of Science & Industry
Museum

(MOSI; 813-987-6000; www.mosi.org; 4801 E Fowler Ave; adult/child $25/20; 9am-5pm Mon-Fri, to 6pm Sat & Sun; P) There's something intriguing for all ages at this interactive science museum. Younger kids go straight to Kids in Charge, where a wealth of hands-on activities hides science beneath unadorned play. The frank human body exhibit – with preserved fetuses and cautionary looks at pregnancy and health – is best for older kids. Don't miss the IMAX movie; it's included with admission.

From downtown, take I-275 north to exit 51, and go east on Fowler Ave.

Florida Museum of Photographic Arts
Museum

(FMoPA; 813-221-2222; www.fmopa.org; The Cube, 400 N Ashley Dr; suggested donation $10; 10am-5pm Tue-Thu & Sat, to 8pm Fri, noon-5pm Sun) This small, intimate photography museum is housed on the 2nd and 3rd story of The Cube, a five-story atrium, in downtown Tampa. In addition to a permanent collection from Harold Edgerton and Len Prince, temporary exhibits have included the work of Ansel Adams, Andy Warhol and contemporary photographers such as David Hilliard. Three-hour ($55), one day ($60) and multi-week photography courses are also offered.

Tampa Bay History Center
Museum

(813-228-0097; www.tampabayhistorycenter.org; 801 Old Water St; adult/child $13/8; 10am-5pm) This first-rate history museum presents the region's Seminole and Miccosukee people, Cracker pioneers and cattle breeders, and Tampa's Cuban community and cigar industry. The cartography collection, spanning six centuries, dazzles.

Greater Tampa Bay

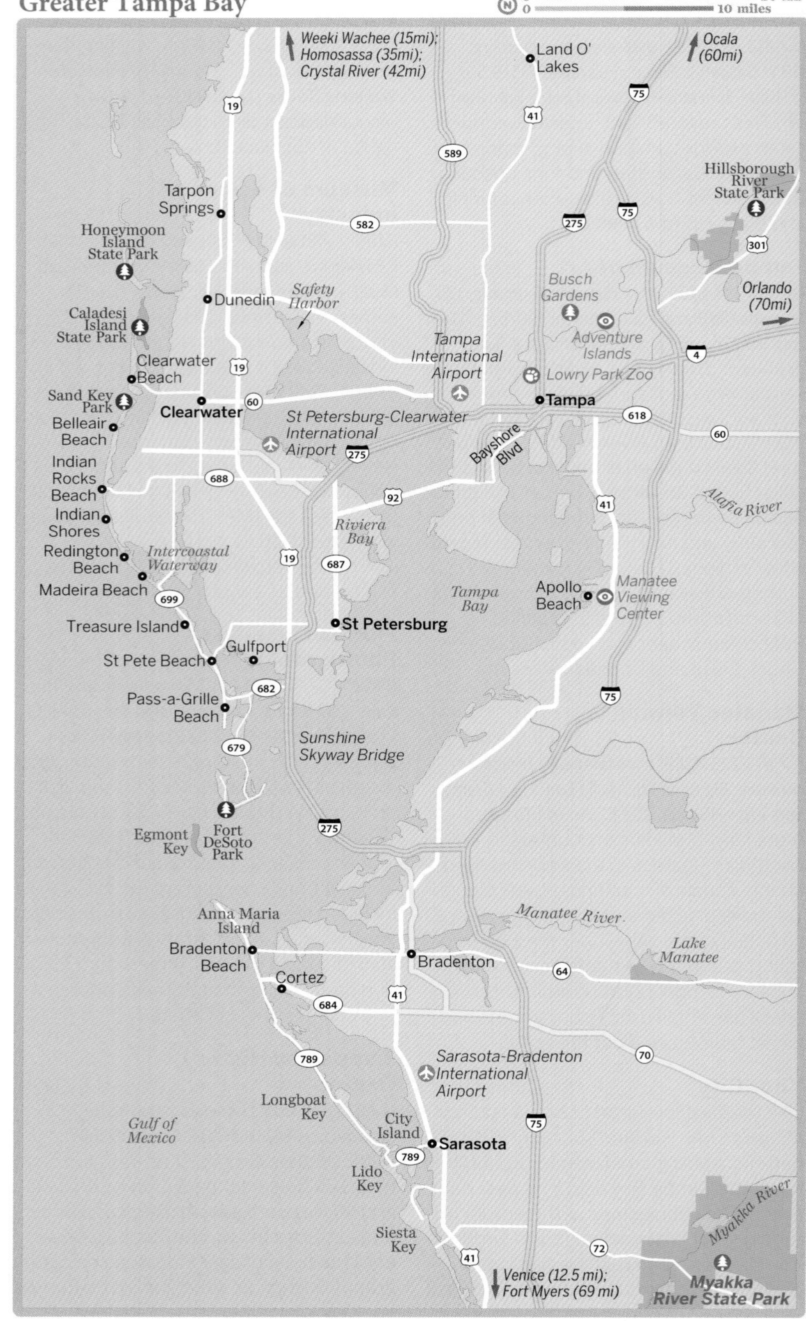

Ybor City Museum State Park Museum

(☎813-247-6323; www.ybormuseum.org; 1818 E 9th Ave; adult/child $4/free; ⏰9am-5pm) This dusty, old-school history museum preserves a bygone era, with cigar-worker houses and wonderful photos. Best is the museum store; get expert cigar advice and pick-up its self-guided **walking tour** (☎813-428-0854; online/audio tour $10/20). The tour is narrated by 24 significant members of the community, including Rafael Martinez-Ybor, great-grandson of Ybor City's founder, and Casey Gonzmart, a fourth-generation member of the Columbia Restaurant clan.

Sleeping

Travelers are best situated in Ybor City or downtown. An abundance of midrange chains are also north of downtown, close to Busch Gardens and the University of South Florida.

Hilton Garden Inn Ybor City Hotel $$

(☎813-769-9267; www.hiltongardeninn.com; 1700 E 9th Ave; r $160-230; P ❄ 📶 🏊) The best option in Tampa is this attractive, efficient and friendly branch of the Hilton Garden chain located just a few blocks from 7th Ave. Rooms are vast and comfortable, there's a nice, private pool area, and the breakfast is generous and cooked to order. An on-call free shuttle is also available for those who want to head downtown.

Gram's Place Hostel Hostel $

(☎813-221-0596; www.grams-inn-tampa.com; 3109 N Ola Ave; dm $23, r $25-60; ❄ @ 📶) As charismatic as an aging rock star, Gram's is a tiny, welcoming hostel for international travelers who prefer personality over perfect linens. Dig the in-ground hot tub and Saturday night jams. Breakfast is not included, but there are two fully serviced kitchens. Gram's Place is in Tampa Heights, 2 miles north of the Museum of Art.

Don Vicente de Ybor Historic Inn Historic Hotel $$

(☎813-241-4545; www.donvicenteinn.com; 1915 Republica de Cuba; r incl breakfast $139-219; P ❄ 📶) Slightly faded, the 1895 Don Vicente recalls Ybor City's glory days. Unfortunately, rooms are less warmly dramatic than the atmospheric Old World public spaces.

Epicurean Hotel Hotel $$$

(☎813-999-8700; www.epicureanhotel.com; 1207 S Howard Ave; r $180-280; P ❄ 📶 🏊) Although part of the Marriott collection, the brand-new Epicurean in South Tampa is a collaboration between six businesses. Bern's Steak House (p270) chef, Chad Johnson, designed the menu of the Élevage restaurant and Dean Hurst plans cutting-edge cocktails at the Edge Social Drinkery rooftop bar. Then there's the Pi patisserie, a fine wine-and-food shop and a culinary classroom. It's hard to see how you'll find time to enjoy the health club, pool or full-service spa, although after all that gourmet gorging they'll be in high demand.

Hampton Inn & Suites Ybor City Hotel $$

(☎813-247-6700; www.hamptoninn.hilton.com; 1301 E 7th Ave; r $130-180; P ❄ 📶 🏊) The red-brick Hampton Inn offers a good level of comfort, a free shuttle downtown and a tiny pool. Its location on 7th Ave means rooms at the front can be noisy.

Eating

Tampa has an excellent restaurant scene, though precious little is downtown.

DOWNTOWN

Oxford Exchange American $$

(☎813-253-0222; www.oxfordexchange.com; 420 W Kennedy Blvd; mains $17-32; ⏰7:30am-5pm Mon-Wed & Fri, to 9pm Thu, 9am-5pm Sat, 9am-8pm Sun) Built in 1891 as a stable for the Plant Hotel, the re-imagined Oxford Exchange takes its inspiration from the venerable Wolseley in London. Chef Erin Guggino's American menu is served beneath sculptural palm fronds in a greenhouse atrium. There's also a tiny wood-paneled bookstore, a Buddy Brew coffee stand and TeBella bar. In 2014 it was granted a liquor license, which meant an exciting new wine and cocktail menu powered by cold-pressed juices.

Downtown Tampa

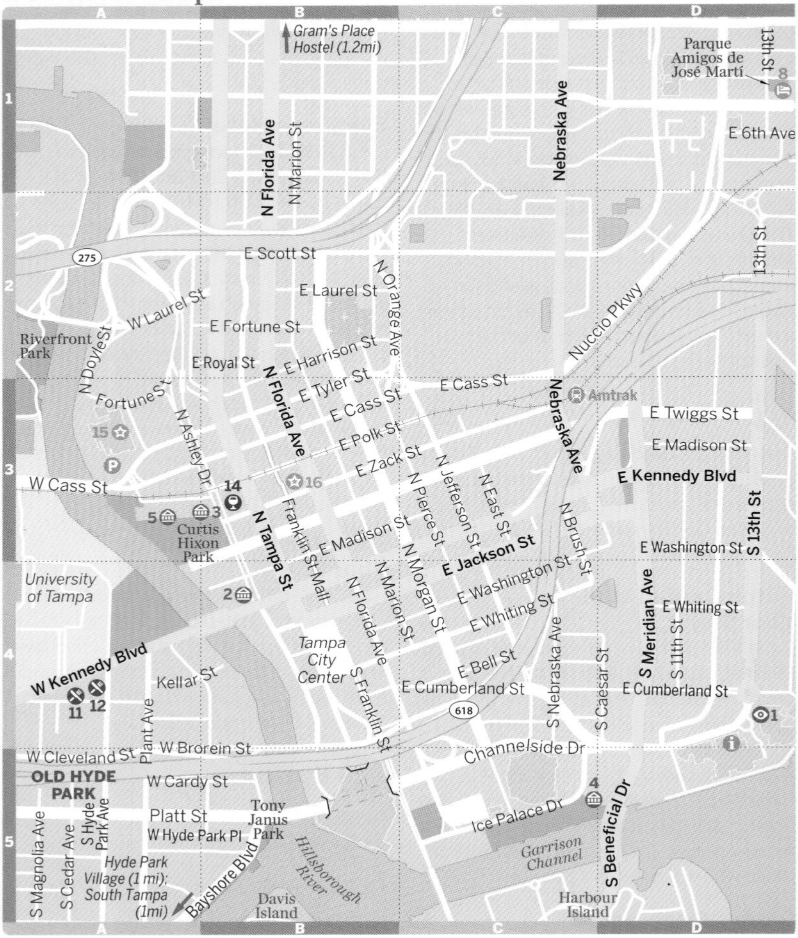

Mise en Place Modern American **$$$**
(**813-254-5373; www.miseonline.com; 442 W Kennedy Blvd; lunch $10-15, dinner $20-35; 11:30am-2:30pm & 5:30-10pm Tue-Fri, 5:30-11pm Sat**) This landmark Tampa restaurant has been a destination for romantic, sophisticated dining for more than 25 years. The menu emphasizes contemporary American cuisine with Floribbean accents, and constantly evolves with nods to culinary fashions without ever feeling pretentious or 'trendy.' Go all out with the great-value 'Get Blitzed' tasting menu ($55).

YBOR CITY

Columbia Restaurant Spanish **$$$**
(**813-248-4961; www.columbiarestaurant.com; 2117 E 7th Ave; mains lunch $9-15, dinner $18-29; 11am-10pm Mon-Thu, to 11pm Fri & Sat, noon-9pm Sun**) Celebrating its centennial in 2015, this Spanish Cuban restaurant is the oldest in Florida. Occupying an entire block, it consists of 13 elegant dining rooms and romantic, fountain-

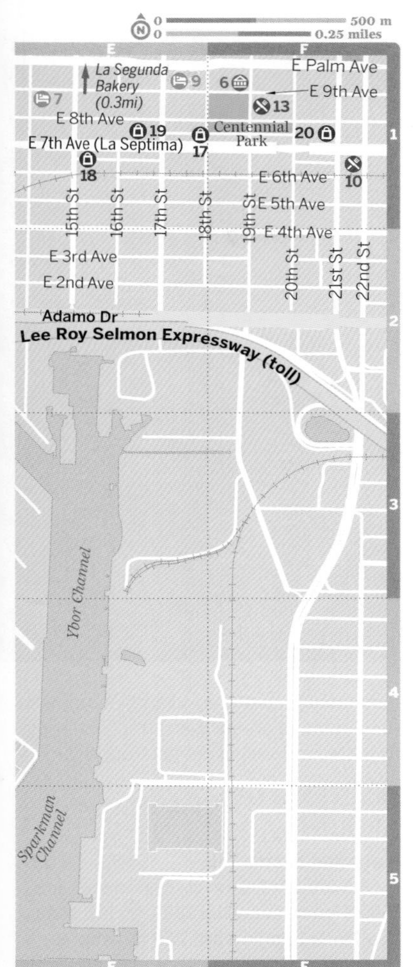

Downtown Tampa

Sights

1	Florida Aquarium	D4
2	Florida Museum of Photographic Arts	B4
3	Glazer Children's Museum	B3
4	Tampa Bay History Center	C5
5	Tampa Museum of Art	A3
6	Ybor City Museum State Park	F1

Sleeping

7	Don Vicente de Ybor Historic Inn	E1
8	Hampton Inn & Suites Ybor City	D1
9	Hilton Garden Inn Ybor City	E1

Eating

10	Columbia Restaurant	F1
11	Mise en Place	A4
12	Oxford Exchange	A4
13	Tre Amici @ the Bunker	F1

Drinking & Nightlife

14	Anise Global Gastrobar	B3

Entertainment

15	Straz Center for the Performing Arts	A3
16	Tampa Theatre	B3

Shopping

17	El Sol	E1
18	King Corona Cigar Factory	E1
19	La France	E1
20	Metropolitan Cigars	F1

centered courtyards. Many of the gloved waiters have been here a lifetime, and owner Richard Gonzmart is zealous about authentic Spanish and Cuban cuisine. Reserve ahead for twice-nightly flamenco and look out for one helluva good birthday party.

Tre Amici @ the Bunker Cafe $

(813-247-6964; www.yborbunker.com; 1907 19th St N; items $3-8; 8am-4pm Mon-Wed, Fri & Sat, to 11pm Thu) Ybor City's hipster contingent wake up at this relaxed community coffeehouse, which offers a range of breakfast burritos, soups and sandwiches all day. Come evening, it hosts open mics, movie nights and even GLBT speed dating.

La Segunda Bakery Bakery $

(www.lasegundabakery.com; 2512 N 15th St; items $1-8; 6:30am-5pm Mon-Fri, 7am-3pm Sat, 7am-1pm Sun) At 15th Ave and 15th St, just outside Ybor's main drag, this authentic Spanish bakery cranks out delicious breads and pastries, rich Cuban coffee and maybe Tampa's best Cuban sandwich. Here since 1915, it bustles every morning with a cross-section of Tampa society.

SOUTH TAMPA

Wright's Gourmet House Sandwiches $

(www.wrightsgourmet.com; 1200 S Dale Mabry Hwy; sandwiches & salads $5-10; 7am-6pm Mon-Fri, 8am-4pm Sat) From the outside this

place looks like it could be a paint store. The inside isn't much better; green vinyl tablecloths and bare white walls. But the red velvet cake, pecan pie and monster sandwiches (try the beef martini with roast beef, wine-marinated mushrooms and bacon), well, these explain what all the fuss is about.

Bern's Steak House Steak **$$$**
(**☎813-251-2421; www.bernssteakhouse.com; 1208 S Howard Ave; mains $25-60; ⏰5-10pm Sun-Thu, to 11pm Fri & Sat**) This legendary, nationally renowned steakhouse is an event as much as a meal. Dress up, order caviar and on-premises dry-aged beef, ask to tour the wine cellar and kitchens, and *don't* skip dessert in the specially designed Harry Waugh Dessert Room.

Restaurant BT Fusion **$$$**
(**☎813-258-1916; www.restaurantbt.com; 2507 S MacDill Ave, Palma Ceia; mains lunch $10-15, dinner $23-32; ⏰11:30am-2:30pm & 5:30-10pm Mon-Sat, to 11pm Fri & Sat**) Chef Trina Nguyan-Batley has combined her high-fashion background and Vietnamese upbringing to create this ultrachic temple to sustainable, locavore gastronomy.

SEMINOLE HEIGHTS & AROUND

Rooster & the Till Fusion **$$**
(**☎813-374-8940; www.roosterandthetill.com; 6500 N Florida Ave; plates $8-19; ⏰3:30-10pm Mon-Thu, to 11pm Fri & Sat**) With an impressive culinary pedigree behind them, Ferrell Alvarez and Ty Rodriguez launched Seminole Heights' most recent and ambitious farm-to-table restaurant. Don't come here for big portions or national brand beverages, instead come for small plates bursting with flavor. Try the Mangalitsa pork belly complemented by pickled apple and peppercorn honey, or smoked shimeji and oyster mushrooms with tart green tomato and Point Reyes blue cheese.

Refinery Modern American **$$**
(**☎813-237-2000; www.thetamparefinery.com; 5137 N Florida Ave; mains $9-24; ⏰5-10pm Sun-**

Left: Manatees; **Below:** Glazer Children's Museum (p265)
(LEFT) PETER PEARSON/GETTY IMAGES ©; (BELOW) RICHARD CUMMINGS/GETTY IMAGES ©

Thu, to 11pm Fri & Sat, brunch 11am-2:30pm Sun;) This blue-collar gourmet joint promises chipped plates and no pretensions, just playful, delicious hyperlocal cuisine that cleverly mixes a sustainability ethic with a punk attitude. Owners Michelle and Greg Baker are among a tiny number of Florida restauranteurs who are known outside the area, thanks no doubt to Greg's three James Beard nominations. From 5pm to 7pm there are $5 chef plates.

Ella's Americana Folk Art Cafe American $$
(813-234-1000; www.ellasfolkartcafe.com; 5119 N Nebraska Ave; mains $11-22; 5-11pm Tue-Thu, to midnight Fri & Sat, 11am-8pm Sun) After one too many Boozy Suzys the visionary outsider art on Ella's walls starts to make a lot of sense. But it's not just the eccentric art and cocktails that keep locals loyal: it's the cosy vibe, the heartwarming soul food and the weekly roster of events from live music to dough-nut- and beer-tasting evenings.

Drinking & Entertainment

For nightlife, Ybor City is party central, though SoHo and Seminole Heights are also hip and happening.

Ybor City is also the center of Tampa's GLBT life; to connect with it, check out the **GaYbor District Coalition** (www.gaybor.com) and **Gay Tampa** (www.gaytampa.com).

Skipper's Smokehouse Live Music
(813-971-0666; www.skipperssmokehouse.com; 910 Skipper Rd; cover $5-25; 11am-midnight Tue-Fri, from noon Sat, from 1pm Sun) Like it blew in from the Keys, Skipper's is a beloved, unpretentious open-air venue for blues, folk, reggae and gator-swamp rockabilly. It's 9 miles directly north of downtown on N Nebraska Ave.

Tampa Theatre Cinema
(☎813-274-8981; www.tampatheatre.org; 711 N Franklin St; tickets $11) This historic 1926 theater in downtown is a gorgeous venue in which to see an independent film. The mighty Wurlitzer organ plays before most movies. Too bad showtimes are so limited: only one evening screening midweek and three on weekends. Look for special events.

Independent Bar Bar
(☎813-341-4883; www.independenttampa.com; 5016 N Florida Ave; ⏲noon-midnight Sun-Wed, to 1am Thu-Sat) If you appreciate craft brews, roll into this converted gas station, now a low-key hip bar in Seminole Heights. You can count on one or more local Cigar City Brews, and it serves some mean pub grub.

Cigar City Brewing Brewery
(☎813-348-6363; www.cigarcitybrewing.com; 3924 West Spruce St; ⏲11am-11pm Sun-Thu, to 1am Fri & Sat) This is Tampa's premier craft brewery. It has dozens of crafted brews on tap, some exclusive to the brewery. On Friday nights there are food trucks in the parking lot and you can take tours of the brewery for $5 (with one beer included). You'll find it west of downtown, north off I-275.

Anise Global Gastrobar Cocktail Bar
(☎813-225-4272; 777 N Ashley Dr; ⏲4-10pm Mon-Thu, to midnight Fri, 11am-midnight Sat, 11am-10pm Sun) Located at the base of the soaring SkyPoint building, Anise has a long sleek bar and a short, smart cocktail list. Even mixers are taken seriously here, from Fever Tree Tonic to Mexican Coke (sweetened with sugar cane not high-fructose corn syrup). There's also a globetrotting wine list and an Asian-inspired tapas menu (from $8 to $11).

Cinebistro Cinema
(☎813-514-8300; www.cobbcinebistro.com; 1609 W Swann Ave, Hyde Park Village) Cross a trendy South Beach nightclub with a plush art-house cinema, and you get this: a snazzy lobby cocktail bar and upscale munchies (mains from $10 to $20) so you can nosh at your seat while you watch. It's movie-going with style.

Straz Center for the Performing Arts Performing Arts
(☎813-229-7827; www.strazcenter.org; 1010 MacInnes Pl) This enormous, multivenue complex draws the gamut of fine-arts performances: touring Broadway shows, pop concerts, opera, ballet, drama and more.

Shopping

On 8th Ave between 15th and 17th Sts, **Centro Ybor** (www.centroybor.com) is an attractive shopping, dining and entertainment complex. In addition, the **Ybor City Farmers Market** (www.ybormarket.com; 8th Ave & 18th St, Centen-

Sign, Tampa Theatre

nial Park; 9am-3pm Sat) emphasizes arts and crafts.

Inkwood Books Books

(813-253-2638; www.inkwoodbooks.com; 216 S Armenia Ave; 10am-9pm Mon-Thu, to 7pm Fri & Sat, 1-5pm Sun) In a small house close to Hyde Park, Tampa's best independent bookstore has a fantastic selection of new Florida titles, both nonfiction and mysteries, and wonderful children's books. It also hosts a whole roster of readings and signing events.

La France Vintage

(813-248-1381; 1612 E 7th Ave, Ybor City; 11am-8pm Mon-Thu, to 10pm Fri & Sat, noon-7pm Sun) Thanks to an influx of wealthy snowbirds, Tampa has a thriving vintage scene. With four streetfront windows rotating displays of flapper dresses, ornamental umbrellas, feathered hats and men's leisure suits, La France is like a living museum without a cover charge. Inside you can browse racks of 1930s maxi-dresses, sparkling 1940s swing dresses and Mod suits from the 60s. Some items are newly made from period designs, while others come from estate sales and private sellers.

If You Like... Cigars

The old Tampa Sweethearts factory still stands (at 1301 N 22nd St), but the most personalized experience for cigar fanatics is the Ybor City Museum walking tour (p267), run by PhD Wallace Reyes, who currently holds the world record for rolling the longest cigar (196ft ⅜in!).

The most knowledgeable (and legitimate) places to buy cigars in Ybor City are:

1 **METROPOLITAN CIGARS** (2014 E 7th Ave; 9:30am-8pm Mon-Fri, 10:30am-5:30pm Sat) The store itself is actually a humidor; perhaps the best cigar shop in Tampa Bay.

2 **KING CORONA CIGAR FACTORY** (www.kingcoronacigars.com; 1523 E 7th Ave; 8am-midnight Mon-Wed, to 1am Thu, to 2am Fri, 10-2am Sat, noon-midnight Sun) The city's largest cigar emporium, complete with an old-fashioned cigar bar.

3 **EL SOL** (www.elsolcigars.com; Suite L, 10549 North Florida Avenue; 10:30am-5:30pm Mon-Sat) Established in 1929, and the oldest cigar store in Ybor City.

4 **GONZALES Y MARTINEZ CIGAR COMPANY** (2025 E 7th Ave; 11am-9pm Mon-Thu, to 11pm Fri & Sat) Within the Columbia Restaurant gift store.

Information

Medical Services

Tampa General Hospital (813-844-7000; www.tgh.org; 1 Tampa General Circle, Davis Island; 24hr) South of downtown on Davis Island.

Tourist Information

Tampa Bay Convention & Visitors Bureau (813-223-1111; www.visittampabay.com; 615 Channelside Dr; 10am-5:30pm Mon-Sat, 11am-5pm Sun) The visitor center has good free maps and lots of information. Book hotels directly through the website.

Getting There & Around

Air

The region's major airport, and the state's third-busiest airport, is **Tampa International Airport** (TPA; 813-870-8700; www.tampaairport.com; 4100 George J Bean Pkwy), about 13 miles west of downtown, off Hwy 589. It's an easy, pleasant airport to negotiate.

All major car agencies have desks at the airport. By car, take the I-275 to N Ashley Dr, turn right and you're in downtown.

Trolley & Streetcar

In-Town Trolley (fare 25¢; 6am-8:30am & 3:30-6pm Mon-Fri) Within downtown, HART's inexpensive trolley runs up and down Florida Ave, Tampa St and Franklin St every 15 minutes.

TECO Line Streetcars (www.tecolinestreetcar.org; adult/child $2.50/1.25; noon-10pm Mon-Thu, 11-2am Fri & Sat, noon-8pm Sun) HART's old-fashioned electric streetcars connect downtown's Marion Transit Center with Ybor City, running every 20 minutes.

St Petersburg

727 / POP 244,700

St Petersburg has a bawdy reputation as a party town, but in fact, the bay area's two cities are more alike than they are different. Both are working hard to revitalize and restore their historic neighborhoods and waterfront districts. Both are succeeding admirably and are well worth visiting.

Sights & Activities

When taking in the sights, visitors can confine themselves to a walkable, T-shaped route: along Central Ave, mainly from 8th St to Bayshore Dr, and along Bayshore Dr from the Dalí Museum to the bayfront parks in the Old Northeast neighborhood.

St Petersburg Museum of Fine Arts Museum
(727-896-2667; www.fine-arts.org; 255 Beach Dr NE; adult/child $17/10; 10am-5pm Mon-Sat, to 8pm Thu, from noon Sun) The Museum of Fine Arts collection is as broad as the Dalí Museum's is deep, traversing the world's antiquities and following art's progression through nearly every era.

Old Northeast Neighborhood
The Old Northeast, or Coffee Pot Bayou, begins around 9th Ave NE and goes to 30th Ave NE; it extends inland from the bay to about 4th St. At about 10th Ave NE the **North Shore Aquatic Complex** (901 N Shore Dr NE; adult/child $5/4.50; 9am-4pm Mon-Fri, 10am-4pm Sat, 1-4pm Sun) has three gorgeous swimming pools, including a kids' pool with waterslide. Adjacent grassy public parks include the **Gizella Kopsick Palm Arboretum** (sunrise-sunset) FREE, essentially an open 2-acre garden of more than 500 palms, all signed and lovingly landscaped. There are also large parking lots here and a long, white-sand **swimming beach**. Keep going along the paved trail, past pretty homes and private docks, all the way to small **Coffee Pot Park**, where manatees can occasionally be spotted.

Morean Arts Center Arts Center
(727-822-7872; www.moreanartscenter.org; 719 Central Ave; 10am-5pm Mon-Sat, from noon Sun) FREE This lively community arts center hosts interesting rotating exhibits in all media. If you love glass, don't miss Morean's attached **Hot Shop** (727-827-4527; adult/child $9/5; noon-5pm Mon-Sat) where full-blast glassmaking demonstrations occur every half-hour. Reserve ahead for a one-on-one 'hot glass experience' ($75) and take home your own creation.

Chihuly Collection Gallery
(727-896-4527; www.moreanartscenter.org; 400 Beach Dr; adult/child $20/13; 10am-5pm Mon-Sat, from noon Sun) Dale Chihuly's glass works are displayed at the Metropolitan Museum of Art in New York, the Victoria and Albert Museum (V&A) in London and the Louvre in Paris. But his permanent collection resides here in St Petersburg, in an understated wood-and-marble gallery designed to off-set dramatic installations such as the *Ruby Red Icicle Chandelier* or the multicolored *Persians* ceiling.

Weedon Island Preserve Hiking, Kayaking
(727-453-6500; www.weedonislandpreserve.org; 1800 Weedon Dr NE; 7am-sunset) Like a patchwork quilt of variegated greens tossed out over Tampa Bay, this 3700-acre preserve protects a diverse aquatic and wetland ecosystem. At the heart of the preserve is the excellent **Cultural and Natural History Center** (open from 9am to 4pm) where you can browse exhibits about the natural environment and the early Weeden Island people. Sign-up also for interpretive hikes over miles of **boardwalk** or go it alone with the online map. Alternatively rent a kayak from **Sweetwater Kayaks**

JOHN COLETTI/GETTY IMAGES ©

Don't Miss
Salvador Dalí Museum

Unveiled in 2011, the theatrical exterior of the Salvador Dalí Museum augurs great things: out of a wound in the towering white shoebox oozes the 75ft geodesic atrium Glass Enigma. Even better, what unfolds inside is like a blueprint of what a modern art museum should be, or at least, one devoted to understanding the life, art and impact of a single revolutionary artist like Dalí.

The Dalí's 20,000 sq ft of gallery space is designed specifically to display all 96 oil paintings in the collection, along with 'key works from every moment and in every medium': drawings, prints, sculptures, photos, manuscripts, even movies, everything arranged chronologically and explained in context. The museum is so sharp it includes a 'contemplation area' with nothing but white walls and a window. Another great breather is the garden, which is small but, like everything, shot through with cleverness.

Excellent, free docent tours occur hourly (on the half hour); these are highly recommended to help crack open the rich symbolism in Dalí's works. Topping this off, the Spanish cafe is first rate, and the gift store is the region's best, hands down.

THINGS YOU NEED TO KNOW

727-823-3767; www.thedali.org; 1 Dali Blvd; adult/child 6-12yr $21/7, after 5pm Thu $10; 10am-5:30pm Mon-Sat, to 8pm Thu, noon-5:30pm Sun

(727-570-4844; www.sweetwaterkayaks.wordpress.com; 10000 Gandy Blvd N; kayaks 1/4hr $17/40; 10am-6pm Mon-Tue & Thu-Sat, 9am-3pm Sun) and head out on the 4-mile **South Trail loop** through the idyllic mangrove islands.

Sleeping

For southwest Florida, St Petersburg has a notable selection of nice B&Bs; contact the local **Association of Bed & Breakfast Inns** (www.spaabbi.com).

St Petersburg

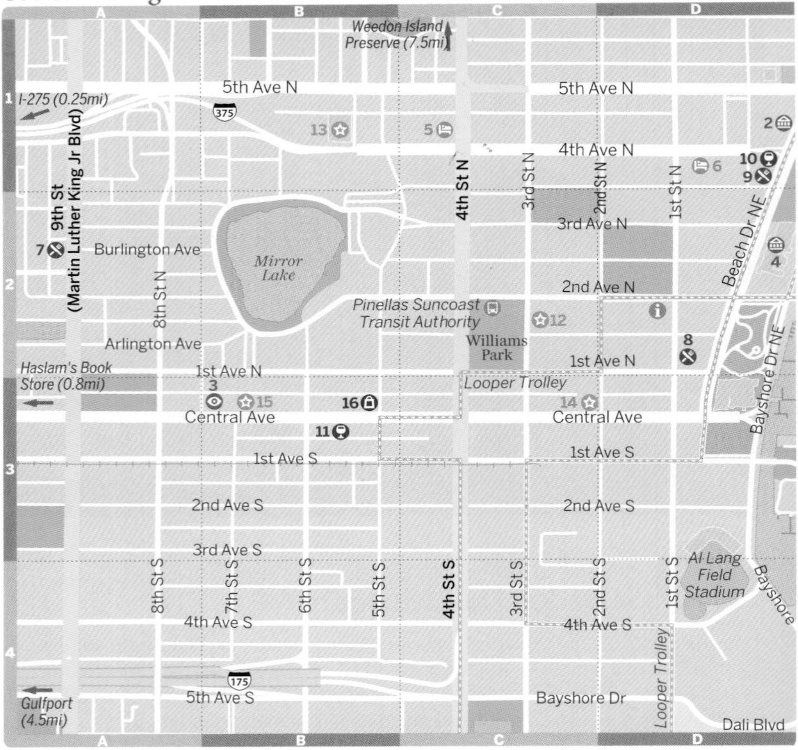

Dickens House B&B **$$**
(☎727-822-8622; www.dickenshouse.com; 335 8th Ave NE; r $119-245; P ❄ @ 📶) Five lushly designed rooms await in this passionately restored arts-and-crafts-style home. The gregarious, gay-friendly owner whips up a gourmet breakfast.

Watergarden Inn at the Bay Inn **$$**
(☎727-822-1700; www.innatthebay.com; 126 4th Ave N; r $130-190, ste $175-290; P ❄ 📶 🏊) This fabulous 1910 inn carved from two old neighborhood houses offers 14 rooms and suites in a mature, half-acre garden. Outside a bright tropical palette and palm-fringed pool gives the complex a beachy Key West vibe, while inside four-poster beds, two-person Jacuzzis and fluffy robes conjure romance.

Hollander Hotel Boutique Hotel **$$**
(☎727-873-7900; www.hollanderhotel.com; 421 4th Ave N; r $98-140; P ❄ 📶) Stepping assuredly into St Pete's hotel scene, the Hollander can do no wrong with its art-deco flavor, 130ft porch, convivial Tap Room, full-service spa and serious Brew D Licious coffee shop. Common areas feature gorgeous period detailing and rooms retain a hint of 1930s romance with their polished wooden floors, lazy ceiling fans and cane furniture.

Eating

Beach Dr along the waterfront is a warm, friendly scene lined with attractive mid-range restaurants; stroll at sunset and let your palate guide you.

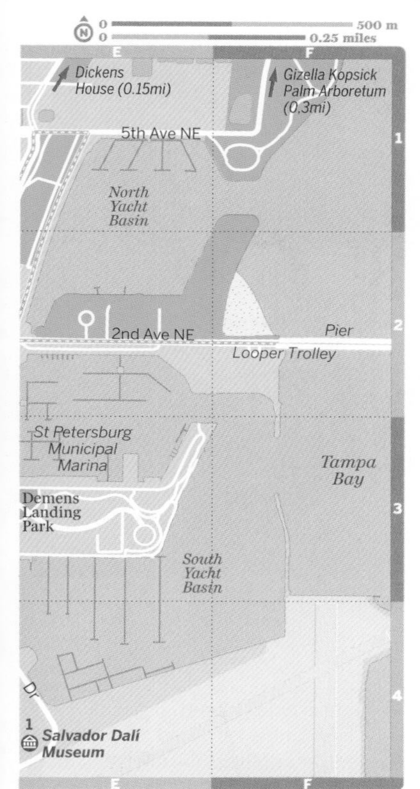

St Petersburg

Don't Miss Sights
1 Salvador Dalí Museum E4

Sights
2 Chihuly Collection D1
3 Morean Arts Center B3
4 St Petersburg Museum of Fine Arts D2

Sleeping
5 Hollander Hotel C1
6 Watergarden Inn at the Bay D1

Eating
7 Coney Island Hot Dog A2
8 DeLucia Italian Bakery Café D2
9 Moon Under Water D1

Drinking & Nightlife
10 Canopy D1
11 Cycle Brewing B3

Entertainment
12 American Stage C2
13 Coliseum Ballroom B1
14 Jannus Live C3
15 State Theatre B3

Shopping
16 Florida Craftsmen Gallery B3

Coney Island Hot Dog Fast Food **$**
(250 9th St N; items $2-3; 10am-7pm Mon-Fri, to 3:30pm Sat) Collectors of Americana and hot-dog fanatics: order two delicious chili dogs, slaw and a milkshake and savor the vinyl-booth charm of this authentic, unvarnished old St Pete institution. Cash only. Near 3rd Ave N.

DeLucia Italian Bakery Café Bakery **$**
(727-824-2874; 119 1st Ave N; pizza $10.50; 7am-9pm Mon-Sat, 7am-2pm Sun) With a master baker on hand to see that the pizza dough, bread and baked goods meet authentic Italian standards and baristas who have been trained by Illy, this new downtown bakery promises great things. Order a super-thin-crust pizza to share or just go for the cookies and a shot of Illy espresso.

Alésia French, Vietnamese **$$**
(727-345-9701; http://alesiarestaurant.com; 7204 Central Ave; mains $7.50-18; 11:30am-2:30pm & 5:30-9pm Tue-Fri, from 10am Sat) Lovely Alésia with its big windows, laid-back soundtrack and umbrellaed courtyard is the brainchild of Sandra Ly-Flores, Erika Ly and Paul Hsu, who wanted to recreate the French Vietnamese cafes of their Parisian youth. Agonise over the selection of pastries tiered on the counter; breakfast on crepes or *croques monsieur;* and linger over bowls of spicy pho and plates of crunchy summer rolls. One thing's for sure: you'll probably be back.

Moon Under Water Indian **$$**
(727-896-6160; www.themoonunderwater.com; 332 Beach Dr NE; mains $9-17; 11am-11pm, to midnight Fri & Sat) Sporting an upbeat, 19th-century British-colonial

ST. PETERSBURG TIMES/ZUMAPRESS.COM/ALAMY ©

Don't Miss Gulfport

Gulfport is the cutest, quirkiest little beach town not on the barrier islands. Beach Blvd is a four-block stretch of funky boutiques, friendly locals, little cafes and surprisingly good restaurants. Get the full dose of wry local sensibilities during the twice-monthly art walk, essentially a low-key street party, every first Friday and third Saturday from 6pm to 10pm.

Peg's Cantina (727-328-2720; www.pegscantina.com; 3038 Beach Blvd; mains $10-16; 5-9pm Wed-Thu, noon-9:30pm Tue, Fri & Sat, noon-9pm Sun) is ripe with Gulfport mojo. This brewpub in a woodsy bungalow perfectly pairs fanciful Mexican dishes with creamy handcrafted beers, ideally enjoyed in the wonderful gardens.

If you're tempted to spend the night, the historic **Peninsula Inn** (727-346-9800; www.innspa.net; 2937 Beach Blvd; r $130-180;), pictured above, has been renovated into a pretty romantic choice. It also has a recommended restaurant with jazz music on weekends.

atmosphere, Moon Under Water serves admirably flavorful Indian curries; ask for a capsicum 'enhancer' to adjust the heat to your palate. The British side of the menu specializes in fish and chips, shepherd's pie and bangers and mash. Both imported British and local Cigar City brews are on tap.

Drinking

Kicking off each month, 'First Friday' is an evening block party and giant pub crawl with live music on Central Ave.

Jannus Live Concert Venue
(727-565-0551; www.jannuslive.com; 16 2nd St N) Well-loved outdoor concert venue

inside an intimate courtyard; national and local bands reverberate downtown.

Cycle Brewing Brewery
(☎727-320-7954; 534 Central Ave; ⌚3pm-midnight Mon-Thu, to 3am Fri, noon-3am Sat, noon-10pm Sun) Hipster brewhouse with sidewalk seating serving 12 rotating taps of world-class beer.

Canopy Cocktail Bar
(☎727-896-1080; www.thebirchwood.com; The Birchwood, 340 Beach Dr NE; ⌚4pm-2am) The 5th-floor rooftop bar of the Birchwood Hotel is currently the hottest ticket in town for late-night drinking thanks to its sexy ambience and panoramic views of Beach Dr. Couples loiter in the hope of snagging one of the private cabanas, while party-lovers lounge on long sofas warmed by the glow of fire pits.

State Theatre Concert Venue
(☎727-895-3045; www.statetheatreconcerts.com; 687 Central Ave; tickets $14-26) Up-and-coming bands of all stripes, and occasional national acts, play this restored art-deco theater (built in 1927).

Coliseum Ballroom Dance
(☎727-892-5202; www.stpete.org/coliseum; 535 4th Ave N; tea dances $7-10) This old-fashioned 1924 ballroom hosts occasional events and has regular tea dances on the first and third Wednesday every month.

American Stage Theater
(☎727-823-7529; www.americanstage.org; 163 3rd St N; tickets $29-59) One of the Tampa Bay area's most highly regarded regional theaters presents American classics and recent Tony winners (such as *August: Osage County* and *The Wiz*). Its 'In the Park' series presents Broadway musicals.

Shopping

The main shopping corridor is along Central Ave between 5th and 8th Sts and also between 10th and 13th Sts.

Haslam's Book Store Books
(☎727-822-8616; www.haslams.com; 2025 Central Ave; ⌚10am-6:30pm Mon-Sat, noon-5pm Sun) A half-block long, with a tremendous selection of new and used books and a fantastic Florida section, Haslam's claims to be the largest independent bookstore in the US Southeast.

Florida Craftsmen Gallery Arts & Crafts
(☎727-821-7391; www.floridacraftsmen.net; 501 Central Ave; ⌚10am-5:30pm Mon-Sat) A non-profit association runs this gallery-store dedicated to Florida craftspeople. Find unusual, unique, high-quality ceramics, jewelry, glass, clothing and art.

Information

All Children's Hospital (☎727-898-7451; www.allkids.org; 501 6th St S; ⌚24hr) The area's largest hospital.

Bayfront Medical Center (☎727-823-1234; www.bayfront.org; 701 6th St S; ⌚24hr) A convenient option downtown.

St Pete Downtown Arts Association (www.stpetearts.org) Information on galleries, craftspeople and artists, plus a locator map.

St Petersburg Area Chamber of Commerce (☎727-821-4069; www.stpete.com; 100 2nd Ave N; ⌚9am-5pm Mon-Fri) Helpful, staffed chamber office has good maps and a driving guide.

Getting There & Around

Air

St Petersburg-Clearwater International Airport (www.fly2pie.com; Roosevelt Blvd & Hwy 686, Clearwater) Mainly regional flights; two international services to Toronto and Halifax, Nova Scotia.

Bus

Pinellas Suncoast Transit Authority (PSTA; www.psta.net; 340 2nd Ave N; adult/student $2/1.25) St Petersburg buses serve the barrier-island beaches and Clearwater; unlimited-ride Go Cards cost $4.50 per day.

Trolley Car

Downtown Looper (www.loopertrolley.com; fare 50¢; ⏱10am-5pm Sun-Thu, to midnight Fri & Sat) Old-fashioned trolley cars run a downtown circuit every 15 minutes; great for sightseeing.

St Pete Beach & Barrier Island Beaches

☎727 / POP 9300

In just 20 minutes from downtown St Petersburg, you can reach the legendary barrier-island beaches that are the sandy soul of the peninsula. This 30-mile-long stretch of sun-faded towns, soft-sand beaches, and sun-kissed azure waters is the perfect antidote to city life and the primary destination of most vacationers.

Sights & Activities

Fort DeSoto Park Park, Beach

(☎727-552-1862; www.pinellascounty.org/park; 3500 Pinellas Bayway S; ⏱sunrise-sunset) FREE Fort DeSoto's 1136-acres of unspoiled wilderness is unquestionably one of Florida's premier beach parks – with the accolades to prove it. It includes 7 miles of beaches, two fishing piers and an extensive nature trail hopping over five interconnected islands. Of its two swimming areas, the long, silky stretch of **North Beach** is the best. It's accessed by huge parking lots and offers grassy picnic areas, a cafe and gift store (open from 10am to 4pm weekdays and to 5pm weekends). The cafe organizes bike ($10 per hour) and kayak ($23 per hour) rentals. **East Beach**, meanwhile, is smaller and coarser, and consequently less crowded.

Pass-a-Grille Beach Beach

(www.pass-a-grillebeach.com; Gulf Blvd) The epic sliver of sand that is Pass-a-Grille Beach is the most idyllic barrier-island beach, backed only by beach houses and a long stretch of metered public parking. Here you can watch boats coming through Pass-a-Grille Channel, hop aboard the **Shell Key Shuttle** (www.shellkeyshuttle.com; Merry Pier, Pass-a-Grille; adult/child $25/12.50; ⏱shuttles 10am, noon & 2pm) to unspoiled **Shell Key**, and retire for eats and ice cream in the laid-back village center.

Birds, Fort DeSoto Park

Suncoast Seabird Sanctuary Wildlife Reserve

(☎727-392-4291727-392-4291; www.seabirdsanctuary.com; 18328 Gulf Blvd, Indian Shores; admission by donation; ⏲9am-sunset) The largest wild-bird hospital in North America, this sanctuary has up to 600 sea and land birds for public viewing at any one time, including a resident population of birds that are too injured to be released. Thousands of birds are treated and released back to the wild annually.

Sleeping

Inn on the Beach Motel $$

(☎727-360-8844; www.innonbeach.com; 1401 Gulf Way, Pass-a-Grille; r $115-250, cottages $185-295; P ❄ wi-fi) For a quiet, relaxing seaside getaway, these 12 rooms and four cottages are unqualified gems. With bright coral and teal accents, functional kitchenettes and lovely tile bathrooms, these quarters are a pleasure to return to in the evening; a couple of 2nd-floor rooms have luscious gulf views and the top-floor Ibis honeymoon suite is swoonworthy.

Fort DeSoto Park Campground Campground $

(☎727-582-2100; www.pinellascounty.org/park; 3500 Pinellas Bayway S; tent sites $34-36, RV sites $40-42; ⏲office 9am-6pm Sat-Thu, to 9pm Fri; P) For tent camping, the Gulf Coast hardly offers better than the more than 200 sites here. Well shaded by thick-growing palms, many face the water, and there are good facilities, hot showers, a grassy field and small camp store, in addition to other park concessions. Online reservations can be made three months in advance, but a few first-come, first-served sites are made available every Friday.

Eating

Walt'z Fish Shak Seafood $

(☎727-395-0732; www.waltzfishshak.com; 224 Boardwalk Pl E, Madeira Beach; mains $4-12; ⏲5-9pm Tue-Fri, noon-3pm Sun) The MO at Water Gerbase's fish shack is simple: the day's domestic-only catch (often featuring grouper, cobia and amberjack) is chalked on the board; you choose one grilled, fried or blackened and served with coleslaw, salad or raw veg. When they run out, that's it for the night. Get there early

If You Like... Islands

Two of the best beaches in Florida are just north of Greater Tampa: Honeymoon Island, which you can drive to, and ferry-only Caladesi Island.

1 **HONEYMOON ISLAND STATE PARK**

(☎727-469-5942; www.floridastateparks.org/honeymoonisland; 1 Dunedin Causeway; car/cyclist $8/2; ⏲8am-sunset; 🐾) **Honeymoon Island State Recreation Area** began life as a grand prize in a 1940s contest. Paramount newsreels and *Life* magazine were giving away all-expenses-paid honeymoons to newlyweds who'd stay in thatched huts lining the beach. A road connecting the island to the mainland was built in 1964 and the state bought the land in the early 1970s. Today, the park offers diverse birdlife, good swimming and great shelling. Coastal plants include mangrove swamps, rare virgin slash pine, strand and salt marshes. There are also nature trails and bird observation areas.

2 **CALADESI ISLAND STATE PARK**

(☎727-469-5918; www.floridastateparks.org/caladesiisland; boat/kayak $6/2; ⏲8am-sunset) Just south of Honeymoon Island, **Caladesi Island State Park** ranks at the top of national surveys for best natural beaches. Reach it by canoe or take the Caladesi Connection ferry (☎727-734-1501; www.caladesiferry.org; adult/child $14/7) from Honeymoon Island. In addition to nature trails and an unspoiled, palm-lined 3-mile beach, it's nice for picnicking, swimming and shelling. You might see armadillos, tortoises, raccoons, turtles and all manner of birds. Keep your eyes open and stay light on your feet.

JAMES SCHWABEL/ALAMY ©

Don't Miss
Cayo Costa State Park

Unspoiled and all natural, as slim as a supermodel and just as lovely, Cayo Costa Island is almost entirely preserved as a 2500-acre state park. Bring a snorkel mask to help scour sandbars for shells and huge conchs – delightfully, many still house colorful occupants (who, by law, must be left there). Bike dirt roads to more-distant beaches, hike interior island trails, kayak mangroves. The ranger station near the dock sells water and firewood, and rents bikes and kayaks, but otherwise bring everything you need. There's a 30-site campground plus 12 cabins, or you can sleep on the beach, although by May, heat and no-see-ums get unpleasant.

The only access is by boat, which doubles as a scenic nature-and-dolphin cruise operated by the park's official concessionaire, Tropic Star. Day-trip ferries ($25) take an hour one-way; a range of other options include stops at Cabbage Key for lunch. It also offers private water taxis ($150 per hour), which are much faster.

THINGS YOU NEED TO KNOW

Cayo Costa State Park (941-964-0375; www.floridastateparks.org/cayocosta; admission $2; 8am-sunset); Tropic Star (239-283-0015; www.cayocostaferry.com; Jug Creek Marina, Bokeelia)

to grab a table and the best of the day's selection.

Guppy's Seafood $$
(727-593-2032; www.3bestchefs.com; 1701 Gulf Blvd, Indian Rocks; lunch $9-14, dinner $13-25; 11:30am-10pm) For variety, quality and price, it's hard to beat Guppy's, which packs diners in nightly. Preparations are diverse, skillfully spanning styles (and budgets), from Italian cioppino to Hawaiian seared-ahi and Caribbean spice-rubbed grouper. The only problem:

it doesn't take reservations, though its 'call-ahead seating' gets your name on the wait list before arrival.

Fetishes French **$$$**
(☎727-363-3700; www.fetishesrestaurant.com; 6305 Gulf Blvd, St Pete Beach; mains $19-60; ⏲5-10pm Tue-Sat) Under Bruce Caplan's eagle eye, sumptuous classics such as steak Diane, duck *a l'orange, coquilles* St Jacques and sole *meunière* are sautéed, brandied and flambéed tableside for tongue-tingling flavor. Go the whole hog and splash out on a spicy, black-cherry flavored Silver Oak Alexander Valley cabernet from the glassed-in wine cellar.

Information

Tampa Bay Beaches Chamber of Commerce
(☎727-360-6957; www.tampabaybeaches.com; 6990 Gulf Blvd, at 70th Ave; ⏲9am-5pm Mon-Fri) Extremely helpful; excellent maps and advice.

SOUTH OF TAMPA

People who prefer Florida's Gulf side over its Atlantic one generally fall in love with this stretch of sun-kissed coastline.

Sarasota

☎941 / POP 51,900

Entire vacations can be spent soaking up the sights and culture, and the egregiously pretty beaches, of sophisticated Sarasota. In fact, base your stay here, and the majority of the Tampa Bay area's highlights are within easy reach.

Sights & Activities

Mote Marine Laboratory Aquarium
(☎941-388-4441; www.mote.org; 1600 Ken Thompson Pkwy, City Island; adult/child $20/15; ⏲10am-5pm) A research facility first and an aquarium second, the Mote is one of the world's leading organizations for shark study, and glimpsing its work is a highlight: marvel at seahorse 'fry' born that very day, and time your visit for **shark training**. Above-average exhibits include a preserved giant squid (37ft long when caught), a stingray touch tank, a dramatic shark tank, and a separate building with intimate encounters with sea turtles, manatees and dolphins. An interactive immersion theater is perfect for kids. Note that animal welfare groups suggest interaction with dolphins and other sea mammals held in captivity creates stress for these creatures.

St Armands Circle Square
(www.starmandscircleassoc.com) Conceived by John Ringling in the 1920s, St

St Armands Circle
IMAGES-USA/ALAMY©

ICIMAGE/ALAMY©

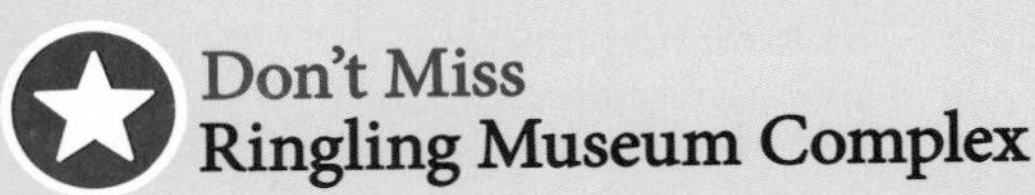

Don't Miss Ringling Museum Complex

The 66-acre winter estate of railroad, real-estate and circus baron John Ringling and his wife, Mable, is one of the Gulf Coast's most eclectic attractions. There's a lot to see, and several ways to see it. For the complete experience, plan a full day or several shorter visits. For instance, the landscaped grounds and rose gardens are free to the public during open hours. The art museum (alone) is free Monday, while 5pm till 8pm Thursday both the art and circus museums are discounted (adult/child $10/5).

In addition to the sights below, the historic Asolo Theater (p286) shows a highly recommended, 30-minute PBS-produced film on Ringling's life (included with admission). The theater is itself an attraction – its ornate Italian interior dating to 1798 – and at night hosts a Hollywood film series and special events.

- **John & Mable Ringling Museum of Art** The Ringlings amassed a vast, impressive collection of European tapestries and paintings ranging from the 14th to the 18th centuries. One wing, though, presents rotating exhibits of contemporary art. In 2012, the Searing Wing plans to open a new atrium, a stunning James Turrell-designed 'Sky Space.'

- **Cá d'Zan** Ringling was a showman, and his winter home Cá d'Zan (1924–26), or 'House of John,' displays an unmistakable theatrical flair.

- **Circus Museum** This is actually several museums in one, all as delightful as the circus itself. One building preserves the hand-carved animal wagons, calliopes, silver cannons and artifacts from Ringling Bros' original traveling show.

THINGS YOU NEED TO KNOW

941-359-5700; www.ringling.org; 5401 Bay Shore Rd; adult/child 6-17yr $25/5; 10am-5pm daily, to 8pm Thu;

Armands Circle is essentially an upscale outdoor shopping mall surrounded by posh residences on St Armands Key. Yet even more than downtown, this traffic circle is Sarasota's social center; it's where everyone strolls in the early evening, window shopping while enjoying a Kilwin's waffle cone. Numerous restaurants, from diners to fine dining, serve all day.

Anna Maria Island Island, Beach

The perfect antidote to party-loving Siesta Key, Anna Maria Island appears beached in a 1950s time warp, with sun-faded clapboard houses, teenagers hanging outside ice-cream stores and a clutch of good seafood restaurants. The island is made up of three beach towns: at the southern end is Bradenton Beach, mid-island is Holmes Beach, which is considered the hub, and at the northern tip is Anna Maria village.

Tours

Legacy Trail Cycling

(www.scgov.net; 6am-sunset) This 20-mile bike run from Casperson Beach in Venice to Palmer Ranches just east of downtown Sarasota is a great way to get off the beaten track. Cutting through a landscape of suburban backyards, forested state park and traversing the Intracoastal Waterway over three trestle bridges, it offers a pleasant variety of scenery with well-planned rest stops every mile along the trail. In addition, the 1400-acre Oscar Scherer State Park has another 15 miles of sandy off-road tracks, plus a handy campsite midway along the route.

Sarasota Bay Explorers Boat Tour

(941-388-4200; www.sarasotabayexplorers.com; 1600 Ken Thompson Pkwy, Mote Marine Laboratory) Under the supervision of marine biologists, boat cruises trawl a net and then examine the sponges, sea horses and various fish you catch. The marine safari (adult/child $45/40) heads out to Lido Key and nearby sandbars where participants get out into the grass flats to comune with crabs, sea horses and sea stars under the guidance of a marine biologist. It also offers guided kayak tours (adult/child $55/45). To get to Mote Marine Laboratory, head to St Armands Circle, take John Ringling Blvd north to Ken Thompson Pkwy; follow it to the end.

Sleeping & Eating

SARASOTA

Hotel Ranola Boutique Hotel $$

(941-951-0111; www.hotelranola.com; 118 Indian Pl; r $109-155, ste $209-270; P) The nine rooms feel like a designer's brownstone apartment: free-spirited and effortlessly artful, but with real working kitchens. It's urban funk, walkable from downtown Sarasota.

Jim's Small Batch Bakery Bakery, Cafe $

(941-922-2253; 2336 Gulf Gate Dr; items $1-10; 8am-4pm Mon-Fri, 9am-3pm Sat) Real small-batch, scratch baking makes Jim's a delicious stop for breakfast and lunch. All-butter hand-laminated croissants, candied bacon BLTs, creamy quiches and cups of soup for a dollar.

Indigenous Modern American $$$

(941-706-4740; www.indigenoussarasota.com; 239 S Links Ave; mains $14-26; 5:30-9pm Tue-Sat) Focusing on the popular farm-to-table movement, chef Steve Phelps whips up innovative American creations such as American-harvested shrimp with grits *lyonnaise* (grits blended with caramelized onions, butter, eggs and Parmesan) and Mote marine sturgeon with sweet potatoes. It's a lot of fun, too, housed in a funky, Old-Florida bungalow with a broad deck and an intimate 'wine cottage' serving biodynamic and small-production wine labels.

SIESTA KEY

Beach Bistro Modern American $$$

(941-778-6444; www.beachbistro.com; 6600 Gulf Dr, Anna Maria Island; mains $20-60;

(⌚5-10pm) Sean Murphy's Beach Bistro is Anna Maria's best date night. Perfectly executed Floridian dishes showcase the best locally and nationally sourced farm products, including fresh line-caught seafood, Hudson Valley foie gras and prime USA beef tenderloin. The Bistro Bouillabaisse is legendary, stacked with lobster tail, jumbo shrimp, shellfish and calamari and stewed in a fresh tomato, saffron and anise flavored broth.

Entertainment

Asolo Repertory Theatre Theater
(☎941-351-8000; www.asolorep.org; 5555 N Tamiami Trail; tickets $20-50; ⌚Nov-Jul) This lauded regional theater company is also an acting conservatory (in partnership with Florida State University). It presents a mix of commissioned works, classics and current Tony-winning dramas on two main stages. The **Sarasota Ballet** (www.sarasotaballet.org) also performs here.

Information

Medical Services

Sarasota Memorial Hospital (☎941-917-9000; www.smh.com; 1700 S Tamiami Trail; ⌚24hr) The area's biggest hospital.

Getting There & Around

Sarasota is roughly 60 miles south of Tampa and 75 miles north of Fort Myers. Main roads are Tamiami Trail/US 41 and I-75.

Sarasota-Bradenton International Airport (SRQ; ☎941-359-2777; www.srq-airport.com; 6000 Airport Circle) Served by many major airlines. Go north on Hwy 41, and right on University Ave.

Fort Myers

☎239 / POP 62,300

Nestled inland along the Caloosahatchee River, Fort Myers is a family-friendly town within striking distance of the region's top beaches.

Sights & Activities

The historic district is a tidy, six-block grid of streets along 1st St between Broadway and Lee St.

Edison & Ford Winter Estates Museum
(☎239-334-7419; www.edisonfordwinterestates.org; 2350 McGregor Blvd; adult/child $20/11; ⌚9am-5:30pm) Florida's snowbirds can be easy to mock, but not this pair. Thomas Edison built his winter home in 1885 and lived in Florida seasonally until his death in 1931. Edison's friend Henry Ford built his adjacent bungalow in 1916. Together, and sometimes side by side in **Edison's lab**, these two inventors, businessmen and neighbors changed our world. The **museum** does an excellent job of presenting the overwhelming scope of their achievements.

Six Mile Cypress Slough Preserve Nature Reserve
(☎239-533-7550; www.sloughpreserve.org; 7791 Penzance Blvd; parking per hr/day $1/5; ⌚dawn-dusk) FREE A 2000-acre slough (pronounced 'slew'), this park is a great place to experience southwest Florida's flora and fauna. A 1.2-mile **boardwalk trail** is staffed by volunteers who help explain the epiphytes, cypress knees, migrating birds and nesting alligators you'll find. Wildlife-watchers should target the winter dry season. The wet summer season is also dramatic of course: at its peak, the entire slough becomes a forested stream up to 3ft deep. The **nature center** (open from 10am to 4pm Tuesday to Sunday) has excellent displays and offers free guided wallks.

Great Calusa Blueway Kayaking
(www.calusablueway.com) With almost 200 miles of kayaking routes, the Great Calusa Blueway is like a watery circulation system that snakes throughout Lee County, much of it hugging the coast of Pine Island, and extending further afield to the shores of Cayo Costa, Captiva and Sanibel Islands, Fort Myers Beach and down to Bonita Springs. The warm, calm

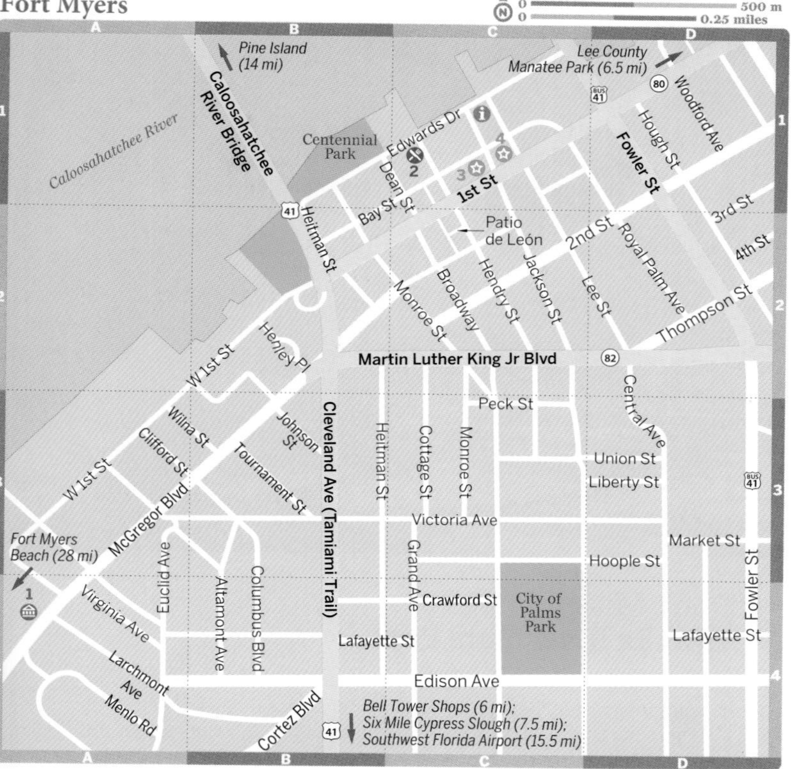

Fort Myers

Sights
1 Edison & Ford Winter Estates A4

Eating
2 Spirits of Bacchus............................... C1

Entertainment
3 Arcade Theatre C1
4 Davis Art Center.................................... C1

waters are a joy to paddle, and there's a lot you miss on land that's only visible by boat. Check the website for 'trails' and where they can be accessed.

Lee County Manatee Park Wildlife Reserve
(**239-690-5030; www.leeparks.org; 10901 State Rd 80; parking per hr/day $2/5; 8am-sunset daily**) FREE November through March, manatees flock up the Orange River to this warm-water discharge canal from the nearby power plant. The waterway is now a protected sanctuary, with a landscaped park and playground in addition to viewing platforms at water's edge, where manatees swim almost at arm's reach. **Calusa Blueway Outfitters** (**239-481-4600; www.calusablueway outfitters.com; 10901 Palm Beach Blvd**) rents kayaks.

Eating

The historic downtown has attractive choices, and more are hidden within strip malls further out.

Cantina Laredo Mexican $$
(**239-415-4424; www.cantinalaredo.com; 5200 Big Pine Way, Bell Tower Shops; mains $12-23;**

IMAC/ALAMY©

Don't Miss
Myakka River State Park

Florida's oldest resident – the 200-million-year-old American alligator – is the star of this 57-sq-mile wildlife preserve. Between 500 and 1000 alligators make their home in Myakka's slow-moving river and its shallow, lily-filled lakes, and you can get up close and personal with these toothsome beasts via canoe, kayak and pontoon-style airboat. During mating season in April and May, the guttural love songs of males rings out across the waters and some 38 miles of trails.

THINGS YOU NEED TO KNOW

941-361-6511; www.myakkariver.org; 13207 State Rd 72; per car $6; 8am-sunset
Myakka Outpost (941-923-1120; www.myakkaoutpost.com; canoes/bikes $20/15; 9:30am-5pm Mon-Fri, 8:30am-6pm Sat & Sun)

11am-10pm Sun-Thu, noon-11pm Fri & Sat) Maybe it's the margarita talking, but this atmospheric Mexican chain does everything right: sharp service, low and romantic lighting, top-shelf tequila, Mexican beer on tap and guacamole made fresh tableside. The *poblano asado* (steak-wrapped *poblano* pepper) is delicious. From downtown, it's a 15-minute drive south along S Cleveland Ave to Bell Tower Shops.

Spirits of Bacchus Tapas **$$**
(239-689-2675; www.spiritsofbacchus.com; 1406 Hendry St; small plates $7-12; 4pm-late Mon-Fri, 6-8pm Sat, 1-8pm Sun) This stylish exposed-brick saloon is a favorite Fort Myers watering hole. It serves a range of fancy tapas, sandwiches and bar food, along with wine and cocktails. Nosh and slosh your way through an evening on the vine-wrapped patio.

Drinking & Entertainment

The historic district becomes a veritable street party twice monthly: for the first-Friday **Art Walk** (www.fortmyersartwalk.com) and the third-Saturday **Music Walk** (www.fortmyersmusicwalk.com).

Arcade Theatre Theater
(☎239-332-4488; www.floridarep.org; 2267 1st St; tickets $17-40; ⏱Oct-May) The 1908 Arcade Theatre is home to the **Florida Repertory Theatre**, one of the best regional theaters in the state. It produces popular comedies, musicals and recent Tony winners, such as *The Seafarer*.

Davis Art Center Performing Arts
(☎239-333-1933; www.sbdac.com; 2301 1st St; ⏱Oct-Jun) This downtown performance space produces an eclectic slate of drama, children's theater, dance, music and film.

SPORTS

March in Fort Myers means major-league baseball's spring training. **Boston Red Sox** (www.redsox.com) fans literally camp out for tickets to **JetBlue Park** (www.leeparks.org; 11500 Fenway S Dr) on Hwy 876. The **Minnesota Twins** (www.mntwins.com) play in Hammond Stadium at **Lee County Sports Complex** (14100 Six Mile Cypress Pkwy), just southwest of the intersection of Daniels Pkwy and Six Mile Cypress Pkwy. During the regular season, the Fort Myers Miracles (the Minnesota Twins' class A minor-league baseball team) play here.

Information

Greater Fort Myers Chamber of Commerce (☎239-332-3624; www.fortmyers.org; 2310 Edwards Dr; ⏱9am-5pm Mon-Fri) Lots of info and can help you find a room.

Lee Memorial Hospital (☎239-343-2000; www.leememorial.org; 2776 Cleveland Ave; ⏱24hr) The area's largest hospital.

Getting There & Around

US 41/S Cleveland Ave is the main north–south artery. From downtown, both Summerlin Rd/Hwy 869 and McGregor Blvd/Hwy 867 eventually merge and lead to Sanibel Island; they also connect with San Carlos Blvd/Hwy 865 to Fort Myers Beach.

Southwest Florida International Airport (RSW; ☎239-590-4800; http://flylcpa.com; 11000 Terminal Access Rd) Take I-75 from Fort Myers and exit 131/Daniels Pkwy. This is also the main airport for nearby Naples.

Sanibel & Captiva Islands

☎239 / POP SANIBEL 6500, CAPTIVA 580

The beautiful barrier islands of Sanibel and Captiva may largely be inhabited by the wealthy, yet by preference and design, island life is informal and egalitarian. Whether for a few days or few weeks, the islands make a genteel escape from balance sheets, status and traffic lights, of which there are none.

Sights & Activities

The quality of **shelling** on Sanibel is so high that dedicated hunters are identified by their hunchbacked 'Sanibel stoop.' However, if you're serious, buy a scoop net, get a shell guide from the visitor center, and peruse the blog www.iloveshelling.com.

Beaches Beach
Modest-size parking lot limits access at **Tarpon Bay Beach**; the sand is not quite as good as Bowman. The same can be said for **Gulfside City Park**.

Captiva's main beach at its northern end, **Alison Hagerup Beach** has a frustratingly small lot; arrive very early. Nice sand ideally positioned for sunset.

JN 'Ding' Darling National Wildlife Refuge Wildlife Reserve
(☎239-472-1100; www.fws.gov/dingdarling; 1 Wildlife Dr; car/cyclist $5/1; ⏱7am-7pm Sat-Thu Apr-Oct, to 5:30pm Nov-Mar) Named for cartoonist Jay Norwood 'Ding'

PRISMA BILDAGENTUR AG/ALAMY©

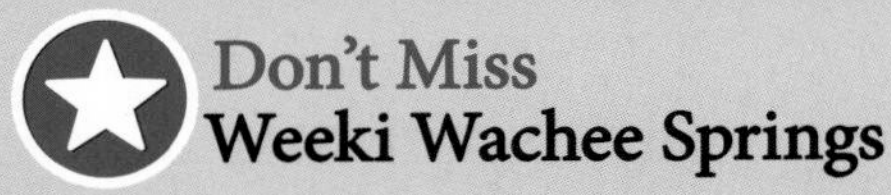

Don't Miss
Weeki Wachee Springs

Were the 'City of Mermaids' ever to close up shop, a bit of Florida's soul would wink out forever. The 'city' of Weeki Wachee is almost entirely constituted by this **state park** (352-592-5656; www.weekiwachee.com; 6131 Commercial Way, Spring Hill; adult/child 6-12yr $13/8; 9am-5:30pm), and the park is almost entirely dedicated to the underwater mermaid show that has entertained families and the famous since 1947. Esther Williams, Danny Thomas and Elvis Presley have all sat in the glass-paneled underwater theater and watched as graceful mermaids perform pirouettes and adagios in the all-natural spring while turtles and fish swim past. The three daily half-hour shows (at 11am, 12:30pm and 2:30pm) remain celebrations of nostalgic kitsch.

The park also offers animal shows, a riverboat cruise, and a modest, weekend-only **waterpark** (combined admission adult/child $26/12), that make for an afternoon's entertainment. Parking is free.

The spring itself is actually the headwater of the crystal-clear Weeki Wachee River. Kayaking or canoeing this river is one of the region's best paddles; at the back of the Weeki Wachee parking lot, follow signs to **Paddling Adventure** (352-597-8484; www.paddlingadventures.com; kayaks $30-35; 8am-2pm). The 7-mile route includes beach areas with good swimming and rope swings, plus you'll see lots of fish and even manatees in winter and spring. It's about 45 minutes from Tampa via I-75 north to Hwy 50 west.

THINGS YOU NEED TO KNOW

352-592-5656; www.weekiwachee.com; 6131 Commercial Way/US 19 at Hwy 50; adult/child 6-12yr $13/5; 10am-3pm Mar, to 4pm Apr-Aug

Darling, an environmentalist who helped establish more than 300 sanctuaries across the USA, this 6300-acre refuge is home to an abundance of seabirds and wildlife, including alligators, night herons, red-shouldered hawks, spotted sandpipers, roseate spoonbills, pelicans and anhinga. The refuge's 5-mile **Wildlife Drive** provides easy access, but bring binoculars; flocks sometimes sit at expansive distances. Only a few very short walks lead into the mangroves. For the best, most intimate experience, canoe or kayak Tarpon Bay.

Bailey-Matthews Shell Museum Museum

(239-395-2233; www.shellmuseum.org; 3075 Sanibel-Captiva Rd, Sanibel; adult/child 5-16yr $9/5; 10am-5pm) Like a mermaid's jewelry box, this museum is dedicated to shells, yet it's much more than a covetous display of treasures. It's a crisply presented natural history of the sea, detailing the life and times of the bivalves, mollusks and other creatures who reside inside their calcium homes. It also shows the role of these animals and shells in human culture, medicine and cuisine. Fascinating videos show living creatures. It's nearly a must after a day spent combing the beaches.

Tarpon Bay Explorers Kayaking

(239-472-8900; www.tarponbayexplorers.com; 900 Tarpon Bay Rd, Sanibel; 8am-6pm) Within the Darling refuge, this outfitter rents canoes and kayaks ($25 for two hours) for easy, self-guided paddles in Tarpon Bay, a perfect place for young paddlers. Guided kayak trips (adult from $30 to $40, child from $20 to $25) are also excellent, and there's a range of other trips and deck talks. Reserve ahead or come early, as trips book up.

Tours

Boats and cruises are nearly as ubiquitous as shells on the islands. **Sanibel Marina** (239-472-2723; www.sanibelmarina.com; 634 N Yachtsman Dr) is the main small-boat harbor with a ton of boat rentals (from $125) and charters (from $350). On

Local Knowledge

Sanibel & Captiva Islands Don't Miss List

RICHARD & SARAH FORTUNE ARE PHOTOGRAPHERS WITH THROUGH THE LENS NATURE PHOTOGRAPHY (WWW.THROUGHTHELENSGALLERY.COM)

1 JN 'DING' DARLING NATIONAL WILDLIFE REFUGE

High on the list for any birders and nature-lovers. The best time to visit is at low tide and early morning to see a feeding frenzy of bird species along Wildlife Drive (p289), especially Lagoons 2 and 3.

2 CAPTIVA CRUISES

Explore **barrier islands** on the pristine Gulf Coast. The *Lady Chadwick* takes in Cabbage Key (promoted by Jimmy Buffett in *Cheeseburger in Paradise*), while Useppa Key has natural beauty not found anywhere else. No cars are allowed on this private island; footpaths are the main arteries. An added bonus is bottlenose dolphins that follow the boat during its one-hour cruise.

3 SUNSETS IN SANIBEL

A Gulf of Mexico **sunset** is second to none. The anticipation for that mystical moment is what vacationers and locals set their clocks for. The best viewing areas are Blind Pass (the beach between Sanibel and Captiva), and the Mucky Duck off Sandy Ross Lane in Captiva. Also very popular is the Causeway between Fort Myers and Sanibel.

4 SANIBEL THRILLER

A high-speed 50ft twin-diesel-powered catamaran (p292) departs Sanibel Marina daily to circumnavigate Sanibel and Captiva Islands. The highly educational narration covers the island's history and uniqueness in protecting and preserving the barrier island's ecological environment.

Detour: Cabbage Key

As all Parrotheads know, Jimmy Buffett's famous song 'Cheeseburger in Paradise' was allegedly inspired by a meal at the **Cabbage Key Inn** (239-283-2278; www.cabbagekey.com; r $100-150, cottages $180-405; 7:30-9am, 11:30am-3pm & 6-8:30pm). Truth be told, the burger is only average, and it wouldn't be worth writing a song about if it weren't served on this 100-acre, mangrove-fringed key in the Gulf of Mexico. Built atop a Calusa shell mound, and originally the 1938 home of writer Mary Roberts Rinehart, the inn has the romantic air of a secluded semitropical port for global wayfarers, one that receives ferry loads of tourists every lunchtime. The bar is certainly a sight: the walls are matted and spongy with perhaps $80,000 in signed $1 bills, including framed bills from ex-president Jimmy Carter and of course Mr Buffett. Bills flutter to the floor daily, which the inn collects, annually donating $10,000 to charity. Staying in the inn, which lacks TVs, pools and a swimming beach but drips with character, is a worthwhile choice.

To get here, contact Tropic Star and Captiva Cruises.

Captiva, **McCarthy's Marina** (239-472-5200; www.mccarthysmarina.com; 11401 Andy Rosse Lane, Captiva) is where **Captiva Cruises** (239-472-5300; www.captivacruises.com; 11400 Andy Rosse Lane) departs from. It offers everything from dolphin and sunset cruises (from $25) to various island excursions (from $35), like Cayo Costa, Cabbage Key and Useppa Key. The **Sanibel Thriller** (239-472-2328; www.sanibelthriller.com; adult/child $43/35) does tours that circumnavigate Sanibel and Captiva; on the way you'll get great lessons on the islands' ecology and conservation.

Sleeping

If you're interested in a one-week vacation rental, contact **Sanibel & Captiva Accommodations** (800-656-9111; www.sanibelaccom.com)

'Tween Waters Inn Resort $$$
(239-472-5161; www.tween-waters.com; 15951 Captiva Dr, Captiva; r $185-285, ste $270-410, cottages $265-460;) For great resort value on Captiva, choose 'Tween Waters Inn. Rooms are attractive roosts with rattan furnishings, granite counters, rainfall showerheads and Tommy Bahama–style decor. All have balconies; those directly facing the Gulf are splendid, and tidy little cottages are romantic. Families make good use of the big pool, tennis courts, full-service marina and spa. Multinight discounts are attractive.

Tarpon Tale Inn Motel $$
(239-472-0939; www.tarpontale.com; 367 Periwinkle Way, Sanibel; r $99-260;) The five charming tile-floored rooms evoke a bright blue-and-white seaside mood and are well located for Sanibel's Old Town; each has its own shady porch and tree-strung hammock. Two rooms have efficiencies and three have full kitchens. With communal hot tub and loaner bikes, it does a nice imitation of a B&B without the breakfast.

Eating & Drinking

Mad Hatter Restaurant American $$$
(239-472-0033; www.madhatterrestaurant.com; 6467 Sanibel-Captiva Rd, Sanibel; mains $29-45; 6-9pm) Vacationing Manhattan and Miami urbanites flock to what is

widely regarded as Sanibel's best locavore gourmet restaurant. Contemporary seafood is the central focus, with creative appetizers such as oysters and a seafood martini, while mains emphasize bouillabaisse, crab cakes, pan-seared grouper and so on. As the name suggests, it's not stuffy, but it is for culinary mavens whose concern is quality, whatever the price.

Sweet Melissa's Cafe American **$$$**
(**239-472-1956; www.sweetmelissascafe.net; 1625 Periwinkle Way, Sanibel; tapas $9-16, mains $26-34; 11:30am-2:30pm & 5-9pm Mon-Fri, 5-9pm Sat)** From menu to mood, Sweet Melissa's offers well-balanced, relaxed refinement. Dishes are creative without trying too hard, and most mains can be served tapas size, which encourages experimenting. Try the shrimp with grits, seared scallops over curried cauliflower, grilled romaine and the refreshing watermelon salad. Service is attentive and the atmosphere upbeat.

Mucky Duck Pub Food **$$**
(www.muckyduck.com; 11546 Andy Rosse Lane, Captiva; mains $10-25; 11:30am-3pm & 5-9:30pm Mon-Sat) The unpretentious, shingle-roofed Mucky Duck is perfectly positioned for Captiva sunsets, and devoted locals jockey for beach chairs and picnic tables each evening. The extended menu offers more than just pub grub, with pasta, steak, chicken and seafood. Really, though, it's the friendly bar and toes-in-the-sand Gulf views that keep 'em coming.

Information

Sanibel & Captiva Islands Chamber of Commerce (239-472-1080; www.sanibel-captiva.org; 1159 Causeway Rd, Sanibel; 9am-5pm;) One of the more helpful visitor centers around; keeps an updated hotel-vacancy list with dedicated hotel hotline.

Getting There & Around

Driving is the only way to come. The Sanibel Causeway (Hwy 867) charges an entrance toll (cars/motorcycles $6/2).

Corkscrew Swamp Sanctuary

The crown jewel in the **National Audubon Society's (239-348-9151; www.corkscrew.audubon.org; adult/child 6-18yr $12/4; 7am-5:30pm Oct–mid-Apr, 7am-7:30pm mid-Apr–Sep)** sanctuary collection, this property provides an intimate exploration of six pristine native habitats, including sawgrass, slash pine and marsh, along a shady, 2.25-mile boardwalk trail. The centerpiece is North America's oldest virgin bald-cypress forest, with majestic specimens over 600 years old and 130ft tall.

NORTH OF TAMPA

The Gulf Coast north of Tampa (and south of the Panhandle) is relatively quiet and often bypassed. As such, it preserves more of that oft-promised, hard-to-find 'Old Florida' atmosphere.

Homosassa Springs

352 / POP 13,800

Signed along US 19, **Homosassa Springs Wildlife State Park (352-628-5343; www.floridastateparks.org/homosassasprings; 4150 S Suncoast Blvd; adult/child 6-12yr $13/5; 9am-5:30pm)** is essentially an old-school outdoor Florida animal encounter – aka, zoo – that features Florida's wealth of headliner species: American alligators, black bears, bobcats, whooping cranes, Florida panthers, tiny Key deer, eagles, hawks and – especially – manatees. Homosassa's highlight is an underwater observatory directly over the springs, where through glass windows you can gawk eyeball to eyeball with enormous schools of some 10,000 fish and ponderous manatees nibbling lettuce. Various animal presentations happen daily, but time your visit for the manatee program (11:30am, 1:30pm and 3:30pm). The park itself is a short, narrated boat ride from the visitor center.

The park is about 20 miles north of Weeki Wachee and 75 miles north of Tampa; US 19 north leads to the park entrance.

Detour: Busch Gardens & Adventure Island

Orlando doesn't hold a monopoly on Florida theme parks. In Tampa, Busch Gardens presents two enormous thrill-seeker destinations: the Africa-themed Busch Gardens, with some of the country's best roller coasters, and the adjacent Adventure Island water park. If you'll be visiting both, get combo tickets.

Both parks are about 7 miles north of downtown Tampa; take I-275 north to exit 50/Busch Blvd and follow signs.

BUSCH GARDENS

This **theme park** (888-800-5447; http://seaworldparks.com/en/buschgardens-tampa; 10165 McKinley Dr; adult/child 3-9yr $92/87, discounts online; 10am-7pm) has nine named African regions, but these flow together without much fuss. The entire park is walkable. In **Egypt**, Busch Gardens has unveiled its newest coaster: Cheetah Hunt, an epic, low-to-the-ground scream-fest meant to mimic a cheetah's acceleration. The 80-acre **Serengeti Plain** recreates African plains, with hundreds of free-roaming animals. Other attractions include the formidable Kumba roller coaster and kid-friendly **Safari of Fun & Bird Gardens**.

ADVENTURE ISLAND

This 30-acre **water park** (888-800-5447; www.adventureisland.com; 10001 McKinley Dr; adult/child 3-9yr $42/38; 10am-5pm) has everything a modern, top-flight water park requires: long, lazy river, huge wave pool, bucket-dumping splash zones, swimming pool, sandy lounge areas, and enough twisting, plunging, adrenaline-fueled waterslides to keep teens lining up till closing.

Crystal River

352 / POP 3100

Every winter, about 20% of Florida's Gulf Coast manatee population meanders into the 72°F, spring-fed waters of Kings Bay, near the town of Crystal River, and for this reason the bay is almost entirely protected within the **Crystal River National Wildlife Refuge** (352-563-2088; www.fws.gov/crystalriver; 1502 SE Kings Bay Dr; 8am-5:30pm Mon-Fri). Up to 560 of these gentle, endangered sea creatures have been counted in a single January day, and like any wildlife spectacle, this draws crowds of onlookers. Nearly 40 commercial operators offer rentals and guided tours of Kings Bay, via every type of nautical conveyance, and the chance to swim with wild manatees is a truly wondrous opportunity not to miss. However, whether visitors should be allowed to actively touch manatees is an ongoing controversy.

There is no public viewing area on land to view manatees; the only access to the refuge is by boat. However, a new boardwalk is in the works.

Best of the Rest

Daytona & Around (p296)

Fast cars, Spring Break, white sand, hot tans and sea turtles.

St Augustine & Amelia Island (p297)

St Augustine is North America's oldest European settlement. Amelia Island meshes the historic with gorgeous beaches.

Tallahassee & Apalachicola (p299)

Experience the hospitality and rustic beauty of North Florida, along with Tallahassee's history.

Destin (p301)

Gulf Coast beauty and true-blue Americana on the Southern-fried Florida panhandle.

ABOVE: Daytona International Speedway (p296);
LEFT: Ponce de Leon Inlet Lighthouse (p297)

Daytona & Around

Daytona Beach
MITTELHAEUSER PHOTOGRAPHY/ALAMY ©

HIGHLIGHTS

1. **Daytona International Speedway** Fabled racing track of the South.
2. **Daytona Beach** Prime swathe of sand for car or bicycle cruising.
3. **Marine Science Center** Cares for injured turtles and seabirds.
4. **Boardwalk & Pier** (p297) Sabal palms and sand overlooking the ocean.

Sights & Activities

Daytona Beach — Beach

(per car $5; beach driving 8am-7pm May-Oct, sunrise-sunset Nov-Apr) This perfectly planar stretch of sand was once the city's raceway. Sections of the beach still welcome drivers to the sands at a strictly enforced top speed of 10mph. The most popular strip is a one-way stretch heading south between International Speedway Blvd and and Dunlawton Ave. Beachside rentals for ATVs, fat-tired cruisers, recumbent trikes and all manner of water sports are ubiquitous. Of course, you're free to frolic anywhere on the beach, off the roadway.

Daytona International Speedway — Racetrack

(800-748-7467; www.daytonainternationalspeedway.com; 1801 W International Speedway Blvd; tickets from $20) The Holy Grail of raceways has a diverse race schedule. Ticket prices skyrocket for good seats at big races, headlined by the **Daytona 500** in February. It's worth wandering the massive stands for free on non-race days. First-come, first-served **tram tours** take in the track, pits and behind-the-scenes areas.

The 30-minute Speedway Tour **(adult/child $16/10; 11:30am, 1:30pm, 3:30pm & 4pm)** covers the basics. Die-hard revheads may wish to up the ante with the hour-long All Access **(adult/child $23/17; hourly 10am-3pm)** or three-hour VIP **(adult/child $50; Tue, Thu, Sat 1pm)** tours. The latter covers everything NASCAR from the comfort of an air-conditioned coach. Real fanatics can indulge in the Richard Petty Driving Experience **(800-237-3889; www.drivepetty.com)**, where you can either ride shotgun around the track or take a day to become the driver.

Marine Science Center — Aquarium

(386-304-5545; www.marinesciencecenter.com; 100 Lighthouse Dr, Ponce Inlet; adult/child $5/2; 10am-4pm Tue-Sat, noon-4pm Sun;) We were impressed by this center's rescue, rehab and release programs for sea turtles and seabirds that nest on Daytona's beaches. It's a fun and environmentally conscious place where adults and kids can enjoy learning about our underwater friends. Exhibits include a 5000-gallon reef aquarium, a stingray touch pool and a bird-observation tower.

Boardwalk & Pier Waterfront, Pier

(admission free; rides $3-5) Follow Main St E and you'll cross Daytona's sabal-palm-lined, ocean-fronting Boardwalk, bedecked with dollar-grabbing ice-cream shops, amusement arcades, rides and patios where you can sip beer from plastic cups. It's fun for the family with a side order of sleaze. Follow Main St further east toward the unmissable coral-colored pier, once a summer-vacation icon and still the longest in the US. Reopened after restoration in 2012, the 85-year-old wooden structure still feels a bit shabby, but perhaps that's to be expected when you jut 237m out into the wild Atlantic Ocean.

Ponce de Leon Inlet Lighthouse & Museum Lighthouse

(386-761-1821; www.ponceinlet.org; 4931 S Peninsula Dr, Ponce Inlet; adult/child $5/1.50; 10am-6pm Sep-May, to 9pm Aug-Sep) Those prone to vertigo may wish to forgo the 203-spiral-step climb to the top of Florida's tallest lighthouse, and enjoy the interesting historical displays of the museum buildings instead. For everyone else, the views of the Atlantic Ocean from the top of the 53m structure, completed in 1887, are breathtaking. The lighthouse and museum are located 6 miles south of Daytona Beach.

St Augustine & Amelia Island

HIGHLIGHTS

1. **Colonial Quarter** (p298) Living history in the USA's oldest city.
2. **Lightner Museum** (p298) Crazy palace with diverse collection of artifacts.
3. **Hotel Ponce de León** (p298) Spanish-style grand hotel – one of Florida's finest historical buildings
4. **Amelia Island** (p298) Take a stroll into the past or hunt for St Augustine's ghosts.

Guard room, Fort Clinch State Park (p298)

Sights & Activities

ST AUGUSTINE

Colonial Quarter Historic Buildings

(☎904-342-2857; www.colonialquarter.com; 33 St George St; adult/child $13/7; ⊙10am-6pm) See how they did things back in the 18th century at this re-creation of Spanish-colonial St Augustine, complete with craftspeople demonstrating blacksmithing, leatherworking and other trades.

Discounted combination tickets, including admission to the Pirate & Treasure Museum and the First Colony exhibit at Government House, are available (adult/child $28/16).

Lightner Museum Museum

(☎904-824-2874; www.lightnermuseum.org; 75 King St; adult/child $10/5; ⊙9am-5pm) Henry Flagler's former Hotel Alcazar is now home to this wonderful museum with a little bit of everything, from ornate Gilded Age furnishings to collections of marbles and cigar-box labels. The dramatic and imposing building itself is a must-see, dating back to 1887 and designed in the Spanish Renaissance Revival style by New York City architects Carrère and Hastings.

Hotel Ponce de León Historic Building

(☎904-823-3378; http://legacy.flagler.edu/pages/tours; 74 King St; tours adult/child $10/1; ⊙tours hourly 10am-3pm summer, 10am & 2pm during school year) Unmissable in town, this striking former luxury hotel, built in the 1880s, is now the world's most gorgeous dormitory, belonging to Flagler College who purchased and saved it in 1967. Guided tours are recommended to get a sense of the detail and history of this magnificent Spanish Renaissance building. At the very least, take a peek inside the lobby for free.

Castillo de San Marcos National Monument Fort

(☎904-829-6506; www.nps.gov/casa; 1 S Castillo Dr; adult/child under 16 $7/free; ⊙8:45am-5:15pm; 👪) This incredibly photogenic fort is another atmospheric monument to longevity: it's the country's oldest masonry fort, completed by the Spanish in 1695. Park rangers lead programs hourly and shoot off cannons most weekends.

Spanish Military Hospital Museum Museum

(☎904-342-7730; www.spanishmilitaryhospital.com; 3 Aviles St; adult/child $7/5; ⊙10am-6pm) Not for the faint of heart, guided tours of this museum discuss Colonial-era medical techniques in all their gory glory: amputations, leeching, the whole shebang. Housed in a reconstruction of the original hospital, the museum will make you very glad you're not a patient in 1791! Discounted tickets can be reserved online.

St Augustine Beach Beach

There's a visitor-information booth at the foot of **St Johns Pier**, where you can rent a rod and reel ($3 for two hours, $1 for each additional hour).

St Augustine City Walks Walking Tour

(☎904-825-0087; www.staugcitywalks.com; 4 Granada St; tours $12-49; ⊙9am-8:30pm) Extremely fun walking tours of all kinds, from silly to serious. A variety of free tours are also available.

AMELIA ISLAND

Thirteen miles from Georgia, this glorious sea island combines the moss-draped charm of the Deep South with the beach culture of Florida.

Fort Clinch State Park Park

(☎904-277-7274; www.floridastateparks.org/fortclinch; 2601 Atlantic Ave; park pedestrian/car $2/6; ⊙park 8am-sunset, fort 9am-5pm) Although construction commenced in 1847, rapid technological advancements rendered Fort Clinch's masonry walls obsolete by as early as 1861, when the fort was easily taken by Confederate militia in the Civil War and later evacuated. Federal troops again occupied the fort during WWII. Today, the park offers a variety of activities, a half-mile-long fishing pier, serene beaches for shelling (of the nonmilitary kind) and 6 miles of peaceful, unpaved trails for hiking and cycling.

Amelia Island Museum of History Museum

(☎904-261-7378; www.ameliamuseum.org; 233 S 3rd St; adult/student $7/4; ⏰10am-4pm Mon-Sat, 1-4pm Sun) Housed in the former city jail (1879–1975), Florida's only oral-history museum has tiny but informative exhibits exploring Native American history, the Spanish-mission period, the Civil War and historic preservation. A variety of tours are available, including the eight-flags tour (11am and 2pm Monday to Saturday and 2pm Sunday), providing lively interpretations of the island's fascinating history, and architecture tours, pub crawls and cellphone walking tours ($5).

Pipeline Surf Shop Surfing

(☎904-277-3717; www.pipelinesurfshop.com; 2022 1st Ave; rentals from $35; ⏰9am-6pm) From fall through spring when nor'easters bluster through, surfable beach breaks are common, especially at Main Beach. Pipeline rents all kinds of boards and wetsuits, and gives surf lessons from beginner to advanced. They even run SUP yoga classes: yoga on stand-up paddle boards!

Eating

ST AUGUSTINE

Collage International $$$

(☎904-829-0055; www.collagestaug.com; 60 Hypolita St; mains $28-45; ⏰5:30-9pm) This upscale dinner-only restaurant is renowned for its impeccable service, intimate atmosphere and the consistency of its cuisine: the menu makes the most of St Augustine's seaside locale and nearby local farms. It's all here: artisan salads, chicken, lamb, veal and pork, lobster, scallops and grouper. A subtle melange of global flavors enhance the natural goodness of the freshest produce.

Tallahassee & Apalachicola

HIGHLIGHTS

1. **Museum of Florida History** (p300) An extensive, family-fun peek into the story of Florida.
2. **Apalachicola National Forest** (p300) The best wilderness area in North Florida.
3. **Mission San Luis** (p300) Beautifully restored Spanish mission settlement.
4. **Tallahassee Museum of History & Natural Science** (p300) Excellent Florida-centric living history museum.

Apalachicola National Forest (p300)
SCOTT J. FERRELL/CONGRESSIONAL QUARTERLY/ALAMY ©

Sights & Activities

Museum of Florida History Museum
(850-245-6400; www.museumoffloridahistory.com; 500 S Bronough St; 9am-4:30pm Mon-Fri, from 10am Sat, from noon Sun) FREE Here it is: Florida's history splayed out in fun, crisp exhibits, from mastodon skeletons to Florida's Paleo-Indians and Spanish shipwrecks to the Civil War.

Tallahassee Museum of History & Natural Science Museum
(850-575-8684850-575-8684; www.tallahasseemuseum.org; 3945 Museum Rd; adult/child $9/6; 9am-5pm Mon-Sat, from 11am Sun) Occupying 52 acres of pristine manicured gardens and wilderness on the outskirts of Tallahassee, near the airport, this stunning natural-history museum features living exhibits of Floridian flora and fauna and has delighted visitors for over 50 years. Check out the otters in their new home or try zip-lining above the canopy in the fun-for-most, scary-for-others Tree to Tree Adventures – a variety of scenarios are available, from $25.

Apalachicola National Forest Park
(325 John Knox Rd; day-use areas $5; 8am-sunset) The largest of Florida's three national forests, the Apalachicola National Forest occupies almost 938 sq miles – more than half a million acres – of the Panhandle from just west of Tallahassee to the Apalachicola River. Made up of lowlands, pine, cypress hammocks and oaks, dozens of species call the area home including mink, gray and red foxes, coyotes, six bat species, beavers, red cockaded woodpeckers, alligators, Florida black bears and the elusive Florida panther. A total of 68.7 miles of the Florida National Scenic Trail extends through the forest as well.

Mission San Luis Historic Site
(850-245-6406; www.missionsanluis.org; 2100 W Tennessee St; adult/child $5/2; 10am-4pm Tue-Sun) This 60-acre site is home to a 17th-century Spanish and Apalachee mission that's been wonderfully reconstructed, especially the soaring Council House.

Mary Brogan Museum of Art & Science Museum
(850-513-0700; www.thebrogan.org; 350 S Duval St; adult/child $7.50/5; 10am-5pm Mon-Sat, from 1pm Sun) Affiliated with the Smithsonian, this museum mixes a kid-friendly, hands-on science center with the Tallahassee Art Museum.

Florida Historic Capitol Museum Museum
(850-487-1902; www.flhistoriccapitol.gov; 400 S Monroe St; 9am-4:30pm Mon-Fri, from 10am Sat, from noon Sun) FREE Adorned by candy-striped awnings and topped with a reproduction of the original glass dome, the 1902 Florida capitol building now houses this interesting political museum, including a restored governor's reception area, numerous portraits, and exhibits on immigration, state development and the infamous 2000 US presidential election.

Florida State Capitol Notable Building
(www.myfloridacapitol.com; cnr S Duval & W Pensacola Sts; 8am-5pm Mon-Fri) FREE The stark and imposing 22-story Florida State Capitol's top-floor observation deck affords wonderful 360-degree views of the city and its edge of rolling green hills.

Eating

Kool Beanz Café Fusion $$
(850-224-2466; www.koolbeanz-cafe.com; 921 Thomasville Rd; mains $17-24; 11am-10pm Mon-Fri, 5:30-10pm Sat, 10:30am-2pm Sun) It's got a corny name but a wonderfully eclectic and homey vibe – plus great, creative fare. The menu changes daily, but you can count on finding anything from hummus plates to jerk-spiced scallops to duck in blueberry-ginger sauce.

Andrew's American $$
(850-222-3444; www.andrewsdowntown.com; 228 S Adams St; mains $9-36; 11:30am-10pm) Downtown's see-and-be-seen political hot spot. At this split-level place, the downstairs (Andrew's Capital Grill and Bar) serves casual burgers and beer, while upstairs (Andrew's 228) serves upscale neo-Tuscan dishes.

Destin

HIGHLIGHTS

1. **Indian Temple Mound & Museum** A major site for Florida's Native Americans.
2. **Southern Star** Excellent dolphin tours on calm Gulf waters.
3. **Grayton Beach State Park** One of the state's most beautiful beach parks.

Indian Temple Mound
TOM UHLMAN/ALAMY ©

Sights & Activities

Grayton Beach State Park — Park

(**850-267-8300; www.floridastateparks.org/graytonbeach; 357 Main Park Rd, Santa Rosa Beach; vehicle $5; 8am-sunset)** An 1133-acre stretch of marble-colored dunes rolling down to the water's edge, this state park's beauty is genuinely mind-blowing. The park sits nestled against the wealthy but down-to-earth community of Grayton Beach, home to the famed Red Bar and the quirky **Dog Wall** – a mural on which residents paint portraits of their dogs. The park also contains the Grayton Beach Nature Trail, which runs through the dunes, magnolias and pine flatwoods and onto a boardwalk to a return trail along the beach.

Indian Temple Mound & Museum — Archaeological Site

(**850-833-9595; fwb.org/museums/indian-temple-mound-museum; 139 Miracle Strip Pkwy SE, Fort Walton Beach; 10am-4:30pm Mon-Sat Jun-Aug, noon-4:30pm Mon-Fri, from 10am Sat Sep-May)** FREE One of the most sacred sites for local Native American culture to this day, the 17ft-tall, 223ft-wide ceremonial and political temple mound, built with 500,000 basket-loads of earth and representing what is probably the largest prehistoric earthwork on the Gulf Coast, dates back to somewhere between AD 800 and 1500. On top of the mound you'll find a recreated temple housing a small exhibition center. The museum offers an extensive overview of 12,000 years of Native American history, and houses flutes, ceramics and artifacts fashioned from stone, bone and shells, as well as a comprehensive research library.

Southern Star Dolphin Cruises — Cruise

(**850-837-7741; www.dolphin-sstar.com; 100 Harbor Blvd, Suite A, Destin; adult/child $29/15.50; 9am-6pm Mon-Sat)** This environmentally conscious operator has been sailing for over 20 years, observing the bottlenose dolphins that live in these waters. Two-hour cruises operate year round from an 80ft glass-bottom boat. Check the website for schedules.

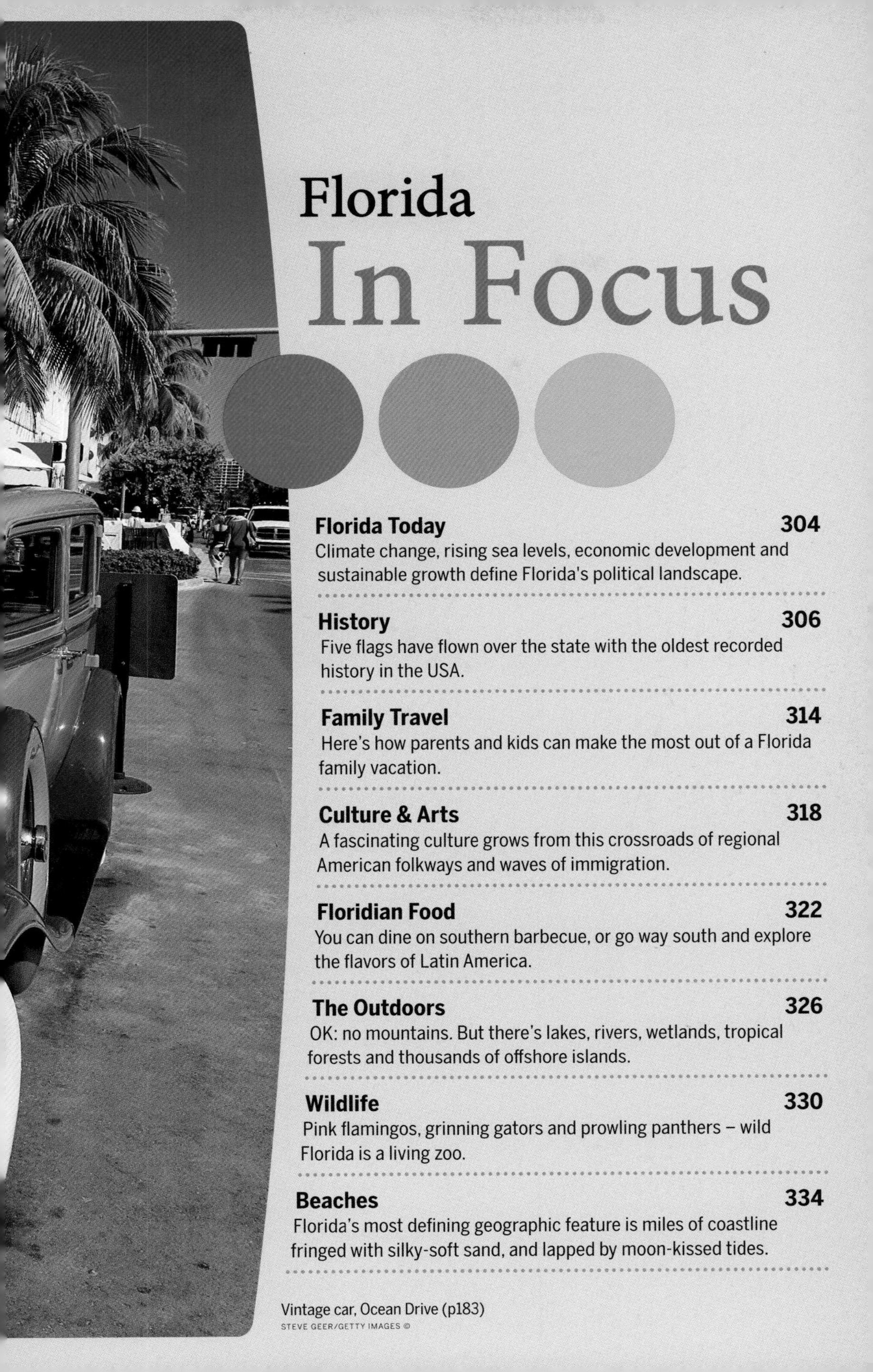

Florida In Focus

Vintage car, Ocean Drive (p183)

Florida Today

> *Florida has always been a place where settlers tried to bend the world to fit their dreams*

Key West (p223)

Preserving the Peninsula

One of Florida's deepest cultural fault lines runs across the debate over development versus conservation. For years development held sway in the state, which has long had one of the most robust housing markets in the country and, not coincidentally, one of the fastest growing populations. At the time of writing, Florida was poised to overtake New York as the third-most populous state.

All of those people need places to live, and in Florida, the need for housing and businesses has traditionally taken precedence over preservation. But a new check on growth has emerged that even some of the most gung-ho developers are noting. In the environmental debates of the 21st century, low-lying Florida is on the ecological frontlines of the climate change and water table debates.

Florida is a largely below-sea-level peninsula, and the ocean is rising even as the peninsula is crumbling. The culprits behind the crumble are artificial canals and waterways dredged in the early 20th century. Those public works

belief systems
(% of population)

if Florida were 100 people

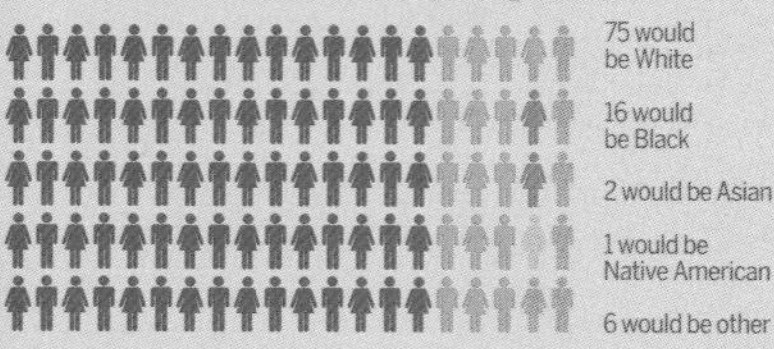

* According to the US Census Bureau, Hispanics may be of any race so are included in applicable race categories

population per sq miles

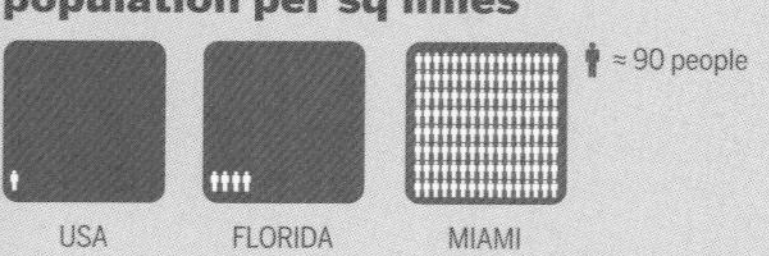

CRISTIAN LAZZARI/ALAMY ©

directed water away from the Everglades and the South Florida aquifer, eroding the wetlands and depleting freshwater reserves. State leaders seem to have recognized how untenable the situation is, and at the time of research, it seems that the Florida legislature may have the political will to redirect the natural flow of run-off water from Lake Okeechobee.

While the interior of the state is trying to re-establish a base of water, coastal areas are trying to ward water away. Rising sea levels can be traced to climate change; rains in Miami that would have been an afterthought a decade ago are now flooding main thoroughfares. Local governments are moving forward with climate change plans to deter the worst fallout of a potential ecological disaster.

A House Divided

From Stand Your Ground laws to political redistricting, some of the most intense debates over American rights and responsibilities occur in Florida. This has always been a place where settlers tried to bend the world to fit their dreams, from Disney World emerging from Central Florida to Miami sprouting from a swamp. This can-do attitude usually comes hand in hand with a pro-business environment that stresses deregulation and individual liberty over public welfare. The frontier mentality that feeds this attitude has traditionally incubated in Florida's sprawling suburbs and agricultural zones.

But as Florida's city spaces grow, so do city ideals, values and policy priorities such as public infrastructure and mass transit. Governor Rick Scott's decision to void a high-speed train between Orlando and Tampa was seen as fiscal prudence by supporters from the countryside and exurbs, but urban opponents felt like a chance at alleviating the state's ubiquitous car culture had been squandered.

As these debates rage, the rifts between rural, white, culturally conservative North Florida and multiethnic South Florida are deepening. South Floridians feel political redistricting has led to them being frozen out of the Florida statehouse; while the state is consistently a toss-up between Democrats and Republicans at the national level, at the state level Republicans have carved out numerous small districts and as a result dominate the legislature.

On the other hand, North Floridians feel like they are being demographically eclipsed by the increasingly ethnically diverse southern part of the state. The irony is that the children of those immigrants tend to Americanize quickly, and some would likely lean conservative if the anti-immigrant rhetoric coming from the American right wasn't so fiery. These kinds of views were what caused Pablo Pantoja, director of the Republican National Party's Hispanic Outreach program in Florida, to defect to the Democratic Party in 2013.

History

Statue of Pedro Menéndez de Aviles outside Flagler College

DENNIS K JOHNSON/GETTY IMA

Florida has the oldest recorded history of any US state. Native Americans were here thousands of years before the first Europeans planted a flag at St Augustine. The state has switched hands between three European and two American flags, and evolved from an agricultural citrus and sugar basket into the tourism capital and international center of commerce it is today.

From Tycoons to Disney

Florida's history isn't just extensive; it's always been a little bizarre too. Spanish explorers chased golden cities, antiaging water and mermaids, but if they found none of those, only a funhouse mirror separates them from us: in Florida, mermaids perform daily, aging snowbirds flock for rejuvenation, Disney World promises a Magic Kingdom and

AD 500

Indigenous peoples settle in year-round villages and begin farming, cultivating corn, beans and squash.

real-estate developers long ago discovered how to get gold from a swamp. Simply drain it.

Florida's modern history truly begins with the late-19th-century tycoons who dried the marshes, built railroads and resorts, and then ceaselessly promoted Florida as an 'emerald kingdom by southern seas.' Since then, each era has been marked by wild-eyed speculation inspiring great tides of immigration – from the 1920s real-estate mania to the 1950s orange boom to the 1960s Cuban exodus to the 1980s influx of Latin Americans – each inevitably followed by a crash: the Great Depression, race riots, cartel cocaine wars, 1992's Hurricane Andrew, and so on.

Today, Florida's boom-and-bust cycle continues. Whatever else, it makes for great storytelling.

First Inhabitants & Seminoles

Florida's original inhabitants never organized into large, cohesive tribes. For some 11,500 years, they remained split into numerous small chiefdoms or villages, becoming more settled and agricultural in the north and remaining more nomadic and warlike in the south.

The Apalachee in Florida's Panhandle developed the most complex agriculture-based society, but other tribes included the Timucua in northern Florida, the Tequesta along the central Atlantic Coast, and the fierce Calusa in southern Florida. Legends say it was a poison-tipped Calusa arrow that killed Ponce de León.

The most striking evidence of these early cultures are shell mounds or middens. Florida's ancestral peoples ate well, and their discarded shells reached 30ft high and themselves became the foundations of villages, as at Mound Key.

When the Spanish arrived in the 1500s, the indigenous population numbered perhaps 250,000. Over the next 200 years, European diseases, war and slavery killed 80% of them. As the 18th century unfolded, Creeks and other tribes fleeing European colonies (and later, the new USA) migrated into Florida. These tribes intermingled and intermarried, and in the late 1700s they were joined by numerous runaway black slaves.

At some point, these uncooperative, fugitive, mixed peoples occupying Florida's interior were dubbed 'Seminoles,' a corruption of the Spanish word *cimarrones*, meaning 'free people' or 'wild ones.' Defying European rule and ethnic category, they were soon considered too free for the newly independent United States, who brought war to them.

10,000 BC
After crossing the Bering Strait from Siberia, humans arrive in Florida.

1513
Ponce de León lands near Cape Canaveral and names it La Florida, 'Feast of Flowers.'

1565
Pedro Menéndez de Aviles founds St Augustine, the first permanent European settlement in the New World.

The Unconquered Seminoles

From 1817 to 1858, the US waged war on Florida's Seminoles three times, always to conquer territory and punish the tribe for sheltering escaped slaves. Of the three conflicts, the Second Seminole War is the most well-known. The war was fought guerrilla-style by 2000 or so Seminoles in swamps and hammocks, led by the famous Osceola, eventually captured under a flag of truce. After the Third Seminole War, 200 to 300 Seminoles refused to sign a peace treaty and slipped away into the Everglades. Technically, these Seminoles never surrendered and remain the only 'unconquered' American Indian tribe. In 1957, the US officially recognized the **Seminole Tribe** (www.semtribe.com), and in 1962, the **Miccosukee Tribe** (www.miccosukee.com). For more history, visit the **Ah-Tah-Thi-Ki Museum** (www.ahtahthiki.com).

Five Flags: Florida Gets Passed Around

Spain claimed Florida in 1513 – when explorer Ponce de León arrived. Five more Spanish expeditions followed (and one French), and nothing bore fruit until 1565, when St Augustine was settled. A malarial, easily pillaged outpost, St Augustine truly succeeded at only one thing: spreading the Catholic religion. Spanish missionaries founded 31 missions across Florida, converting and educating Indians, occasionally with notable civility.

In 1698 Spain established a permanent military fort at Pensacola, which was then variously captured and recaptured by the Spanish, French, English and North Americans for a century. Pensacola set the trend for Florida as a state: as a piece of real estate to be fought over. From now till 1865 Florida would be ruled by five flags: Spain, France, Britain, the US and the Confederacy.

From Civil War to Civil Rights

In 1838 the Florida territory was home to about 48,000 people, of whom 21,000 were black slaves. By 1860, 15 years after statehood, Florida's population was 140,000, of whom 40% were slaves, most of them working on highly profitable cotton plantations. Thus, unsurprisingly, when Abraham Lincoln was elected president on an antislavery platform, Florida joined the confederacy of Southern states that seceded from the Union in 1861. During the ensuing Civil War, which lasted until 1865, only moderate fighting occurred in Florida.

After Southern surrender the US government imposed 'Reconstruction' on all ex-Confederate states. Reconstruction protected the rights of freed blacks, and led to

1702
The British burn St Augustine; two years later they destroy 13 Spanish missions.

1776
The American Revolution begins, but Florida's two colonies don't rebel, instead remaining loyal to the British crown.

1823
Tallahassee is established as Florida's capital because it's halfway between Pensacola and St Augustine.

19 blacks becoming elected to Florida's state congress. Yet this radical social and political upheaval led to a furious backlash. When federal troops finally left, Florida 'unreconstructed' in a hurry, adopting a series of Jim Crow laws that segregated and disenfranchised blacks in every sphere of life – in restaurants and parks, on beaches and buses – while a poll tax kept blacks and the poor from voting. From then until the 1950s, black field hands in turpentine camps and cane fields worked under a forced-labor 'peonage' system, in which they couldn't leave till their wages paid off their debts, which of course never happened.

The Ku Klux Klan thrived, its popularity peaking in the 1920s, when Florida led the country in lynchings. Racial hysteria and violence were commonplace; most infamously, a white mob razed the entire town of Rosewood in 1923.

In 1954 the US Supreme Court ended legal segregation in the US with Brown vs Board of Education, but in 1957 Florida's Supreme Court rejected this decision, declaring it 'null and void.' This sparked protests but little change until 1964, when a series of race riots and demonstrations, some led by Martin Luther King Jr, rocked St Augustine and helped spur passage of the national Civil Rights Act of 1964. More race riots blazed across Florida cities in 1967 and 1968, after which racial conflict eased as Florida belatedly and begrudgingly desegregated itself.

The Best... Historical Homes

1 Flagler Museum (p142)

2 Vizcaya Museum & Gardens (p196)

3 Edison & Ford Winter Estates (p286)

4 Hemingway House (p223)

Florida's racial wounds healed equally slowly – as evidenced by more race riots in the early 1980s. Today, despite much progress and the fact that Florida is one of the nation's most ethnically diverse states, these wounds still haven't completely healed.

Draining Swamps & Laying Rail

By the middle of the 19th century, the top half of Florida was reasonably well explored, but South Florida was still a swamp. So, in the 1870s, Florida inaugurated its first building boom by adopting laissez-faire economic policies centered on three things: unrestricted private development, minimal taxes, and land grants for railroads.

In 10 years, from 1881 to 1891, Florida's railroad miles quintupled, from 550 to 2566. Most of the track crisscrossed northern and central Florida, but one rail line went south to nowhere. In 1886, railroad magnate Henry Flagler started building a railroad down the coast on the spectacular gamble that once he built it, people would come.

In 1896 Flagler's line stopped at muddy Fort Dallas, which incorporated as the city of Miami that same year. Then, people came, and kept coming, and Flagler is largely

1845
Florida is admitted to the Union as the 27th state.

1861
Voting 62–7, Florida secedes from the USA, raising the stars-and-bars of the Confederacy.

1912
'Flagler's Folly,' Henry Flagler's 128-mile overseas railroad connecting the Florida Keys, reaches Key West.

The Best... Florida Histories

1 *The New History of Florida*, Michael Gannon

2 *The Everglades: River of Grass*, Marjory Stoneman Douglas

3 *Reamers, Schemers & Scalawags*, Stuart McIver

4 *The Enduring Seminoles*, Patsy West

5 *Miami Babylon*, Gerald Posner

credited with founding every town from West Palm Beach to Miami.

In 1900 Governor Napoleon Bonaparte Broward, envisioning an 'Empire of the Everglades,' set in motion a frenzy of canal building. Some 1800 miles of canals and levees were etched across Florida's limestone. These earthworks successfully drained about half the Everglades (about 1.5 million acres) below Lake Okeechobee, replacing it with farms, cattle ranches, orange groves, sugarcane and suburbs.

From 1920 to 1925, the South Florida land boom swept the nation. In 1915, Miami Beach was a sandbar; by 1925, it had 56 hotels, 178 apartment buildings, and three golf courses. In 1920, Miami had one skyscraper; by 1925, 30 were under construction. In 1925 alone, 2.5 million people moved to Florida. Real-estate speculators sold undeveloped land, undredged land, and then just promises of land.

Then, two hurricanes struck, in 1926 and 1928, and the party ended. The coup de grâce was the October 1929 stock-market crash. Florida plunged into depression, though the state rode it relatively well due to New Deal public works, tourism, and a highly profitable foray into rum running – smuggling being a popular illicit means of income in a state intersected by thousands of miles of tiny waterways.

Tin Can Tourists, Retirees & A Big-Eared Mouse

For the record, tourism is Florida's number-one industry, and this doesn't count retirees – the tourists who never leave.

Tourism didn't become a force in Florida until the 1890s, when Flagler built his coastal railroad and hoity-toity Miami Beach resorts. In the 1920s, middle-class 'tin can tourists' arrived via the new Dixie Hwy – driving Model Ts, sleeping in campers and cooking their own food.

In the 1930s, savvy promoters created the first 'theme parks': Cypress Gardens and Silver Springs. But it wasn't until after WWII that Florida tourism exploded. During the war, Miami was a major military training ground, and afterward, many of those GIs returned with their families.

1926–28
Hurricanes take a toll of some 2400 lives across the state.

1933–40
New Deal public-works projects employ 40,000 Floridians and build the Overseas Highway, replacing Flagler's railroad.

1935
Dick Pope opens Cypress Gardens, the USA's first theme park.

In addition, after the war, Social Security kicked in, and the nation's aging middle class migrated south to enjoy a new concept; retirement. Many came from the East Coast, and quite a few were Jewish: by 1960, Miami Beach was 80% Jewish.

Then one day in 1963, so the story goes, Walt Disney flew over central Florida, spotted the intersection of I-4 and the Florida Turnpike, and said, 'That's it.' In secret, he bought 43 sq miles of Orlando-area wetlands. Exempt from a host of state laws and building codes, largely self-governing, Disney World opened in 1971. How big did it become? In 1950, Florida received 4.5 million tourists, not quite twice its population. By the 1980s, Disney alone drew 40 million visitors a year, or four times the state population.

Disney had the Midas touch. In the shadow of the Magic Kingdom, Florida's old-school attractions – Weeki Wachee, Seminole Village, Busch Gardens; all the places made famous through billboards and postcards – seemed hokey, small-time. The rules of tourism had changed forever.

Hemingway House (p223), Key West
ROBERT J. BENNETT/GETTY IMAGES ©

1946
Frozen concentrated orange juice is invented, leading to Florida's orange boom.

1947
Everglades National Park is established, successfully culminating a 19-year effort to protect the Everglades.

1961
Brigade 2506, a Miami-based 1300-strong volunteer army, invades Cuba but is defeated by Castro.

The Best... Historical Hotels

1 Curry Mansion Inn (p228)

2 Hotel Ponce de León (p298)

3 Breakers (p143)

4 Biltmore Hotel (p197)

5 Cardozo Hotel (p205)

Viva Cuba Libre!

South Florida has an intimate relationship with Cuba. In the 20th century, so many Cuban exiles sought refuge in Miami, they dubbed it the 'Exile Capital.' Later, as immigration expanded, Miami simply became the 'Capital of Latin America.'

From 1868 to 1902, during Cuba's long struggle for independence from Spain, Cuban exiles settled in Key West and Tampa, giving birth to Ybor City. Then, in 1959, Fidel Castro's revolution (plotted partly in Miami hotels) overthrew the Batista dictatorship. This triggered a several-year exodus of over 600,000 Cubans to Miami, most of them white, wealthy, educated professionals.

In April 1961, Castro declared Cuba communist, setting the future course for US–Cuban relations. The next day, President Kennedy approved the ill-fated Bay of Pigs invasion, which failed to overthrow Castro, and in October 1962, Kennedy blockaded Cuba to protest the presence of Russian nuclear missiles. Khrushchev famously 'blinked' and removed the missiles, but not before the US secretly agreed never to invade Cuba again.

None of this sat well with Miami's Cuban exiles, who agitated for the USA to free Cuba (chanting *'Viva Cuba libre':* long live free Cuba). Between 1960 and 1980, a million Cubans, or 10% of the island's population, emigrated; by 1980, 60% of Miami was Cuban.

In the 1980s and '90s, poorer immigrants flooded Miami from all over Latin America and the Caribbean – particularly El Salvador, Nicaragua, Mexico, Colombia, Venezuela, the Dominican Republic and Haiti. These groups did not always mix easily, but they found success in a city that already conducted business in Spanish. By the mid-1990s, South Florida was exporting $25 billion in goods to Latin America, and Miami's Cubans were more economically powerful than Cuba itself.

Today, Miami's Cubans are firmly entrenched, and the younger generation no longer consider themselves exiles, but residents. Although younger Cubans remain firmly anti-Castro, some call for more moderate dealings with the motherland, arguing for limited trade and engagement.

Hurricanes, Politics & the Everglades

Florida has a habit of selling itself too well. The precarious foundation of its paradise was driven home in 1992, when Hurricane Andrew ripped across South Florida, leaving a wake of destruction that stunned the state and the nation. Plus, mounting evidence

1969
Apollo 11 lifts off from Cape Canaveral and lands on the moon.

1971
Walt Disney World® Resort opens and around 10,000 people arrive on the first day.

1984
Miami Vice debuts. The glamorous but gritty show raises South Beach's international profile.

of rampant pollution – fish kills, dying mangroves, murky bays – appeared like a bill for a century of unchecked sprawl and population growth.

Newcomers were trampling what they came for. From 1930 to 1980, Florida's population growth rate was 564%. Florida had gone from the least-populated to the fourth-most-populated state, and its infrastructure struggled to keep up with the strain.

In particular, saving the Everglades became a moral, as well as environmental, crusade. Would one of the Earth's wonders become a subdivision? The Florida Forever Act and the Comprehensive Everglades Restoration Plan were both signed into law in 2000, but at time of writing, the impetus for these programs was slowed by delays from the Army Corps of Engineers.

As the 21st century dawned, Florida's historic tensions – between its mantra of growth and development and the demands that places on society and nature, between its white Southern north and its multiethnic immigrant-rich south – seemed as entrenched as ever. At the same time, the state continues to attract millions of visitors and immigrants, domestic and international, seeking the better life the 'Feast of Flowers' has promised for over 400 years.

Great blue heron, Everglades National Park
ALEX POTEMKIN/GETTY IMAGES ©

1999
Despite wild protests in Miami, the US returns refugee Elián Gonzalez to Cuba.

2000
The US presidential election is determined by 537 votes in Florida.

2014
The 0.75-mile Port of Miami Tunnel, connecting the MacArthur Causeway with the Port of Miami is due to open.

Family Travel

Surfers with longboard

WILLIAM GOLDSMITH/GETTY IMAGES ©

Florida does two things better than just about any place in America – beaches and theme parks. If you're traveling with kids, you may want to stop reading right now, because that's pretty much your itinerary. Indeed, a Florida family trip can easily achieve legendary status with just a few well-placed phone calls. That's why so many families return year after sandy, sunburned year.

Florida for Kids

Every tourist town in Florida has already anticipated the needs of every age demographic in your family. With increasing skill and refinement, nearly every Florida museum, zoo, attraction, restaurant and hotel aims to please traveling families of all stripes.

Your only real trouble is deciding what to do. Florida offers so much for kids and families that planning can be tough. That simple beach-and-theme-park itinerary can suddenly become a frantic dawn-to-dusk race to pack it all in. We can't help you there. In fact, we can't even fit everything in this book.

Eating Out

Most midrange Florida restaurants have a dedicated kid's menu, along with high chairs, crayons for coloring, and changing tables in restrooms. And nearly every restaurant, even high-end ones, is happy to make a kid's meal on request. As a rule, families with infants or toddlers will get better service earlier in the dinner hour (by 6pm). Only a few truly snooty big-city gourmet temples will look askance at young diners; if you're unsure, simply ask when making reservations.

Theme Parks

Walt Disney World® Resort, Universal Studios, SeaWorld, Discovery Cove, Busch Gardens: Florida's biggest theme parks are verily worlds unto themselves. You can visit for a day, or make them your sole destination for a week, even two.

Beaches

The prototypical Florida family beach is fronted by or near very active, crowded commercial centers with lots of watersports and activities, tourist shops, grocery stores and midrange eats and sleeps. Some may be known for Spring Break–style party scenes, but all have family-friendly stretches and usually only get rowdy in the late evening.

Zoos, Museums & Attractions

Up-close animal encounters have long been a Florida tourist staple, and the state has some of the best zoos and aquariums in the country. Florida's native wildlife is truly stunning, and it's easy to see. Florida's cities also have an extremely high number of top-quality hands-on children's museums, and there's a wealth of smaller roadside attractions and oddities designed for, or that appeal to, kids.

The Best... Family Friendly Wildlife Encounters

1 Shark Valley, Everglades National Park (p243)

2 National Key Deer Refuge (p222)

3 Bill Baggs Cape Florida State Recreation Area (p193)

4 Myakka River State Park (p288)

Getting into Nature

Don't overlook unpackaged nature. Florida is exceedingly flat, so rivers and trails are frequently ideal for short legs and little arms. Raised boardwalks through alligator-filled swamps make perfect pint-size adventures. Placid rivers and intercoastal bays are custom-made for first-time paddlers, adult or child. Never snorkeled a coral reef or surfed? Florida has gentle places to learn. Book a sea-life cruise, a manatee swim or nesting sea-turtle watch.

Rules of the Road

Florida carseat laws require that children under three must be in a carseat, and children under five in at least a booster seat (unless they are over 80lb and 4'9" tall, allowing seat belts to be positioned properly). Rental-car companies are legally required to provide child seats, but only if you reserve them in advance; they typically charge $10 to $15 extra. Avoid surprises by bringing your own.

Best Regions for Kids

Orlando (p89)Two words: theme parks. No, seven words: the theme park capital of the world.

Miami (p183) Kid-focused zoos and museums, plus amazing beaches, but also Miami itself, one of the USA's great multicultural cities.

Florida Keys (p223) Active families with older kids will adore the snorkeling, diving, fishing, boating and all-around no-worries vibe.

Tampa Bay & Gulf Coast (p264) Top-flight zoos, aquariums and museums, plus some of Florida's prettiest, most family-friendly beaches.

Daytona & Space Coast (p99 & p296) Surfing, sandcastles, four-wheeling on the beach, kayaking mangroves: all ages love this stretch of Atlantic coastline.

Panhandle Beaches (p336) Frenetic boardwalk amusements, family-friendly resorts, stunningly white sand: Panama City and Pensacola beaches aim to please everyone.

Planning

If you're a parent, you already know that luck favors the prepared. But in Florida's crazy-crowded, overbooked high-season tourist spots, planning can make all the difference. Before you come, plot your trip like a four-star general: pack everything you might need, make reservations for every place you might go, schedule every hour. Then, arrive, relax and go with the flow.

Accommodations

The vast majority of Florida hotels stand ready to aid families: they have cribs and rollaway beds (perhaps charging extra); they have refrigerators and microwaves (but ask to confirm); and they have adjoining rooms and suites. Particularly in beach towns, large hotels and resorts can go toe-to-toe with condos for amenities: including partial or full kitchens, laundry facilities, pools and barbecues, and various activities. Properties catering specifically to families are marked by a family icon (👪).

The only places that discourage young kids (they aren't allowed to discriminate) are certain romantic B&Bs and high-end boutique hotels. If you're unsure, ask, and they'll tell you what minimum age they prefer.

Need to Know

- **Change Facilities** Found in most towns, theme parks, malls and many chain restaurants
- **Cots** Available in midrange and top-end establishments
- **Health** See the general health section (p342)
- **Highchairs** Widely available in restaurants, as are booster seats
- **Nappies** (diapers) Widely available
- **Strollers** Can be rented at many theme parks and hotels, and folks on public transport will give you a helping hand
- **Transport** All public transport caters for young passengers

Date Night

Traveling with kids doesn't necessarily mean doing everything as a family. Want a romantic night on the town? Several child-care services offer in-hotel babysitting by certified sitters; a few run their own drop-off centers. For more resources while staying at Walt Disney World® Resort, see p91.

- **Kid's Nite Out** (www.kidsniteout.com)
- **Sittercity** (www.sittercity.com)
- **Sunshine Babysitting** (www.sunshinebabysitting.com) Statewide.

Travel Advice & Baby Gear

If you prefer to pack light, several services offer baby gear rental (high chairs, strollers, car seats, etc), while others sell infant supplies (diapers, wipes, formula, baby food, etc), all delivered to your hotel; book one to two weeks in advance. These and other websites also provide family-centered travel advice. Most focus on Orlando, Miami and Tampa, but a few are statewide.

Baby's Away (www.babysaway.com) Rents baby gear.

Traveling Baby Company (www.travelingbabyco.com) Rents baby gear.

Babies Travel Lite (www.babiestravellite.com) Sells baby supplies for delivery; also offers general and Florida-specific family travel advice.

Jet Set Babies (www.jetsetbabies.com) Sells baby supplies, plus general infant travel advice.

Travel For Kids (www.travelforkids.com) Florida-specific family travel; helpful planning advice.

Family Vacation Critics (www.familyvacationcritics.com) Trip Advisor-owned, parent-reviewed hotels, sights and travel.

Florida-Themed Books for Kids

We're big fans of getting reading-age kids in a Florida mood. Try these great books.

Hoot (2002) by Carl Hiaasen: Hiaasen's same zany characters, snappy plot twists and environmental message, but PG-rated. If you like it, pick up *Flush* (2005) and *Scat* (2009).

Because of Winn-Dixie (2000) by Kate DiCamillo: Heart-warming coming-of-age tale about a 10-year-old girl adjusting to her new life in Florida.

The Yearling (1938) by Marjorie Kinnan Rawlings: Pulitzer-prize-winning literary classic about a boy who adopts an orphaned fawn in Florida's backwoods.

The Treasure of Amelia Island (2008) by MC Finotti: Historical fiction that re-creates Spanish-ruled Florida through the eyes of an 11-year-old.

Bad Latitude (2008) by David Ebright: Pirate adventure for tween boys, with a dash of historical realism.

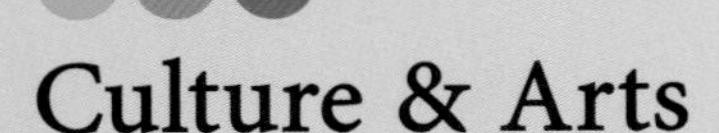

Culture & Arts

Dancing the tango

DOUGLAS MENUEZ/GETTY IMAGES ©

Florida's peoples and culture are a compelling mix of accents and rhythms, pastel hues and Caribbean spices, rebel yells and Latin hip-hop, Jewish retirees and Miami millionaires. Florida is, in a word, diverse. Like the prehistoric swamp at its heart, it is both fascinatingly complex and too watery to pin down, making for a very intriguing place to explore.

Portrait of a Peninsula

Pessimists say Florida is so socially and culturally fractured that it will never have a coherent identity. Optimists, strangely enough, embrace the diversity and say nearly the same thing.

In terms of geography, Florida is a Southern state. Yet culturally, only Florida's northern half is truly Southern. In the Panhandle, Jacksonville and the rural north, folks speak with that distinctive Southern drawl, serve sweet tea as a matter of course, and still remember the Civil War.

Central Florida and the Tampa Bay area were favoured by Midwesterners, and here you often find a plainspoken, Protestant worker-bee sobriety. East Coast Yankees have carved a definable presence in South Florida – such as the Atlantic Coast's Jewish retirement communities, in Miami and the southern Gulf Coast.

Rural Florida, north or south, can still evoke America's western frontier. In the 19th century, after the West was won, Florida became one of the last places where pioneers could simply plant stakes and make a life. Today, even if they live in cookie-cutter suburbs, many Floridians like to feel they share that same streak of fierce, undomesticated self-reliance.

In parts of Miami and Tampa you won't feel like you're in the US at all. The air is filled with Spanish, the majority of people are Roman Catholic, and the politics of Cuba, Haiti or Colombia animate conversations.

Ultimately, Florida satisfies and defies expectations. You might find Cuban lawyers more politically conservative than Confederate flag-waving construction workers, and fixed-income retirees more liberal than gay South Beach restaurateurs. This is one reason why it's so hard to predict Florida elections, and why sometimes they turn on a handful of votes.

The Capital of Latin America

Modern Florida has been redefined by successive waves of Hispanic immigrants from Latin America. What sets Florida apart is the teeming diversity of its Latinos and their self-sufficient, economically powerful, politicized, Spanish-speaking presence.

How pervasive is Spanish? One in four Floridians speak a language other than English at home, and three-quarters of these speak Spanish (many of the rest speak Haitian Creole). Spanish is the first language for over 90% of the population of Hialeah, a suburb of Miami.

Today, every Latin American country is represented in South Florida. Argentines can be found in North Miami Beach, Colombians in Coral Gables and Downtown, and Cubans, of course, are everywhere. The children of Cuban exiles are now called YUCAs, 'young urban Cuban Americans,' while the next generation of Latinos has been dubbed Generation Ñ (pronounced enyey).

With each other, young Latinos slip seamlessly between English and Spanish, typically within the same sentence, reverting to English in front of Anglos and Spanish in front of relatives.

Immigration by Numbers

Before WWII, Florida was the least populated state (with under two million people); today it's the fourth most populated, with 18.8 million in 2010.

Florida's growth rate was an astonishing 44% during the 1970s. While that rate has declined since, it was still over 17% for the 21st century's first decade, twice the national average.

Florida ranks fourth in the nation for the largest minority population (approximately 8.6 million), and the largest number and percentage of foreign-born residents (3.7 million people, who make up 19.5%). In Miami, the foreign-born population exceeds 60% – easily tops among large US cities.

The Best... Performing-Arts Venues

Floridians at Play

Floridians are passionate about sports. For the majority of Floridians, college football is the true religion. Florida has three of the country's best collegiate teams – the University of Miami Hurricanes, the University of Florida Gators (in Gainesville), and the Florida State University Seminoles (in Tallahassee).

Florida boasts three pro football teams (Miami Dolphins, Tampa Bay Buccaneers and Jacksonville Jaguars) and two pro basketball teams (Orlando Magic and Miami Heat). The Stanley Cup–winning Tampa Bay Lightning is one of several pro and semipro hockey teams in the state, including the Miami-based Florida Panthers.

Major-league baseball's spring training creates a frenzy of excitement in March, when 13 pro teams practice across southern Florida. These stadiums then host minor-league teams, while two pro teams are based here: the Florida Marlins (in Miami) and Tampa Bay Rays (in St Petersburg).

Nascar originated among liquor bootleggers who needed fast cars to escape the law. Fast outgrowing its Southern roots, Nascar is near and dear to Floridians and hosts regular events in Daytona.

Imported sports also flourish in South Florida. One is the dangerous Basque game of jai alai, popular with Miami's wagering types (betting is still legal at jai alai matches). Cricket, surprisingly enough, is popular in South Florida thanks to large Jamaican and West Indian populations.

Literature

Beginning in the 1930s, Florida developed its own bona-fide literary voice, courtesy mainly of three writers. The most famous was Ernest Hemingway, who settled in Key West in 1928. 'Papa' wrote For Whom the Bell Tolls and A Farewell to Arms here, but he only set one novel in Florida, *To Have and Have Not* (1937).

The honor of 'most Floridian writer' is generally bestowed on Marjorie Kinnan Rawlings, who lived in Cross Creek between Gainesville and Ocala. She turned her sympathetic eye on Florida's pioneers and the elemental beauty of the state's swampy wilderness. Her novel *The Yearling* (1938) won the Pulitzer Prize, while *Cross Creek* (1942) is a much-lauded autobiographical novel.

Zora Neale Hurston, an African-American writer who was born in all-black Eatonville, near Orlando, became a major figure in New York's Harlem renaissance of the 1930s. Her most famous novel, *Their Eyes Were Watching God* (1937), evokes the suffering of Florida's rural blacks, particularly women.

Florida writing is perhaps most famous for its eccentric take on hard-boiled crime fiction. Carl Hiaasen almost singlehandedly defines the genre; his stories are hilarious gumbos of misfits and murderers, who collide in plots of thinly disguised environmentalism, in which bad guys are developers and the true crimes are against nature. Other popular names are Randy Wayne White, John D MacDonald, James Hall, and Tim Dorsey.

Painting & Visual Arts

Florida has an affinity for modern art, and modern artists find Florida allows them to indulge their inner pink. In 1983, Bulgarian artist Christo 'wrapped' 11 islands in Biscayne Bay in flamingo-colored fabric, so they floated in the water like giant discarded flowers, dwarfing the urban skyline.

Everyone loved it; it was so Miami.

Cartoon-hued grandeur and exhibitionism seem Miami's calling cards. That certainly applies to Brazilian émigré Romero Britto, whose art graces several buildings, such as the Miami Children's Museum (p200). Miami's prominence in the contemporary art world was cemented in 2002, when the Art Basel festival arrived, and Miami's gallery scene is arguably unmatched outside of LA and Manhattan.

The rest of the state does not lack for high-quality art museums. In addition to Miami, other notable cities are Fort Lauderdale, West Palm Beach, St Petersburg, Tampa, Sarasota, Naples and Orlando.

The Best... Art Museums

1 Morikami Museum & Japanese Gardens (p154)

2 Salvador Dalí Museum (p275)

3 Bass Museum of Art (p184)

4 Lowe Art Museum (p19)

5 Orlando Museum of Art (p90)

Music

Tom Petty, Lynyrd Skynyrd and the Allman Brothers form Florida's holy rock trio, while Matchbox Twenty and Dashboard Confessional also got their start in Florida. Tampa is the home to both punk and 'death metal.' And yet, the popular musician who most often defines Florida is Jimmy Buffett, whose heart lives in Key West, wherever his band may roam.

Rap and hip-hop have flourished in Tampa and Miami, most notoriously with 2 Live Crew, while Orlando (by way of mogul and now jailbird Lou Pearlman) bestowed to the world the boy bands N Sync and Backstreet Boys.

Miami is a tasty mélange of Cuban salsa, Jamaican reggae, Dominican merengue, and Spanish flamenco, plus mambo, rumba, cha-cha, calypso and more. Gloria Estefan and the Miami Sound Machine launched a revival of Cuban music in the 1970s, when they mixed Latin beats with disco with 'Conga.'

Cinema & Television

Some of the more notable popular films filmed in Florida include the Marx Bros farce *Cocoanuts*, *Creature from the Black Lagoon* (filmed at Wakulla Springs), *The Truman Show* (filmed at Seaside), *Ulee's Gold, Donnie Brasco, Get Shorty, Hoot* and *Miami Blues.*

Florida, as setting, has been a main character in a number of TV shows. In the 1960s, the most famous were *Flipper,* about a boy and his dolphin, and *I Dream of Jeannie,* about an astronaut and his one-woman harem.

In the 1980s, Miami was never the same after *Miami Vice* hit the air: a groundbreaking drama that made it OK to wear sport coats over T-shirts and helped inspire the renovation of South Beach's then-dilapidated historic district. Today's popular *CSI: Miami* owes a debt to Don Johnson and *Miami Vice* it can never repay.

Floridian Food

Grilled shrimp at a restaurant in Key West (p228)

DANA HOFF/GETTY IMAGES ©

Florida offers as much culinary excellence and adventure as you'd like. The state draws from sublime fresh bounty from land and sea, and menus playfully nick influences from a hemisphere's worth of cultures: Southern, Creole, Cuban, Caribbean, and Central and South American, but also Jewish, Asian, Spanish, and more. Gourmets can genuflect before celebrity chefs, while gourmands hunt Florida's bizarre delicacies, like boiled peanuts, frog's legs, snake, and gator.

Destination Dining

Florida has a rich culinary heritage, but the state wasn't known as a place for good restaurants until the 1990s, when a wave of gourmet chefs transformed the Miami dining scene. They dedicated themselves to pleasing sophisticated urban palates by spicing up menus with South Florida's unique combination of Cuban, Caribbean and Latin American influences, which came to be dubbed Floribbean cuisine.

Today, Miami remains the epicenter of all things gourmet, and has the greatest selection of ethnic cuisines, but the ripples have spread statewide. In big cities and anywhere moneyed tourists and snowbirds land, you will find upscale restaurants and skilled chefs plying their trade, often in contemporary dining rooms framing ocean views.

North of Miami and Miami Beach, Fort Lauderdale, Palm Beach and West Palm Beach offer the well-heeled foodie oodles of fun. Key West is, as in all things, more laid-back, but its dining scene is notably stocked with creative-fusion cool.

The southern Gulf Coast is similarly satisfying: Tampa is riding the cusp of a culinary renaissance, with everything from Old World Iberian to locavore-inspired modern gastronomy. Skip south through the rich beach towns of Sarasota, Sanibel Island and Naples, and a memorable meal is a reservation away.

As you go north, robust Southern cuisine comes to dominate, and high-end dining favors classic Italian, French and seafood. Though lacking gourmet 'scenes,' great choices are sprinkled around Orlando and its theme parks. Along the Atlantic Coast, Amelia Island and St Augustine are foodie havens.

Bounty of the Sea

Florida has always fed itself from the sea, which lies within arm's reach from nearly every point. If it swims or crawls in the ocean, you can bet some enterprising local has shelled or scaled it, battered it, dropped it in a fryer and put it on a menu.

Grouper is far and away the most popular fish. Grouper sandwiches are to Florida what the cheesesteak is to Philadelphia or pizza to Manhattan – a defining, iconic dish, and the standard by which many places are measured. Hunting the perfect grilled or fried grouper sandwich is an obsessive Floridian quest, as is finding the creamiest bowl of chowder.

Of course, a huge range of other fish is offered. Popular species include snapper (with dozens of varieties), mahimahi and catfish.

Florida shines when it comes to crustaceans: try pink shrimp and rock shrimp, and don't miss soft-shell blue crab – Florida is the only place with blue-crab hatcheries, making them available fresh year-round. Winter (October to April) is the season for Florida spiny lobster and stone crab (out of season, both will be frozen). Florida lobster is all tail, without the large claws of its Maine cousin, and stone crab is heavenly sweet, served steamed with butter or the ubiquitous mustard sauce.

Finally, the Keys popularized conch (a giant sea snail); now fished out, most conch is from the Bahamas. It's best served 'cracked,' or fried, with a variety of dipping sauces, or curried in a spicy gravy and served with rice; the latter dish is popular in many Caribbean restaurants.

Cuban & Latin American Cuisine

Cuban food, once considered 'exotic,' is itself a mix of Caribbean, African and Latin American influences, and in Tampa and Miami, it's a staple of everyday life. Sidle up to a Cuban *loncheria* (snack bar) and order a *pan cubano:* a buttered, grilled baguette stuffed with ham, roast pork, cheese, mustard and pickles.

Integral to many Cuban dishes are *mojo* (a garlicky vinaigrette, sprinkled on sandwiches), *adobo* (a meat marinade of garlic, salt, cumin, oregano and sour orange juice) and *sofrito* (a stew-starter mix of garlic, onion and chili peppers). Main-course meats are typically accompanied by rice and beans and fried plantains.

With its large number of Central and Latin American immigrants, the Miami area offers plenty of authentic ethnic eateries. Seek out Haitian griots (marinated fried pork), Jamaican jerk chicken, Brazilian BBQ, Central American gallo pinto (red beans and rice) and Nicaraguan *tres leches* ('three milks' cake).

In the morning, try a Cuban coffee, also known as *café cubano* or *cortadito.* This hot shot of liquid gold is essentially sweetened espresso, while *café con leche* is just *café au lait* with a different accent: equal parts coffee and hot milk.

The Best... Cuban Restaurants

1 Versailles (p212)

2 Islas Canarias (p212)

3 La Segunda Bakery (p269)

4 Exquisito Ristorante (p212)

Another Cuban treat is *guarapo,* or fresh-squeezed sugarcane juice. Cuban snack bars serve the greenish liquid straight or poured over crushed ice, and it's essential to an authentic mojito. It also sometimes finds its way into *batidos,* a milky, refreshing Latin American fruit smoothie.

Southern Cooking

The further north you travel, the more Southern the cooking, which makes up in fat what it may lack in refinement. 'Meat and three' is Southern restaurant lingo for a main meat – like fried chicken, catfish, barbecued ribs, chicken-fried steak or even chitlins (hog's intestines) – and three sides: perhaps some combination of hush puppies, cheese grits, cornbread, coleslaw, mashed potatoes, black-eyed peas, collard greens or buttery corn. End with pecan pie, and that's living. Po' boys are merely Southern hoagies, usually filled with fried nuggets of goodness.

Cracker cooking is Florida's rough-and-tumble variation on Southern cuisine, but with more reptiles and amphibians. And you'll find a good deal of Cajun and Creole as well, which mix in spicy gumbos and bisques from Louisiana's neighboring swamps. Southern Floridian cooking is epitomized by writer Marjorie Kinnan Rawlings' famous cookbook *Cross Creek Cookery.*

Ice tea is so ubiquitous it's called the 'wine of the South,' but watch out for 'sweet tea,' which is an almost entirely different Southern drink – tea so sugary your eyes will cross.

Florida Specialties

From north to south, here are dishes strange and sublime, but 100% Florida; try not to leave without trying them at least once.

Boiled peanuts In rural north Florida, they take green or immature peanuts and boil them until they're nice and mushy, sometimes spicing them up with Cajun or other seasonings. Sure, they feel weird in the mouth, but they're surprisingly addictive.

Alligator Alligator tastes like a cross between fish and pork. The meat comes from the tail, and is usually served as deep-fried nuggets, which overwhelms the delicate flavor and can make it chewy. Try it grilled. Most alligator is legally harvested on farms and is often sold in grocery stores. It's also healthier than chicken, with as much protein but half the fat, fewer calories and less cholesterol.

Frog's legs Those who know say the 'best' legs come from the Everglades; definitely ask, since you want to avoid imported ones from India, which are smaller and disparaged as 'flavorless.'

Stone crabs The first recycled crustacean: only one claw is taken from a stone crab – the rest is tossed back in the sea (the claw regrows in 12 to 18 months, and crabs plucked again are called 'retreads'). The claws are so perishable that they're always cooked before selling. October through April is less a 'season' than a stone-crab frenzy. Joe Weiss of Miami Beach is credited with starting it all.

Key lime pie Key limes are yellow, and that's the color of an authentic Key lime pie, which is a custard of Key lime juice, sweetened condensed milk and egg yolks in a cracker crust, then topped with meringue. Avoid any slice that's green or stands ramrod straight. The combination of extra-tart Key lime with oversweet milk nicely captures the personality of Key West Conchs.

Libations

Is it the heat or the humidity? With the exception of the occasional teetotaling dry town, Florida's embrace of liquor is prodigious, even epic. And as you ponder this legacy – from Prohibition-era rumrunners, Spring Break hedonists and drive-thru liquor stores to Ernest Hemingway and Jimmy Buffett – it can seem that quantity trumps quality most of the time.

Yet as with Florida's cuisine, so with its bars. Surely, Anheuser-Busch's Jacksonville brewery will never go out of business, but Tampa also boasts several handcrafted local microbreweries. Daytona's beaches may be littered with gallon-size hurricane glasses, but Miami mixologists hone their reputations with their designer takes on martinis and mojitos.

Indeed, Cuban bartenders became celebrities in the 1920s for what they did with all that sugarcane and citrus: the two classics are the *Cuba libre* (rum, lime and cola) and the mojito (rum, sugar, mint, lemon and club soda), traditionally served with *chicharrónes* (deep-fried pork rinds).

As for Hemingway, he favored piña coladas, lots of them. Jimmy Buffett memorialized the margarita – so that now every sweaty beach bar along the peninsula claims to make the 'best.' Welcome, good friends, to Margaritaville.

The Best... Florida Food Blogs

1 Jan Norris (www.jannorris.com)

2 Jeff's Eats (http://jeffseats.com)

3 Meatless Miami (www.meatlessmiami.com)

4 Mega Yummo (http://megayummo.com)

5 Food for Thought (http://foodforthoughtmiami.com)

The Outdoors

Diving (p328) in the Atlantic

STEPHEN FRINK/GETTY IMAGES ©

Florida's beaches are justifiably her claim to fame, and we explore them in-depth later. But the state's waters do more than frame a coastline. Under the ocean is the largest coral reef system in North America, while the peninsula is crisscrossed with 11,000 miles of rivers and streams. The flat topography is perfect for cycling and conceals a trove of hiking trails.

Hiking

One thing Florida hikers never have to worry about is elevation gain. But the weather more than makes up for it. Particularly if your destination is South Florida, hike and camp from November through March. This is Florida's 'dry season,' when rain, temperature, humidity and mosquitos decrease to tolerable levels. In summer, make sure to hike first thing, before noon, to avoid the midday heat and afternoon thundershowers.

Florida National Scenic Trail (FSNT; www.floridatrail.org) is one of 11 national scenic trails and covers 1400 not-yet-contiguous miles. It runs north from the swamps of **Big Cypress National Preserve** (p247); around Lake Okeechobee; through the **Ocala National Forest** (fs.usda.gov/ocala); and then west to the **Gulf Islands National Seashore (www.nps.gov/guis)** near Pensacola. All the parks above are rife with great hikes.

Other prime hiking areas include the remote pine wilderness, karst terrain and limestone sinkholes of **Apalachicola National Forest** (p300), while **Wekiwa Springs State Park** (p91) rewards hikers, paddlers and snorkelers.

South Florida swamps tend to favor 1- to 2-mile boardwalk trails; these are excellent, and almost always wheelchair accessible. But to really explore the swamps, get in a kayak.

The Best... Canoeing & Kayaking

1 Hell's Bay (p246)

2 JN 'Ding' Darling National Wildlife Refuge (p289)

3 Bill Baggs Cape Florida State Recreation Area (p193)

4 Indian Key Historic State Park (p220)

5 10,000 Islands (p247)

Canoeing & Kayaking

To really experience Florida's swamps and rivers, its estuaries and inlets, its lagoons and barrier islands, you need watercraft, preferably the kind you paddle. The intimate quiet of dipping among mangroves, startling alligators and ibis, stirs wonder in the soul.

As with hiking, the winter 'dry' season is best for paddling. If it's summer, canoe near cool freshwater springs and swimming beaches.

Some unforgettable rivers include: Orlando's 'Wild and Scenic' **Wekiva River** (p91); and the Tampa region's alligator-packed **Myakka River** (p288).

You'll tell your grandchildren about kayaking **Everglades National Park** (p242); **Hell's Bay paddling trail** (p246) is heavenly. The nearby **10,000 Islands** (p247) are just as amazing, and nothing beats sleeping in the Everglades in a chickee (wooden platform above the waterline; p252). Explore the serenity of the southern Gulf Coast via the azure spaces of the **Great Calusa Blueway**.

And don't forget the coasts. You'll kick yourself if you don't kayak Miami's **Bill Baggs Cape Florida State Recreation Area** (p193); Tampa Bay's **Caladesi Island** (p281) and Sanibel Island's **JN 'Ding' Darling National Wildlife Refuge** (p289). Plus, on Florida's Atlantic Coast, more mangroves, waterbirds, dolphins and manatees await in the **Canaveral National Seashore (www.nps.gov/cana)**, particularly Mosquito Lagoon. Also seek out **Indian River Lagoon (www.indianriverlagoon.org)**. **Big and Little Talbot Islands (☎904-251-2320; www.floridastateparks.org/bigtalbotisland)** provide more intercoastal magic.

For paddling organizations, see p339.

Surfing

Ten-time world champion surfer Kelly Slater is from Cocoa Beach, and four-time women's champion Lisa Anderson is from Ormond Beach. Both first learned how to carve in Space Coast waves, in the shadow of rockets, and Slater honed his aerials at Sebastian Inlet.

All of which is to say that while Florida's surf may be considered 'small' by Californian and Hawaiian standards, Florida's surfing community and history are not. Plus, Florida makes up in wave quantity what it may lack in wave size.

The Best... Diving & Snorkeling

1 John Pennekamp Coral Reef State Park (p218)

2 Biscayne National Park (p251)

3 Dry Tortugas National Park (p229)

Nearly the entire Atlantic Coast has rideable waves, but the best spots are gathered along the Space Coast: shoot for **Cocoa Beach** (p99). You'll also find tiny, longboard-friendly peelers from **Fort Lauderdale** (p159) down to Miami's **South Beach** (p179).

Florida's northern Atlantic Coast is less attractive, partly due to chilly winter water, but consistent, 2ft to 3ft surf can be had at **Daytona Beach** (p296); at **St Augustine** (p298), and around **Amelia Island** (p299).

Diving & Snorkeling

For diving and snorkeling, most already know about Florida's superlative coral reefs and wreck diving, but northern Florida is also the 'Cave Diving Capital of the US.' The peninsula's limestone has more holes than Swiss cheese, and most are burbling goblets of diamond-clear water.

If you prefer coral reefs teeming with rainbow-bright tropical fish, you're in luck...Florida has the continent's largest coral reef system. The two best spots are **John Pennekamp Coral Reef State Park** (p218) and **Biscayne National Park** (p251) but you won't be disappointed at **Bahia Honda State Park** (p222). Named for their abundant sea turtles, the **Dry Tortugas** (p229) islands are well worth the effort to reach them.

Wreck diving in Florida is also epic, and some are even accessible to snorkelers; check out **Fort Lauderdale** (p160) and **Biscayne National Park** (p252).

Many spots line the Suwannee River: try **Peacock Springs State Park** (www.floridastateparks.org/peacocksprings), one of the continent's largest underwater cave systems or **Troy Springs State Park** (www.floridastateparks.org/troyspring). Another fun dive is **Blue Spring State Park** (386-775-3663; www.floridastateparks.org/bluespring), near Orlando. Note you need to be cavern certified to dive springs (open-water certification won't do), and solo diving is usually not allowed. But local dive shops help with both (for dive organizations and resources, see p340.

Biking

Florida is too flat for mountain biking, but there are plenty of off-road opportunities, along with hundreds of miles of paved trails for those who prefer to keep their ride clean. As with hiking, avoid biking in summer, unless you like getting hot and sweaty.

Top off-roading spots include **Big Shoals State Park** (www.floridastateparks.org/bigshoals), with 25 miles of trails along the Suwannee River. Also recommended are the **Ocala National Forest** (fs.udsa.gov/ocala) and the **Apalachicola National Forest** (p300), particularly the sandy Munson Hills Loop.

With so many paved cycling trails, it's hard to choose. Two of the most unforgettable? Palm Beach's **Lake Trail** (561-966-6600; www.pbcgov.com/parks), aka the 'Trail of Conspicuous Consumption' for all the mansions and yachts, and the 15-mile **Shark Valley Tram Road Trail** (p243), which pierces the Everglades' gator-infested sawgrass river.

For more-involved overland adventures, do the **Florida Keys Overseas Heritage Trail** (p226), which mirrors the Keys Hwy for 70 noncontiguous miles, and the urban-and-coastal **Pinellas Trail** (727-549-6099; www.pinellascounty.org/trailgd), which goes 43 miles from St Petersburg to Tarpon Springs. For more biking advice, see p339.

Tread Lightly, Explore Safely

These days, it should go without saying that any wilderness, even a swamp, is a fragile place. Whether hiking, biking, paddling, or snorkeling, always practice 'Leave No Trace' ethics (see www.lnt.org for comprehensive advice). In short, this boils down to staying on the trail, cleaning up your own mess, and observing nature rather than plucking or feeding it.

As you enjoy Florida's natural bounty, take care of yourself, too. In particular, carry lots of water, up to a gallon per person per day, and always be prepared for rain. Line backpacks with plastic bags, and carry rain gear and extra clothes for when (not if) you get soaked. Reid Tillery's *Surviving the Wilds of Florida* will help you do just that, while Tillery's website **Florida Adventuring** (www.floridaadventuring.com) covers backcountry essentials.

Fishing

The world may contain seven seas, but there's only one Fishing Capital of the World: Florida. No, this isn't typically overwrought Floridian hype. Fishing here is the best the US offers, and for variety and abundance, nowhere else on Earth can claim an indisputable advantage.

In Florida's abundant rivers and lakes, largemouth bass are the main prize. Prime spots, with good access and facilities, are **Lake Manatee State Park** (www.floridastateparks.org/lakemanatee), south of St Peterburg; fly-fishing at **Myakka River State Park** (p288); and **Jacksonville** (www.jacksonvillefishing.com), which has charters to the St Johns River and Lake George for freshwater fishing, to the bay for ocean fishing, plus kayak fishing.

Near-shore saltwater fishing means redfish and mighty tarpon, snook, spotted seatrout and much more, up and down both coasts. In the Keys, **Bahia Honda** (p222) offers shore-fishing highlights.

However, as 'Papa' Hemingway would tell you, the real fishing is offshore, where majestic sailfish leap and thrash. Bluefish and mahimahi are other popular deep-water fish. For offshore charters, aim for **Fort Lauderdale** (p159), **Lauderdale-by-the-Sea** (p157), **Destin** (p301), and **Key West** (p223). The best strategy is to walk the harbor, talking with captains, till you find one who speaks to your experience and interests.

Note that you usually need a license to fish, and there are a slew of regulations about what you can catch; see p356 for fishing organizations and details.

Sailing

If you prefer the wind in your sails, Florida is your place. Miami is a sailing sweet spot, with plenty of marinas for renting or berthing your own boat – **Key Biscayne** (p191) is a particular gem. **Fort Lauderdale** (p159) is chock full of boating options. In **Key West** (p223), sail on a schooner with real cannons, though tour operators are plentiful throughout the Keys.

Wildlife

Cooter turtle, Lakeland

STEVEN BLANDIN/BIRD-WILDLIFEPHOTOGRAPHY.COM/GETTY IMAGE

With swamps full of gators, rivers full of snakes, manatees in mangroves, sea turtles on beaches, and giant flocks of seabirds taking wing at once, how is it that a squeaky-voiced mouse became Florida's headliner (especially when one of the state's flagship species is a hunting cat)? Dinosaurs, diving birds and the wild heart of a tropical wilderness await you...

Birds

Nearly 500 avian species have been documented in the state, including some of the world's most magnificent migratory waterbirds: ibis, egrets, great blue herons, white pelicans and whooping cranes.

Nearly 350 species spend time in the Everglades, the prime birding spot in Florida. But you don't have to brave the swamp. Completed in 2006, the **Great Florida Birding Trail** (http://floridabirdingtrail.com) runs 2000 miles and includes nearly 500 bird-watching sites. Nine of these are 'gateway' sites, with staffed visitor centers and free 'loaner' binoculars; see the website for downloadable guides, and when driving, look for brown road signs.

Among the largest birds, white pelicans arrive in winter (October to April), while brown pelicans, the only pelicans to dive for their food, live here year-round. To see the striking pale-pink roseate spoonbill, a member of the ibis family, visit **JN 'Ding' Darling National Wildlife Refuge** (p289), the wintering site for a third of the US population.

About 5000 nonmigratory sandhill cranes are joined by 25,000 migratory cousins each winter. White whooping cranes, at up to 5ft the tallest bird in North America, are nearly extinct; about 100 winter on Florida's Gulf Coast near Homosassa.

Songbirds and raptors fill Florida skies, too. The state has over 1000 mated pairs of bald eagles, the most in the southern US, and peregrine falcons migrate through in spring and fall.

The Best... Wildlife Sanctuaries

1 Suncoast Seabird Sanctuary (p281)

2 JN 'Ding' Darling National Wildlife Refuge (p289)

3 Turtle Hospital (p221)

4 Florida Keys Wild Bird Rehabilitation Center (p218)

Land Mammals

Florida's most endangered mammal is the Florida panther. Though hunting was stopped in 1958, it was too late for panthers to survive on their own. Without a captive breeding program, begun in 1991, the Florida panther would now be extinct, and with only some 120 known to exist, they're not out of the swamp yet.

You're not likely to see a panther, but black bears have recovered to around 3000; as their forests diminish, bears are occasionally seen traipsing through suburbs in northern Florida.

White-tailed deer are an all-too-common species that troubles landscaping everywhere. Endemic to the Keys are Key deer, a Honey-I-Shrunk-the-Ungulate subspecies: less than 3ft tall and lighter than a 10-year-old boy, they live mostly on **Big Pine Key** (p222).

Marine Mammals

Florida's coastal waters are home to 21 species of dolphins and whales. By far the most common is the bottlenose dolphin, which is frequently encountered around the entire peninsula. Bottlenose dolphins are the species most often seen in captivity.

Winter is the manatee season; they seek out Florida's warm-water springs and power-plant discharge canals beginning in November. These lovable, lumbering creatures are another iconic Florida species whose conservation both galvanizes and divides state residents.

Reptiles & Amphibians

Boasting an estimated 184 species, Florida has the nation's largest collection of reptiles and amphibians. Uninvited guests add to the total, many after being released by pet owners. Some of the more problematic invasive species include Burmese pythons, black and green iguanas and Nile monitor lizards.

The American alligator is Florida's poster species, and they are ubiquitous in Central and South Florida. South Florida is also home to the only North American population of American crocodile. Florida's crocs number around 1500; they prefer saltwater, and to distinguish them from gators, check their smile – a croc's snout is more tapered and its teeth stick out.

Turtles, frogs and snakes love Florida, and nothing is cuter than watching bright skinks, lizards and anoles skittering over porches and sidewalks. Of 44 species

The Best... State Parks

1 Cayo Costa State Park (p282)

2 John Pennekamp Coral Reef State Park (p218)

3 Wekiwa Springs State Park (p91)

4 Homosassa Springs Wildlife State Park (p29)

5 Indian Key Historic State Park (p220)

of snakes, six are poisonous, and only four of those are common. Of the baddies, three are rattlesnakes (diamondback, pygmy, canebrake), plus copperheads, cottonmouths, and coral snakes. While cottonmouths live in and around water, *most* Florida water snakes are not cottonmouths.

Sea Turtles

Predominantly three species create over 80,000 nests in Florida annually, mostly on southern Atlantic Coast beaches but extending to all Gulf Coast beaches. Most are loggerhead, then far-fewer green and leatherback, and historically hawksbill and Kemp's ridley as well; all five species are endangered or threatened.

During the May-to-October nesting season, sea turtles deposit 80 to 120 eggs in each nest. Infants can become confused by artificial lights and noisy human audiences. For the best, least-disruptive experience, join a sanctioned turtle watch; for a list, visit http://myfwc.com/seaturtle, then click on 'Educational Information' and 'Where to View Sea Turtles.'

National, State & Regional Parks

About 26% of Florida's land lies in public hands, which breaks down to three national forests, 11 national parks, 28 national wildlife refuges (including the first, Pelican Island), and 160 state parks. Overall attendance is up, with over 20 million folks visiting state parks annually. Florida's state parks have twice been voted the nation's best.

For specific park information:

Florida State Parks (www.floridastateparks.org)

National Forests, Florida (www.fs.usda.gov/florida)

National Park Service (NPS; www.nps.gov)

National Wildlife Refuges, Florida (NWR; www.fws.gov/southeast/maps/fl.html)

Recreation.gov (www.recreation.gov) National lands campground reservations.

The **Florida Fish & Wildlife Commission** (http://myfwc.com) manages Florida's mostly undeveloped Wildlife Management Areas (WMA). The website is an excellent resource for wildlife viewing, as well as boating, hunting, fishing and permits.

A Kinder, Gentler Wilderness Encounter

Everyone has an obligation to consider the best ways to experience nature without harming it in the process. For most activities, there isn't a single right answer; specific impacts are often debated. However, there *are* a few clear guidelines.

Airboats and swamp buggies While airboats have a much lighter 'footprint' than big-wheeled buggies, both are motorized (and loud) and have larger impacts than canoes for exploring wetlands. As a rule, nonmotorized activities are least damaging.

Coral-reef etiquette Never touch the coral reef. Coral polyps are living organisms. Touching or breaking coral creates openings for infection and disease.

Dolphin encounters Captive dolphins are typically rescued animals already acclimated to humans. For a consideration of dolphin swims, see p238. However, when encountering wild dolphins in the ocean, federal law makes it illegal to feed, pursue, or touch them. Habituating any wild animal to humans can lead to the animal's death, since approaching humans often leads to conflicts and accidents (as with boats).

Feeding wild animals Don't. Kind animals like deer and manatees may come to rely on human food (to their detriment), while feeding bears and alligators just encourages them to hunt you.

Manatee swims When swimming near manatees, a federally protected endangered species, look but don't touch. 'Passive observation' is the standard.

Sea-turtle nesting sites It's a federal crime to approach nesting sea turtles or hatchling runs. Most nesting beaches have warning signs and a nighttime 'lights out' policy. If you encounter turtles on the beach, keep your distance and no flash photography.

Beaches

Smathers Beach, Key West (p223)

FRANZ MARC FREI/GETTY IMAGES

Here's a telling statistic: 80% of Florida's population lives along its coastline. So it's not just visitors who come to Florida for the beach; it's the natives too. The word 'coastline' is a loaded term, as Florida has two coasts, Atlantic and Gulf, and different beaches for each body of water. Whatever coast you choose to chill on, remember that in Florida, life is always a beach.

Florida's beaches are the best in the country outside of Hawaii, and incredibly diverse, so let's start with two questions: Do you prefer sunrise or sunset? Do you prefer surfing and boogie boarding or sunbathing and sandcastles? For the former, hit the bigger, east-facing waves of the Atlantic Coast; for the latter, choose the soporific, west-facing waters of the Gulf Coast.

With few exceptions, Florida's beaches are uniformly safe places to swim; the most dangerous surf will occur just before and after a storm. Also, stingrays in summer and occasional jellyfish can trouble swimmers (look for posted warnings).

Be careful about driving down any old road and popping onto the sand in Florida; you may be on someone's property, and folks here can get prickly about that sort of thing. Parking lots for public beaches and public beaches themselves are always well signed. Expect to pay a dollar or two an hour to park at a public beach.

Florida's best beach? Aaw, why not ask us to choose a favorite child. But visitors do have to make decisions. Also consult Dr Beach (www.drbeach.org).

The Atlantic Coast

The Atlantic Coast is the adult coast of Florida beaches. While there are family friendly options, the beaches here, in terms of their main marketing thrust, tend to cater to a more adult crowd. The Atlantic Ocean brings decent waves and occasionally unpredictable swells and riptides. The presence of the Bahamas means that most of the water that filters in below Jupiter is pretty uniformly calm.

The Keys

The Keys are islands, but they're fringed more by mangroves than sand and as such aren't great for beaches. Exceptions include **Sombrero Beach** in Marathon and the **Bahia Honda State Park**.

South Beach

Famed for celebrities, skin, parties, speedos and thongs. South Beach isn't all glam jetsetters, Latin American aristocrats and European fashionistas – there's plenty of Middle Americans out there too – but there's more than a grain of truth to that stereotype. The exception: **South Pointe Park**, at the bottom of South Beach, was specifically designed to be family-friendly.

The Best... Atlantic Coast Beaches

1 Bahia Honda (p222)

2 Bill Baggs Cape Florida State Recreation Area (p193)

3 Fort Lauderdale (p159)

4 Lake Worth (p152)

5 Hollywood Beach & Broadwalk (p166)

Other Miami Beaches

Further north you'll run into sedate **Mid-Beach** and **North Miami Beach**. Haulover Beach Park in North Miami Beach is clothing optional! Miami locals also like to party on the sand in North Miami Beach, but this tends to be a nighttime activity. The lovely beaches of **Key Biscayne** are popular with families and water-sports enthusiasts.

Fort Lauderdale

The main beach is a magnificent stretch of sand, as is the **promenade** that accompanies it. The north end of Fort Lauderdale beach is gay-friendly, while the southern end caters more to families. **Hollywood Beach & Broadwalk** is aimed at all types, lacks pretension and is great.

Come Sail Away

Miami is a sailing sweet spot, with plenty of marinas for renting or berthing your own boat – **Key Biscayne** (p191) is a particular gem. Fort Lauderdale is chock-full of boating options. In **Key West** (p223) you can sail on a schooner with real cannons, though tour operators are plentiful throughout the Keys. There are sailing schools in all of the major coastal cities in Florida, including Tampa, St Petersburg, Fort Lauderdale, Ft Myers and Sarasota.

Gold Coast

As you head up to Palm Beach you'll find great beaches all along the coast. Some of the best include **Lake Worth Beach**, an extraordinarily pretty slice of seashore, any of the sand near **Delray Beach** and well-kept **Palm Beach Municipal Beach**.

Space Coast

Cocoa Beach is popular with college students, surfers and water-sports enthusiasts, while **Apollo Beach** is a 6-mile coastline that draws in a family crowd. **Vero Beach** is the spot for those who want a bit of peace, quiet, pedestrian walkways and a cozy arts scene to complement their beach experience.

Northeast Florida

Amelia Island is a quirky getaway for the family crowds and history buffs, while **Daytona Beach** is a bit more... down to earth (read: fun boardwalk with crass T-shirts).

The Best... Gulf Coast Beaches

1 Fort DeSoto Park (p280)

2 Caladesi Island State Park (p281)

3 Sanibel Island (p289)

4 Pass-a-Grille Beach (p281)

The Gulf Coast

The Gulf Coast is warm and calm as bathwater. This is where you find a mom, dad and 2.5 children having the time of their lives. Spring Breakers make their way here too, but in general, the beach scene here is peaceful.

Naples

We give Naples immense credit for keeping **Naples City Beach** entirely free of concession stands. It helps that this is a postcard-perfect snapshot of snowy white sand.

Fort Myers

Fort Myers Beach is full of bars, restaurants and kids looking for a good time, but it's popular with parents and their little ones too. There's pretty, silky sand on **Sanibel** and **Captiva** islands, which also happen to be some of the best beaches in the world for shelling. Offshore **Cayo Costa State Park** is an all-natural, peaceful escape from reality.

Sarasota

Sarasota is packed with beaches, including the immensely popular, family-oriented **Bradenton Beach**, beautiful **Lido Beach** and quiet **Turtle Beach**, a popular nesting spot for its namesake reptiles from May to November.

St Petersburg

The beaches on 'St Pete' are some of the best on the Gulf Coast. Favorites include the natural beauty of family-friendly **Fort DeSoto Park & Beach**, the vintage charm of **Pass-a-Grille** and the bright lights and flash of **St Pete Beach**. Just 30 minutes north of St Petersburg is **Clearwater Beach**, a decidedly party-oriented locale; nearby **Sand Key Park** is tamer.

The Panhandle

The 'Redneck Riviera' of **Destin** is actually a fantastic slice of old-school seaside Americana, while raucous **Panama City** is (in)famously Spring Break central. **Pensacola** and surrounding beaches are geared towards Southern families on weekend breaks.

Survival Guide

Jupiter, North Palm Beach, the Gold Coast
PHOTOGRAPHER: CREDIT

Directory

Accommodations

Our reviews (and rates) use the following room types:

- single occupancy (s)
- double occupancy (d)
- room (r), same rate for one or two people
- dorm bed (dm)
- suite (ste)
- apartment (apt)

Many places have certain rooms that cost above or below their standard rates, and seasonal/holiday fluctuations can see rates rise and fall dramatically, especially in Orlando and tourist beach towns. Specific advice for the best rates varies by region, and is included throughout: on the one hand, booking in advance for high-season tourist hotspots (like beaches and Orlando resorts) can be essential to ensure the room you want. On the other, enquiring at the last minute, or even same-day, can yield amazing discounts on any rooms still available.

The following price ranges refer to a standard double room at high season rates, unless rates are distinguished as winter/summer or high/low season. Note that 'high season' can mean summer or winter depending on the region. Unless otherwise stated, rates do not include breakfast, bathrooms are private and all lodging is open year-round. Rates don't include taxes, which vary considerably between towns; in fact, hotels almost never include taxes and fees in their rate quotes, so always ask for the total rate with tax. Florida's sales tax is 6%, and some communities tack on more. States, cities and towns also usually levy taxes on hotel rooms, which can increase the final bill by 10% to 12%.

- **$** less than $100
- **$$** $100–$200
- **$$$** more than $200

Hotels

We have tried to highlight independently owned hotels in this guide, but in many towns, members of hotel chains offer the best value in terms of comfort, location and price. The calling-card of chain hotels is reliability: acceptable cleanliness, unremarkable yet inoffensive decor, a comfortable bed and a good shower. Air-conditioning, mini-refrigerator, microwave, hair dryer, safe and, increasingly, flat-screen TVs and free wi-fi are now standard amenities in most midrange chains. A recent trend, most evident in Miami and beach resorts, is an emergence of funky new brands, such as Aloft (www.starwoodhotels.com/alofthotels), which are owned by more recognizable hotel chains striving for a share of the boutique market.

High-end hotel chains like Four Seasons and Ritz-Carlton overwhelm guests with their high levels of luxury and service: Les Clefs d'Or concierges, valet parking, 24-hour room service, dry cleaning, health clubs and decadent day spas. These special touches are reflected in the room rates. If you're paying for these five-star properties and finding they're not delivering on any of their promises, you have every right to speak politely with the front-desk manager to have your concerns addressed – you deserve only the best.

You'll find plenty of boutique and specialty hotels in places such as Miami's South Beach and Palm Beach. While all large chain hotels have toll-free reservation numbers, you may find better savings by calling the hotel directly, or paying upfront using the hotel website or a third-party booking site.

Note that it is customary to tip in most hotels of any size or stature in the US.

Book Your Stay Online

For more accommodations reviews by Lonely Planet authors, check out http://hotels.lonelyplanet.com. You'll find independent reviews, as well as recommendations on the best places to stay. Best of all, you can book online.

Anywhere between $1 and $5 is usually always appreciated by the porter who carries your bags, the bellman who greets you by name daily, and the guy who drives the 'free' airport shuttle. Some people find it a nice gesture to leave a tip for the housekeeping staff. Conversely, if you're given attitude or any sense of entitlement by any hotel staff member, do feel free to save your bucks for the bar.

Chain-owned hotels include the following:

Four Seasons (☎ 800-819-5053; www.fourseasons.com)

Hilton (☎ 800-445-8667; www.hilton.com)

Holiday Inn (☎ 888-465-4329; www.holidayinn.com)

Marriott (☎ 888-236-2427; www.marriott.com)

Radisson (☎ 888-201-1718; www.radisson.com)

Ritz-Carlton (☎ 800-542-8680; www.ritzcarlton.com)

Sheraton (☎ 800-325-3535; www.starwoodhotels.com/sheraton)

Wyndham (☎ 877-999-3223; www.wyndham.com)

Resorts

Florida resorts, much like Walt Disney World® Resort, aim to be so all-encompassing you'll never need, or want, to leave. Included are all manner of fitness and sports facilities, pools, spas, restaurants, bars and so on. Many also have on-site babysitting services. However, some also tack an extra 'resort fee' onto rates, so always ask.

Practicalities

- **Electricity** Voltage is 110/120V, 60 cycles.
- **Measurements** Distances are measured in feet, yards and miles; weights are tallied in ounces, pounds and tons.
- **Newspapers** Florida has three major daily newspapers: *Miami Herald* (in Spanish, *El Nuevo Herald*), *Orlando Sentinel* and the *St Petersburg Times*.
- **Smoking** Florida bans smoking in all enclosed workplaces, including restaurants and shops, but excluding 'stand-alone' bars (that don't emphasize food) and designated hotel smoking rooms.
- **Time** Most of Florida is in the US Eastern Time Zone: noon in Miami equals 9am in San Francisco and 5pm in London. West of the Apalachicola River, the Panhandle is in the US Central Time Zone, one hour behind the rest of the state. During daylight-saving time, clocks 'spring forward' one hour in March and 'fall back' one hour in November.
- **TV** Florida receives all the major US TV and cable networks. **Florida Smart** (www.floridasmart.com/news) lists them all by region. Video systems use the NTSC color TV standard.

Activities

Biking

Note that the state organizations also discuss biking trails. Florida law requires that all cyclists under 16 must wear a helmet (under 18 in national parks).

Bike Florida (www.bikeflorida.org) Nonprofit organization promoting safe cycling and organized rides, with good biking links.

Florida Bicycle Association (www.floridabicycle.org) Advocacy organization providing tons of advice, a statewide list of cycling clubs, and links to off-road-cycling organizations, racing clubs, a touring calendar and more.

Canoeing & Kayaking

Water-trail and kayaking information is also provided by the Florida State Parks and Florida Greenways & Trails websites. Here are more resources:

American Canoe Association (ACA; www.americancanoe.org) ACA publishes a newsletter, has a water-trails database and organizes courses.

Climate

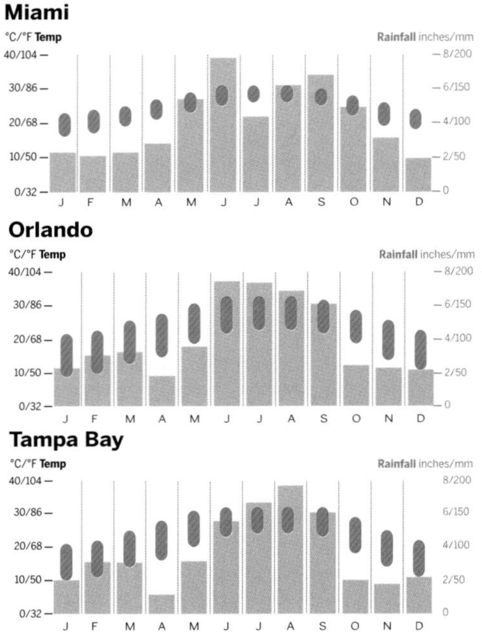

Miami

°C/°F Temp — Rainfall inches/mm

40/104 – 30/86 – 20/68 – 10/50 – 0/32 — 8/200 – 6/150 – 4/100 – 2/50 – 0

J F M A M J J A S O N D

Orlando

°C/°F Temp — Rainfall inches/mm

40/104 – 30/86 – 20/68 – 10/50 – 0/32 — 8/200 – 6/150 – 4/100 – 2/50 – 0

J F M A M J J A S O N D

Tampa Bay

°C/°F Temp — Rainfall inches/mm

40/104 – 30/86 – 20/68 – 10/50 – 0/32 — 8/200 – 6/150 – 4/100 – 2/50 – 0

J F M A M J J A S O N D

Florida Professional Paddlesports Association (www.paddleflausa.com) Provides a list of affiliated member kayak outfitters.

Kayak Online (www.kayakonline.com) A good resource for kayak gear, with links to Florida outfitters.

Diving

Ocean diving in Florida requires an Open Water I certificate, and Florida has plenty of certification programs (with good weather, they take three days). To dive in freshwater springs, you need a separate cave-diving certification, and this is also offered throughout the state.

National Association for Underwater Instruction (NAUI; www.naui.org) Information on dive certifications and a list of NAUI-certified Florida dive instructors.

Professional Diving Instructors Corporation (PDIC; www.pdic-intl.com) Similar to NAUI, with its own list of PDIC-certified Florida dive instructors.

Fishing

All non-residents 16 and over need a fishing license to fish and crab, and Florida offers several short-term options. There are lots of regulations about what and how much you can catch, and where. Locals can give you details, but please do the right thing and review the official word on what's OK and what's not; visit the Florida Fish & Wildlife Conservation Commission website.

Florida Fish & Wildlife Conservation Commission (FWC; www.myfwc.com) The official source for all fishing regulations and licenses (purchase online or by phone). Also has boating and hunting information.

Florida Fishing Capital of the World (www.visitflorida.com/fishing) State-run all-purpose fishing advice and information.

Florida Sportsman (www.floridasportsman.com) Get the lowdown on sport fishing, tournaments, charters, gear and detailed regional advice.

Surfing

Looking for lessons, surf reports or competitions? Start here:

Florida Surfing (www.floridasurfing.com) Instructors, contests, webcams, weather, equipment, history: it's all here.

Florida Surfing Association (FSA; www.floridasurfing.org) Manages Florida's surf competitions; also runs the surf school at Jacksonville Beach.

Surf Guru (www.surfguru.com) East Coast Florida surf reports.

Surfer (www.surfermag.com) *Surfer*'s travel reports cover Florida and just about every break in the USA.

Discount Cards

There are no Florida-specific discount cards. Florida is a *very* competitive tourist destination, so persistence, patience and research pay.

Being a member of certain groups also gives access to discounts (usually about 10%) at many hotels, museums and sights, with the right ID.

Students Any student ID is typically honored; international students might consider an **International Student Identity Card** (ISIC; www.isiccard.com).

Seniors Generally refers to those 65 and older, but sometimes those 60 and older. Join the **American Association of Retired Persons** (AARP; ☎ 888-687-2277; www.aarp.org) for more travel bargains.

Electricity

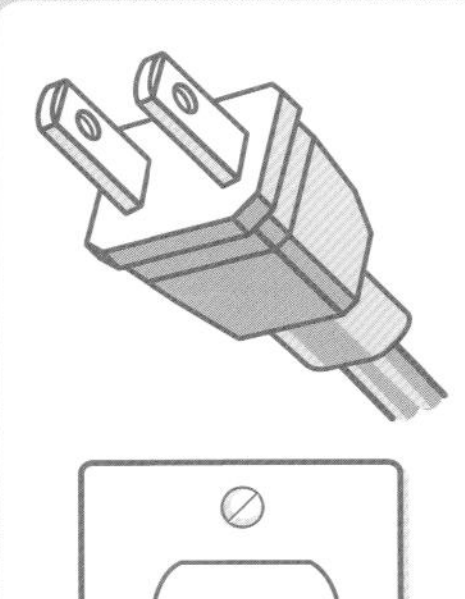

120V/60Hz

120V/60Hz

Food

The following price ranges refer to a typical dinner main course. The Florida state sales and use tax is 6%, which will be added to the total of your bill. Some counties and municipalities may charge an additional percentage, but this is the exception and not the rule. For good to excellent service, always tip 15% to 25% of the total bill.

For Miami and Orlando:

- **$** less than $15
- **$$** $15–30
- **$$$** more than $30

Elsewhere:

- **$** less than $10
- **$$** $10–20
- **$$$** more than $20

Gay & Lesbian Travelers

Florida is not uniformly anything, and it's not uniformly embracing of gay life. The state is largely tolerant, particularly in major tourist destinations, beaches and cities, but this tolerance does not always extend into the more rural and southern areas of northern Florida. However, where Florida does embrace gay life, it does so with a big flamboyant bear hug. Miami and South Beach are as 'out' as it's possible to be, with some massive gay festivals. Fort Lauderdale, West Palm Beach and Key West have long supported vibrant gay communities and are now regarded as some of the 'gayest' destinations in the world. Notable gay scenes and communities also exist in Orlando, Jacksonville, Pensacola, and, to far lesser degrees, in Daytona Beach, Tampa, and Sarasota.

Good gay-and-lesbian resources:

Damron (https://damron.com) Damron, an expert in LGBT travel, offers a searchable database of LGBT-friendly and specific travel listings. Publishes popular national guidebooks, including *Women's Traveller, Men's Travel Guide* and *Damron Accommodations.*

Gay Cities (www.gaycities.com) Everything gay about major US cities and beyond.

Gay Yellow Network (www.glyp.com) City-based yellow-page listings include six Florida cities.

Gayosphere (www.gayosphere.com) The new website from the creators of Fun Maps, bringing you all the naughty and nice hotspots for gay travelers in Florida's major cities and beyond.

Out Traveler (www.outtraveler.com) Magazine specializing in gay travel.

Purple Roofs (www.purpleroofs.com) Lists queer accommodations, travel agencies and tours worldwide.

Health

Florida (and the USA generally) has a high level of hygiene, so infectious diseases are not a significant concern for most travelers. There are no required vaccines, and tap water is safe to drink. Despite Florida's plethora of intimidating wildlife, the main concerns for travelers are sunburn and mosquito bites – as well as arriving with adequate health insurance in case of accidents.

Animal & Spider Bites

Florida's critters can be cute, but they can also bite and sting. Here are a few to watch out for:

Alligators & snakes Neither attack humans unless startled or threatened. If you encounter them, simply back away calmly. Florida has several venomous snakes, so always immediately seek treatment if bitten.

Bears & wildcats Florida is home to a small population of black bears and predatory felines such as the lynx and Florida panther: one of the rarest and most endangered species on the planet. All are generally incredibly hard to spot and live deep in wilderness areas. Should you be lucky (or unlucky) enough to encounter these critters in the wild, stay calm, do not provoke the animal and don't be afraid to make a little noise (talking, jiggling keys) to alert the animal of your presence. In the rare and unfortunate event of an attack, do your best to defend yourself and retreat to a covered position as soon as possible.

Jellyfish & stingrays Florida beaches can see both; avoid swimming when they are present (lifeguards often post warnings). Treat stings immediately; they hurt but aren't dangerous.

Spiders Florida is home to two venomous spiders – the black widow and the brown recluse. Seek immediate treatment if bitten by any spider.

Health Care

In general, if you have a medical emergency, go to the emergency room of the nearest hospital. If the problem isn't urgent, call a nearby hospital and ask for a referral to a local physician; this is usually cheaper than a trip to the emergency room. Stand-alone, moneymaking urgent-care centers provide good service, but can be the most expensive option.

Pharmacies (called drugstores) are abundantly supplied. However, some medications that are available over the counter in other countries require a prescription in the US. If you don't have insurance to cover the cost of prescriptions, these can be shockingly expensive.

Health Insurance

The US offers some of the finest health care in the world. The problem is that it can be prohibitively expensive. It's essential to purchase travel health insurance if your policy doesn't cover you when you're abroad.

Citizens of some Canadian provinces may have a certain level of reciprocal health cover within the US: check with your provincial health-care provider before traveling to the US. Citizens from all other nations should not even think about travel to the States without adequate travel insurance covering medical care. Find out in advance whether your insurance plan will make payments directly to the providers or if they will reimburse you later for any overseas health expenditures.

Accidents and unforeseen illnesses do happen and horror stories are common of people's vacations turning into nightmares when they're hit with hefty hospital bills for seemingly innocuous concerns. On a more serious note, hospital bills for car accidents, falls or serious medical emergencies can run into the tens of thousands of dollars. Look for an insurance policy that provides at least $1 million of medical coverage. Policies with unlimited medical coverage are also available at a higher premium, but are usually not necessary. You may be surprised at how inexpensive good insurance can be.

Bring any medications you may need in their original containers, clearly labeled. A signed, dated letter from your physician that describes all of your medical conditions and medications (including generic names) is also a good idea.

Infectious Diseases

In addition to more common ailments, there are several infectious diseases that are unknown or uncommon outside North America. Most are acquired by mosquito or tick bites.

Giardiasis Also known as traveler's diarrhea. A parasitic infection of the small intestines, typically contracted by drinking feces-contaminated fresh water. Never drink untreated stream, lake or pond water. Easily treated with antibiotics.

HIV/AIDS HIV infection occurs in the US, as do all sexually transmitted diseases: incidences of syphilis are on the rise. Use condoms for all sexual encounters.

Lyme disease Though more common in the US northeast than Florida, Lyme disease occurs here. It is transmitted by infected deer ticks, and is signaled by a bull's-eye rash at the bite and flulike symptoms. Treat promptly with antibiotics. Removing ticks within 36 hours can prevent infection.

Rabies Though rare, the rabies virus can be contracted from the bite of any infected animal; bats are most common, and their bites are not always obvious. If bitten by any animal, consult with a doctor, since rabies is fatal if untreated.

West Nile virus Extremely rare in Florida, West Nile virus is transmitted by culex mosquitoes. Most infections are mild or asymptomatic, but serious symptoms and even death can occur. There is no treatment for West Nile virus. For the latest update on affected areas, see the **US Geological Survey disease maps** (http://diseasemaps.usgs.gov).

Useful Websites

Consult your government's travel health website before departure, if one is available. There is a vast wealth of travel-health advice on the internet.

Two good sources:

MD Travel Health (www.mdtravelhealth.com) Provides complete, updated and free travel-health recommendations for every country.

World Health Organization (www.who.int/ith) The superb book *International Travel and Health* is available free online.

Insurance

It's expensive to get sick, crash a car or have things stolen from you in the US. Make sure you have adequate coverage before arriving. To insure yourself for items that may be stolen from your car, consult your homeowner's (or renter's) insurance policy or invest in travel insurance.

Worldwide travel insurance is available at www.lonelyplanet.com/travel-insurance. You can buy, extend and claim online anytime – even if you're already on the road.

Internet Access

The USA and Florida are wired. Nearly every hotel and many restaurants and businesses offer high-speed internet access. With few exceptions, most hotels and motels offer in-room wi-fi: it's generally free of charge, but do check for connection rates.

Many cafes and all McDonald's offer free wi-fi and most transport hubs are wi-fi hotspots. Public libraries provide free internet terminals, though sometimes you must get a temporary nonresident library card ($10).

For a list of wi-fi hotspots (plus tech and access info), visit **Wi-Fi Alliance** (www.wi-fi.org) and **Wi-Fi Free Spot** (www.wififreespot.com).

Legal Matters

In everyday matters, if you are stopped by the police, note that there is no system for paying traffic tickets or other fines on the spot. The patrol officer will explain your options to you; there is usually a 30-day period to pay fines by mail.

If you're arrested, you are allowed to remain silent,

though never walk away from an officer; you are entitled to have access to an attorney. The legal system presumes you're innocent until proven guilty. All persons who are arrested have the right to make one phone call. If you don't have a lawyer or family member to help you, call your embassy or consulate. The police will give you the number on request.

Drinking & Driving

To purchase alcohol, you need to present a photo ID to prove your age. Despite what you sometimes see, it's illegal to walk with an open alcoholic drink on the street. More importantly, don't drive with an 'open container'; any liquor in a car must be unopened or else stored in the trunk. If you're stopped while driving with an open container, police will treat you as if you were drinking and driving. Refusing a breathalyzer, urine or blood test is treated as if you'd taken the test and failed. A DUI (driving under the influence) conviction is a serious offense, subject to stiff fines and even imprisonment.

Money

Prices quoted in this book are in US dollars ($).

The ease and availability of ATMs have largely negated the need for traveler's checks. However, traveler's checks in US dollars are accepted like cash at most midrange and top-end businesses (but rarely at budget places). Personal checks not drawn on US banks are generally not accepted. Exchange foreign currency at international airports and most large banks in Miami, Orlando, Tampa and other Florida cities.

Major credit cards are widely accepted, and they are required for car rentals. Most ATM withdrawals using out-of-state cards incur surcharges of $2 or so.

Tipping

Tipping is standard practice across America. In restaurants, for satisfactory to excellent service, tipping 15% to 25% of the bill is expected; less is OK at informal diners. Bartenders expect $1 per drink; cafe baristas a little change in the jar. Taxi drivers and hairdressers expect 10% to 15%. Skycaps at airports and porters at nice hotels expect $1 a bag or so. If you spend several nights in a hotel, it's polite to leave a few dollars for the cleaning staff.

Opening Hours

Standard business hours are as follows:

Banks 8:30am to 4:30pm Monday to Thursday, to 5:30pm Friday; sometimes 9am to 12:30pm Saturday.

Bars Most bars 5pm to midnight; to 2am Friday and Saturday.

Businesses 9am to 5pm Monday to Friday.

Post offices 9am to 5pm Monday to Friday; sometimes 9am to noon Saturday.

Restaurants Breakfast 7am to 10:30am Monday to Friday; brunch 9am to 2pm Saturday and Sunday; lunch 11:30am to 2:30pm Monday to Friday; dinner 5pm to 9:30pm, later Friday and Saturday.

Shops 10am to 6pm Monday to Saturday, noon to 5pm Sunday; shopping malls keep extended hours.

Public Holidays

On the following national public holidays, banks, schools and government offices (including post offices) are closed, and transportation, museums and other services operate on a Sunday schedule. Many stores, however, maintain regular business hours. Holidays falling on a weekend are usually observed the following Monday.

New Year's Day January 1

Martin Luther King, Jr Day Third Monday in January

Presidents Day Third Monday in February

Easter March or April

Memorial Day Last Monday in May

Independence Day July 4

Labor Day First Monday in September

Columbus Day Second Monday in October

Veterans Day November 11

Thanksgiving Fourth Thursday in November

Christmas Day December 25

Safe Travel

When it comes to crime, there is Miami, and there is the rest of Florida. As a rule, Miami suffers the same urban problems facing other major US cities such as New York and Los Angeles, but it is no worse. The rest of Florida tends to have lower crime rates than the rest of the nation, but any tourist town is a magnet for petty theft and car break-ins.

If you need any kind of emergency assistance, such as police, ambulance or firefighters, call 911. This is a free call from any phone.

Hurricanes

Florida's hurricane season extends from June through November, but the peak is September and October. Relatively speaking, very few Atlantic Ocean and Gulf of Mexico storms become hurricanes, and fewer still are accurate enough to hit Florida, but the devastation they wreak when they do can be enormous. Travelers should take all hurricane alerts, warnings and evacuation orders seriously.

Hurricanes are generally sighted well in advance, allowing time to prepare. When a hurricane threatens, listen to radio and TV news reports. For more information on storms and preparedness, contact the following:

Florida Division of Emergency Management (www.floridadisaster.org) Hurricane preparedness.

Florida Emergency Hotline (800-342-3557) Updated storm warning information.

National Weather Service (www.nws.noaa.gov)

Telephone

Always dial 1 before toll-free (800, 888 etc) and domestic long-distance numbers. Some toll-free numbers only work within the US. For local directory assistance, dial 411.

To make international calls from the US, dial 011 + country code + area code + number. For international operator assistance, dial 0. To call the US from abroad, the international country code for the USA is 1.

Pay phones are readily found in major cities, but are becoming rarer. Local calls cost 50¢. Private prepaid phonecards are available from convenience stores, supermarkets and drugstores.

Most of the USA's mobile-phone systems are incompatible with the GSM 900/1800 standard used throughout Europe and Asia. Check with your service provider about using your phone in the US. In terms of coverage, Verizon has the most extensive network, but AT&T, Sprint and T-Mobile are decent. Cellular coverage is generally excellent, except in the Everglades and parts of rural northern Florida.

Tourist Information

Most Florida towns have some sort of tourist information center that provides local information; be aware that chambers of commerce typically only list chamber members, not all the town's hotels and businesses. This guide provides visitor center information throughout.

To order a packet of Florida information prior to coming, contact **Visit Florida** (www.visitflorida.com).

Travelers with Disabilities

Because of the high number of senior residents in Florida, most public buildings are wheelchair accessible and have appropriate restroom facilities. Transportation services are generally accessible to all, and telephone companies provide relay operators for the hearing impaired. Many banks provide ATM instructions in braille, curb ramps are common and many busy intersections have audible crossing signals.

A number of organizations specialize in the needs of disabled travelers:

Access-Able Travel Source (www.access-able.com) An excellent website with many links.

Flying Wheels Travel (507-451-5005; http://flyingwheelstravel.com) A full-service travel agency specializing in disabled travel.

Mobility International USA (www.miusa.org) Advises disabled travelers on mobility issues and runs an educational exchange program.

Travelin' Talk Network (www.travelintalk.net) Run by the same people as Access-Able Travel Source; a global network of service providers.

Work

Seasonal service jobs in tourist beach towns and theme parks are common and often easy to get, if low-paying.

If you are a foreigner in the USA with a standard non-immigrant visitors visa, you are expressly forbidden to take paid work in the USA and will be deported if you're caught working illegally. In addition, employers are required to establish the bona fides of their employees or face fines. In particular, southern Florida is notorious for large numbers of foreigners working illegally, and immigration officers are vigilant.

To work legally, foreigners need to apply for a work visa before leaving home. For non-student jobs, temporary or permanent, you need to be sponsored by a US employer, who will arrange an H-category visa. These are not easy to obtain.

Student-exchange visitors need a J1 visa, which the following organizations will help arrange:

American Institute for Foreign Study (AIFS; ☎866-906-2437; www.aifs.com)

BUNAC (☎203-264-0901; www.bunac.org) British Universities North American Club.

Camp America (☎800-727-8233; www.campamerica.aifs.com)

Council on International Educational Exchange (CIEE; ☎800-407-8839; www.ciee.org)

InterExchange (☎212-924-0446; www.interexchange.org) Camp and au-pair programs.

Climate Change & Travel

Every form of transport that relies on carbon-based fuel generates CO_2, the main cause of human-induced climate change. Modern travel is dependent on airplanes, which might use less fuel per kilometer per person than most cars but travel much greater distances. The altitude at which aircraft emit gases (including CO_2) and particles also contributes to their climate change impact. Many websites offer 'carbon calculators' that allow people to estimate the carbon emissions generated by their journey and, for those who wish to do so, to offset the impact of the greenhouse gases emitted with contributions to portfolios of climate-friendly initiatives throughout the world. Lonely Planet offsets the carbon footprint of all staff and author travel.

Transportation

Getting There & Away

Nearly all international travelers to Florida arrive by air, while most US travelers prefer air or car. Florida is bordered by Alabama to the west and north, and Georgia to the north. Major interstates into Florida are the I-10 from the west (Alabama), and the I-75 and I-95 from the north (Georgia).

Getting to Florida by bus is a distant third option, and by train an even more distant fourth. Major regional hubs in Florida include Miami, Fort Lauderdale, Orlando, Tampa and Jacksonville.

Flights, cars and tours can be booked online at lonelylanet.com/bookings.

Bus

For bus trips, **Greyhound** (☎800-231-2222; www.greyhound.com) is the main long-distance operator in the US. It serves Florida from most major cities. It also has the only scheduled statewide service.

Standard long-distance fares can be relatively high: bargain airfares can undercut buses on long-

Bus Fares

Sample one-way advance-purchase and standard fares between Miami and some major US cities:

CITY	FARE (ADVANCE/ STANDARD)	DURATION (HR)	FREQUENCY (PER DAY)
Atlanta	$82/148	16-18	4-6
New Orleans	$139/154	23-24	3-4
New York City	$166/184	33-35	4-6
Washington, DC	$154/178	27-29	4-6

distance routes; on shorter routes, renting a car can be cheaper. Nonetheless, discounted (even half-price) long-distance bus trips are often available by purchasing tickets online seven to 14 days in advance. Then, once in Florida, you can rent a car to get around. Inquire about multiday passes.

Car & Motorcycle

Driving to Florida is easy; there are no international borders or entry issues. Incorporating Florida into a larger USA road trip is very common, and having a car while in Florida is often a necessity: there's lots of ground to cover and some of the most interesting places and state parks are only accessible by car.

Train

From the East Coast, **Amtrak** (800-872-7245; **www.amtrak.com**) makes a comfortable, affordable option for getting to Florida. Amtrak's *Silver Service* (which includes *Silver Meteor*and *Silver Star-* trains) runs between New York and Miami, with services that include Jacksonville, Orlando, Tampa, West Palm Beach and Fort Lauderdale, plus smaller Florida towns in between.

There is no direct service to Florida from Los Angeles, New Orleans, Chicago or the Midwest. Trains from these destinations connect to the *Silver Service* route, but the transfer adds a day or so to your travel time.

Amtrak's *Auto Train* takes you and your car from the Washington, DC, area to the Orlando area; this saves you gas, the drive and having to pay for a rental car. The fare for your vehicle isn't cheap, though, depending on its size and weight. The *Auto Train* leaves daily from Lorton, VA, and goes only to Sanford, FL. It takes about 18 hours, leaving in the afternoon and arriving the next morning. On the *Auto Train,* you pay for your passage, cabin and car separately. Book tickets in advance. Children, seniors and military personnel receive discounts.

Sea

Florida is nearly completely surrounded by the ocean, and it's a major cruise-ship port. Fort Lauderdale is the largest transatlantic harbor in the US. Adventurous types can always

Car Travel Times

Sample distances and times from various points in the US to Miami:

CITY	DISTANCE (MILES)	DURATION (HR)
Atlanta	660	10½
Chicago	1380	23
Los Angeles	2750	44
New York City	1280	22
Washington, DC	1050	17

Train Fares

Sample one-way fares (from low to high season) and durations from NYC to points in Florida:

FROM	TO	FARE	DURATION (HR)
New York City	Jacksonville	$172-291	18-20
New York City	Miami	$185-314	28-31
New York City	Orlando	$175-297	22-23
New York City	Tampa	$176-299	26

sign up as crew members for a chance to travel the high seas.

Getting Around

Once you reach Florida, traveling by car is the best way of getting around – it allows you to reach areas not otherwise served by public transportation.

Air

The US airline industry is reliable, safe and serves Florida extremely well, both from the rest of the country and within Florida. However, the industry's continuing financial troubles have resulted in a series of high-profile mergers in recent years: Midwest joined Frontier; Orlando-based Air Tran merged into Southwest; Continental merged with United, and the American Airlines merger with US Airways to form the world's largest airline finalized in 2014.

In general, this has led to the abolition of some routes, fewer flights, fuller airplanes, less perks, more fees and higher fares. Airport security screening procedures also keep evolving; allow extra time.

Air service between Florida's four main airports – Fort Lauderdale, Miami, Orlando International, and Tampa – is frequent and direct. Smaller destinations such as Key West, Fort Myers, Pensacola, Jacksonville, Tallahassee and West Palm Beach are served, but less frequently, indirectly and at higher fares.

Airlines in Florida

Domestic airlines operating in Florida:

American (AA; ☎ 800-433-7300; www.aa.com) Has a Miami hub and service to and between major Florida cities.

Cape Air (9K; www.flycapeair.com) Convenient connections between Fort Myers and Key West.

Delta (DL; ☎ 800-455-2720; www.delta.com) International carrier to main Florida cities, plus flights from Miami to Orlando and Tampa.

Frontier (F9; ☎ 800-432-1359; www.frontierairlines.com) Services Tampa, Orlando and Fort Lauderdale from Denver, Minneapolis and the Midwest.

JetBlue (JB; ☎ 800-538-2583; www.jetblue.com) Serves Orlando, Fort Lauderdale and smaller Florida cities from the East and West Coast.

Southwest (WN; ☎ 800-435-9792; www.southwest.com) One of the US's leading low-cost carriers, offering free baggage and, at times, extremely low fares.

Spirit (NK; ☎ 801-401-2220; www.spiritair.com) Florida-based discount carrier serving Florida cities from East Coast, US, Caribbean, and Central and South America.

United (UA; ☎ 800-824-6400; www.united.com) International flights to Orlando and Miami; domestic flights to and between key Florida cities.

Air Passes

International travelers who plan on doing a lot of flying, both in and out of the region, might consider buying an air pass. Air passes are available only to non-US citizens, and must be purchased in conjunction with an international ticket.

Conditions and cost structures can be complicated, but all include a certain number of domestic flights (from three to 10) that must be used within a set time frame, generally between 30 and 60 days. In most cases, you must plan your itinerary in advance, but dates (and even destinations) can sometimes be left open. Talk with a travel agent to determine if an air pass would save you money based on your plans.

The two main airline alliances offering air passes are Star Alliance (www.staralliance.com) and One World (www.oneworld.com).

Bicycle

Regional bicycle touring is very popular. Flat countryside and scenic coastlines make for great itineraries. However, target winter to spring; summer is unbearably hot and humid for long-distance biking.

Some Florida biking organizations operate bike tours. Renting a bicycle is easy throughout Florida.

Some other things to keep in mind:

Helmet laws Helmets are required for anyone aged 16 and younger. Adults are not required to wear helmets, but should for safety.

Road rules Bikes must obey auto rules; ride on the right-hand side of the road, with traffic, not on sidewalks.

Transporting your bike to Florida Bikes are considered checked luggage on airplanes, but often must be boxed and fees can be high (more than $200).

Theft Bring and use a sturdy lock (U-type is best). Theft is common, especially in Miami Beach.

For more information and assistance, a few organizations can help:

Better World Club (☎ 866-238-1137; www.betterworldclub.com) Offers a bicycle roadside assistance program.

International Bicycle Fund (www.ibike.org) Comprehensive overview of bike regulations by airline, and lots of advice.

League of American Bicyclists (www.bikeleague.org) General advice, plus lists of local cycle clubs and repair shops.

Boat

Florida is a world center for two major types of boat transport: privately owned yachts and cruise ships.

Each coastal city has sightseeing boats that cruise harbors and coastlines. It really pays (in memories) to get out on the water. Water-taxi services along Intracoastal Waterways are a feature in Fort Lauderdale and around Sanibel Island and Pine Island on the Gulf.

Cruises

Florida is a huge destination and departure point for cruises of all kinds. Miami likes to brag that it's the 'cruise capital of the world,' and Walt Disney World® runs its own **Disney Cruise Line** (☎ 800-951-3532; www.disneycruise.disney.go.com), which has a number of three- to seven-night cruises throughout the Caribbean, including to Disney's own private island, Castaway Cay.

For specials on other multinight and multiday cruises, see the following:

Cruise.com (www.cruise.com)

CruiseWeb (www.cruiseweb.com)

Vacations to Go (www.vacationstogo.com)

CruisesOnly (www.cruisesonly.com)

Florida's main ports:

Port Canaveral (www.portcanaveral.com) On the Atlantic Coas; gives Miami a run for its money.

Port Everglades (www.porteverglades.net) Near Fort Lauderdale, and the third-busiest Florida port.

Port of Miami (☎ 305-347-4800; www.miamidade.gov/portofmiami) At the world's largest cruise-ship port, trips offered are to the Bahamas, Caribbean, Key West and Mexico.

Port of Tampa (www.tampaport.com) On the Gulf Coast; rapidly gaining a foothold in the cruise market.

Major cruise companies:

Carnival Cruise Lines (☎ 800-764-7419; www.carnival.com)

Norwegian Cruise Line (☎ 866-234-7350; www.ncl.com)

Royal Caribbean (☎ 866-562-7625; www.royalcaribbean.com)

Bus

The only statewide bus service is by Greyhound (p346), which connects all major and mid-sized Florida cities, but not always smaller towns (even some popular beach towns). Regional or city-run buses cover their more limited areas much better; used together, these bus systems make travel by bus possible, but time-consuming.

Greyhound Bus Fares

To get you started, here are some round-trip Greyhound bus fares and travel times around Florida:

FROM	TO	FARE	DURATION (HR)
Daytona Beach	St Augustine	$29	1
Fort Lauderdale	Melbourne	$58	4
Jacksonville	Tallahassee	$54	3
Melbourne	Daytona Beach	$34	3½
Miami	Key West	$58	4½
Miami	Naples	$46	3
Panama City	Pensacola	$49	3
St Augustine	Jacksonville	$24	1
Naples	Tampa	$59	5
Tampa	Orlando	$38	2
Tallahassee	Panama City	$39	2½

It's always a bit cheaper to take a Greyhound bus during the week than on the weekend. Fares for children are usually about half the adult fare.

Car & Motorcycle

By far the most convenient and popular way to travel around Florida is by car. While it's quite possible to avoid using a car on single-destination trips – to Miami, to Orlando theme parks or to a self-contained beach resort – relying on public transit can be inconvenient for even limited regional touring. Even smaller, tourist-friendly towns such as Naples, Sarasota or St Augustine can be frustrating to negotiate without a car. Motorcycles are also popular in Florida, given the flat roads and warm weather (summer rain excepted).

Automobile Associations

The **American Automobile Association** (AAA; ☎ 800-874-7532; www.aaa.com) has reciprocal agreements with several international auto clubs (check with AAA and bring your membership card). For members, AAA offers travel insurance, tour books, diagnostic centers for used-car buyers and a greater number of regional offices, and it advocates politically for the auto industry. It also has a handy online route planner that can help you calculate the exact mileage and estimated fuel costs of your intended itinerary.

An ecofriendly alternative is the Better World Club (p349), which donates 1% of earnings to assist environmental cleanup; offers ecologically sensitive choices for services; and advocates politically for environmental causes. Better World also has a roadside-assistance program for bicycles.

In both organizations, the central member benefit is 24-hour emergency roadside assistance anywhere in the USA. Both clubs also offer trip planning and free maps, travel-agency services, car insurance and a range of discounts (car rentals, hotels etc).

Driver's License

Foreign visitors can legally drive in the USA for up to 12 months with their home driver's license. However, getting an International Driving Permit (IDP) is recommended; this will have more credibility with US traffic police, especially if your home license doesn't have a photo or is in a foreign language. Your automobile association at home can issue an IDP, valid for one year, for a small fee. You must carry your home license together with the IDP at all times. To operate a motorcycle, you need either a valid US state motorcycle license or an IDP specially endorsed for motorcycles.

Insurance

Don't put the key into the ignition if you don't have insurance: it's legally required, and you risk financial ruin without it if there's an accident. If you already have auto insurance (even overseas), or if you buy travel insurance, make sure that the policy has adequate liability coverage for a rental car in Florida; it probably does, but check.

Rental-car companies will provide liability insurance, but most charge extra for the privilege. Always ask. Collision-damage insurance for the vehicle is almost never included in the US. Instead, the provider will offer an optional Collision Damage Waiver (CDW) or Loss Damage Waiver (LDW), usually with an initial deductible of $100 to $500. For an extra premium, you can usually get this deductible covered as well. However, most credit cards now offer collision-damage coverage for rental cars if you rent for 15 days or less and charge the total rental to your card. This is a good way to avoid paying extra fees to the rental company, but note that if there's an accident, you sometimes must pay the rental car company first and then seek reimbursement from the credit-card company. Check your credit-card policy. Paying extra for some or all of this insurance increases the cost of a rental car by as much as $10 to $30 a day.

Travel insurance, either specific paid policies or free insurance provided by your credit-card company (when your travel arrangements are purchased on their credit cards), often includes cover for rental-car insurances up to the full amount of any deductible. If you plan on renting a vehicle for any significant period of time, the cost of travel insurance, which includes coverage for rental vehicles, is often way cheaper than purchasing the optional insurance from the car-rental company directly. Be prudent and do your research to avoid getting a shock when you go to sign your car-rental contract and discover all the additional charges.

Rental

Car rental is a very competitive business. Most rental companies require that you have a major credit card; that you be at least 25 years old; and that you have a valid driver's license (your home license will do). Some national companies may rent to drivers between the ages of 21 and 24 for an additional charge. Those under 21 are usually not permitted to rent at all.

Additional drivers are not usually covered under the base rate and an additional daily surcharge will be applied. If someone other than the parties authorised on the rental contract is driving the vehicle and has an accident, all paid insurances will be void: you don't want this to happen. If anyone else is likely to drive the vehicle, they need to be present at the time of collection and are required to submit their driver's license and pay the extra fee. If the additional driver is not able to be present at the time of collection, it is possible to drive into any branch of the rental company and add the additional driver on to your rental agreement at a later date. Charges may be backdated to the day of collection.

Good independent agencies are listed by **Car Rental Express** (www.carrentalexpress.com), which rates and compares independent agencies in US cities; it's particularly useful for searching out cheaper long-term rentals.

National car-rental companies:

Alamo (☎ 877-222-9075; www.alamo.com)

Avis (☎ 800-331-2112; www.avis.com)

Budget (☎ 800-527-0700; www.budget.com)

Dollar (☎ 800-800-4000; www.dollar.com)

Enterprise (☎ 800-261-7331; www.enterprise.com)

Hertz (☎ 800-654-3131; www.hertz.com)

National (☎ 800-468-3334; www.nationalcar.com)

Rent-a-Wreck (☎ 877-877-0700; www.rentawreck.com)

Thrifty (☎ 800-367-2277; www.thrifty.com)

Rental cars are readily available at all airport locations and many downtown city locations. With advance reservations for a small car, the daily rate with unlimited mileage is about $35 to $55, while typical weekly rates are $200 to $400, plus a myriad of taxes and fees. If you rent from a downtown location, you can save money by avoiding the exorbitant airport fees.

An alternative in Miami is **Zipcar** (www.zipcar.com),

a car-sharing service that charges hourly and daily rental fees with free gas, insurance and limited mileage included; prepayment is required.

Note that one-way rentals (picking up in one city and dropping off in another) will often incur a prohibitive one-way drop fee. Experimenting with your routing, or returning the vehicle to the same or a nearby city to where you collected your vehicle, may help avoid this penalty. Also check if the location that you're collecting the car from is franchised or centrally owned: sometimes the latter will help get any one-way fees waived.

Motorcycle

To straddle a Harley across Florida, contact **EagleRider** (☎ 888-900-9901; www.eaglerider.com), which has offices in Daytona Beach, Fort Lauderdale, Miami, St Augustine and Orlando. It offers a wide range of models, which start at $150 a day, plus liability insurance. Adult riders (over 21) are not required by Florida law to wear a helmet, but you should for your own safety.

Motorhome (RV)

Forget hotels. Drive your own. Touring Florida by recreational vehicle (RV) can be as low-key or as over-the-top as you wish.

After settling on the vehicle's size, consider the impact of gas prices, gas mileage, additional mileage costs, insurance and refundable deposits; these can add up quickly. Typically, RVs don't come with unlimited mileage, so estimate your mileage up front to calculate the true rental cost.

Inquire about motorhome relocations: sometimes you can get amazing deals where you're effectively being paid to move the vehicle between cities for its owner – but you'll need to be extremely flexible with your dates and routes.

Adventures On Wheels (☎ 800-943-3579; www.wheels9.com) Office in Miami.

CruiseAmerica (☎ 800-671-8042; www.cruiseamerica.com) The largest national RV-rental firm has offices across South Florida.

Recreational Vehicle Rental Association (☎ 703-591-7130; www.rvda.org) Good resource for RV information and advice, and helps find rental locations.

Road Rules

If you're new to Florida or US roads, here are some basics:

- The maximum speed limit on interstates is 75mph, but that drops to 65mph and 55mph in urban areas. Pay attention to the posted signs. City-street speed limits vary between 15mph and 45mph.

- Florida police officers are strict with speed-limit enforcement, and speeding tickets are expensive. If caught going over the speed limit by 10mph, the fine is $155. Conversely, you may be fined if you're driving too slowly on an interstate.

- All passengers in a car must wear seat belts; the fine for not wearing a seat belt is $30. All children under three must be in a child safety seat.

- As in the rest of the US, drive on the right-hand side of the road. On highways, pass in the left-hand lane (but anxious drivers often pass wherever space allows).

- Right turns on a red light are permitted after a full stop. At four-way stop signs, the car that reaches the intersection first has right of way. In a tie, the car on the right has right of way.

Local Transportation

Bus

Local bus services are available in most cities; along the coasts, service typically connects downtown to at least one or two beach communities. Some cities (such as Tampa and Jacksonville) have high-frequency trolleys circling downtown, while some coastal stretches are linked by seasonal trolleys that ferry beach-goers between towns (such as between St Pete Beach and Clearwater).

Fares generally cost between $1 and $2. Exact change upon boarding is usually required, though some buses take $1 bills. Transfers – slips of paper that will allow you to change buses – range from free to 25¢. Hours of operation differ from city to city, but generally buses run from approximately 6am to 10pm.

Metro

Walt Disney World® Resort has a monorail and Tampa has an old-fashioned, one-line streetcar, but the only real metro systems are in and near Miami. In Miami, a driverless Metromover circles downtown and connects with Metrorail, which connects downtown north to Hialeah and south to Kendall.

Meanwhile, north of Miami, Hollywood, Fort Lauderdale and West Palm Beach (and the towns between them) are well connected by Tri-Rail's double-decker commuter trains. Tri-Rail runs all the way to Miami, but the full trip takes longer than driving.

Train

Amtrak trains (p347) run between a number of Florida cities. For the purpose of getting around Florida, its service is extremely limited, and yet for certain specific trips its trains can be very easy and inexpensive. In essence, daily trains run between Jacksonville, Orlando and Miami, with one line branching off to Tampa. In addition, the Thruway Motorcoach (or bus) service gets Amtrak passengers to Daytona Beach, St Petersburg and Fort Myers.

Behind the Scenes

Author Thanks

Adam Karlin

To my crew: Paula, Benedict and Jennifer, for giving me a painless turn at the coordinating author's helm; my editors, Jo and Dora, for being understanding, accommodating and supportive; Jaime Levenshon and Bethany Martinez, for an amazing crash-course in Miami dining; my parents, for their unflagging support; Eggy and Gizmo, who have made writing from home more zoo-keeping, cuddling joy than chore; Rachel Houge, my lovely wife, for the same, and for her humor, smiles and laughter, and for following me whenever I paddle too close to crocodiles; and to my dearest daughter Sanda, to whom I wish safe and adventurous journeys now and forever.

Acknowledgments

Climate map data adapted from Peel MC, Finlayson BL & McMahon TA (2007) 'Updated World Map of the Köppen-Geiger Climate Classification', Hydrology and Earth System Sciences, 11, 1633¬44.

Cover photographs
Front: Magic Kingdom, Walt Disney World® Resort, Orlando, Blaine Harrington III/Alamy
Back: Charles Deering Estate, Palmetto Bay, South Miami, Susanna Kremer/4Corners

This Book

This 2nd edition of Lonely Planet's *Discover Florida* was written by Adam Karlin, Jennifer Rasin Denniston, Paula Hardy and Benedict Walker. The previous edition was written by Adam Karlin and Jennifer Rasin Denniston along with Jeff Campbell and Emily Matchar. This guidebook was commissioned in Lonely Planet's London office and produced by the following:

Destination Editor Dora Whitaker
Product Editor Martine Power
Senior Cartographer Alison Lyall
Book Designer Clara Monitto
Assisting Editors Kate Chapman, Justin Flynn, Jodie Martire
Cartographer James Leversha
Cover Researcher Naomi Parker
Thanks to Isabel Arzberger, Sasha Baskett, Elin Berglund, Brendan Dempsey, Ryan Evans, Larissa Frost, Anna Harris, Alexander Howard, Andi Jones, Gabriel Lindquist, Chris Love, Kate Mathews, Samantha Russell-Tulip, Dianne Schallmeiner, Ellie Simpson, Luna Soo, Dante Tatipata, John Taufa, Angela Tinson, Samantha Tyson, Juan Winata

SEND US YOUR FEEDBACK

We love to hear from travelers – your comments keep us on our toes and help make our books better. Our well-traveled team reads every word on what you loved or loathed about this book. Although we cannot reply individually to your submissions, we always guarantee that your feedback goes straight to the appropriate authors, in time for the next edition. Each person who sends us information is thanked in the next edition, the most useful submissions are rewarded with a selection of digital PDF chapters.

Visit **lonelyplanet.com/contact** to submit your updates and suggestions or to ask for help. Our award-winning website also features inspirational travel stories, news and discussions.

Note: We may edit, reproduce and incorporate your comments in Lonely Planet products such as guidebooks, websites and digital products, so let us know if you don't want your comments reproduced or your name acknowledged. For a copy of our privacy policy visit lonelyplanet.com/privacy.

Index

000 Map pages

000 Map pages

H

I

J

K

000 Map pages

L

M

N

O

P

Q

R

S

000 Map pages

T

U

V

W

Y

Z

NOTES

How to Use This Book

These symbols give you the vital information for each listing:

- Telephone Numbers
- Opening Hours
- Parking
- Nonsmoking
- Air-Conditioning
- Internet Access
- Wi-Fi Access
- Swimming Pool
- Vegetarian Selection
- English-Language Menu
- Family-Friendly
- Pet-Friendly
- Bus
- Ferry
- Metro
- Subway
- London Tube
- Tram

All reviews are ordered in our authors' preference, starting with their most preferred option. Additionally:

Sights are arranged in the geographic order that we suggest you visit them, and within this order, by author preference.

Eating and Sleeping reviews are ordered by price range (budget, mid-range, top end) and within these ranges, by author preference.

Look out for these icons:

No payment required

A green or sustainable option

Our authors have nominated these places as demonstrating a strong commitment to sustainability – for example by supporting local communities and producers, operating in an environmentally friendly way, or supporting conservation projects.

Map Legend

Sights
- Beach
- Buddhist
- Castle
- Christian
- Hindu
- Islamic
- Jewish
- Monument
- Museum/Gallery
- Ruin
- Winery/Vineyard
- Zoo
- Other Sight

Activities, Courses & Tours
- Diving/Snorkelling
- Canoeing/Kayaking
- Skiing
- Surfing
- Swimming/Pool
- Walking
- Windsurfing
- Other Activity/Course/Tour

Sleeping
- Sleeping
- Camping

Eating
- Eating

Drinking
- Drinking
- Cafe

Entertainment
- Entertainment

Shopping
- Shopping

Information
- Post Office
- Tourist Information

Transport
- Airport
- Border Crossing
- Bus
- Cable Car/Funicular
- Cycling
- Ferry
- Monorail
- Parking
- S-Bahn
- Taxi
- Train/Railway
- Tram
- Tube Station
- U-Bahn
- Underground Train Station
- Other Transport

Routes
- Tollway
- Freeway
- Primary
- Secondary
- Tertiary
- Lane
- Unsealed Road
- Plaza/Mall
- Steps
- Tunnel
- Pedestrian Overpass
- Walking Tour
- Walking Tour Detour
- Path

Boundaries
- International
- State/Province
- Disputed
- Regional/Suburb
- Marine Park
- Cliff
- Wall

Population
- Capital (National)
- Capital (State/Province)
- City/Large Town
- Town/Village

Geographic
- Hut/Shelter
- Lighthouse
- Lookout
- Mountain/Volcano
- Oasis
- Park
- Pass
- Picnic Area
- Waterfall

Hydrography
- River/Creek
- Intermittent River
- Swamp/Mangrove
- Reef
- Canal
- Water
- Dry/Salt/Intermittent Lake
- Glacier

Areas
- Beach/Desert
- Cemetery (Christian)
- Cemetery (Other)
- Park/Forest
- Sportsground
- Sight (Building)
- Top Sight (Building)

Our Story

A beat-up old car, a few dollars in the pocket and a sense of adventure. In 1972 that's all Tony and Maureen Wheeler needed for the trip of a lifetime – across Europe and Asia overland to Australia. It took several months, and at the end – broke but inspired – they sat at their kitchen table writing and stapling together their first travel guide, *Across Asia on the Cheap*. Within a week they'd sold 1500 copies. Lonely Planet was born.

Today, Lonely Planet has offices in Franklin, London, Melbourne, Oakland, Beijing and Delhi, with more than 600 staff and writers. We share Tony's belief that 'a great guidebook should do three things: inform, educate and amuse'.

Our Writers

ADAM KARLIN

Coordinating Author, Miami & the Keys, The Everglades Adam's grandmother sheltered him from winter weather in West Palm Beach throughout his childhood, and he worked for a stint at the *Key West Citizen*, covering hyperbolic politicians, Cuban exiles, mosquito-control initiatives and trailer park evictions. It was the sort of journalism gig you supplement with a try at being a local-radio DJ and a few nights' bouncing at Keys bars. After that adventure, Adam went on to Lonely Planet, where he has written or co-authored well over 40 guidebooks, including three editions of *Florida* and *Miami & the Keys*.

JENNIFER RASIN DENNISTON

Walt Disney World® Resort & Orlando, Universal Orlando Resort Jennifer, her geologist husband Rhawn, and their two daughters Anna and Harper spend three or four months every year road-tripping through the US and beyond, including annual weeks-long trips to Florida. They've explored beaches from the Panhandle to the Keys, kayaked Space Coast estuaries and searched the Gulf Coast for ice-age fossils, screamed hands-free on coasters and sidled up to Cinderella.

PAULA HARDY

Palm Beach & the Gold Coast, Tampa Bay & the Gulf Coast Born in Kenya, based in London and married to a man who's lived half his life on Gulf Coast islands, Paula has spent an awful lot of days at the beach. Who can complain? When not squabbling over shells or the merits of grouper sandwiches with her second half, she's authored over 30 guidebooks for Lonely Planet, including contributions to *New England*, *USA* and *Eastern USA*. When not researching Lonely Planet guidebooks, Paula writes about culture, travel and food for a variety of websites and travel publications. You can find her tweeting @paula6hardy.

BENEDICT WALKER

The Best of the Rest, Survival Guide Born in Newcastle, Australia, Ben is living the dream, exploring the wilds and the wild things of Florida, Canada, Japan and Australia. Ben dog-eared his first Lonely Planet guide *(Japan)* when he was 14. When he grew up, he'd write chapters for the same book: a dream come true. A Communications graduate, then travel agent by trade, Ben speaks fluent Japanese. He's co-written and directed a play, toured with rock stars and fancies himself as a photographer. Writing for Lonely Planet means that 'home' equals living out of a suitcase between Australia, Canada, Japan and the US, but he loves and is grateful for every second.

Published by Lonely Planet Publications Pty Ltd
ABN 36 005 607 983
2nd edition – Mar 2015
ISBN 978 1 74220 746 9

10 9 8 7 6 5 4 3 2 1
Printed in China